illustrated book of
fighter aircraft

illustrated book of
fighter aircraft

from the earliest planes to the supersonic jets of today

FRANCIS CROSBY
OF IMPERIAL WAR MUSEUM DUXFORD

southwater

Contents

This edition is published by Southwater, an imprint of Anness Publishing Ltd, 108 Great Russell Street, London WC1B 3NA; info@anness.com

www.southwaterbooks.com; www.annesspublishing.com

Anness Publishing has a new picture agency outlet for images for publishing, promotions or advertising. Please visit our website www.practicalpictures.com for more information.

© Anness Publishing Ltd 2014

Publisher: Joanna Lorenz
Project Editor: Felicity Forster
Art Manager: Clare Reynolds
Editors: Peter Moloney and Alan Thatcher
Designer: Steve West
Production Controllers: Rosie Anness

PAGE 1: Grumman F-14 Tomcat.
PAGES 2–3: Hawker Hurricane.

Introduction

"It is not to be expected that aircraft will be able to carry out their duties undisturbed. In war, advantages must be fought for and the importance of aerial reconnaissance is so great that each side will strive to prevent the other side making use of it." Royal Flying Corps manual, 1914.

This observation predates the first true fighter aircraft but neatly sums up how fighter aircraft came to be. World War I reconnaissance aircraft, "scouts", began to gather increasingly valuable information for their forces and effective armament became a necessity so they could carry out their work unmolested. Initially scout crews armed themselves to take the occasional shot at other scouts. The aeroplane, once no more than a sporting contraption, had become a weapon, and a special type of military aircraft soon evolved – the fighter.

From simple beginnings over the bloody trenches of World War I, fighter aircraft have developed into the extraordinarily complex machines in service today. Although air fighting is only a phenomenon of the last century, it is now central to securing military victory on the ground. In 1940, Hitler's Luftwaffe needed to gain control of the sky over southern England before Germany could mount an effective invasion of Britain. Without air superiority Germany risked their ground

TOP: **The Hurricane (top) and Spitfire, two of World War II's classic fighting aircraft.** ABOVE: **A classic fighter pilot pose – an RAF pilot with his Curtiss P-40 Kittyhawk.**

troops coming under constant attack from British bombers. The fighters of Britain's Royal Air Force defended their country's sky in what has become an almost legendary campaign in the summer of 1940 – The Battle of Britain – and Germany's planned invasion was thwarted.

The weapons with which the Spitfires and Messerschmitts fought each other during the Battle of Britain would have been recognized by the pilots from World War I – machine-guns and cannon, the latter basically a heavy machine-gun that fired explosive shells. Although many modern fighters still carry guns, primary weaponry is now the guided air-to-air missile, some with such long ranges that in recent air combats, pilots have seen an enemy only as a blip on their radar screen before loosing off a missile.

In terms of pilot workload, modern fighters are very demanding and in reality today's fighter pilot spends more time managing computerized weapons systems than flying the aircraft, much of which is done by on-board computers. Where fighters once had mechanical linkages from control columns to control surfaces, fighters now employ electronic signalling to move control surfaces. Computer and electronic systems control the fighters of today and pilots manage these systems.

This book attempts to tell the story of fighter aircraft and how they evolved, and highlights particular episodes of history in which fighters have played a key role, such as the Battle of Britain in 1940. The A–Z listing of fighters does not claim to include every fighter ever built. Instead it presents the individual stories of what the author believes to be the most significant fighters. Specification tables are presented in a

TOP: **The McDonnell Douglas F-4 Phantom typified the 1950s trend for higher and faster flying fighters.** ABOVE: **The unique V/STOL Harrier gave military leaders the capability to operate fighters from virtually anywhere.** LEFT: **Bristling with air-to-air missiles, the Saab Gripen is one of the world's most modern fighters.**

consistent manner to enable the reader to readily compare size, weights and capability of aircraft as diverse as the Fokker Dr.I, the P-51 Mustang and the Eurofighter Typhoon. The performance figures quoted in the table for each type should be seen as broad indicators of an aircraft's capabilities. Aircraft performance and capability can vary considerably, even within the same marks of an aircraft type. If drop tanks are fitted, for example, maximum speed can be reduced – even radio aerials can affect performance. Also, the maximum speeds quoted are top speeds achieved at the optimum altitude for that particular aircraft type and should not be seen as the definitive top speed for an aircraft at all altitudes.

The History of Fighter Aircraft

The fighter aircraft, born in World War I, has played a crucial role in modern history. Fighter aircraft have won wars, possibly prevented wars and defended nations from aggressors. Multi-role fighters of today can range over vast areas of airspace and, if required, unleash a range of "smart" weaponry against the enemy. This is a far cry from the first pistol shots exchanged between "scout" aircraft over the trenches of World War I.

Although the speed of fighter aircraft increased remarkably from World War I through to the 1960s, improved agility and manoeuvrability became the goals of the last quarter of the 20th century. This was made possible by the development of special materials allowing large thin wings to be built, optimizing manoeuvrability and aerodynamics without compromising the strength of the aircraft.

Fighters can be used to protect national airspace, escort bomber aircraft on hazardous missions and, with the dawn of true multi-role aircraft, carry out reconnaissance or ground attack missions themselves. As long as air superiority is a military necessity, there will always be fighter aircraft.

LEFT: **Two classic European fighter aircraft, the Tornado ADV (top) and the legendary Spitfire (bottom).**

Birth of the fighter

Although the Wright Brothers pioneered sustained and controllable powered flight in 1903, they were not the first builders of military aircraft. The first contract for a military aeroplane was awarded to Frenchman Clément Ader in February 1892 for the construction of a two-seater capable of lifting a 75kg/165lb bombload. The aircraft failed to fly but the precedent was set – the military were interested in the aeroplane as a weapon.

In 1907 the US Army released the first ever specification for a military aeroplane issued for commercial tender. Within the specification were the requirements that the aircraft should have a speed of at least 64kph/40mph and that it should be designed to carry two persons having a combined weight of 159kg/350lb for 201km/125 miles.

A key year in the development of military air power was 1910. Missiles were first dropped from an aeroplane in January 1910 when Lt Paul Beck of the US Army released sandbags representing bombs over the city of Los Angeles, but, more importantly for this book, the first military firearm to be fired from an aeroplane was a rifle used by Lt Jacob Earl Fickel of the United States Army from a two-seat Curtiss biplane on August 20, 1910. Equally significant was a German patent, taken out in 1910, for a device that allowed a fixed machine-gun to be fired from an aeroplane.

TOP: **The Wright Brothers, Wilbur (second from left) and Orville (far right) and their Wright Military Aeroplane, 1909.**
ABOVE: **Lt Harvey-Kelly's B.E.2a was the first British aircraft to land in France after World War I began.**

The first British aeroplane built as an armed fighting machine was the Vickers Destroyer E.F.B.1 ordered by the British Admiralty in November 1912. A year later, in November 1913, the first aerial combat between aircraft took place during the Mexican civil war – pistol shots were exchanged and, although none seemed to hit the mark, the aircraft was now seen as a weapon of war. But at the outbreak of World War I, military aircraft had a long way to go before they could be described as effective fighting machines.

When World War I broke out in 1914, Britain's Royal Flying Corps had five squadrons. Most of these B.E.2s, Blériot monoplanes, Farman biplanes, Avro 504s and B.E.8s were sent to France in mid-August 1914 – all were unarmed. Blériot had conquered the English Channel just five years earlier and crossing that expanse of water to France by air was still a risky undertaking. When the first Royal Naval Air Service aircraft arrived in France in late August they were promptly fired on by their own troops. British Union Jack flags were quickly painted beneath the wings of British aircraft, being soon replaced by the roundels developed for the Allies.

Arming these early military aircraft was not easy, and a stray friendly bullet could have easily damaged a vital bracing wire or wooden support, not to mention the wooden propeller. At first, aircrew were armed with hand-held weapons – pistols and rifles. Early use of machine-guns like the Lewis gun were not immediately successful as the weapon's weight severely hampered the aircraft's performance. On August 22, 1914 RFC aircraft were scrambled to challenge a German Albatros – a Farman armed with a Lewis Gun took half an hour to reach 305m/1000ft and on landing the pilot was ordered to remove the Lewis and only carry a rifle. Machine-guns were however soon acknowledged to be the best armament and were gradually fitted to the sturdier aircraft entering service on both sides of World War I.

Mounted cavalry did see action early in World War I but the mechanized battlefield was no place for these warriors of another age and the mounted cavalry were driven from the field of combat forever. By early 1915, aircraft began to take over the reconnaissance role of the cavalry. Whereas cavalry could not ride through enemy positions defended by barbed wire and machine-guns, aircraft could simply fly over these positions and gather intelligence about the enemy – the military aircraft was beginning to define its role.

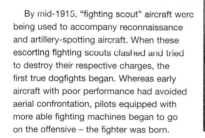

TOP: This dramatic painting of World War I combat shows aircraft attacking out of the sun. ABOVE: The Sopwith Camel was another classic British fighter – note the guns, synchronized to fire between the spinning propeller blades. LEFT: The Bristol Fighter's arrival over the Western Front was bad news for enemy aircrews. BELOW: The Albatros D.Va was the ultimate Albatros D. fighter but was soon outclassed as better Allied aircraft appeared to counter it.

By mid-1915, "fighting scout" aircraft were being used to accompany reconnaissance and artillery-spotting aircraft. When these escorting fighting scouts clashed and tried to destroy their respective charges, the first true dogfights began. Whereas early aircraft with poor performance had avoided aerial confrontation, pilots equipped with more able fighting machines began to go on the offensive – the fighter was born.

The first aces

World War I was a conflict fought on a truly massive scale – the devastation and loss of life on all sides was fantastically high. Almost as an antidote to the grim reports of mass slaughter, the stories of daring pilots in their magnificent machines, locked in aerial combat with a deadly foe, gripped the people back home on all sides of the conflict. The new knights were the men who did battle flying the new, dangerous yet glamorous aeroplane.

Albert Ball – Britain

Ball was the first British ace idolized by the public and was the darling of the British press. An engineering student when the war began, he transferred from the regular army to the Royal Flying Corps in 1915. From his arrival in France in February 1916, Ball established a reputation as a fearless pilot and excellent shot, achieving his first confirmed victory in late June. In just three months over the Somme, he scored 30 victories. With the introduction of the S.E.5, he reluctantly gave up his Nieuport XVII and on May 6, 1917 claimed his 44th and last victim, a German Albatros D.III.

The S.E.5s of Ball's flight encountered Manfred von Richthofen's unit, the all-red Jasta 11 on the evening of May 7, 1917 and Ball was last seen entering a thundercloud. Moments before Ball crashed, a German officer on the ground witnessed Ball's undamaged inverted aircraft emerge alone from the clouds, 61m/200ft above the ground with a dead propeller. He was only 20 years old and was posthumously awarded the Victoria Cross. Ball's death profoundly affected the morale of the Royal Flying Corps.

Manfred von Richthofen – Germany

The most famous ace of World War I, Manfred von Richthofen, joined a cavalry regiment in 1911. He transferred to the German Air Service in May 1915, initially as an observer, and earned his pilot's wings in December that year. After brief service on the Russian Front he transferred to France in August 1916 and on September 17, 1916 claimed the first of his 80 confirmed victories.

On January 16, 1917 he was given command of his own squadron, Jagdstaffel 11 and on June 26 that year, the command of Jagdgeschwader 1, a wing of four staffeln (squadrons) that came to be known as Richthofen's Flying Circus. The wing was made up of Germany's flying élite and Richthofen was keen to let the enemy know they were dealing with the "top guns" of the time – his personal Albatros D.III was painted all red and his men's aircraft were equally conspicuous, earning him the Red Baron nickname. Richthofen was almost killed in a dogfight in July 1917 – he received a serious head wound but managed to crash-land his Albatros D.V. On September 2, 1917, flying the new Fokker Dr.I triplane, he scored his 60th kill. The Red Baron's score continued to climb and on April 20, 1918 he claimed his 80th and last victim, an RAF Sopwith

TOP: **Captain Albert Ball VC, DSO, MC – Britain's first aviation hero of the Great War.** ABOVE: **The Albatros D.V was the type being flown by the "Red Baron" in mid-1917.** RIGHT: **Pilots of Jagdstaffel 11 with von Richthofen in the cockpit of the Albatros D.III.**

Camel. Richthofen was killed the next day as he flew over the trenches in pursuit of Canadian Wilfrid May in his R.E.8. Evidence suggests Richthofen was hit by a single bullet, possibly fired from a machine-gun in the trenches. Richthofen's loss devastated German morale and far outweighed the military value of any further victories he might have achieved.

Edward Rickenbacker – USA

A celebrated racing driver before World War I, Eddie Rickenbacker first went to France in 1917 as the personal chauffeur of General Pershing. Eager to see action, he transferred to the US Army Aviation Section, initially as an engineering officer. After learning to fly, he joined the 94th Aero Squadron in March 1918.

He first flew Nieuport 28s and then SPADs and by the end of the war he had built up the impressive total of 26 victories, even more remarkable as he was hospitalized for two of his eight months of combat flying. Rickenbacker took over as commanding officer of the 94th in September 1918, and having been born in 1890, Rickenbacker was an old man compared to many of the pilots he commanded. Unlike many other famous World War I fighter pilots, he survived the war and returned to a hero's welcome in the USA as America's leading fighter ace.

Charles Nungesser – France

Like Rickenbacker, Charles Nungesser had been a racing driver, and by the end of World War I Nungesser was officially France's third-ranking fighter ace. While racing in South America, the Frenchman learned to fly and on returning to France in 1914 he joined the army. Nungesser got a transfer to the Flying Service and by 1915 he was a reconnaissance pilot, albeit a very aggressive example. In November that year he was posted to a fighter squadron and began to build his impressive total of 45 victories, most of which he won flying Nieuports bearing his favoured skull and crossbones motif.

On January 29, 1916 Nungesser was in a serious crash and broke both legs, but he was flying again within two months. He was wounded many times and in-between his numerous crashes and visits to the hospital, Nungesser was taking his toll of German aircraft – by December 1916, a total of 21 victories.

At one point a German aircraft dropped a message on his aerodrome challenging him to a "duel". When Nungesser arrived at the appointed place he was ambushed by six German fighters. He shot two of them down and the others fled. On the same day, the Frenchman was attacked in the air by an RFC pilot who clearly had poor recognition skills – the British pilot persisted and Nungesser reluctantly shot him down too. The sky over the Western Front was full of danger. By mid-August 1917 he was so physically exhausted that he had to be carried to his aircraft, such was his desire to fight. Nungesser continued the familiar pattern of crashes, injuries and more victories until the war's end.

Although he survived the war, he disappeared over the Atlantic in 1927 while trying to fly from France to the USA.

TOP: **The Fokker Dr.I Triplane was von Richthofen's last mount.** ABOVE. **With his matinee idol looks and outstanding combat record Eddie Rickenbacker was the all-American hero.** LEFT: **Pictured with his Nieuport, Nungesser started the war as a cavalry officer and began his military flying in 1915.**

LEFT: **The cockpit of this Bristol Scout replica is equipped with all the original instruments a 1914 pilot had.** BELOW: **Woodworking tools outnumbered metalworking tools in the early aircraft factories.** BOTTOM: **With two wings generating more lift than one, the biplane was a popular configuration.**

Fighter aircraft technology up to 1945

When Orville and Wilbur Wright built their pioneering Wright Flyer in 1903, they used wood as the main material for wings and fuselage, braced by wires for added strength. By the end of World War II, most fighters were all-metal and flew at speeds the Wrights could have only dreamed of. The Wright Flyer was a biplane and a pusher aircraft, that is the propeller was used to push from behind rather than pull from the front as in later tractor aircraft.

The pusher arrangement was retained for some early fighters, in the days before the invention of interrupter gear, so that a forward-firing gun could be used with no propeller, which had tended to get in the way of the bullets. With no propeller in the way, the front seat was given to the gunner/observer while the pilot occupied the rear seat. The pusher arrangement was ultimately unsuitable for higher-per-formance fighters and dangerous – in the event of a nose-down crash, the engine and associated fuel tended to land on top of the two-man crew. The tractor configuration therefore became the norm for fighters and other aircraft.

The Wrights' aircraft's roll was controlled by wing warping, that is, bracing wires were pulled to twist the wing's outer sections. When World War I broke out, most aircraft designers were favouring the conventional tailplane and fin arrangement using trailing edge ailerons to effect roll in place of the limited wing warping.

As engine technology improved and speeds increased, drag on early aircraft became an issue and aircraft frames were increasingly covered and enclosed with taut fabric for streamlining. This technique was used into the mid-1930s, but by the time of World War II most new fighter aircraft were of all-metal "monocoque" construction. Whereas early fabric-covered fighters got their structural strength from taut metal bracing wires, the metal skin of the monocoque fuselage and ultimately wings and tail, welded or riveted to a light metal interior framework provided an incredibly strong construction.

The Wrights chose a biplane configuration for their Flyer and this form was used in most early World War I fighters as two pairs of wings generated much more lift than a monoplane. A series of pre-World War I accidents had led Britain's government to ban the Royal Flying Corps from using the apparently unstable and unsafe monoplane, and it was not until 1937 that the Royal Air Force deployed a monoplane fighter – the Hurricane. The Hawker Hurricane was an interesting aircraft and was a "crossover" design as it incorporated old and new aircraft construction techniques – it was a monoplane but its fuselage had a metal framework covered with wooden formers with a fabric covering.

As biplanes had succeeded in the first air combats, it was therefore inevitable that triplanes appeared, and in the cases of the Fokker Dr.I and the Sopwith Triplane were very successful.

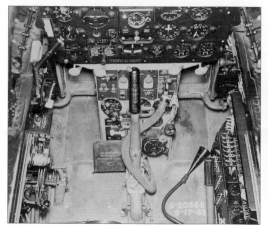

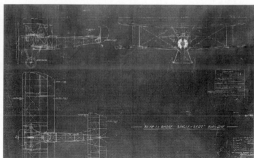

LEFT: **Compare the complexity of this 1945 Grumman Tigercat cockpit with that of the 1914 Bristol Scout.** BELOW: **By the end of World War II, the wood and fabric fighter construction technique was obsolete.**

Sets of two or three wings had to be braced by fairly substantial wires and joined together with interplane struts which in themselves generated drag. A single wing of the same area would generate much less drag and being more aerodynamic would allow the aircraft to go that much faster.

Engine technology developed at an incredible pace in the first four decades of the 20th century. The 1914 Vickers F.B.5 with a top speed of 113kph/70mph was powered by a 100hp rotary engine, and less than three decades later the engine that powered the 697kph/433mph P-47 Thunderbolt was rated at 2535hp. Rotary engines, the principal combat aircraft engine when war broke out, reached their developmental peak by the end of World War I. Although relatively small and light, power output of the rotary dropped off with increased altitude.

By the end of World War I, air-cooled radials and in-line piston engines were clearly the way ahead. Both types of engine had much to commend them and both were developed to the maximum until the jet engine ultimately replaced them both. The importance of engine development in the evolution of fighters cannot be overemphasized. More powerful and efficient engines coupled with improved aerodynamics enabled fighters to fly higher and faster. Without a Merlin engine, would the Spitfire have been the fighter it became?

Although World War I had clearly demonstrated the military value of aircraft, in the years immediately after, fighter development was neglected – it was peacetime uses of aircraft that taxed the designers' ingenuity. However, speed competitions like the Schneider Trophy challenged designers to develop small, fast aircraft. With national pride at stake, these competitions generated huge amounts of worldwide interest. The Schneider Trophy races held annually from 1919 to 1931 did much to encourage innovation in engine and airframe design and showed that fuel science and super-charging were vital elements in the engine equation. Britain won the Schneider Trophy in 1931 with a Supermarine racing floatplane, a design that led directly to the legendary Spitfire.

ABOVE: **A Royal Air Force Spitfire. By 1945, piston engine technology had effectively reached its evolutionary limit.**

But what use is an engine without a good propeller? This vital but often overlooked element of the fighter aircraft "package" was itself dramatically improved between World War I and 1945. World War I fighters had two blades but late mark Spitfires had five-blade examples. As a propeller spins it generates thrust in the same way a wing develops lift. Early propellers were fixed pitch but in the late 1930s variable-pitch propellers were introduced so the pilot could mechanically adjust the propeller blades' angle for maximum efficiency at different speeds.

Towards the end of World War II, German and British jet-powered aircraft appeared and showed aircraft designers around the world the way ahead. The Messerschmitt Me262 could reach speeds of 870kph/540mph compared to the P-51 Mustang's top speed of 703kph/437mph. Designers knew that these early jet engines could take aircraft to speeds almost 25 per cent faster than the best piston-engined fighters in the world. The jet engine was the powerplant of the future.

Fighter armament 1914–45

At the outbreak of World War I, aircraft armament was non-existent or ad hoc. The first fighters were armed with revolvers, rifles or shotguns carried by the pilots or observers but the importance of reliable hard-hitting armament was soon appreciated. Once weapons like the 7.7mm/0.303in Lewis machine-gun were proven, their use was then perfected. At first the guns were mounted on pivot pins or flexible mounts, aimed by the observers or pilots but they became truly effective once the guns were fixed to the aircraft and were synchronized to fire between the spinning propeller blades. To aim at a target, the pilot simply had to fly straight at it.

During World War I, two rifle-calibre machine-guns were usually enough to inflict serious damage on canvas-covered mainly wooden aircraft. By the mid-1930s this was clearly inadequate to destroy the larger, metal bombers coming off the drawing boards at the time. Consequently, more and bigger guns were used to arm fighter aircraft but where was the best location for them? Guns synchronized to fire through the propeller arc usually experienced a 10 per cent reduction in the rate of fire, and the numbers of guns that could be clustered around an engine was physically limited. The other option was to mount the guns in the wings – a far cry from the early days of air fighting when the gun's breech had to be within reach of the pilot so he could free jammed bullets. The down side of the wing-mounted gun, especially as wings became thinner, was the limited amounts of ammunition that could be physically fitted in the wing.

Most British World War I fighters were armed with 7.7mm/0.303in Vickers machine-guns and these remained the standard British armament until the mid-1930s when the Browning 7.7mm/0.303in was adopted. The Browning could fire 1100–1200 rounds per minute compared to the 750rpm of the Lewis. The muzzle velocity of the Browning was also greater than that of the Vickers – 811m/2660ft per second compared to 683m/2240ft per second. These performance figures are important because in most combats, pilots only have time for perhaps a second's burst as an enemy aircraft flashes by.

BELOW: **The synchronizing of fighter aircraft guns eased aiming for the pilots and thus improved the effectiveness of the early fighters.**

During World War I, experiments had been carried out to see if large calibre weapons (cannon) firing explosive ammunition could destroy enemy aircraft. Early British tests found that the recoil of these comparatively large weapons was enough to stop a slow-moving firing aircraft in flight, let alone inflict damage on an enemy. French development work was more successful and a 37mm/1.45in cannon was used in combat by French aces Guynemer and Fonck, both of whom destroyed German aircraft with the weapon. Germany's World War I Becker cannon was later used as the basis for the early 1930s French Hispano-Suiza cannon that became the hugely successful Type 404 Moteur Canon.

In the mid-1930s Britain was behind the other major air forces in the procurement of cannon armament for fighter aircraft so it eventually licence-built the French Hispano-Suiza cannon.

When the legendary Spitfire first went to war its original armament was eight 7.7mm/0.303in Browning machine-guns but as the German Luftwaffe provided their aircraft with more armour and self-sealing fuel tanks it was apparent that the Spitfire's eight machine-guns were not adequate to inflict enough damage on enemy aircraft. Some Spitfire pilots were amazed to learn that enemy bombers claimed as "probably destroyed" had managed to limp home having suffered perhaps over 100 hits from 7.7mm/0.303in ammunition rounds. The Germans' ingenious self-sealing tanks, made of lightweight metal coated with layers of vulcanized and non-vulcanized rubber, must have saved many such aircraft from becoming airborne infernos. When the fuel tank was punctured by a bullet or shrapnel, the leaking fuel reacted with the non-vulcanized layer making it swell thereby plugging the hole. In spite of this, a hit from an exploding cannon round would have caused irreparable damage.

Aircraft like the early Hurricane with its eight machine-guns could unleash 160 bullets per second on a target whereas a 20mm/0.78in cannon carried by a Messerschmitt Bf109 could fire five shells per second – quantity versus destructive capability. The best solution was a compromise and so later Spitfires and Hurricanes carried a combined machine-gun/cannon armament.

TOP LEFT: **Rearming an RAF Hurricane – two of the aircraft's four hard-hitting wing-mounted 20mm/0.78in cannon.** ABOVE: **Preparing to load the guns in USAAF P-51 Mustangs.**

During World War I, pilots had aimed their guns using a ring bead sight but that kept them too focused on the target, unable to see what else was going on in the sky ahead. In the mid-1930s the electric reflector sight was introduced and was a simplistic forerunner of today's Head-Up Display. A bright circle of light with an aiming dot in the centre was projected on to a small glass screen in front of the pilot. As the image was focused on infinity, it also allowed the pilot to be aware of what else was in the sky ahead.

Although the machine-gun and cannon were the most significant air-to-air weapons in the period, unguided rockets were highly developed by the end of World War II. Soviet fighters had in fact been experimentally armed with bomber-destroying 82mm/3.23in unguided rockets in the late 1930s. This Russian rocket was typical of most unguided rockets, having impact-fused explosive warheads that could inflict major damage on a bomber. During World War II, Germany was equally advanced in the development of unguided missiles and was eager to produce any means of knocking enemy bombers from the sky. The Luftwaffe initially used adapted surface-to-surface 21cm/8.27in rockets with 10.22kg/22.5lb high-explosive warheads detonated by a timed fuse. By the end of the war, Luftwaffe fighters were routinely armed with up to 24 unguided air-to-air rockets which, fired as a salvo, represented a deadly threat to Allied bombers. More impressive was the crude but effective radar-linked fire control computer that tracked an enemy aircraft and then launched an unguided missile at optimum range. Luckily for the Allies, Germany's comprehensive guided missile programme did not result in production weapons before the war's end.

LEFT: **In World War I, formal uniforms were the normal flying dress, however impractical they were.**
BELOW: **In winter conditions and as aircraft ceilings increased, thick flying suits were introduced on both sides during World War I.**

Pilot equipment up to 1945

What kind of equipment was at the early fighter pilot's disposal?

Early cockpits had very few instruments – an airspeed indicator, altimeter, fuel and oil pressure gauges and little else. As fighters were able to climb higher and higher, so the aircrew had to wear more and more clothes to counter the effect of the bitter cold. A pilot's efficiency also suffers above heights of 3050m/10,000ft and pressurized oxygen is required above 5,500m/18,000ft or they will ultimately pass out. Face masks were developed to provide oxygen under these conditions and continue to be used today. Cockpit heating was not much use if the pilot's "office" was open to the elements but it did make a difference when enclosed cockpits were introduced.

Before World War I, aircraft had carried radio receivers and transmitters only for experimental purposes – the first use of radio between an aircraft and the ground was in the USA in 1910. Before the days of transistors, those early radios were large heavy pieces of equipment weighing up to 114kg/250lb and as weight was a crucial factor in early aircraft, they were just not practical. When radios were installed they were normally only capable of receiving or sending Morse code signals. The other complication was that due to the wavelengths in use at the time, a trailing aerial of 91m/300ft length had to be used. Improved technology was required to make radio more practical and by the mid-1930s, relatively clear speech exchanges over the air were becoming the norm. Leather flying helmets were produced with earpieces stitched in, while the oxygen mask also had a built-in microphone.

On March 1, 1912 Captain Albert Berry of the United States made the first parachute jump from an aircraft, and from the start of World War I observation balloon crews were equipped with parachutes. The life-saving devices were not, however,

LEFT: **By the end of World War II more practical flying clothing was the norm, as were the parachutes denied to pioneer fighter pilots.** BELOW: **This Spitfire pilot sports the standard RAF oxygen mask with inbuilt microphone fixed to his helmet featuring in-built headphones.** BOTTOM: **The ultimate emergency exit. This unknown pilot leaves his stricken aircraft and prepares to open his 'chute.**

issued to aircrew and this led to many unnecessary deaths on both sides. Early 'chutes were heavy and bulky and would have added greatly to the overall weight of an aircraft. There was also a ludicrous belief among British military leaders that parachutes would undermine a pilot's fighting spirit and that they would "take to the silk" when faced with danger.

By the last year of World War I, however, aircraft performance and better parachute design made the parachute a more practical piece of equipment. Germany had led the way and issued parachutes to its crews in the summer of 1918. The first time a pilot used a parachute as a means of escape and survived was on August 22, 1918 – Lt Frigyes Hefty of the Austro-Hungarian Air Corps left his burning fighter after a dogfight with Italian aircraft, landed safely and lived to tell the tale.

As the higher speed jet fighters entered service towards the end of World War II, parachutes were found to be unsuitable for emergency escape. The high speed airflow made it very difficult and dangerous to bail out in the traditional manner. In the same way that they had led the way with parachutes, the Germans pioneered the use of what came to be known as "ejection seats" that propelled the pilot clear of their aircraft's tail, usually approaching very rapidly from the rear. A Heinkel He219A-0 was experimentally fitted with compressed air ejection seats for both crew, believed to be the first of their kind in service. The Heinkel 280 jet prototype's seat was also fired with compressed air, as opposed to the explosive charges in use today. In January 1942, during a test flight of the Heinkel jet, the pilot lost control of the aircraft and successfully ejected. The pilot, Flugkapitan Otto Schenk, was the first of thousands of aircrew to have their lives saved by ejection seats.

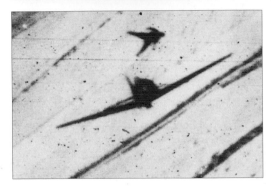

Blitzkrieg fighters

When Germany invaded Poland on September 1, 1939, precipitating World War II, a Blitzkrieg (lightning war) was unleashed on the ill-prepared Poles. The Blitzkrieg strategy was devised to create psychological shock and chaos in enemy forces through the use of surprise, speed and superiority. Proven by the Germans during the Spanish Civil War in 1938, the Blitzkrieg against Poland saw totally co-ordinated air (fighters and bombers) and land forces paralyse Poland's capacity to defend.

The best fighter aircraft in the Polish inventory was the P.Z.L. P.11 – with a top speed of 390kph/242mph the P.11 was still no match for the German Messerschmitt Bf109E that could fly over 177kph/110mph faster than the Polish fighter.

ABOVE: **The Messerschmitt Bf109, one of the all-time great fighter aircraft, was at the forefront of the Blitzkrieg, blasting ill-prepared opposition from the air.**
BELOW: **By the time the Luftwaffe reached France, it met more effective fighters – the Dewoitine D.520s.**

That said, the Polish P.11 pilots made the most of their out-moded machines. Some sources claim that 114 of the P.11s were destroyed in the air battles that raged at the time of the invasion – although the defence of Poland failed, the P.11s did claim 126 Luftwaffe aircraft in the process.

The Luftwaffe deployed 200 Bf109E fighters and fighter-bombers for the invasion of Poland and the more manoeuvrable Bf109 was also better armed than the P.11 and Poland's even more antiquated P.7 fighters. The P.11s were however very nimble and not to be taken lightly, a mistake made by a number of Luftwaffe twin-engine fighter crews.

The Polish air defence ultimately failed partly because of the inflexible military structure of the Polish armed forces. Many fighter and bomber units were assigned to different armies tasked with defending different parts of the country and so there was no co-ordinated fighter response to the armadas of German bombers. A very significant element of the Polish fighter force was the Pursuit Brigade solely tasked with the defence of Warsaw.

The Nazi Propaganda Ministry had claimed that the Polish Air Force had been destroyed on the ground in the first day of battle but this was far from the truth. A formation of Heinkel He111 bombers trying to attack an airfield near Warsaw, was mauled and six were destroyed, the first falling to P.11 pilot Lt Aleksander Gabszwicz. On the afternoon of September 1, 1939, He111 bombers again headed for Warsaw, escorted by Bf109s and Bf110s. The air combats that followed after defending P.11 fighters were scrambled saw six German bombers shot down for the loss of five Polish fighters. So committed were the Polish defenders that one pilot rammed a Bf109 and baled out. The Polish defenders had prevented the Luftwaffe from dropping a single bomb on Warsaw.

The fighters attached to the armies saw much action and accounted for many German aircraft. In the first six days of war, army units claimed 63 Luftwaffe aircraft while the Pursuit Brigade claimed 42. From September 8, as the Germans pushed through and the Polish forces fell back towards Warsaw, the Poles' ability to defend themselves in a concerted manner was severely undermined. As the Polish infrastructure was dismantled by the Blitzkrieg, and starved of fuel, their fighter forces dissolved into chaos. On September 17, Soviet forces, acting in concert with Germany, also crossed into Poland, sealing the fate of the beleaguered nation.

The P.11s and P.7s continued to fight as they could until being ordered by General Rayski, Polish Commander-in-Chief, to evacuate to Romania. Many desperate and courageous Polish pilots had continued to attack large Luftwaffe formations on what were ultimately suicide missions. A number of Polish pilots escaped so they could continue to fight Germany from friendly countries. Some enlisted in the French Air Force and after the Fall of France made their way to Britain to join RAF Fighter Command.

Poland had fallen to the might of the Nazi war machine with Luftwaffe fighters playing a vital role in neutralizing resistance in the air. Blitzkrieg tactics were subsequently employed in the German invasions of Belgium, the Netherlands and France in 1940.

TOP: **German nightfighters, primarily developed to counter the RAF night-time bombing offensive, gave the Luftwaffe the ability to fight around the clock.**
ABOVE: **The P.Z.L. P.11 fighters of Poland were not able to repulse the might of the Nazi Blitzkrieg.** LEFT: **Armadas of Heinkel He111 bombers, having honed their skills in Spain, carried the Blitzkrieg across Europe.**

The Battle of Britain

By June 1940 Belgium, Holland and France had fallen to German forces. The British Army withdrew from the Continent and the British Prime Minister, Winston Churchill, declared "the Battle of France is over; the Battle of Britain is about to begin". The so-called "phoney" war was over and the Third Reich's next objective was the subjugation of Britain. Churchill refused to consider peace on German terms and Hitler realized that he might have to invade Britain, which was protected from the German Army by the waters of the English Channel. On July 16, 1940 Hitler issued a directive ordering the preparation and execution of a plan to invade Britain. With Britain's large and powerful navy to contend with, an amphibious invasion of Britain would only be possible if the Luftwaffe could establish control of the air over the Channel and southern England. The Luftwaffe planned to destroy British air power in a wave of massive raids and clear the way for the invasion. As the Luftwaffe bombing attacks started in July 1940, Goering, leader of the German Air Force, thought that the Luftwaffe would easily beat the Royal Air Force, and so the German Army and Navy prepared to invade. Invasion barges were assembled in Channel ports.

ABOVE: **The Spitfire's well-documented role in the summer of 1940 earned it a place in world history.**

The forces deployed in the Battle of Britain were surprisingly small. The RAF had around 600 front-line fighters, mainly Spitfires and Hurricanes, to defend their country. The Germans had around 1300 bombers and dive bombers, and about 900 single-engined and 300 twin-engined fighters. Despite the importance of the campaign as a prelude to invasion, the Luftwaffe had no systematic or consistent plan of action. In contrast, RAF Fighter Command had prepared themselves for exactly the type of battle that took place. Britain's radar early warning, the most advanced operational system in the world, gave the RAF notice of where and when to direct their fighter forces to repel German raids, thus avoiding costly and misplaced standing patrols. This was a vital lesson which is as valid today as in 1940.

German bombers lacked the bomb-carrying capacity to mount truly strategic bombing raids against key military targets, and British radar largely prevented them from exploiting the element of surprise. Long-range Luftwaffe fighter cover was only partially available from German fighter aircraft, since the latter were operating at the limit of their flying range from bases across the English Channel.

Between July 10 and August 11, German air attacks were directed on ports and most importantly on fighter airfields to draw Fighter Command into combat. From August 12 to 23 the battle became more intense as the Luftwaffe launched Adlerangriff (Eagle Attack) hitting radar stations and trying to destroy Fighter Command in combat – inland airfields and communications centres were still heavily attacked. Up to September 6, RAF Fighter Command came close to defeat as the Germans intensified their efforts to destroy Fighter Command and obliterate British defences. Although British aircraft production increased and the Luftwaffe had lost more than 600 aircraft, RAF pilots were being killed more quickly than replacements could be trained. The RAF's effectiveness was further hampered by bombing damage done to the vital radar stations.

At the beginning of September the British retaliated by unexpectedly bombing Berlin, which so angered Hitler that he ordered the Luftwaffe to shift its attacks from Fighter

Command installations to London and other cities. Although this led to many civilian casualties, it gave Fighter Command a short respite and time to regroup. In reality, the Luftwaffe's raids were somewhat formulaic which allowed Fighter Command to concentrate its fighter strength for the first time. By September 6, a huge German invasion fleet appeared to be ready to sail and British forces were put on "Alert No.2" meaning that an attack was probable in the next three days.

On September 15, the RAF's Spitfires and Hurricanes destroyed 185 German aircraft, showing the Luftwaffe that it could not gain air ascendancy over Britain. British fighters were simply shooting down German bombers faster than German industry could produce them. After the decisive RAF victories on September 15, the threat of invasion faded. The Battle of Britain was won, principally by the fighters of the Royal Air Force, and Hitler's invasion of Britain was postponed indefinitely.

ABOVE: **Messerschmitt Bf109s on patrol over the English Channel.** ABOVE RIGHT: **The fate of many Luftwaffe aircraft during the Battle.** RIGHT: **The Hawker Hurricane in fact destroyed more enemy aircraft than Spitfires, balloons and anti-aircraft defences combined. This photograph shows No.310 (Czechoslovakian) Squadron, Duxford 1940.**

Nightfighters

As early as World War I, German night bombing of Britain had been countered by defending fighters such as the Bristol Fighter and Sopwith Camel. Relying only on their eyesight and the hope of a bright moon, early nightfighter pilots did not constitute a practical deterrent and achieved only marginal success.

By World War II, defenders were assisted by ground radars, which could guide nightfighters to the general area where the enemy might be found, again by visual means. Truly effective night interception had to await the development of a radar small enough to be carried by the fighter itself. An airborne radar of this kind could aid in finding, stalking and bringing the nightfighter into firing range.

The USA, Germany, and Britain were all developing airborne radar early in World War II. Britain modified existing aircraft to fill the nightfighter gap. The Bristol Blenheim could not match the performance of day fighters like the German Bf109 so many became nightfighters, ultimately carrying the new and highly secret airborne radar. But even before the Blenheim IFs were equipped with radar, the RAF achieved some night-time victories – in June 1940 No.23 Squadron destroyed a Heinkel 111 bomber over Norfolk. However, the first radar interception came in late July 1940 when a Blenheim IF of the RAF's Fighter Interception Unit destroyed a German Dornier Do 17.

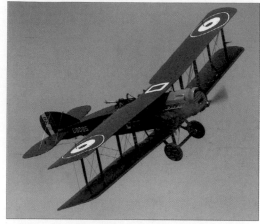

ABOVE: **The only specialized equipment carried by early nightfighters like the Bristol Fighter was the pilot's keen eyesight.** BELOW: **The Spitfire, with its narrow undercarriage track, was far from ideal for night operations.**

The Bristol Beaufighter was the world's first high-performance purpose-designed nightfighter and was a very advanced aircraft for its time. At the time of its combat début in 1940 the Beaufighter's devastating armament of four 20mm/0.78in cannon and six 7.7mm/0.303in machine-guns was the heaviest carried by any front-line aircraft. The closing months of 1940 saw the machine-guns fitted to the

LEFT: **The Northrop P-61 Black Widow – the first purpose-designed US nightfighter.** BELOW: **Only a handful of the Focke Wulf Ta154 dedicated nightfighters were ever built but indicated the realization that nightfighting was a specialized business.**

ABOVE: **A Junkers Ju 88 Ñ-1 nightfighter.** RIGHT: **As aircraft were developed for nightfighting, so the cockpit began to accumulate new forms of equipment. The right seat position of this RAF Mosquito XIII nightfighter is dominated by the viewing apparatus of the AI Mk VIIIB radar.**

Beaufighters and, after a period of trial and error mastering the new radar with its range of 6.4km/4 miles, the aircraft's night victories began to increase.

Meanwhile, the United States directed its attentions to the interim Douglas P-70 and to the new Northrop P-61 Black Widow, the first US aircraft designed from the outset as a nightfighter. Lacking sufficient suitable US aircraft, USAAF units in Europe operated the British Beaufighter and later the Mosquito with good effect. In the Pacific, USAAF nightfighter squadrons operated the P-70 nightfighter version of the Douglas A-20 until P-61s could be delivered in 1944. By the end of World War II, the P-61 was the standard USAAF nightfighter and was in service with 15 of the 16 nightfighter squadrons operating in combat theatres worldwide.

German nightfighting began in the same way as the British – day fighters used in conjunction with a pilot's eyesight and searchlights on the ground below as the only means of seeing enemy aircraft in the dark. But by the summer of 1942 dedicated nightfighter groups were equipped with airborne radar. The RAF then began to use "Window", bundles of aluminium strips which, when dropped from the bombers, filled the sky with erroneous radar targets rendering German radar useless at a stroke. The Luftwaffe response in mid-1943 was the Wilde Sau nightfighters (Bf109 and Fw190) that relied on the illumination of enemy bombers by flares, searchlights or fires from below. Fighters guided from the ground by radar and helped by the ground lighting were then able to engage the enemy. German flak units were ordered to limit their fire to altitudes of 7000m/22,967ft so that the friendly nightfighters could operate in safety. Messerschmitt Bf110 and Junkers Ju 88 nightfighters equipped with radar and upward firing cannon did take a heavy toll of Allied bombers – literally hundreds were shot down.

The first uncertain steps in nightfighting led to the radar-equipped fighters of today, equally at home in day, bad weather and night conditions.

Fleet fighters: the rise of naval air power

The year 1910 was a key year in the development of military air power. On November 14 that year a Curtiss biplane became the first ever to take-off from a ship. The aircraft flown by Eugene B. Ely flew from a 25.3m/83ft platform built over the bows of the US Navy cruiser USS *Birmingham*. Within two months Ely had succeeded in landing a Curtiss on a ship, this time the USS *Pennsylvania*. These feats were considered by many as nothing more than stunts but Ely had shown that aircraft actually did not need dry land from which to operate. By combining one of man's oldest means of transport, the boat, with his newest, the aeroplane, a new means of waging war was born.

Britain's first deck take-off came on January 10, 1912, when the Royal Navy's Lt C.R. Samson flew a Short biplane from staging erected over the gun turret of the cruiser HMS *Africa*. By 1915 Britain had two ships with 36.6m/120ft-long flying-off decks but they were far from operational. Flying-off platforms were, however, fitted to a handful of Royal Navy ships and a Sopwith Pup using the HMS *Yarmouth* flying platform was launched against and subsequently destroyed a German Zeppelin – this action is believed to have been the earliest use of a "carrier-borne" fighter for air defence.

The first significant use of carrier-borne air power came in the 1931–2 war between China and Japan. In January 1932, carrier-borne aircraft operated in support of Japanese land forces in action near Shanghai. It was not, however, until World War II that aircraft carriers and fighters came into their own.

TOP: **Three thoroughbred Grumman fighters – the Hellcat (foreground), Bearcat and Wildcat (rear).** ABOVE: **Early fleet fighter – a Sopwith 1½ Strutter takes off from the deck of HMS *Argus*.**

The carrier was vital in the World War II Japanese campaigns in the Pacific and enabled them to project power over vast distances. Carriers were able to make or break campaigns by providing strike aircraft and air cover for other ships, convoys and assault ships, making their protection vital. Each carrier had fighter aircraft to defend the ships and carriers from air attack. The US Navy developed defensive fighter "nets" over carrier groups to protect them from enemy aircraft by a combination of radar early-warning and standing patrols of fighters, some up to 64km/40 miles away from the carrier. A carrier that could be protected from air attack was a massive strategic asset in any theatre of war.

LEFT: **A typical scene from the flight deck of a Pacific theatre carrier.**

ABOVE: **Martlet/Wildcats prepare for take-off from the deck of a Royal Navy carrier.** RIGHT: **The deck of a wartime carrier was fraught with dangers. Here a US Navy Hellcat burns while another, wings folded, awaits orders.**

While Britain at first had second-rate or obsolete aircraft deployed as carrier-borne fighters, other nations developed high-performance hard-hitting fighters designed from the outset as carrier aircraft. One of the first true fighters deployed by the Royal Navy was the Sea Hurricane, the navalized version of the famous Battle of Britain fighter. RAF Hurricanes had flown on and off HMS *Glorious* during the Norwegian campaign in 1040 and shown that high-performance fighters could be operated from carriers. It was followed into Royal Navy service by the American-built Grumman Martlet (known as the Wildcat in the US Navy and later in the Royal Navy). The Wildcat proved itself almost immediately in its first carrier deployment on convoy protection in September 1941 by driving away or destroying enemy aircraft. Meanwhile the Sea Hurricanes soldiered on, tackling German torpedo aircraft while newer high-performance fighters were awaited from America.

World War II Japanese carrier-borne air power was formidable. Six aircraft carriers took part in the devastating December 1941 attack on Pearl Harbor which devastated the US Pacific Fleet. In this and other attacks, Japanese strike aircraft were only able to carry out their deadly missions because they were escorted by fighters such as the Mitsubishi Zero that fought with the defending fighters. The Zero was a formidable enemy to take on but its excellent manoeuvrability was achieved at the price of pilot safety. Every weight-saving measure was taken – there was no armour protecting the pilot and often there was not even a radio in the aircraft.

ABOVE: **Dramatic rocket-sled take-off by an early Sea Hurricane. Launched from a ship without a flight deck, the pilot had to find land or ditch.**

One carrier fighter in particular could be described as a war winner – the Grumman F6F Hellcat. Following its arrival in combat in August 1943, this tough fighter was able to turn the tables on the Zero and gave US Navy and Marine Corps pilots the upper hand until the end of World War II. Aircraft carriers had been shown to be as good as their defences, and in particular the fighters that protected them.

Higher and faster

By the end of World War II, the piston-engined fighter had effectively been developed to the limits of its possibilities. The future lay with a greater knowledge of aerodynamics and fighters with jet power. Less than a decade after the end of the war, there were fighter aircraft on the drawing board that were planned to travel at up to three times the speed of sound. But jet propulsion also opened up new horizons for bomber aircraft design. While bombers were designed to go higher and faster, fighters were also developed to go higher and faster to intercept and destroy them. Speeds that man had only dreamed of were now within reach.

Whereas propellers would not have looked out of place on some early straight-wing jet fighters, aerodynamicists began to understand more about the special design requirements of high-speed jet aircraft. Wartime German research had found that by sweeping back the wings and tailplanes, the buffeting, vibration and drag experienced by early jets near the speed of sound could be reduced. Designers hoped that this feature could help the aircraft ease through the Mach 1 sound barrier.

TOP: **The Panavia Air Defence Tornado is capable of patrolling and defending huge expanses of airspace.** ABOVE: **The BAC Lightning reached RAF units in 1960. It was the fastest British fighter ever.**

At the same time the experts were trying to get their aircraft higher and higher. The fast climb was essential because it gave defending fighters the chance to reach the "high ground" from which to mount the most effective attack on enemy fighters and bombers – the aim of fighter pilots since World War I.

During the Korean War of 1950–3, the North American F-86 Sabre and the MiG-15 represented the state of the art and both had been designed with the benefit of wartime German research data. Both of these highly successful fighters tried to use their performance to achieve a height advantage

LEFT: **The F-16 has a maximum speed of 2125kph/1320mph and a ceiling in excess of 15,250m/50,000ft which it can reach in one minute.**
BELOW: **The ubiquitous MiG-21, still widely deployed today, was one of the first high-performance all-weather fighters.**

ABOVE: **Much of the performance data of the Saab Gripen remains secret.**

over the enemy, with the result that most fighter actions were fought 8–13km/5–8 miles above the ground. The Korean War had shown that the straight-wing jets had had their day and that high-performance and therefore the most effective fighters would have swept wings and other aerodynamic innovations.

Third-generation jet fighters such as the F-100 Super Sabre and MiG-19 were the first production jet fighters capable of supersonic speeds in level flight but were still essentially fair-weather fighters. It was not until the next wave of jet fighters that the interceptor was born. High-performance fast-climbing

aircraft such as the MiG-21 and F-104 could reach speeds of Mach 2 and operate in all weathers.

The 1950s was the golden age of the strategic bomber – the USA, USSR and Britain all had fleets of long-range strategic bombers. High-performance, fast-climbing radar-equipped interceptors such as the English Electric Lightning and Convair F-102 appeared, and in the case of the Lightning could climb at 15,240m/50,000ft per minute.

In 1957 Britain's Defence Minister, Duncan Sandys, said the manned fighter would soon be a thing of the past, replaced by missiles. While this debate raged in the UK, elsewhere larger, often two-seat, fighters armed with missiles were in favour.

While Mach 2 performance and rapid climb are taken for granted in modern fighters, manoeuvrability is just as important. Modern interceptors like the Tornado ADV, F-16 and Gripen have an advantage over even slightly older fighters in that although they have to be able to climb quickly to high altitudes, the pilots don't actually have to see the enemy target aircraft. The powerful radars carried by today's fighters can pick up "bogies" over great distances and air-to-air missiles can be launched at targets beyond visual range.

Korea: the first jet v. jet war

Although jet fighter aircraft did enter service with Germany, Britain and the United States towards the end of World War II, it was not until the Korean War of 1950–3 that jet fought jet in the first major air war since World War II. When the war broke out following the North Korean invasion of South Korea on June 25, 1950, both sides were equipped with piston-powered aircraft, the North Korean Air Force having among other combat aircraft a total of 70 aged Soviet Yakovlev Yak-9 fighters. The Communist aggression against South Korea, whose air arm consisted of 16 unarmed trainers, drew the United States and the United Nations to the aid of the South.

The early days of the air war saw World War II types like F- (formerly P-) 51 Mustangs taking on Lavochkin La-7s although the USAF quickly deployed the F-80, the USAF's main fighter in the theatre. This straight-winged jet arrived just too late to see action in World War II but by 1950 was virtually obsolete. Nevertheless it began to rack up significant numbers of kills against the older North Korean types.

On July 3, US Navy jets flew in anger for the first time ever as F9F-3 Panthers escorted a bombing mission. Although the Panther too was a straight-wing jet, it remained the standard US Navy fighter throughout the conflict.

And so for the first six months of the war, the UN were to retain the upper hand in the air and on the ground. But then on November 1, 1950 some USAF Mustang pilots reported coming under fire by six swept-wing jet fighters that had flown across the Yalu river from Manchuria – the Russian-built Mikoyan-Gurevich MiG-15 was in the Korean War. The first jet

against jet air combat soon followed on November 8, when four MiGs were seen to fly into Korean air space and were challenged by F-80Cs of the 51 Fighter-Interceptor Wing. Lt Russell J. Brown attacked and destroyed one of the MiGs in mid-air. This historic combat was followed next day by the first jet kill by a US Navy jet when a Panther flown by Lt Commander

TOP: **Two classic jet fighters – the F-86 Sabre (left) and MiG-15.** ABOVE: **Royal Navy Lt Peter Carmichael on the day he downed a MiG jet with his piston-powered Sea Fury.**

W.T. Amen shot down another MiG-15. The Russian jets were starting to enjoy victories of their own against USAF B-29 bombers which had previously operated in relative safety. Flying from Chinese bases immune from UN attack, the MiGs were used to defend North Korean installations and represented a major threat to UN air superiority in the north where they created the very dangerous "MiG Alley". UN aircraft could range across the battlefields but faced deadly opposition when they neared areas in range of the MiG bases.

The USAF were quick to respond to the MiG threat and on November 8 ordered the F-86 Sabre-equipped 4th Fighter Group from the USA to Korea. The 27th Fighter-Escort Wing and their F-84 Thunderjets followed soon after. The F-86A was the most modern USAF fighter available but was later shown

TOP: The F-51 Mustang was widely deployed by the USAF in the early days of the air war. ABOVE: A Sea Fury FB Mk II of No.804 Sqdn, Royal Navy leaves the deck of HMS *Glory*. LEFT: The remarkable F-82 Twin Mustang was among the first USAF aircraft to operate over Korea.

to have a slightly inferior performance to that of the MiG. The Sabre's armament of six 12.7mm/0.5in machine-guns was no match for the two 23mm/0.9in and one 37mm/1.46in cannon of the MiG although the Sabre was a steadier gun platform. Tactically, the Communist pilots did themselves no favours, preferring to fly in gaggles of 20 or more aircraft compared to the section of four favoured by Western tacticians.

The first Sabre versus MiG air battle occurred on December 17, 1950 when four F-86s came upon four MiGs at an altitude of 7620m/25,000ft. Lt Colonel Bruce H. Hinton, leader of the F-86 section, fired 1500 rounds of ammunition and sent one MiG down to its destruction. On December 22, eight Sabres took on 15 MiGs and in the dogfights that followed from 9145m/30,000ft down to 305m/1000ft, the USAF pilots destroyed no fewer than six of the MiGs.

The Royal Australian Air Force, initially equipped with F-51 Mustangs, converted to Gloster Meteor F.8s but they were no match for the fast and manoeuvrable MiGs, which inflicted unacceptable losses on the F.8s.

The Republic F-84 Thunderjet was widely used in the war as a fighter-bomber and is credited with a number of air-kills, the first of which came on January 21, 1951. During a dive-bombing attack, F-84s were bounced by MiGs and in the dogfights that followed, Lt Colonel William E. Bertram scored the F-84's first MiG kill.

The MiGs did well to avoid all UN aircraft, not just the jets. The Hawker Sea Fury, operated by the Royal Navy, is known to have destroyed more Communist aircraft than any other non-US type and even shot down a number of North Korean MiGs. During August 1952, while flying the piston-engined Sea Fury off HMS *Ocean*, Royal Navy Lt Peter Carmichael destroyed a MiG-15 jet and earned himself a place in history.

By the end of the Korean War, USAF Sabres had achieved 757 victories for 103 losses. The first jet versus jet war was over and had demonstrated that tactics were as vital as effective weaponry. Straight-winged jets such as the F-80, F-84 and Meteor were shown to have had their day and the swept-winged fighters were on the ascendancy.

Fighter aircraft technology: 1945 to the present day

For most of the latter half of the 20th century, the designers of fighter aircraft continued to do what their predecessors had done – improve performance through more powerful engines and a better understanding of aerodynamics. Piston-engined fighters had virtually reached the end of their evolutionary line by 1945 although many remained in service for some years after the end of World War II. Jet powered fighters began to make their mark toward the end of the war, and within a decade supersonic speeds were regularly achieved, albeit in dives.

A greater understanding of "area rule" – the design technique that produces a fuselage contour with the lowest possible transonic wave drag – came in the 1950s and helped aircraft designers break through the "sound barrier" and produce aircraft capable of supersonic speeds in level flight. The quest for performance as opposed to manoeuvrability was typified by the Lockheed F-104 Starfighter that first flew in 1954.

Jet engine technology progressed rapidly in the 1950s resulting in engines like the F-104's General Electric 7076kg/15,600lb afterburning thrust J79 turbojet. This engine generated more than twice the output of the F-86 Sabre's 3402kg/7500lb thrust J47 turbojet. Compare them both to the 11,340kg/25,000lb thrust engines that power the F-15s in service today. Afterburner or reheat capability was developed in the late 1940s to give fighters an emergency boost of energy if required. When a pilot engages afterburner, additional fuel is simply burned in the jetpipe to generate extra thrust. This does consume considerable amounts of fuel and is used sparingly.

At first, jet fighters continued to use the construction techniques and materials employed on piston-engined aircraft. With the dawn of high speed flight and the extreme stresses placed on an airframe, designers began to look beyond aluminium and magnesium alloys and used titanium alloys and specially developed steel. Carbon or graphite fibre composites are also now commonly used and weigh half as much as

aluminium alloys but have three times the strength. This major weight saving reduces the overall weight of fighters and allows them to carry more fuel or weaponry if required.

Jet fighter designers have always grappled with the problem of trying to reduce the take-off and landing runs of high speed swept-wing aircraft and thus enable fighters to operate from shorter runways or even sections of road.

A truly innovative solution was the development of swing-wing or variable geometry in which the wings can move automatically from the swept to the spread position to maximize the aircraft's aerodynamic performance as required.

On take-off the spread position generates more lift and gets the aircraft off the ground sooner. Once in the air, the wings can be swept back for high-speed performance. Only a handful of swing-wing fighters have entered service – the F-14 Tomcat, the MiG-23 and the Tornado.

The ultimate solution to the short take-off requirement is the Harrier – the only single-engined vertical or short take-off and landing (V/STOL) aircraft in service. The key to the Harrier's truly remarkable vertical take-off capability lies with the vectored thrust from the Harrier's Rolls-Royce Pegasus engine, directed by four jet nozzles. The nozzles swivel as one, directing thrust from directly to the rear to just forward of vertical. In air combat the nozzles can be used to rapidly decelerate the aircraft so that an enemy aircraft, previously on the Harrier's tail, shoots by, unable to stop, thus becoming the Harrier's prey instead.

Where fighters once had mechanical linkages from control columns to control surfaces, modern fighters have fly-by-wire. This form of electronic signalling eliminates the need for mechanical linkages and a control column – the F-16 for example has a small side stick instead. Computers are now as fundamental to fighters as engines and weapons.

FAR LEFT: **The revolutionary vertical take-off Harrier is equally at home operating from an airfield or a supermarket car park.** INSET LEFT: **The Lockheed F-104 epitomized the quest for better performance.** BELOW: **A Rolls-Royce Spey jet engine. The development of powerplants such as these gave designers the thrust to achieve the required performance.**

Fighter armament: 1945 to the present day

In the years immediately after World War II it became apparent that jet fighters needed better armament than the machine-guns then available, some of which were based on World War I designs. By the end of World War II, Germany was leading the way in fighter armament development and some of their weapons were adopted and improved by the Allies after the war. The highly advanced Mauser MG-213 cannon for example was copied by the USA, Switzerland, France, the Soviet Union and Britain amongst others, and equipped most of the world's air forces in the post-war period. The British version of the Mauser gun, the Aden, is still used today. Even highly evolved cannon have their limitations and cannot for instance be effective over great distances.

The single most important development in aircraft armament since World War II has in fact been the guided Air-to-Air Missile (AAM) with its high explosive warhead. Unguided missiles, many of them developed in World War II, continued to be used into the 1950s. Perhaps the most remarkable of all unguided missiles was the Douglas Genie AAM which to this day is undoubtedly the most devastating of all AAMs. First tested in 1957, the Genie had a 1.5 kiloton nuclear warhead (equivalent to 1500 tons of TNT) with a lethal radius in excess of 305m/1000ft. The launch aircraft's

TOP: **A Royal Air Force Harrier looses off a Sidewinder AAM.** ABOVE: **A Matra Magic II AAM carried by a French Navy Super Etendard.**

on-board computer used radar to track the target and detonated the warhead at the optimum time. Pinpoint accuracy was not necessary with warheads of such destructive power.

Guided air-to-air missiles are now used by fighters to attack enemy aircraft from a minimum of 1.6km/1 mile away and up to distances in excess of 161km/100 miles. Air-to-air missiles

LEFT: **A Tornado F.3 armed with four Sky Flash and two Sidewinder AAMs.** BELOW: **A Royal Air Force F-4 Phantom pictured in 1974 with its armament of SRAAM Sidewinders under the wing, MRAAM Sparrows on the trolley and to the extreme right the pod-mounted 20mm/0.78in Vulcan gun.**

were first used in anger in 1958 when Taiwanese F-86 Sabres clashed with MiG-15s of the People's Republic of China. Armed with early examples of the AIM-9 Sidewinder, the F-86s downed a number of Chinese MiGs with the new weapon.

Modern AAMs are usually infra-red (IR) guided (the missile sensors make it follow a high temperature source such as an engine exhaust) or radar guided (the missile homes in on a target illuminated by a radar from the aircraft, and then follows on its own radar). The latter type normally uses a technique called Semi-Active Radar Homing which allows the radar to operate in pulses, to avoid making itself a target to radar-homing missiles. Some missiles use both the IR and radar guidance methods being radar-guided to within a few miles range and then IR guided to terminate in destruction.

Whatever the guidance, the AAM must reach its target quickly as most only have enough fuel for a few minutes' run. In those missiles with speeds of three or four times the speed of sound, the run can be counted in seconds.

AAMs are usually proximity armed, and, having detected that they are within lethal range, explode rather than having to hit the target. This is to counter last second evasive manoeuvres by the target aircraft and even if a missile just misses the target, the detonation will still cause substantial damage.

Air-to-air missiles are categorized according to their range, into short-range missiles (SRAAMs), medium range missiles (MRAAMs), and long-range missiles (LRAAMs).

The SRAAM is designed for use in close air combat and distances up to 18km/11 miles and a typical SRAAM would be the well-known and widely used American Sidewinder (AIM-9) series.

The Medium-Range Air-to-Air Missile is mainly used to intercept targets beyond SRAAM range and uses a radar homing system with a greater detection range and better all-weather properties than the infra-red guidance system.

Long-Range Air-to-Air missiles are truly remarkable weapons and perhaps the most impressive of all is the Phoenix carried exclusively by the US Navy F-14 Tomcat. Probably the world's most sophisticated and expensive AAM the Phoenix has a speed of five times the speed of sound, and can be launched from over 200km/124 miles distance from a target, before the F-14 has even appeared on an enemy aircraft radar screen.

With no real alternatives on the horizon, air-to-air missiles will remain the prime armament of fighters for some years to come.

LEFT: **An artist's impression of a Saab Gripen test firing a BVRAAM (Beyond Visual Range Air-to-Air Missile).**

Fighters at war: 1950s–70s

M any fighters developed since the end of World War II have never fired a shot in anger. However, wars have raged around the globe since then, and those that did not directly involve the superpowers often became testing grounds for their equipment. Fighter aircraft have played a key part in most of these conflicts from the Arab-Israeli War to the Falklands, and from the Indian-Pakistan wars to the Gulf War. The performance of these fighters influenced fighter design.

After Korea, the next significant use of fighters came in the 1958 exchanges between Taiwan and the People's Republic of China over disputed territory. In a replay of some of the classic air battles of the Korean War, Taiwanese F-86s took on Chinese MiG-15s. This time the Sabres were armed with air-to-air missiles as well as guns.

India and Pakistan's first air battles took place in 1965. While the Indians deployed the Hawker Hunter, Folland Gnat, Mystère IV and MiG-21, Pakistan had Lockheed F-104s and Sabres which, like the Taiwanese examples, were armed with Sidewinders. Although the Mach 2 F-104 was able to shoot down two Indian Mystères it was shown to be no dogfighter. Indian Hunters were able to outperform enemy Sabres but the F-86 air-to-air missile capability more than evened up the fight.

Fighters entered the fray in Vietnam from 1965 and battled almost constantly until 1973. North Vietnam relied on Soviet equipment including the MiG-17 much favoured by North Vietnam's aces. The MiGs were agile and very dangerous in close combat whereas the USA deployed large, complex missile-armed fighters like the F-4 Phantom designed to hit enemy aircraft from some distance away. The US Navy Crusader, known as the last of the gunfighters, actually achieved 19 out of 20 air victories using AAMs. Despite claims that the dogfight was a thing of the past, Vietnam proved that close air combat expertise was still a vital skill for modern fighter pilots. The US Navy was so concerned with the poor air-combat results from early in the Vietnam War that it set up the now famous Top Gun programme. US Navy pilots were taught how to fight and not just how to fly, and the programme continues to this day.

When the Arab-Israeli War erupted in 1967 the Israelis had Mirage IIIs and, later, the F-4 Phantom, while their Arab opponents flew MiG-19s and MiG-21s. The Mirage III was able to outfly and outgun any aircraft it met in the war and when the F-4 entered Israeli service, the nation had one of the most potent and combat experienced fighter forces in the world. In September 1973 a patrol of Arab MiG-21s attacked a flight of Israeli Mirages and Phantoms off the Syrian coast – 13 MiGs were lost for one Mirage. Fighter aircraft had come a long way since the Korean War but were still only as good as the air fighting system that backed them.

LEFT: **Royal Air Force F-4s. The Phantom saw considerable combat in Vietnam and the Middle East.** TOP AND UPPER MIDDLE: **The MiG-15 (top) and F-86 Sabre (upper middle) had a post-Korea rematch in air battles between Taiwan and the People's Republic of China.** LOWER MIDDLE: **The Hawker Hunter, widely exported from Britain, was used in action by the Indian Air Force during the Indo-Pak war of 1965.** BOTTOM: **The ubiquitous MiG-21.**

Fighters at war: 1980s–90s

Israel's fighter actions against Syria over the Lebanon in 1982 demonstrated how fighters, as part of an integrated strike plan, can win wars. Eighty-two Syrian fighters, mainly MiG-21s and -23s were destroyed without loss by the Israeli fighter force of F-15s and F-16s. Israeli use of all-aspect Sidewinder air-to-air missiles for the first time in combat, allowed their fighters to attack enemy aircraft from any angle and not just the traditional "six o'clock" position to the rear. Ground radar, AWACS and ELINT aircraft all passed information to the Israeli fighters bestowing their pilots with exceptional situational awareness – in short, they knew exactly where the Syrian fighters were and what they were doing.

In 1982 the Falklands War between Britain and Argentina also broke out. Compared to other conflicts, fighter operations over the Falklands were limited but nevertheless absolutely determined the outcome of the war. Fighting a numerically superior enemy, the British pilots had to achieve air superiority over the islands so the ground campaign could begin. British Sea Harriers were tasked with defending the British fleet and

ABOVE: **The swing-wing F-14 Tomcat.** BELOW: **The Mirage 2000, deployed during the Gulf War by France, is an extraordinarily manoeuvrable fighter. Although it has been flying since 1978, the 2000's agility stops the show when it appears at air displays.**

faced the Argentine Mirage IIIs and Daggers. The Argentine fighters, forced to withdraw to the mainland after RAF Vulcan bombing raids on the Port Stanley runway, were operating hundreds of miles from their home bases. In the air combats that took place, British Sea Harriers accounted for 23 enemy aircraft including the very capable Mirages and Israeli-built Daggers – no Sea Harriers were lost in air combat. If the Sea Harriers had not protected the British Task Force so effectively,

Britain's attempt to retake the Falklands could have ended in defeat with the Task Force at the bottom of the South Atlantic.

The rather more one-sided Gulf War of 1991 saw Iraq take on most of the Western world as a result of their invasion of Kuwait. The best fighter in the Iraqi inventory was the Mach 2 plus MIG-29. This very capable, incredibly agile high-performance fighter was developed in the Cold War to take on the best of the West's fighters. With a radar that can track ten targets simultaneously up to 245km/152 miles away, the MiG-29 pilot's helmet-mounted sight allows them to direct air-to-air missiles wherever the pilot looks. Complemented by MiG-21s, -23s, -25s and Mirage F1s, the Iraqi fighter force of MiG-29s was not to be taken lightly. The coalition forces boasted a fighter force of Tornado F.3s, Mirage 2000Cs, F-15Cs, F-16Cs, F-14s and F/A-18s provided by the United States (Air Force, Navy and Marine Corps), Britain (Royal Air Force), Saudi Arabia, France, Qatar and Canada. Although the Iraqi aircraft were very capable in absolute terms, compared to the highly trained coalition pilots backed by the biggest military machine since World War II, Iraqi pilots had little chance of success. The coalition had systematically destroyed the Iraqi military infrastructure piece by piece using bombs and cruise missiles. Despite the massive deployment of coalition fighters only 45 victories were achieved because most Iraqi fighters had fled to safe havens as soon as the shooting began. Without their complex support system, the Iraqi fighters would have been sitting ducks. Thirty-six of the victories were achieved by USAF F-15 Eagles, demonstrating the war-winning ability of the McDonnell Douglas fighter. A further two "kills" were credited to a single Royal Saudi Air Force F-15 that simultaneously shot down two Iraqi Mirage F1s with air-to-air missiles.

The overwhelming weight of coalition fighter power drove the Iraqi Air Force from the sky and allowed the Allied air attacks to continue unopposed. The cease-fire was signed on March 3, 1991 and the fighter had once again helped bring a war to a swift conclusion.

Inflight refuelling

Inflight refuelling (IFR) is vital to the world's major air forces and most recently played a key role in NATO's 1999 air offensive over the Balkans. In the early days of military aviation however, the refuelling of aircraft in flight was seen as nothing more than a stunt and it took some time for the military to be convinced of its value.

In June 1923 the US Army Air Service (USAAS) used two DH4 biplanes to prove a workable, if risky, system consisting of 500 litres/110 gallons of fuel, large funnels, and a 15.25m/50ft hose with an "on/off" nozzle on the end. Despite the dangers, by 1935 the record for sustained flight courtesy of inflight refuelling was pushed to 653 hours and 33 minutes – a record that stands to this day.

Although the USA had an early lead it was Britain's Sir Alan Cobham who turned IFR from a stunt to a workable technique. In 1934 Cobham's company Flight Refuelling Ltd developed a system consisting of a weighted cable let out from the tanker and a grapnel fired from the receiving aircraft to grab the cable. The hose was then drawn into the receiver aircraft – it was known as the looped hose system. However, just as World War II was coming to an end, Flight Refuelling perfected a new technique, still in use today – the probe and drogue

TOP: **A Royal Navy Sea Harrier tops up its tanks from a Royal Air Force VC-10 tanker using the probe and drogue technique.** ABOVE: **A USAF "flying boom" prepares to connect to an F-16.**

method. The tanker aircraft trails a hose with a stabilizing conical drogue at its end. Receiving aircraft are fitted with fixed probes which accept fuel flow when connected to the drogue. Valves are automatically opened on the probe and drogue when locked together and shut once contact is broken.

LEFT: **Converted Handley Page Victor bombers served as RAF tankers.**
BELOW: **Tanker operations have been central to fighter operations in a number of conflicts. Here a KC-135 refuels a USAF F4E during the Vietnam War. Two F4Ds (foreground) and two more F4Es (background) await their turn.**

The probe and drogue method was developed and perfected in the late 1940s and was widely adopted, representing a major improvement on the old line and grapnel method. On August 7, 1949 an RAF Meteor Mk 3 was kept airborne for 12 hours and 3 minutes and pilot comfort appeared to be the only limiting factor. In 1951 a specially modified USAF B-29 bomber with three refuelling points became the world's first triple point tanker. In spite of trials in which this B-29 simultaneously kept six RAF Meteor 8s aloft for four hours at a time, the RAF appeared to lose interest in IFR. The triple point tanker was however taken up by the USAF and in the mid-1950s, unlike their British counterparts, all new American fighters were built with IFR probes.

The US Navy also adopted the probe and drogue system in 1954. The Douglas company created the "buddy pack" so that aircraft could carry an air refuelling pod as an external store as easily as a drop tank. This makes for wonderful flexibility as any "buddy-equipped" aircraft can be a tanker or receiver. From the mid-1950s most US Navy and Marine aircraft were also fitted with folding probes.

Meanwhile in the USA, the Boeing company set about developing their own system to improve on the British technique. They wanted to pass fuel at a faster rate down a shorter hose which ultimately evolved into a rigid pipe. So was born the flying boom method used by the USAF today.

The rigid pipe is actually telescopic and joined to the tanker by a universally pivoted coupling. The boom is pressurized by the fuel itself and has aerodynamic control surfaces near the "business" end, controlled by a boom operator or "boomer" who "fires" the telescopic boom to make a fuel-tight seal.

The Boeing KC-135 tanker, developed from the 707 airliner, first flew in August 1956 and swiftly took its place as the tanker aircraft of all time. The KC-135 had a performance that allowed it to fuel thirsty aircraft at jet speed and heights using a high-speed boom transferring 3773 litres/1000 US gallons of fuel per minute. The French Air Force were so impressed by the KC-135 they ordered 12, modified for probe and drogue use, to exclusively refuel the Armée de l'Air Mirage IVA nuclear attack force. In Vietnam, KC-135s transferred almost 3.6 billion kg/8 billion lb of fuel in over 160,000 missions. USAF KC-135s are still in widespread use today and were in the air around the clock during the 1999 NATO action against Serb forces.

During the Gulf War in 1990–1 and the extensive 1999 air campaign against Serb forces, IFR was used throughout both to keep the Allies' aircraft aloft. As long as combat aircraft cannot carry enough fuel to complete lengthy missions, the flying fuel stations of the world's air forces will remain crucial to the plans of aerial warfare strategists.

Pilot equipment in the 21st century

No matter how advanced fighters may become in years to come, as long as there are human pilots they will always need a means of safely abandoning the aircraft in an emergency. One of the most fundamental pieces of pilot equipment is the ejection seat, pioneered during World War II. They are more than just a means of getting pilots and other aircrew out of the aircraft in an emergency – they also have to be comfortable and will be sat on, possibly for thousands of hours without ever being fired. When an ejection seat is fired usually by a handle between the legs or on top of the seat headrest, it draws the occupant's legs in close to the seat with garters (through which the legs are threaded) to keep them from harm's way as the seat rockets from the aircraft. The garters release at the same time as the main harness holding the pilot in the seat is opened.

For a seat to be a true life-saver it must be capable of being fired from ground level and propel itself high enough for the parachute to deploy while not subjecting the pilot to unacceptably dangerous acceleration forces. If a high altitude ejection takes place, modern ejection seats carry their own supply of oxygen so the occupant can breathe easily as soon as ejection has occurred. In reality many aircrew lose their face masks on ejection – some even lose their boots, such can be the violence of an ejection.

When the seat falls below 3050m/10,000ft a barostatic gauge senses the altitude and releases a drogue chute to draw

ABOVE: **Split-second decisions are essential in combat. The Head-Up Display of modern fighters projects vital data on to an angled screen so that the pilot does not waste time constantly looking down at an instrument panel.** LEFT: **A true life-saver – although ejection is a physically traumatic experience, it gives aircrew a means of escape from a stricken aircraft at virtually any altitude.**

out the main parachute. Another drogue chute is deployed as soon as the seat leaves the aircraft and slows the seat's descent. All of these functions are automatic in case the occupant is unconscious.

Once clear of the aircraft, the seat automatically releases the occupant from the seat and deploys the main parachute. Although aircrew can suffer injuries due to the rapid acceleration during ejection and the battering they receive as they hit the airflow, possibly at hundreds of miles per hour, they do at least have a means of escape, unlike their 1914 counterparts.

The future?

Cockpit instrumentation has been revolutionized in recent years to relieve the pilot's workload as much as possible so that they can manage the aircraft's systems and fight more effectively.

Helmet-mounted sights have been in use since the mid-1990s but helmet-mounted displays are likely to become the only means of providing the pilot with information. Computers will "clean" the information so that the pilot does not become overloaded with data. A 3-D moving map, painted on the pilot's retina using eye-friendly lasers, will maximize a pilot's situational awareness letting them know exactly where they are in relation to potential enemies.

Pilots are already bombarded with huge volumes of data from on board and other sensors, all of which has to be assimilated by the pilot whilst flying and perhaps fighting.

ABOVE: **Radar equipment carried by today's fighters is far more powerful than that carried during World War II.**

There is however a limit to the amount of information and activities a human can handle simultaneously. Incredibly intelligent software will ultimately be able to provide pilots with instantaneous decision support by assimilating information and recommending an action.

Pilots have relied mainly on sight for flying and fighting whereas systems already under development for the Space Shuttle and the US Navy's Joint Strike Fighter use other senses. Pilots wear a vest bristling with what the manufacturers call "tactors" that vibrate against the pilot's body as a non-visual means of providing information on aircraft orientation. If the aircraft rolls left a tactor vibrates against the pilot's left side and so on.

Complementing visual displays, 3-D audio can also make fuller use of the pilot's senses – a left engine failure for

TOP: **The Eurofighter cockpit is dominated by a wide-angle Head-Up Display and three colour monitors displaying all instrument information and flight data. The pilot has a helmet-mounted sight for weapon aiming and direct voice input allows the pilot to control certain aspects of the flight just by talking to the aircraft.** ABOVE: **Helmet-mounted sights were introduced in the mid-1990s.**

example could be signalled to the pilot via an audible tone in the left ear.

Some experts are claiming, not for the first time in the history of fighter aircraft, that the days of the manned fighter may be coming to an end. Time will tell, but for the foreseeable future, air combat will be fought with humans in the cockpit.

A–Z of World War Fighter Aircraft

1914–45

At the outbreak of World War I there were no fighter aircraft as such. Early aerial battles between aircraft with top speeds of around 135kph/84mph consisted of the pilots or observers shooting at their opposite number with pistols or hand-held rifles. Armed reconnaissance aircraft gave way to fighting scouts, the first true fighter aircraft. By the end of the war, one of the fastest fighters was the SPAD S.XIII with a top speed of 215kph/134mph. Compare this to the 660kph/410mph Gloster Meteor that flew into action late in World War II or the remarkable rocket-powered Messerschmitt Me163 Komet, which could reach 960kph/596mph.

These remarkable advances were made in only three decades. Piston engines were developed to their limits and jet engines, like those that equipped the Meteor, were produced as viable powerplants. Biplanes eventually gave way to monoplanes, and pilots came to be enclosed in heated cockpits as air fighting was forced higher and higher by attackers trying to evade defenders. But by the end of World War II, new aircraft designs and other technological advances were under development that would make the finest World War II fighters seem primitive by comparison.

LEFT: **A pair of North American P-51 Mustangs.**

LEFT: **The widely produced Albatros D.Va was an early example of fuselage streamlining.**

BELOW: **In early 1917 the D.I won air superiority for the Germans over the Western Front.**

Albatros D. Fighters – I, II, III, V, Va

The D series of Albatros fighters illustrates very well just how short-lived air superiority could be over the Western Front in World War I. As one side introduced a more effective type and achieved the upper hand, the enemy would develop a superior aircraft and very quickly redress the balance. The D.V was the last of a line of Albatros fighters that began with the D.I, developed into the D.II and then the D.III. As each version joined the fray it enjoyed only relatively short-lived success.

The Albatros D.I was introduced by the Germans to counter the Allied de Havilland and Nieuport fighting scouts, which had ended the "Fokker Scourge" of early 1916 and regained air superiority from the Germans. The D.I played a major role in swinging the pendulum back in favour of the Germans in early 1917. Apart from the fuselage, the D.I was built using components or building methods employed in the Albatros C series. The fighter's fuselage was elliptical in section and represented an advance in aerodynamic design over the earlier models.

The aircraft was powered by either a Benz Bz.III or a Mercedes D.III engine, which were then the most powerful engines fitted in a scout. This, coupled with the fact that the D.I was armed with two synchronized machine-guns, made it a hard-hitting fighter capable of climbing to 1000m/3280ft in six minutes – an impressive climb rate for the time. These factors made it attractive to the German "top guns" of the time, such as von Richthofen and Boelcke, who used the aircraft to regain air superiority for the Germans over the Western Front.

The D.II introduced a few fundamental improvements, including the lowering of the top wing so that the pilot could see over it and the aerodynamically improved installation of the radiator in the upper wing centre section. Climbing to 1000m/3280ft now took a mere five minutes.

The D.III was an improved version of the D.II, designed for better manoeuvrability. Changes to the wing set-up required the introduction of v-shaped struts between the upper and lower wings to improve rigidity. By late 1917 the D.III was in turn outclassed by the newer Allied fighters like the S.E.5 and was replaced by the D.V, the ultimate Albatros. The D.V had a wonderfully streamlined plywood-skinned fuselage and was produced in vast numbers. Over 1500 alone served on the Western Front, making up for any combat shortcomings by sheer weight of numbers. Heavy losses were

experienced, not only as a result of enemy action but also to the Albatros's tendency to break up in flight, due to inherent structural weaknesses in the lower wing.

ABOVE: **The D.II had its upper wing lowered so that the pilot could see over the top.**

Albatros D.V

First flight: Spring 1917

Power: Mercedes 180hp DIIa six-cylinder in-line engine.

Armament: Two belt-fed fixed 7.92mm/0.31in Spandau machine-guns

Size: Wingspan – 9.05m/29ft 8in
Length – 7.33m/24ft 0.5in
Height – 2.7m/8ft 10.25in
Wing area – 21.28m^2/229sq ft

Weights: Empty – 687kg/1511lb
Maximum loaded – 937kg/2061lb

Performance: Maximum speed – 187kph/116mph
Ceiling – 5700m/18,700ft
Range – 2 hours endurance
Climb – 1000m/3280ft in 4 minutes

LEFT: **An all-metal Siskin IIIA of No.49 Squadron Royal Air Force, pictured in 1929.**

Armstrong Whitworth Siskin IIIA

First flight: October 20, 1925
Power: Armstrong Siddeley Jaguar IV radial piston engine
Armament: Two synchronized 7.7mm/0.303in Vickers machine-guns in forward fuselage
Size: Wingspan – 10.11m/33ft 2in
　　Length　7.72m/25ft 4in
　　Height – 3.1m/10ft 2in
　　Wing area – 27.22m^2/293sq ft
Weights: Empty – 935kg/2061lb
　　Maximum loaded – 1366kg/3012lb
Performance: Maximum speed – 251kph/156mph
　　Ceiling – 8230m/27,000ft
　　Range – 1 hour, 12 minutes at full throttle
　　Climb – 3050m/10,000ft in 6 minutes, 20 seconds

Armstrong Whitworth Siskin

This fighter had its origins in the Siddeley Deasy S.R.2 Siskin, produced by Armstrong Whitworth's parent company in 1919 and constructed mainly of wood. Britain's Air Ministry only wanted all-metal fighters and so the Siskin was redesigned. When the Siskin III joined No.41 Squadron at Northolt in May 1924 it became the first all-metal fighter in RAF service.

In total, 465 Siskin IIIs were produced, including some examples for export to Estonia and Canada. The improved Siskin IIIA, powered by a supercharged Armstrong Siddeley Jaguar IV engine, first flew in October 1925 and went on to equip eleven RAF squadrons from September 1926 – the newer model can be identified by the lack of the ventral fin beneath the tail.

Royal Air Force Siskin squadrons pioneered aerobatics in the service, some Siskins even being flown literally tied together at the famous Hendon Air Displays.

The last Siskin in RAF service was phased out in October 1932, although IIIAs supplied to the Royal Canadian Air Force soldiered on until replaced by Hawker Hurricanes in 1939.

LEFT: The Avia 534, arguably the best fighter of its time.

Avia 534

First flight: August 1933
Power: Hispano Suiza 860hp HC 12Ydrs in-line piston engine
Armament: Four fixed 7.7mm/0.303in synchronized machine-guns in front fuselage plus underwing racks for six 20kg/44lb bombs
Size: Wingspan – 9.4m/30ft 10in
　　Length – 8.2m/26ft 10.75in　Height – 3.1m/10ft 2in
　　Wing area　23.56m^2/253.61sq ft
Weights: Empty – 1460kg/3219lb
　　Maximum loaded – 2120kg/4674lb
Performance: Maximum speed – 394kph/245mph
　　Ceiling – 10,600m/34,775ft
　　Range – 580km/360 miles
　　Climb – 900m/2953ft per minute

Avia B. 534-IV

This little-known fighter has been described as the finest fighter aircraft of its time, because of its combination of impressive armament, excellent handling and high speed. It was certainly the most important Czech aircraft of the inter-war years and was almost at the pinnacle of biplane fighter design, lacking only a retractable under-carriage. Construction of the 534 was an

interesting combination of steel wings covered with fabric, and a fuselage of riveted and bolted steel tubes covered with metal panels or fabric. In April 1934 the second prototype set a Czech national speed record of 365.74kph/227.27mph.

Front-line Czech fighter units were equipped with over 300 of these fine aircraft during the Munich Crisis of

September 1938, and after the German occupation of Czechoslovakia, Slovak Air Force units flew 534s against the Red Army in July 1941.

The Avia 534 interested the Luftwaffe sufficiently for it to form in late 1939, albeit briefly, a unit equipped solely with the captured Czech fighter. These robust and manoeuvrable fighters were later relegated to target towing duties.

LEFT: **The P-39, widely used by the Soviet Union.**

Bell P-39M Airacobra

First flight: April 6, 1938
Power: Allison 1200hp V-1710-83
in-line piston engine
Armament: One 37mm/1.46in T9 cannon,
two 12.7mm/0.5in machine-guns and four
7.62mm/0.3in machine-guns
Size: Wingspan – 10.36m/34ft
Length – 9.19m/30ft 2in   Height – 3.61m/11ft 10in
Wing area – 19.79m²/213sq ft
Weights: Empty – 2545kg/5610lb
Maximum take-off – 3810kg/8400lb
Performance: Maximum speed – 621kph/386mph
Ceiling – 10,970m/36,000ft
Range – 1046km/650 miles
Climb – 4575m/15,000ft in 4 minutes, 30 seconds

Bell P-39 Airacobra

The P-39 was the first fighter with a tricycle undercarriage. The type was also unorthodox because its engine was installed behind the pilot, as it was armed with a large-calibre cannon that fired through the propeller hub. The aircraft had in fact been designed around the 37mm/1.46in weapon from the outset. Initially ordered for the French Air Force, the aircraft were instead supplied to Britain.

The P-39 entered USAAF service in February 1941, and in September the same year, No.601 Squadron became the first and only RAF unit to operate the type. During the aircraft's test programme, a decision was made to exclude the engine's turbocharger and the consequent relatively poor performance did not endear the P-39 to the RAF, who only used the type for

ground attack missions between October and December 1941. The USAAF, however, did use the P-39 with some success in North Africa in a ground attack role and around 5000 were supplied to the USSR, where they were used for similar missions. From 1942–4 the P-39, together with the P-40, were the main front-line USAAF fighters in the Pacific theatre.

LEFT: **At first the F4B had no engine cowling, but later a ring cowling was added to improve streamlining. The F4B equipped both the US Navy and Marine Corps, while the P-12 variants were operated by the USAAC.**

Boeing F4B

First flight: June 25, 1928
Power: Pratt and Whitney 550hp R-1340-16
Wasp nine-cylinder radial engine
Armament: Two fixed forward-firing 7.62mm/0.3in
machine-guns
Size: Wingspan – 9.14m/30ft
Length – 6.12m/20ft 1in
Height – 2.84m/9ft 4in
Wing area – 21.13m²/227.5sq ft
Weights: Empty – 1068kg/2354lb
Maximum loaded – 1638kg/3611lb
Performance: Maximum speed – 303kph/188mph
Ceiling – 8200m/26,900ft
Range – 595km/370 miles
Climb – 1525m/5000ft in 2 minutes, 42 seconds

Boeing F4B/P-12

Boeing developed the F4B as a private venture to possibly replace the US Navy's Boeing F2B and F3B. The new aircraft was smaller and lighter than its forerunners but retained the Wasp engine of the F3B and included some design changes that together resulted in improved performance. Accordingly the

F4B was ordered in great quantities for the US Navy and, later, the US Army who gave it the designation P-12. Both the US Navy and Army utilized a host of different variants many of which served on into World War II. Brazil was the only major customer outside the USA. Total production reached 586.

Boeing P-26

The "Peashooter" as it was known, was an aircraft that spanned two eras. America's first all-metal fighter produced in quantity is also notable as it was the last to have a fixed undercarriage and open cockpit. Boeing first proposed the P-26 to the US Army in 1931 having designed it around the trusted Pratt and Whitney R-1340 radial engine. The first prototype was built and flown in only nine weeks, taking to the air for the first time in March 1932 at Wright Field. The P-26's top speed of 365kph/227mph may seem sedate by today's transonic standards but it represented an increase of over 20 per cent compared to the performance of the P-12 it replaced. The order placed by the US Army Air Corps (USAAC) in January 1933 was at the time the biggest ever for a US military aircraft.

By the time the P-26 joined the USAAC squadrons in early 1934, a number of refinements and improvements had been incorporated including strengthening of the pilot's headrest fairing. An early version of the

aircraft had overturned after landing on soft ground, killing the pilot as the headrest collapsed. The Peashooter was popular with pilots as it was light and responsive, and it was the fastest USAAC fighter until 1938. It remained in service until as late as 1942.

Boeing widely exported the P-26, but the aircraft had a high landing speed for the time, around 117kph/73mph, which was found to be rather high for the rough airfields of foreign air forces. Split landing flaps were fitted to reduce the speed at the critical landing time. In September 1934 the first of ten examples sold to China arrived at Canton. Over the next year or so the Peashooters were in action against the invading Japanese on an almost daily basis and succeeded in destroying some of the enemy's aircraft in air combat. Ex-USAAC P-26s were also supplied to Guatemala where they comprised the Guatemalan Military Air Corps' first fighter unit and remained in service until 1955.

TOP: **The Peashooter was the fastest USAAC fighter aircraft until 1938, and the type remained in Guatemalan service until 1955.** ABOVE: **The agile P-26 was America's first mass-produced all-metal fighter.**

Boeing P-26A

First flight: March 20, 1932

Power: One Pratt and Whitney 500hp nine-cylinder air-cooled radial piston engine

Armament: Two synchronized forward-firing 7.62mm/0.3in machine-guns on sides of nose

Size: Wingspan – 8.52m/27ft 11.5in
Length – 7.26m/23ft 10in
Height – 3.17m/10.5ft
Wing area – 13.89m^2/149.5sq ft

Weights: Empty – 1031kg/2271lb
Maximum take-off – 1366kg/3012lb

Performance: Maximum speed – 365kph/227mph
Ceiling – 8350m/27,400ft
Range – 579km/360 miles
Climb – 719m/2360ft per minute

LEFT: **Defiants of No.264 Squadron, RAF.**

Boulton Paul Defiant Mark II

First flight: August 11, 1937
Power: Rolls-Royce 1280hp Merlin XX piston engine
Armament: Four 7.7mm/0.303in machine-guns in power-operated dorsal turret
Size: Wingspan – 11.99m/39ft 4in
Length – 10.77m/35ft 4in
Height – 3.45m/11ft 4in
Wing area – 23.23m²/250 sq ft
Weights: Empty – 2849kg/6282lb
Maximum loaded – 3821kg/8424lb
Performance: Maximum speed – 504kph/313mph
Ceiling – 9250m/30350ft
Range – 748km/465 miles
Climb – 580m/1900ft per minute

Boulton Paul Defiant

The Defiant was the RAF's first four-gun fighter in squadron service, making its first flight in August 1937. Tactically, the Defiants were a departure for two-seat fighters as all of their firepower was concentrated in the rear turret and no forward armament was carried. They went into action for the first time on May 12, 1940 and by the end of the month had destroyed 65 enemy aircraft over France. The success was partly due to the devastating firepower that could be unleashed on any fighter that got on a Defiant's tail. The "honeymoon" was soon over. In dogfights the Defiant was no match for the Luftwaffe's best fighters and losses began to increase. With no front-firing guns, the Defiant was vulnerable to head-on attacks and in August 1940 they were withdrawn.

Defiants were then "recycled" as nightfighters and fitted with the new and highly secret Airborne Interception radar. Over the winter of 1940–1 the Defiant had more kills per interception than any other RAF type. At the height of their use, Defiant nightfighters equipped 13 RAF squadrons, and played a vital role in the night defence of Britain.

LEFT: **Buffaloes entered RAF service in 1940.**

Brewster F2A-3 Buffalo

First flight: December 1937
Power: Wright 1200hp R-1820-40 Cyclone radial piston engine
Armament: Four fixed forward-firing 12.7mm/0.5in machine-guns
Size: Wingspan – 10.67m/35ft
Length – 8.03m/26ft 4in   Height – 3.68m/12ft 1in
Wing area – 19.41m²/208.9sq ft
Weights: Empty – 2146kg/4723lb
Maximum take-off – 3247kg/7159lb
Performance: Maximum speed – 517kph/321mph
Ceiling – 10,120m/33,200ft
Range – 1553km/965 miles
Climb – 935m/3070ft per minute

Brewster F2A Buffalo

The F2A was designed to meet a US Navy specification for a carrier-based monoplane and was awarded the contract, making it the Navy's first monoplane fighter. Of the 54 ordered only 11 made it into service, the rest being sold to Finland. Further contracts from the US Navy brought the F2A-2 and the more heavily armed and armoured F2A-3 into service. US Marine Corps aviators used the Buffalo to the best of their ability in the first Battle of Midway, when 13 out of 19 were destroyed.

Orders placed by Britain (where the F2A was named Buffalo by the RAF and was found to be inadequate for the war in Europe) and the Netherlands East Indies brought more Buffaloes to the war in the Far East, where they were out-classed by Japanese fighters. The aircraft's failure was due to its poor manoeuvrability, heavy weight and basic instability. In spite of this, by the time of the fall of Singapore in February 1942, RAF Buffaloes had destroyed 30 Japanese aircraft in the air.

Only in Finland did the Buffalo hold its own, when from mid-1941 until September 1944 it successfully opposed Soviet forces in the Russo-Finnish War.

Bristol Beaufighter

The Beaufighter was not designed to an official specification – the Bristol company simply proposed a versatile heavily armed aircraft that they thought the RAF needed. Britain's Air Ministry was impressed by the proposal and the devastating fire power this aircraft could unleash, realizing they had found the heavily armed long-range fighter missing from the RAF inventory. Using the major airframe elements of the Beaufort torpedo-bomber already in production, the two-seat Beaufighter was produced quickly and joined front-line squadrons at the height of the Battle of Britain in 1940, only 13 months after the prototype first flew.

TOP: **A Beaufighter of No.235 Squadron RAF.**
ABOVE: **Nicknamed "Whispering Death" by the Japanese, the Beaufighter was a robust aircraft well suited to hot and tropical conditions.**
LEFT: **A well-worn Beaufighter IIF.**

The "Beau" was the world's first high-performance purpose-designed nightfighter and was a very advanced aircraft for its time. At the time of its combat début with the Fighter Interception Unit in 1940, the Beaufighter's armament of four 20mm/0.78in cannon and six 7.7mm/0.303in machine-guns was the heaviest carried by any front-line aircraft. Crews found the "Beau" to be quite fast

and manoeuvrable and experienced Blenheim pilots were able to manage the aircraft's demanding take-off swing. When Beaufighters joined front line Royal Air Force squadrons in early September 1940, most only carried their cannon armament – the much needed machine-guns were retained for the all-important Spitfires and Hurricanes, should a shortage have arisen. The closing months of 1940 saw machine-guns fitted to the Beaufighters and, after a period of trial and error mastering the new AI radar, the aircraft's night victories against the Luftwaffe began to increase.

Day fighter versions saw action in the Western Desert and Malta while RAF Coastal Command also used the "Beau" to great effect, particularly over the Bay of Biscay against Luftwaffe Junkers Ju 88s. Bomber and torpedo-carrying versions also saw wartime service with the RAF and after the war's end, Beaufighters served with Coastal Command and in the Far East until 1950 and as target towing aircraft until 1960.

Bristol Beaufighter VIF

First flight: July 17, 1939
Power: Two Bristol 1,635hp Hercules VI 14-cylinder air-cooled sleeve valve radials
Armament: Four 20mm/0.78in cannon in nose, plus six 7.7mm/0.303in machine-guns in wings
Size: Wingspan – 17.65m/57ft 10in
Length 12.6m/41ft 8in
Height – 4.84m/15ft 10in
Wing area – 46.74m^2/503sq ft
Weights: Empty – 6631kg/14,600lb
Maximum take-off – 9810kg/21,600lb
Performance: Maximum speed – 536kph/333mph
Ceiling – 8083m/26,500ft
Range – 2381km/1480 miles
Climb – 4575m/15,000ft in 7.8 minutes

Bristol Blenheim

The three-seat Bristol Blenheim first flew in 1935 and was a technological quantum leap among RAF aircraft at the time. With a top speed of around 428kph/266mph, the Blenheim bomber was considerably faster than the 290kph/180mph Hind biplane it replaced and it could outrun many contemporary fighters. The first Blenheim fighter, the IF, was proposed as a long-range fighter that could escort bombers over hostile territory and also carry out ground attack missions of its own. Around 200 Blenheims were modified for these fighter duties, additionally armed with a gun pack beneath the fuselage consisting of four machine-guns.

The type had first entered service in December 1938 and by September 1939 there were 111 Blenheim fighters in use with the RAF. Unfortunately the Blenheim could not match the performance of aircraft such as the Messerschmitt Bf109 and so many became nightfighters, ultimately carrying the new and highly secret airborne radar.

Even before the IFs were equipped with radar they achieved some night-time victories – in June 1940 No.23 Squadron destroyed a Heinkel 111 bomber over Norfolk. The first ever radar interception came in late July when a Blenheim IF of Tangmere's Fighter Interception Unit destroyed a Dornier Do 17 near Brighton.

The pioneers of the Blenheim night-fighters were a flight of No.25 Squadron who were in fact the first unit in the world to operate radar-equipped night-fighters. But Blenheim fighters continued to operate in daylight too and as late as August 15, 1940, during the Battle of Britain, No.219 Squadron were in action against a German raid on north-east England. Between November 1939 and March 1940, RAF Coastal Command also operated IFs, providing top cover for shipping. The Mark IVF was again a long-range fighter version of the Mark IV bomber, carrying the same gun pack. Around 125 served with Coastal Command, providing shipping with air cover, as had the IF. In April 1940 a pilot of No.254 Squadron shot down a Heinkel 111 that posed a threat to British ships off the coast of Norway.

TOP: **This Blenheim, preserved and flown in the UK is a rare survivor.** ABOVE: **A Blenheim Mk IF of No.248 Squadron RAF – note the ventral gun pack beneath the rear of the cockpit area.**

Bristol Blenheim IF

First flight: April 12, 1935
Power: Two Bristol 840hp Mercury VIII nine-cylinder air-cooled radial engines
Armament: Four 7.7mm/0.303in Browning machine-guns in ventral gun pack, plus one Browning gun in port wing and one in gun turret
Size: Wingspan – 17.17m/56ft 4in
Length – 12.12m/39ft 9in Height – 3m/9ft 10in
Wing area – 43.57m^2/469sq ft
Weights: Empty – 3674kg/8100lb
Maximum take-off – 5670kg/12,500lb
Performance: Maximum speed – 458kph/285mph
Ceiling – 8315m/27,280ft
Range – 1810km/1125 miles
Climb – 4570m/15,000ft in 11 minutes, 30 seconds

LEFT: **The prototype Bulldog II, J9480. The Bulldog was an unequal span biplane with a metal frame and a fabric covering.** BELOW: **A Bulldog IIA, preserved at a UK aviation museum. The type was the standard RAF fighter for seven years.**

Bristol Bulldog II

First flight: May 17, 1927
Power: Bristol 440hp Jupiter VII radial piston engine
Armament: Two fixed forward-firing synchronized Vickers machine-guns
Size: Wingspan – 10.34m/33ft 11in
Length – 7.62m/25ft
Height – 3m/9ft 10in
Wing area – 28.47m²/306.6sq ft
Weights: Empty – 998kg/2200lb
Maximum loaded – 1583kg/3490lb
Performance: Maximum speed – 280kph/174mph
Ceiling – 8230m/27,000ft
Range – 443km/275 miles
Climb – 6096m/20,000ft in 14 minutes, 30 seconds

Bristol Bulldog

The Bulldog was designed in response to a 1926 Air Ministry specification for a single-seat day- or nightfighter armed with two Vickers machine-guns able to take on the bombers of the era. The Mark I was used for development and it was the Mark II that replaced the RAF's Siskins and Gamecocks and first entered RAF service with No.3 Squadron at Upavon in June 1929. The Bulldog's fuselage was all-metal with a fabric covering, and it had a shock-absorbing tail skid, as operations were still exclusively from grass strips. Innovations for the Bulldog included an oxygen supply for the pilot and a short-wave two-way radio.

By 1932 the Bulldog equipped ten RAF squadrons and it remained the service's standard fighter until 1936. The 312 Bulldogs that entered service comprised about 70 per cent of the UK's air defence capability.

The last RAF Bulldogs were phased out in 1937, being replaced by Gloster Gauntlets. Many were exported to other countries, including Australia, Denmark, Siam (now Thailand), Sweden, Estonia and Finland. A two-seat trainer version was also produced.

Bristol Fighter

The arrival of the Bristol F.2B Fighter, powered by the new Rolls-Royce Falcon engine, over the Western Front ultimately proved to be very bad news for the German opposition. The aircraft had two crew – a pilot and an observer gunner in the rear cockpit. Each could engage an enemy aircraft independently – the pilot with a fixed forward-firing machine-gun and the observer with a Lewis gun (or two if he was strong).

Designed by Capt. Frank Barnwell around the Falcon engine, the armament of the Bristol Fighter was integral to its design from the outset, crew visibility was excellent and they had an unobstructed field of fire. The April 5, 1917 combat début of the "Brisfit" at the Battle of Arras was, however, far from successful as the Royal Flying Corps pilots used the standard two-seater tactic of leaving the aircraft's defence with the observer. This tactical error, coupled with oil freezing, which rendered a number of observers' guns useless, led to the loss of four out of six Brisfits on their first mission. Within days, the British pilots began to use the aircraft's forward-firing Vickers gun to full effect and flew the F.2B as if it were a single-seat fighter – the aircraft became something to be feared. The Bristol Fighter was to become the best two-seat fighter of World War I. When the Royal Air Force was established on April 1, 1918 it was a Bristol Fighter that flew the first combat mission of Britain's newly formed independent air arm. It proved popular with pilots because it was fast, manoeuvrable, could dive faster than any other aircraft in the theatre and it could take a lot of punishment.

The Vickers machine-gun mounted on the Bristol Fighter's centreline was beneath the engine cowling. Its location required a "tunnel" to be provided for the gun through the upper fuel tank.

Post-war the type was used as an Army co-operation aircraft and a trainer. Production of the Bristol Fighter continued until 1927 and the RAF took

TOP: **The combat début of the Bristol Fighter in April 1917 was far from auspicious, with four out of six aircraft being lost on their first mission.** ABOVE: **When both crew members used their guns, the Brisfit was a formidable fighter to contend with.**

delivery of its last Bristol Fighter in December 1926. Fourteen foreign air forces, including Canada, Greece and Mexico, also operated the type. Fifteen years after entering RFC service, the Brisfit was still serving with the RAF in Iraq and India, at which time they were replaced by Fairey Gordons. The Royal New Zealand Air Force continued to operate Bristol Fighters until 1938.

TOP: **The Bristol Fighter equipped RAF units in Turkey, India, Iraq, Palestine, Egypt and Syria.** ABOVE: **The Brisfit went on to become one of the best two-seat fighters of World War I.** BELOW: **Pilots and observers of No.22 Squadron of the newly formed Royal Air Force, pictured at Vert Galland on April 1, 1918.**

Bristol F.2B Fighter

First flight: September 9, 1916
Power: Rolls-Royce 275hp Falcon III in-line
   piston engine
Armament: One fixed forward-firing synchronized
   Vickers machine-gun and one or two "flexible"
   7.7mm/0.303in Lewis guns in rear cockpit
Size: Wingspan – 11.96m/39ft 3in
   Length – 7.87m/25ft 10in
   Height – 2.97m/9ft 9in
   Wing area – 37.63m²/405 sq ft
Weights: Empty – 975kg/2150lb
   Maximum loaded – 1474kg/3250lb
Performance: Maximum speed – 198kph/123mph
   Ceiling – 5485m/18,000ft
   Range – 3 hours endurance
   Climb – 3048m/10,000ft in 11 minutes, 30 seconds

Bristol Scout

The Scout was derived from a pre-World War I racing aircraft and, had it been designed with armament from the outset, could have been a great fighter. Widely described as a very "clean" design, the Scout was certainly fast for its day and was used initially as a fast "scout", or reconnaissance aircraft. Soon after its appearance at the Front in February 1915, with its high performance, single-seat Scouts were allocated to two-seater squadrons as escorts. Armament on these first fighters varied widely at first, sometimes simply consisting of rifles bolted to the sides of the fuselage. In spite of this, on July 25, 1915 Captain L.G. Hawker used his Bristol Scout C to shoot down three enemy aircraft, themselves armed with machine-guns. For this action he was awarded the Victoria Cross, the first for aerial combat. At this point, Scouts equipped both the Royal Flying Corps and the Royal Naval Air Service, the latter using the Scout for anti-Zeppelin patrols armed with explosive "darts" thrown over the side.

When No.11 Squadron RFC was formed in February 1915 equipped with, among other types, Bristol Scouts, its sole purpose was the interception and destruction of enemy aircraft – it was one of the first true fighter squadrons. The British ace Albert Ball served with No.11 and liked to fly the Scout D which entered service in November 1915, equipped with a synchronized Vickers machine-gun. During one week in May

ABOVE: **5574 was a Scout D, the version that introduced a synchronized Vickers machine-gun.** BELOW: **A replica Scout D. Once the type was withdrawn from front-line duties the Scout was used for training purposes, and later a number were sold for civil use.**

1916 Albert Ball used his Scout D, serial number 5326, to drive down four enemy aircraft and remove them from the war.

In all, around 370 Scouts were delivered. From mid-1916 they were gradually withdrawn from front-line duties to become training aircraft.

Bristol Scout

First flight: February 23, 1914 (Scout A)
Power: Le Rhône 80hp rotary piston engine
Armament: One 7.7mm/0.303in Lewis machine-gun or local combinations of small arms
Size: Wingspan – 8.33m/27ft4in
Length 6.02m/19ft 9in
Height – 2.59m/8ft 6in
Wing area – 18.39m^2/198sq ft
Weights: Empty – 345kg/760lb
Maximum loaded – 567kg/1250lb
Performance: Maximum speed – 161kph/100mph
Ceiling – 4267m/14,000ft
Range – 2.5 hours endurance
Climb – 3050m/10,000ft in 18.5 minutes

LEFT: **The large and remarkable R. 11.**

Caudron R. 11

First flight: March 1917
Power: Two Hispano-Suiza 215hp 8Bba in-line
piston engines
Armament: Five 7.7mm/0.303in Lewis machine-guns
– two each in front and rear gunner positions, plus
an additional "stinger" under the aircraft nose
Size: Wingspan – 17.92m/58ft 9.5in
Length – 11.22m/36ft 9.5in
Height – 2.8m/9ft 2.25in
Wing area – 54.25m^2/583.96sq ft
Weights: Empty – 1422kg/3135lb
Maximum take-off – 2167kg/4777lb
Performance: Maximum speed – 183kph/114mph
Ceiling – 5950m/19,520ft
Range – 3 hours endurance
Climb – 2000m/6560ft in 8 minutes, 10 seconds

Caudron R.11

The R.11 was designed in 1916 by René Caudron as a heavily armed reconnaissance-bomber, but the twin-engined biplane found its niche as a formidable escort fighter over the Western Front. Armed with five Lewis machine-guns, and fully aerobatic, the R.11 could escort French bombers to targets deep in enemy territory and dish out considerable punishment to German fighters that came near. The three-seat R.11, twice the size of other escort fighters in use at the time, built up an impressive tally of enemy aircraft kills.

A number of features make the R.11 stand out from many aircraft of the time. The engines were housed in streamlined nacelles to minimize drag, and both could be fed from one of two main fuel tanks as required. In late model R.11s the rear sections of the engine nacelles could be jettisoned, together with the auxiliary fuel tanks they contained. Another innovation was the provision of dual controls in the rear gunner's cockpit so that the gunner could take control if the pilot was incapacitated. The R.11 protected France until July 1922.

LEFT: **Developed from an aircraft which was itself derived from another, the Boomerang proved to be a very worthwhile fighter. The example pictured, sole survivor of the type, is preserved in Australia.**

Commonwealth Boomerang II

First flight: May 29, 1942
Power: Pratt & Whitney 1200hp R-1830-S3C4
Twin Wasp radial piston engine
Armament: Four 7.7mm/0.303in machine-guns
and two 20mm/0.78in cannon in wings
Size: Wingspan – 10.97m/36ft
Length – 7.77m/25ft 6in
Height – 2.92m/9ft 7in
Wing area – 20.9m^2/225sq ft
Weights: Empty – 2437kg/5373lb
Maximum take-off – 3742kg/8249lb
Performance: Maximum speed – 491kph/305mph
Ceiling – 10,365m/34,000ft
Range – 2575km/1600 miles
Climb – 896m/2940ft per minute

Commonwealth Boomerang

The Boomerang was born of desperation and the sudden need in December 1941 to defend Australia from the Japanese. The aircraft was based on the Commonwealth Aircraft Corporation's earlier Wirraway which was in turn developed from the North American NA-16 trainer. The Wirraway's wing, undercarriage and tail were mated to a new fuselage and the resulting Boomerang prototype was produced in only three months. The Twin Wasp engine was considered too low powered for fighters elsewhere but the Boomerang design team used it to power their aircraft, which entered service in October 1942. This well-armed, tough and manoeuvrable aircraft first flew into action in April 1943 and proved to be an adversary to be reckoned with. As other fighter types became available the Boomerang was quickly replaced, having served in New Guinea and defended western and northern Australia in the country's time of need.

Curtiss P-36 Hawk

Design work on the second family of Curtiss Hawks began in 1934 and led to the P-36 Hawk, which first flew in May 1935. It incorporated advanced features for the time, including an enclosed cockpit and retractable landing gear. The aircraft impressed the US Army Air Corps so much that Curtiss received an order for 210 machines, the largest peacetime order ever placed by the USAAC for a fighter. Deliveries began in April 1938 but by the time America entered World War II in December 1941, the aircraft was already thought to be obsolete, although some did see early action against the Japanese. P-36As were the main fighters defending Hawaii at the time of Pearl Harbor in December 1941.

Export versions of the P-36, the H75, were supplied to France where they saw limited action before the fall of France in 1940. One Armée de l'Air Hawk claimed the first German aircraft to fall to a French fighter in World War II. Most of the French Hawks were, however, transferred to the UK , where the Royal Air Force designated them "Mohawks". Some of the Hawks seized by the Germans were supplied by them to Finland after being used by the Luftwaffe as fighter trainers.

A further 100 Mohawks came to the UK direct from the USA between July and December 1940. Some were shipped to the Middle East and others were dispatched to India, where they entered service in December 1941. At one point, the fighter defence of the whole of north-east India was provided by just eight Mohawks. The last RAF unit to fly them was No.155 Squadron, which relinquished them in January 1944.

Hawks were also supplied to Norway (and the Free Norwegian Forces based in Canada), the Netherlands (diverted to the Netherlands East Indies) and Persia (now Iran). Vichy France, Finland, India and Peru also operated the type.

In 1937 a less sophisticated version of the P-36, the Hawk 75, was developed for export and supplied to China, Siam (now Thailand) and Argentina, where a further 20 were built. Chinese and Siamese 75s were used against the Japanese.

TOP: **A French H75, the export version of the P-36.** ABOVE: **One of the French H75s transferred to the RAF after the fall of France.**

Curtiss P-36G Hawk

First flight: May 1935
Power: Wright 1200hp R-1820-G205A Cyclone piston radial engine
Armament: Four wing-mounted 7.62mm/0.3in machine-guns, plus two fuselage-mounted 12.7mm/0.5in machine-guns
Size: Wingspan – 11.28m/37ft
   Length – 8.69m/28ft 6in
   Height – 2.82m/9ft 3in
   Wing area – 21.92m^2/236sq ft
Weights: Empty – 2121kg/4675lb
   Maximum loaded – 2667kg/5880lb
Performance: Maximum speed – 518kph/322mph
   Ceiling – 9860m/32,350ft
   Range – 1046km/650 miles
   Climb – 4570m/15,000ft in 6 minutes

Curtiss P-40 Warhawk/Kittyhawk

The next version in the Hawk family tree was the P-40 Warhawk, which mainly differed from the Hawk by having an Allison liquid-cooled engine instead of the air-cooled Wright Cyclone radial. This model, more aerodynamically efficient than the Hawk due to the use of flush rivets, became the principal fighter of US Army Air Corps pursuit (fighter) squadrons. France had placed an order, which was instead sent to the UK after Germany invaded France. Britain had also ordered the new P-40s and designated them "Tomahawks". For the RAF, the Allison engine failed to provide the performance required for air combat in Europe in 1941 and RAF Tomahawks were used purely as low-level tactical reconnaissance aircraft. However, 100 British Tomahawk IIs were diverted to the American Volunteer Group operating in China, where they achieved many victories against Japanese aircraft.

The P-40D first flew in May 1941 and was a major improvement on previous models, with a new, more powerful Allison engine. The nose cross-section was reduced and the guns formerly carried in the nose were dropped. Main armament was now four 12.7mm/0.5in machine-guns in the wings and a rack could be added beneath the fuselage to carry a 227kg/500lb bomb. It was the British who ordered the P-40D and coined the name "Kittyhawk" for their version of the Curtiss fighter. (The name Kittyhawk is often mistakenly applied to the whole Warhawk range.) By now, however, the P-40 was way behind in contemporary fighter performance and it was not capable of holding its own against crack pilots. Nevertheless, the later P-40E model was also supplied to the American Volunteer Group in China, where it continued to achieve kills. Even in the Western Desert, where the RAF's Kittyhawks' fighter-bomber achievements are well known, the type had many victories in the air. Legendary British test pilot Neville Duke scored 12 air victories while flying Kittyhawks there, as well as the five kills he achieved whilst flying Tomahawks, also in the Western Desert.

Total production of the P-40 exceeded 16,800.

ABOVE: **This P-40, preserved in the USA, is painted as an aircraft of the American Volunteer Group.**
BELOW: **A fine wartime photograph of an RAF Kittyhawk in the Western Desert.**

P-40N/Kittyhawk IV

First flight: October 1938 (XP-40)
Power: Allison 1360hpV-1710-81 in-line piston engine
Armament: Six 12.7mm/0.5in machine-guns in wings and provision for one 227kg/500lb bomb under fuselage
Size: Wingspan – 11.42m/37ft 4in
Length – 10.2m/33ft 4in Height – 3.77m/12ft 4in
Wing area – 21.95m²/236sq ft
Weights: Empty – 2724kg/6000lb
Maximum loaded – 4018kg/8850lb
Performance: Maximum speed – 609kph/378mph
Ceiling – 11,630m/38,000ft
Range – 386km/240 miles
Climb – 4590m/15,000ft in 6 minutes, 42 seconds

LEFT: **A French Air Force D.500.**

Dewoitine D.501

First flight: Early 1934
Power: Hispano-Suiza 690hp 12Xcrs in-line
piston engine
Armament: One 20mm/0.78in Oerlikon cannon firing
through propeller hub, plus two wing-mounted
7.55mm/0.295in machine-guns
Size: Wingspan – 12.09m/39ft 8.25in
Length – 7.56m/24ft 9.75in
Height – 2.7m/8ft 10.25in
Wing area – 16.5m²/177.61sq ft
Weights: Empty – 1287kg/2837lb
Maximum loaded – 1787kg/3940lb
Performance: Maximum speed – 335kph/208mph
Ceiling – 10,200m/33,465ft
Range – 870km/541 miles
Climb – 1000m/3280ft in 1 minute, 20 seconds

Dewoitine D.500 series

The French D.500 may have been the most modern-looking fighter of its day but it was a transition design, bridging the gap between open-cockpit fabric-covered biplanes and the new all-metal monoplanes. The D.500, the prototype for the series, was made entirely of light alloy and first flew in 1932, attracting much overseas interest. It was a low wing monoplane with a fixed tailwheel. The D.501 was the first production version of a series that differed in engine and armament installation, resulting in a host of variants.

The ultimate version was the D.510 which, together with a few D.501s, was in widespread use in the French Air Force at the outbreak of World War II. Compared with the earlier models in the series, the D.510 had a more powerful engine and greater fuel capacity but with a top speed of 400kph/249mph, it would have been no match for Hitler's more modern and capable fighters.

It was transferred to French squadrons overseas before the German attack of May 1940. Some exported Dewoitines did battle in China until late 1941.

LEFT: **The long nose of the D.520 presented the pilot with a very poor view from the cockpit, so techniques used by RAF Spitfire pilots were employed – weave while taxiing and sideslip in to land.**

Dewoitine D.520

First flight: October 2, 1938
Power: Hispano-Suiza 850hp 12Y-45 12-cylinder
liquid-cooled piston engine
Armament: One 20mm/0.78in cannon firing through
propeller hub, plus four 7.5mm/0.295in machine-
guns in wings
Size: Wingspan – 10.2m/33ft 5.5in
Length – 8.76m/28ft 8.75in Height – 2.57m/8ft 5in
Wing area – 15.95m²/171.7sq ft
Weights: Empty – 2125kg/4685lb
Maximum take-off – 2790kg/6151lb
Performance: Maximum speed – 535kph/332mph
Ceiling – 10,250m/33,639ft
Range – 1540km/957 miles
Climb – 4000m/13,125ft in 5 minutes, 48 seconds

Dewoitine D.520

The D.520, with the look of a racing aircraft, was certainly the most capable fighter available to the French Armée de l'Air at the start of World War II. Production, in the face of initial official indifference was problematic, but they were rolling off the line at a healthy rate by the time France fell to the Germans. Some did reach French fighter units before the fall, and accounted for 147 German aircraft. Henschel 126s, Messerschmitt Bf109s

and Bf110s, and Heinkel 111s all fell to the guns of the outnumbered D.520s.

Vichy forces used the D.520 extensively and with some success against Allied aircraft in the 1941 Syrian campaign and the North African landings of November 1942. D.520 production continued in Occupied France and these aircraft together with captured examples were supplied to Germany's allies, including Italy, Romania and Bulgaria.

The Luftwaffe itself was also quick to realize the D.520's potential as a fighter-trainer. These aircraft were later seized back by French forces after D-Day in 1944, had their German markings painted over, and were used against Germans in southern France. Post-war, the French Air Force operated D.520s until 1953.

de Havilland/Airco DH.2

In June 1914 Airco hired talented young designer Geoffrey de Havilland, later founder of the company that bore his name, to head their design department and the DH.2 was his second project for the company. The first had been the DH.1 two-seat reconnaissance fighter and the DH.2 was simply a smaller version of it for a one-man crew. The DH.2 used an air-cooled rotary engine instead of the DH.1's water-cooled in-line engine but kept the "pusher" configuration, with the propeller facing behind the aircraft. This was due to the fact that in early 1915 a means had not yet been perfected that would allow a gun to shoot forwards between the spinning blades of propeller blades.

The armament arrangement seems bizarre by today's standards, consisting of a Lewis gun which could be mounted on either side of the cockpit as the pilot wished. He did of course have to manhandle the gun (that weighed 8kg/17.5lb) to the other side if an enemy presented himself there, all while still trying to control the aircraft. The gun was later mounted at the front of the aircraft on the centre line and was normally used as a fixed weapon, aimed by aiming the aircraft itself.

Nevertheless the DH.2 was praised by its pilots for its responsiveness and excellent rate of climb, and the aircraft was certainly central to winning back control of the air over the Western Front in early 1916.

Around 450 were built, but the tide began to turn again, and the DH.2 was outclassed by the latest German fighters by late 1916. The type was eventually withdrawn from March 1917 but not before No.29 Squadron lost five out of six DH.2s in one engagement, with five of the new Albatros D.IIIs on December 20, 1916.

Airco DH.2

First flight: Spring 1915
Power: Gnome Monosoupape 100hp nine-cylinder rotary piston engine
Armament: One 7.7mm/0.303in Lewis machine-gun
Size: Wingspan – 8.61m/28ft 3in
    Length – 7.68m/25ft 2.5in
    Height – 2.91m/9ft 6.5in
    Wing area – 23.13m²/249sq ft
Weights: Empty – 428kg/943lb
    Maximum take-off – 654kg/1441lb
Performance: Maximum speed – 150kph/93mph
    Ceiling – 4265m/14,000ft
    Range – 2 hours, 45 minutes endurance
    Climb – 1830m/6000ft in 11 minutes

de Havilland Mosquito

The Mosquito was a true multi-role combat aircraft, which started life in late 1938 as an outline design for a bomber-reconnaissance aircraft that could fly so fast and high that no defensive armament was needed. The far-sighted design avoided the use of strategic materials, instead using wood for virtually the whole aircraft – this later led to the nickname the "Wooden Wonder". Even so, it was only after World War II began that Britain's Air Ministry seriously considered the proposal, and then with some caution, but in November 1940 the Mosquito first flew and convinced the sceptics that it was a remarkable aircraft. Priority production was ordered for the bomber version and meanwhile the photo-reconnaissance and fighter prototypes were prepared.

The Mosquito fighter prototype flew in May 1941 and was immediately developed as a nightfighter equipped with the latest secret Airborne Interception (AI) radar. It also differed from the bomber version by having strengthened wing spars for air combat and a flat bullet-proof windscreen.

Armed with four cannon in the floor beneath the nose and four machine-guns in the nose itself, the two-man Mosquito NF.II entered Fighter Command service in January 1942, gradually replacing the Beaufighter as the RAF's standard UK-based nightfighter. From December that year, No.23 Squadron's NF.IIs operated from Malta, and in the first few months of 1943 shot down 17 enemy aircraft. They were

TOP: **The bomber version of the Mosquito appeared first.** ABOVE: **The Mosquito sting – four 20mm/0.78in cannon below the cockpit. Later nightfighters had radomes like this NF.XIX, eliminating the external "antler" aerials.**

equally active in daylight and also flew train-busting missions over Italy, Sicily and North Africa, clearly demonstrating the versatility of the Mosquito as a fighter-bomber. The purely dayfighter version was shelved after one prototype, such was the effectiveness of the nightfighter and the later fighter-bomber versions.

The radar carried by nightfighter Mosquitoes was constantly improved (Marks NF.XII, XIII and XVII) and the nose-mounted machine-guns were eventually deleted, leaving four cannon as the only armament. The crews became very adept at finding and destroying enemy aircraft under cover of darkness. On March 19, 1944 a Mk XVII of No.25 Squadron shot down three

Junkers Ju 188s on a single sortie over the Humber. Some of the XVIIs were equipped with a tail-mounted warning radar so that they could themselves avoid becoming the prey.

Fighter-bomber versions were also developed and the FB.Mk VI became the most widely used of all Mosquito fighters. This version was a day or night intruder, able ultimately to carry two 227kg/500lb bombs as well as the usual fighter armament. RAF Coastal Command were quick to see the potential of the type and soon began using the VI, armed with underwing rockets, as a maritime strike aircraft.

Mk VIs were equally at home defending the UK as nightfighters or flying deep into German airspace, wreaking havoc on their nightfighters. Mosquito VIs were also capable of catching and destroying the German V-1 flying bombs that rained down on parts of Britain from June 1944. In all, Mosquito fighters destroyed 428 V-1s, the first being claimed by Flight Lt J.G. Musgrove on the night of June 14–15.

ABOVE: **All Royal Australian Air Force Mosquitoes carried the A52 serial prefix denoting the aircraft type. DH Australia produced a total of 212 Mosquitoes during World War II.** BELOW: **Covered with matt black paint and with aerial arrays on the nose, the NF.II entered service in January 1942.**

In March 1944, a modified IV became the first British twin-engine aircraft to land on an aircraft carrier. This trial, on board HMS *Indefatigable*, proved the feasibility of the Sea Mosquito which, equipped with folding wings and a modified undercarriage, joined the Royal Navy in 1946.

The ultimate wartime Mosquito nightfighter was the NF.30 high-altitude version, which regularly escorted Royal Air Force bombers on missions over Germany. As one pilot later said, "The fact that we might have been there on their tail made some Luftwaffe pilots think twice before attacking our bomber boys".

Post-war, the Mosquito NF.36, fitted with American Mk 10 AI radar, appeared and an export version equipped with British AI radar was supplied to Yugoslavia. The NF.36 was the only all-weather fighter available to the RAF until 1951–2, when the nightfighter Meteors and Vampires entered service. It is hard to think of the Mosquito as a Cold War aircraft but it came to be so due to a technology deficit in the UK.

The last de Havilland Mosquito, out of a total production run of 7781 planes, was an NF.38, completed at Chester in November 1950.

de Havilland Mosquito NF.30

First flight: May 15, 1941 (fighter prototype)

Power: Two Rolls-Royce 1690hp Merlin 113/114 in-line piston engines

Armament: Four 20mm/0.78in cannon

Size: Wingspan – 16.5m/54ft 2in
Length – 13.57m/44ft 6in
Height – 3.81m/12ft 6in
Wing area – 42.19m^2/454sq ft

Weights: Empty – 6086kg/13,400lb
Maximum take-off – 9810kg/21,600lb

Performance: Maximum speed – 655kph/407mph
Ceiling – 11,590m/38,000ft
Range – 2091km/1300 miles
Climb – 869m/2850ft per minute

Dornier Do 17 nightfighters

Nicknamed the "Flying Pencil", Germany's Do 17 was a medium bomber developed from a Dornier high-speed mailplane, whose performance caused much concern outside Germany when it appeared in 1934. The concern was well placed as the Do 17 was extensively used by the Luftwaffe as a bomber, reconnaissance aircraft and glider tug through much of World War II.

The first Do 17 nightfighter variant was the experimental Do 17Z-6 Kauz (Screech Owl), which married a Do 17Z-3 airframe to the nose and forward-firing armament (three MG15 machine-guns and a 20mm cannon) of the Ju 88C-2.

The production Do 17Z-10 Kauz II had a completely new purpose-designed nose, housing four machine-guns, four cannon and an infra-red (IR) detector. Rear-firing machine-guns were retained from the bomber version.

The first unit to operate the three-seat Do 17 Kauz II was 4/NJG 1 based at Deelen, and on October 18, 1940 the Do 17 nightfighter claimed its first kill when a Royal Air Force Wellington bomber was destroyed.

The 4/NJG 1 also achieved some success in the east of England by attacking the streams of bomber aircraft returning to home airfields after night missions over Europe. The vulnerable RAF bombers were classic sitting targets as they dropped their undercarriages for the safe landing that never came.

A small but significant number of Kauz IIs remained active until early 1942. Versions of the Do 17 that had more powerful engines and were designed for export to Yugoslavia were designated Do 215. In all only ten Do 17 nightfighters were built and remained active until early 1942.

ABOVE: **The versatile Dornier Do 17 "Flying Pencil" spawned the very useful nightfighter variants. Although produced in small numbers, they were very effective against RAF bombers. Although only in use for around two years, the Do 17 nightfighters proved the value of dedicated nightfighters.**

Dornier Do 17Z-10 Kauz II

First flight: Early 1938 (Do 17 prototype)
Power: Two Bramo 1000hp 323P radial piston engines
Armament: Four 7.92mm/0.31in machine-guns and four 20mm/0.78in cannon
Size: Wingspan – 18m/59ft 1in
Length – 15.8m/51ft 10in
Height – 4.55m/14ft 11in
Wing area – 55m^2/592sq ft
Weights: Empty – approx 5700kg/12,545lb
Maximum take-off – 9000kg/19,841lb
Performance: Maximum speed – 450kph/280mph
Ceiling – 9500m/31,170ft
Range – 1609km/1000 miles
Climb – 1000m/3280ft in 4 minutes, 30 seconds

Dornier Do 217 nightfighters

The Do 217 was derived from the highly successful Do 17/215 series of bombers, but was very different from the earlier aircraft. The 217 was initially developed as a bomber that could carry a greater load than any other German bomber of the time. Variants soon followed, including the three-seat 217J fighter-bomber and nightfighter versions. Both differed from the 217 bomber by having a solid nose in place of the "greenhouse" nose for a bomb aimer.

The J-1 was a fighter-bomber, operational from February 1942, armed with four nose-mounted 7.92mm/0.31in machine-guns and four 20mm/0.78in cannon, in addition to dorsal and ventral gun positions, each mounting a pair of 13mm/0.51in guns.

The J-2 was an interim nightfighter, armed like the J-1 but without a bomb bay and equipped with the Lichtenstein radar. Both J models entered service in summer 1942 but only over Germany. The Italian Air Force, the Regia Aeronautica, also operated J models over Italy and the Mediterranean.

July 1942 saw the test flight of the improved Do 217N four-seat nightfighter. Powered by higher-performance engines and carrying more "black box" radar equipment than the J-2, the N model also had its rear bomb bay reinstated for missions over the Eastern Front. The upper and lower gun positions were deleted and faired over and this weight reduction improved performance. Replacement fire-power was in the form of four oblique, upward-firing 20mm/0.78in cannon. The 217N was used operationally in the Mediterranean as well as over Germany and in the occupied countries.

In 1943 Hauptmann Hans Krause was awarded the Iron Cross after destroying 12 Allied aircraft over Hungary and the Adriatic while flying Do 217Ns.

Dornier Do 217N-2

First flight: July 31, 1942
Power: Two Daimler Benz 1750hp DB 603A 12-cylinder liquid-cooled engines
Armament: Four 7.9mm/0.31in machine-guns in nose, four 20mm/0.78in cannon in lower nose, four 20mm/0.78in cannon firing obliquely upwards (70 degrees) from centre fuselage
Size: Wingspan – 19m/62ft 4in
Length – 18.9m/62ft, including radar aerials
Height – 5m/16ft 5in Wing area – 57m^2/614sq ft
Weights: Empty – 19,780kg/43,607lb
Maximum take-off – 13,700kg/30,202lb
Performance: Maximum speed – 425kph/264mph
Ceiling – 8418m/27,600ft
Range – 1755km/1090 miles
Climb – 6000m/19,685ft in 17 minutes

A total of 364 J and N models were produced and they were replaced by mid-1944.

BELOW: **The distinctive aerials of the Lichtenstein C-1 radar on the Do 217J-2 were the nightfighters' eyes in the black of night.**

Fairey Firefly

From 1926 Britain's Fleet Air Arm deployed a series of fast two-seat fighter reconnaissance aircraft, and the Fairey Firefly continued the tradition, first flying in December 1941. It replaced the Fairey Fulmar as the Royal Navy's principal carrier-borne fighter from July 1943 and first saw action during attacks on the *Tirpitz* in July 1944. The Firefly's elliptical wings could be folded back manually for beneath-deck stowage and were hydraulically locked into the extended flying position.

Although the Griffon-engined Firefly Mk 1 was around 64kph/40mph faster than the Merlin-engined Fulmar, it was still slower than most contemporary fighters. The Firefly did however have better armament, in the form of four hard-hitting 20mm/0.78in cannons in place of the Fulmar's eight machine-guns. It also had great low-speed handling characteristics – vital for carrier-borne fighters.

Firefly nightfighter variants were developed early in production of the type and carried airborne interception radar in small wing-mounted radomes. The associated extra equipment affected the aircraft's centre of gravity and necessitated a lengthening of the fuselage by 45.7cm/18in. This version of the F.1, the N.F.2, was only produced in limited quantities because an alternative means of accomodating the radar equipment was developed that did not require major structural work. Radar was then being fitted as standard to Fireflies and the non-lengthened Firefly N.F.1 was the nightfighter version of the F.R.1, which was itself basically an F.1 fitted with radar. All Firefly nightfighters were equipped with exhaust dampers so that the glowing exhausts of the Griffon engine would not show up in darkness.

Although the Firefly was never a classic fighter, it excelled in the strike and armed reconnaissance role. The first Firefly air combat victory occurred on January 2, 1945 during a Fleet Air Arm attack on oil refineries in Sumatra, when a No.1770 Squadron aircraft shot down a Japanese "Oscar", a very capable dogfighter.

In the weeks immediately after VJ Day (September 2, 1945), Fleet Air Arm Fireflies carried out supply drops to POW camps on the Japanese mainland. Royal Navy Fireflies went on to see action in the Korean War and then, in 1954, in the ground-attack role in Malaya. Royal Netherlands Air Force Firefly AS4s were in action in Indonesia in early 1962.

Fairey Firefly F.1

First flight: December 22, 1941
Power: Rolls-Royce 1990hp Griffon XII engine
Armament: Four 20mm/0.78in cannon in wings
Size: Wingspan – 13.56m/44ft 6in, spread
  4.04m/13ft 3in, folded
  Length – 11.46m/37ft 7in
  Height – 4.14m/13ft 7in
  Wing area – 30.48m^2/328sq ft
Weights: Empty – 4423kg/9750lb
  Maximum take-off – 6360kg/14,020lb
Performance: Maximum speed – 509kph/316mph
  Ceiling – 8534m/28,000ft
  Range – 2092km/1300 miles
  Climb – 4575m/15,000ft in 9.6 minutes

ABOVE: **The early Fireflies had the radiator beneath the engine.** BELOW: **Later versions had wing leading edge radiators, changing the look of the aircraft.**

Fiat CR.32

This biplane fighter, which first flew in 1933, has been described as one of the greatest ever aircraft in its class. The highly manoeuvrable all-metal aircraft proved itself during the Spanish Civil War, when around 380 flew in support of the Nationalist forces. It was more than a match for the Republicans' Polikarpov I-15 and I-16 monoplanes, and Spain built its own under licence as the Hispano Chirri. Other Fiat-built machines were supplied to China, Hungary and various South American countries. Even as late as 1940 the

CR.32 was widely deployed by Italy's Regia Aeronautica. They were by then outclassed by contemporary fighters but some were modified as nightfighters and others soldiered on, some being used against British troops in Libya. Some of the Spanish Chirri models remained in service up to 1953 as aerobatic trainers.

LEFT: **The CR.30, proven in the Spanish Civil War.**

Fiat CR.32

First flight: April 28, 1933
Power: Fiat 600hp A.30 V-12 water-cooled in-line piston engine
Armament: Two synchronized 7.7mm/0.303in machine-guns
Size: Wingspan – 9.5m/31ft 2in
length, 7.45m/24ft 5.25in
Height – 2.63m/8ft 7.5in
Wing area – 22.1m²/237.89sq ft
Weights: Empty – 1325kg/2921lb
Maximum take-off – 1850kg/4079lb
Performance: Maximum speed – 375kph/233mph
Ceiling – 8800m/28,870ft
Range – 680km/422 miles
Climb – 907m/2000ft per minute

Fiat CR.42 Falco

Italy's air ministry, impressed by the performance of the CR.32 in the Spanish Civil War, believed the biplane fighter still had a place in modern air war. The Falco was really of another age by the time it entered service. With many air forces planning to equip with closed-cockpit metal monoplanes, the fixed-undercarriage Falco was virtually obsolete before it had flown. Nevertheless, the CR.42 was not only ordered for Italy's Regia Aeronautica but also for the air forces of Sweden, Belgium and Hungary. When Italy went to war in June 1940, Falcos flew as

escorts on bombing missions over France. In late 1940 the biplane fighters were based in Belgium for Italian bomber attacks on Britain. This often forgotten aspect of the post-Battle of Britain period climaxed on November 11 when the only major Italian raid saw the Italian attackers severely mauled – Falcos were no match for Hurricanes.

LEFT: **This Falco is preserved in the UK by the Royal Air Force Museum.**

Fiat CR.42 Falco

First flight: May 23, 1938
Power: Fiat A.74 R1C 14-cylinder radial piston engine
Armament: Two fixed synchronized 12.7mm/0.5in machine-guns
Size: Wingspan – 9.7m/31ft 10in
Length – 8.27m/27ft 1.5in
Height – 3.59m/11ft 9.25in
Wing area – 22.4m²/241.12sq ft
Weights: Empty – 1782kg/3929lb
Maximum take-off – 2298kg/5060lb
Performance: Maximum speed – 430kph/267mph
Ceiling – 10,200m/33,465ft
Range – 775km/482 miles
Climb – 6000m/19,685ft in 8 minutes, 40 seconds

Fiat G.50 Freccia

The G.50 was the Regia Aeronautica's first all-metal retractable undercarriage monoplane fighter. Early models were combat-tested in the Spanish Civil War: pilots talked of its manoeuvrability and speed. The pilots did not, however, like the "greenhouse" cockpit canopy and, remarkably, the next 200 G.50s built had an open cockpit. About 120 were in service when Italy entered World War II and some were used on raids against France. G.50s also took part in the Italian Air Force raids on Britain in late

1940 and later participated in the Greek and Western Desert campaigns, sometimes in the fighter-bomber role. Only a handful were left in service at the time of the Italian armistice.

In 1939 Finland bought 35 Freccias (Arrow) and used them in action against the Soviet Union in the Russo-Finnish War between 1941 and 1944.

LEFT: **A Regia Aeronautica G.50.**

Fiat G.50 Freccia

First flight: February 26, 1937
Power: Fiat A.74 RC38 14-cylinder radial piston engine
Armament: Two synchronized 12.7mm/0.5in machine-guns
Size: Wingspan – 10.96m/35ft 11.5in
Length – 7.79m/25ft 6.75in
Height – 2.96m/9ft 8.5in
Wing area – 18.15m²/195.37sq ft
Weights: Empty – 1975kg/4354lb
Maximum take-off – 2415kg/5324lb
Performance: Maximum speed – 472kph/293mph
Ceiling – 9835m/32,265ft
Range – 670km/416 miles
Climb – 6000m/19,685 in 7 minutes, 30 seconds

Focke-Wulf Fw190

The Fw190, considered by many to be the finest Luftwaffe fighter of the war, was first flown in June 1939 and swiftly proved that single-seat fighters powered by air-cooled radials could still take on the best of the in-line engined fighters. When the Fw190 appeared in combat over France in September 1941 claiming three Spitfires, it proved to be bad news for the RAF whose Spitfire V had ruled the sky since its appearance in February 1941. The 190 was more manoeuvrable than the Spitfire V, except in its turning circle, and had a higher top speed. The Focke-Wulf fighter had a considerable period of dominance in the west and was only seriously challenged when the improved Spitfire IX appeared in quantity in the autumn of 1942.

In February 1942 the Fw190A had its combat début, providing air cover for the German battle-cruisers *Scharnhorst* and *Gneisenau* and the heavy cruiser *Prinz Eugen* as they tried to reach north German ports. In one engagement, 190s destroyed all six attacking Royal Navy Swordfish.

From 1942, the 190A began to appear in quantity on all major fronts and in the West served in both the air defence and fighter/bomber roles. Fw190s were in the thick of one of the fiercest air battles of World War II, over the British and Canadian landings at Dieppe on August 19, 1942. Fw190s were in action throughout the day, by the end of which their pilots had claimed a total of 97 RAF aircraft destroyed. One pilot alone, Josef Wurmheller, claimed seven Spitfires.

The A-model was constantly improved, carrying heavier armament and sometimes equipped with water-methanol or nitrous-oxide injection. Over 30 different variants appeared from the simple fighter to torpedo-carriers.

ABOVE: **The Fw190F was a fighter-bomber version. This example, captured by US forces, is seen awaiting evaluation at Freeman Field in the USA, September 1945.**

In the later war years, the Fw190 became the standard home defence fighter for Germany and was in constant action against the Allied bomber streams. On August 17, 1943 a USAAF bomber force was intercepted by over 300 Fw190 fighters who accounted for 60 American bombers destroyed and 100 damaged. Some of the 190s were specially equipped with 210mm/8.19in rockets used to blow the defensive formations apart, making the bombers easier targets for the conventionally armed Fw190s.

In June 1943 a dedicated Fw190 nightfighter unit was formed but the aircraft were not fitted with radar, instead relying on intercepting the bombers over targets where they might be illuminated by flares, searchlights or the light of the fires below. Over 200 RAF heavy bombers are believed to have been destroyed by these aircraft.

In 1943, the Luftwaffe was faced with an urgent need for fighters with better high-altitude performance to face not just the threat of Allied bombers but also the American B-29 that was known to be coming into service. The existing Fw190 was thought to be incapable of intercepting this new American bomber and so Focke-Wulf, under the leadership of Kurt Tank, undertook the development of a high altitude version of his Fw190 fighter to meet the threat.

The result was the long-nosed D model, or "Dora", and the first production version was the Fw190D-9, which attained production status in the early summer of 1944. The Fw190D

LEFT: The versatile Fw190 was an excellent fighter-bomber. This example is shown carrying a bomb below its centre line. BELOW: The D model, or "Dora" was introduced to counter the anticipated threat of USAAF B-29s.

BELOW RIGHT: A captured Ta152H-1 in RAF markings. The Ta152 was an even longer-nosed derivative of the Fw190D. BELOW: This Fw190A-3 landed in the UK by mistake during June 1943, giving the Allies all the information they needed about the type.

was the first production Fw190 fitted with a liquid-cooled engine and was a very good high-altitude interceptor, equal to the P-51D or Spitfire Mk XIV and without the altitude limitations of the Fw190A. Delivery of the Fw190D-9 began in August 1944 and the first Gruppe (group) to convert to the Dora-9 was 3/JG 54. Their first mission was to provide top cover for Me 262 jet fighters during take-off when they were at their most vulnerable. The general opinion of the Fw190D-9 pilots was that it was the finest Luftwaffe propeller fighter of the entire war and many considered it more than a match for the P-51 Mustang.

The D model was the stepping-stone to the high-flying Focke-Wulf Ta152 that saw service in limited numbers towards the end of the war.

Focke-Wulf 190D-9

First flight: June 1, 1939 (Fw190)
Power: Junkers 1776hp Jumo 213A-1 inverted V piston engine
Armament: Two 13mm/0.51in machine-guns, two 20mm/0.79in cannon plus one 500kg/1102lb bomb
Size: Wingspan – 10.5m/34ft 5.5in
Length – 10.2m/33ft 5.5in
Height – 3.35m/11ft
Wing area – 18.3m²/197sq ft
Weights: Empty – 3490kg/7694lb
Maximum take-off – 4848kg/10,670lb
Performance: Maximum speed – 685kph/426mph
Ceiling – 12,000m/39,370ft
Range – 835km/519 miles
Climb – 6000m/19,685ft in 7 minutes, 6 seconds

Fokker Eindecker

The Fokker E (Eindecker or monoplane) was significant because it was the first combat aircraft to be equipped with interrupter gear that allowed bullets from a fixed machine-gun to be fired safely between the spinning blades of a propeller. This gave the Eindecker pilots a significant advantage over their Allied adversaries, who still had to manoeuvre their aircraft into a firing position and then aim their moving guns manually. The interrupter gear synchronized the Eindecker's single gun with the propeller blades so that once the aircraft was pointed at a target, so was the gun.

The Eindecker, not a remarkable aircraft, was developed from the pre-war M.5 design and relied on "wing-warping" for lateral control, but the technical advantage of a single synchronized gun allowed its pilots to rack up a significant number of aerial victories, beginning on August 1, 1915, when the legendary German ace Max Immelmann achieved his and the Eindecker's first "kill". Over the following weeks Royal Flying Corps pilots were alarmed to come across these single-seat "fighters" that could fire along their own line of flight. This was the beginning of a period of German air supremacy over the Western Front that came to be known as the "Fokker Scourge". The Eindecker, with its innovative armament, gave pilots like Immelmann and Oswald Boelcke a string

of victories that made them national heroes in their homeland and possibly the first well-known fighter aces.

In spite of this, for a number of reasons the Eindecker never reached its full potential as a weapon. German paranoia about the "secret" of the interrupter gear falling into British hands made them forbid the use of the Eindeckers over enemy territory. Also, the Eindeckers were only allocated as individual aircraft to fly escort for two-seater aircraft. Production problems meant that even though they were clearly very significant aircraft, there were less than a hundred in service by the end of 1915. Nevertheless, Eindecker pilots honed their tactics and eventually began to operate in fours, while a more organized ground control system had them vectored to airspace where enemy aircraft were known to be. The result was that by the end of 1915 a small number of Eindeckers had effectively removed the enemy's ability to carry out reconnaissance missions. Meanwhile two lone Eindeckers on the Eastern Front kept the Imperial Russian Air Service in their area at bay.

The tactical advantage enjoyed by the Fokker E series (later Es, the EII, III and

TOP: **The very effective Fokker Eindecker destroyed over 1000 Allied aircraft.** ABOVE: **The period of Eindecker supremacy over the Western Front was known as the "Fokker Scourge".**

IV had more powerful engines and/or an additional gun) came to an end, as Allied designers produced purpose-built fighters to counter the "Fokker Scourge" and Eindeckers were gradually replaced during 1916, but they are thought to have destroyed over 1000 Allied aircraft in their short time of supremacy.

Fokker Eindecker

First flight: 1913 (M.5)

Power: Oberursel 100hp U.I nine-cylinder rotary piston engine

Armament: One fixed forward-firing 7.92mm/0.31in machine-gun

Size: Wingspan – 9.5m/31ft 2.75in
Length – 7.2m/23ft 7.5in
Height – 2.4m/7ft 10.5in
Wing area – 16m²/172.23sq ft

Weight: Empty – 399kg/880lb
Maximum take-off – 610kg/1345lb

Performance: Maximum speed – 140kph/87mph
Ceiling – 3500m/11,480ft
Range – 1.5 hours endurance
Climb – 3000m/9845ft in 30 minutes

Fokker Dr.I Triplane

The Dr.I, chosen by the Germans to counter the threat posed by the British Sopwith Triplane, was rushed into production in 1917 and reached front-line units in October that year. Although extremely manoeuvrable the Dr.I (Dr. was short for Dreidecker or triplane) had an enormous amount of induced drag from its three wings and was consequently not as fast as most of the fighter aircraft then in front-line service. It was, however, extremely manoeuvrable and became the mount of some of Germany's finest World War I aces. The Dr.I will be forever linked with the "Red Baron", Manfred von Richthofen.

Lt Werner Voss scored ten victories flying a prototype Dr.I between September 3 and September 23, 1917 when he died in a dogfight with a Royal Flying Corps S.E.5a. Production models first joined Manfred von Richthofen's Jagdgeschwader (fighter squadron) 1 in mid-October but were grounded after a series of fatal crashes. Investigations found defective wing construction and

the Dr.Is were back in action from the end of November only after all wings had been checked and if necessary rebuilt. Its career was, however, short-lived and production ceased in May 1918, at which time all remaining Dr.Is were withdrawn for the air defence of Germany. Although it was manoeuvrable, the Fokker was outclassed in many

other ways and was really the last of the line of rotary-engined fighters. Richthofen, however, liked its agility and excellent climb rate and was flying his personal scarlet machine when he was shot down and killed in April 1918.

Lt Carl Jacobs was the highest scoring Imperial German Air Force Triplane pilot, credited with 41 victories.

ABOVE: **Perhaps best known as the type made famous by the Red Baron, the Dr.I was one of the rotary-engined fighters.** LEFT: **The Fokker Triplane was introduced to counter the British Sopwith Triplane, which was very manoeuvrable.**

Fokker Dr.I Triplane

First flight: June 1917

Power: Oberursel Ur II nine-cylinder rotary piston engine

Armament: Two fixed forward-firing 7.92mm/0.31in machine-guns

Size: Wingspan – 7.2m/23ft 7.5in
Length – 5.77m/18ft 11.25in
Height – 2.95m/9ft 8.25in
Wing area – 18.7m^2/201.29sq ft

Weights: Empty – 406kg/895lb
Maximum take-off – 585kg/1290lb

Performance: Maximum speed – 165kph/103mph
Ceiling – 6095m/20,000ft
Range – 1.5 hours endurance
Climb – 1000m/3280ft in 2 minutes, 54 seconds

Fokker D. VII

The D. VII followed the Dr.I into production at the Fokker factory and went on to become the most famous German fighting scout aircraft of World War I. Like the Dreidecker before it, the D. VII was largely designed by Fokker designer Reinhold Platz and shared a number of common components and features with it. The 160hp engine fitted to early D. VIIs was, however, a major step forward in terms of power and the first test flight was carried out by Manfred Richthofen. It first entered service in April 1918 with Jagdgeschwader 1, Richthofen's old unit, commanded by Hermann Goering after the "Red Baron's" death.

The D. VII was popular with its pilots, who described it as responsive and easy to fly. Pilots of this last World War I Fokker fighter achieved many aerial victories in a short period. Germany's first true naval fighter unit Marine-Feld-Geschwader was formed in May 1917 and it was this unit which on August 12, equipped with D. VIIs, shot down 19 British aircraft without loss to itself. The only Allied

aircraft that could match the D. VII were the Sopwith Snipe and the SPAD S.XIII.

It is believed that over 1000 were built by the time of the Armistice in November 1918. It is interesting to note that one of the conditions of the Armistice Agreement was that "… especially all first-line D. VII aircraft" were to be handed over to the Allies, such was the regard for the Fokker fighter.

The Fokker company had been founded by Dutchman Anthony Fokker, who having had some of his designs rejected by Britain, among others, offered his services to the Central Powers. At the end of World War I, Fokker managed to smuggle some disassembled D. VIIs and components into Holland, where he went on manufacturing D. VIIs after the war. The Dutch Air Force continued to fly D. VIIs in the Netherlands East Indies until the late 1920s. Ex-German D. VIIs also served with many European air forces after the war.

TOP: **The Fokker D. VII was such a potent fighter that it was specifically mentioned in the Armistice Agreement.** ABOVE: **Oberleutnant Ernst Udet with his personal D. VII. His personal "LO" markings are just visible on the side of the fuselage.**

Fokker D. VII

First flight: January 1918
Power: BMW 185hp six-cylinder in-line piston engine
Armament: Two fixed forward-firing 7.92mm/0.3in machine-guns
Size: Wingspan – 8.9m/29ft 2.5in
Length – 6.95m/22ft 9.5in
Height – 2.75m/9ft 0.25in,
Wing area – 20.5m^2/220.67sq ft
Weights: Empty – 735kg/1620lb
Maximum take-off – 880kg/1940lb
Performance: Maximum speed – 200kph/124mph
Ceiling – 7000m/22,965ft
Range – 1.5 hours endurance
Climb – 5000m/16,405ft in 16 minutes

LEFT: **A D. XXI of the Finnish Air Force, 1941.**

Fokker D. XXI

First flight: March 27, 1936
Power: Bristol 830hp Mercury VIII nine-cylinder
radial piston engine
Armament: Four 7.9mm/0.31in machine-guns,
two in upper cowling and two in wings
Size: Wingspan – 11m/36ft 1in
Length – 8.2m/26ft 10.75in
Height – 2.95m/9ft 8in
Wing area – 16.2m²/174.38sq ft
Weights: Empty – 1450kg/3197lb
Maximum take-off – 2050kg/4519lb
Performance: Maximum speed – 460kph/286mph
Ceiling – 11,000m/36,090ft
Range – 950km/590 miles
Climb – 3000m/9842ft in 3 minutes, 30 seconds

Fokker D. XXI

Although the D. XXI was designed to meet a Netherlands East Indies Army Air Service requirement, it became the standard fighter for three European countries – Holland, Finland and Denmark. The first Dutch Air Force aircraft flew in mid-1938 and all were in service by early September 1938. The Dutch Air Force had 28 D. XXIs deployed when Germany invaded the Netherlands

in May 1940. During the five days before Holland surrendered, the Fokker fighters were pitched against overwhelming odds, but on May 10 they destroyed 37 German Junkers 52 transports in one morning. The brave Dutch D. XXI pilots flew on until their ammunition ran out.

Finnish licence production ran from 1939 until 1944, and a number of these machines were modified to take the

825hp Pratt and Whitney Twin Wasp Junior or the Bristol Pegasus engines. Finnish aircraft also differed from the others by having all four guns mounted in the wings, and "snow shoes" for winter operations.

Denmark operated both Dutch-built and Danish licence-built D. XXIs, which saw action in World War II, opposing the German invaders in March 1940.

LEFT: **Royal Air Force Gauntlet Is. The type was
replaced by Gladiators, Spitfires and Hurricanes
from 1938, but soldiered on in RAF service overseas
until late 1940.**

Gloster Gauntlet II

First flight: October 1934 (Gauntlet I)
Power: Bristol 640hp Mercury VIS nine-cylinder
radial piston engine
Armament: Two fixed forward-firing 7.7mm/0.303in
machine-guns
Size: Wingspan – 9.99m/32ft 9.5in
Length – 8.05m/26ft 5in
Height – 3.12m/10ft 3in
Wing area – 29.26m²/315sq ft
Weights: Empty – 1256kg/2770lb
Maximum take-off – 1801kg/3970lb
Performance: Maximum speed – 370kph/230mph
Ceiling – 10,210m/33,500ft
Range – 740km/460 miles
Climb – 701m/2300ft per minute

Gloster Gauntlet

The Gauntlet was the last open-cockpit biplane fighter with the RAF, entering service in 1935. It was the fastest single-seat fighter in service until 1937, when the Hurricane appeared, and served as a day- and nightfighter.

Gauntlets went on to equip 14 squadrons of RAF Fighter Command and remained a front-line aircraft in the UK until June 1939. However, the type

soldiered on with No.6 Squadron in Palestine until April 1940 and a flight of four fought the Italians in East Africa during September-November 1940. On September 7 a Gauntlet downed an Italian Caproni Ca133 bomber.

In November 1937 it was a Gauntlet of No.32 Squadron that became the first fighter ever to carry out an interception under the direction of ground radar.

Seventeen Gauntlets were produced under licence in Denmark, and ex-RAF Gauntlets were supplied to the Royal Australian Air Force, Finland, Rhodesia and South Africa. The Finnish Gauntlets were fitted with ski landing gear.

Gloster Meteor

The Gloster Meteor was the first jet aircraft in RAF squadron service and also the only Allied jet to see action in World War II. The Meteor beat Germany's Messerschmitt Me262 into squadron service and entered the history books by a matter of days to become the world's first operational jet fighter.

The Meteor was designed by George Carter, who began design work in 1940 and chose the twin-engine layout because of the poor thrust produced by the turbojets of the time. The first Meteor to be built was powered by two Frank Whittle-designed W2B turbojets, but the aircraft was only taxied as the engines failed to produce more than 454kg/1000lb of thrust. So when, on March 5, 1943 the first Meteor flew, it was powered by two Halford H1 engines, forerunners of the Goblin engine later used in the de Havilland Vampire, each providing 681kg/1500lb of thrust. Other prototypes soon took to the air, powered by different engines as the most reliable and efficient powerplant was sought. Development and manufacture of the Whittle-designed engine had passed to Rolls-Royce, who produced it as the 772kg/1700lb thrust W2B/23 Welland engine and it was two of these powerplants that took the fourth Meteor prototype into the air for the first time in June 1943. The Welland was subsequently chosen to power the production Meteor I.

The first RAF Meteor squadron was No.616, who received their first delivery of the futuristic fighters on July 12, 1944 and wasted no time in putting the Meteor to the test. The first

TOP: **A Meteor F.8, the only British jet type to see action in the Korean War.**
ABOVE: **Over 1000 Meteor F.8s were in service with the RAF between 1950 and 1955.**

sortie flown by a Meteor was not against manned aircraft but actually against the deadly V-1 flying bombs that began to rain down on Britain in 1944. Problems with the guns frustrated Britain's first jet pilots but on August 4 Flying Officer Dean succeeded in tipping a V-1 over in flight after his guns had jammed. By the end of the month, with gun problems resolved, No.616 had destroyed a total of 13 flying bombs. As the Allies pushed into Europe after D-Day, the next Meteors were readied for fighter v. fighter combat, possibly against the new twin-engined Me262 recently deployed by the Germans. In fact only one inconclusive encounter with Focke-Wulf Fw190s is recorded. As World War II came to an end, the Meteor F. Mk III was the standard version in service, with more powerful Derwent engines and a sliding canopy. These aircraft remained in RAF service for some years after the war and formed the backbone of Fighter Command in the post-war years, retaining the standard wartime armament of four 20mm/0.78in Hispano cannon, carried on the sides of the fuselage forward of the cockpit.

Between 1947 and 1948 the Mk III was superseded in front-line units by the F. Mk 4, which was powered by uprated Derwent 5 engines and which went on to equip 22 RAF squadrons. The F. Mk 8, developed from the F.4 had a longer fuselage, extra internal fuel tankage and an ejection seat as standard. The latter safety feature is taken for granted these days but it was not so in the early days of jet fighter aircraft. The Mk 8 had a top speed of 965kph/600mph and from 1950 until 1955 was the RAF's main day interceptor with a staggering 1090 in service to counter the Soviet bomber threat.

Although not used there by the RAF, F.8s of the Royal Australian Air Force became the only British jet aircraft to see action in Korea, though their performance gave the enemy MiG-15s little to worry about. After the type's poor showing against the MiGs in Korea, many air forces applied the Meteor to the ground-attack role, armed with small bombs and air-to-ground rockets. The Meteor's performance was improved during its operational life but by the early 1950s it was outclassed by swept-wing fighters.

RAF F. Mk 8s were replaced by Hunters from 1955 but some were converted for use as target tugs and continued to fly in the RAF until 1977.

TOP: **The F.4 entered RAF service in 1947 and equipped 22 Fighter Command units.** ABOVE: **The Meteor F. Mk III was in RAF service by the end of World War II.** BELOW: **The Meteor was widely exported and equipped the air arms of at least 13 other nations.**

Over 350 Gloster Meteors were exported to at least 13 other nations (NATO air forces included Belgium, the Netherlands and Denmark) and more than 240 were built under licence by Belgium's Avions Fairey. Total UK production of Meteors reached 2920, and a few aircraft dayfighters of the era remained in service for three decades.

Gloster Meteor F. Mk I

First flight: March 5, 1943

Power: Two Rolls Royce 772kg/1700-lb thrust W2B/23 Welland turbojets

Armament: Four 20mm/0.78in cannon

Size: Wingspan – 13.11m/43ft
Length – 12.57m/41ft 4in
Height – 3.96m/13ft
Wing area 34.74m^2/374sq ft

Weights: Empty – 3692kg/8140lb
Maximum take-off – 6268kg/13,800lb

Performance: Maximum speed – 660kph/410mph
Ceiling – 12,190m/40,000ft
Range – 1610km/1000 miles
Climb – 657m/2155ft per minute

Gloster Gladiator

The Gloster Gladiator was the RAF's last biplane fighter and entered service in February 1937, by which time it was already obsolete. Although largely replaced by the start of World War II, the Gladiators of Nos.607 and 615 auxiliary squadrons were deployed to France with the Air Component of the Allied Expeditionary Force in November 1939. The RAF fighter squadrons were converting to Spitfires and Hurricanes

when the German attack in the west was launched in May 1940, and the Gladiators proved to be no match for the modern Luftwaffe fighters.

Meanwhile in Norway, No.263 Squadron Gladiators were in action defending British forces and one pilot, Flying Officer Jacobsen, destroyed at least five German aircraft on one remarkable mission. Tragically all of No.263's aircraft and all but two of its pilots were lost when the ship carrying them home following the British withdrawal from Norway was sunk by German battleships.

Even during the Battle of Britain, No.247 Squadron's Gladiators based at Roborough protected Plymouth and its dockyard from German attackers.

In June 1940 a handful of Gladiators were responsible for the defence of

LEFT: **Three RAF Gladiators, literally tied together for the ultimate test of formation flying, practice for the Hendon Air Display.** BELOW: **This Gladiator, preserved in the UK by the Shuttleworth Collection, is shown painted as an aircraft of No.247 Squadron at the time of the Battle of Britain.**

Malta and the type was also in action against Italian forces in Egypt. Elsewhere, Gladiators served in the Western Desert until early 1942.

Some Gladiators were fitted with arrester hooks and served with the Fleet Air Arm from December 1938, while fully navalized Sea Gladiators equipped for catapult launches were developed. After withdrawal from front-line duties, Gladiators continued to fly as communications and meteorological aircraft until 1944.

Gloster Gladiator Mk I

First flight: September 12, 1934
Power: Bristol 840hp Mercury IX air-cooled radial piston engine
Armament: Two 7.7mm/0.303in machine-guns in nose, plus two more mounted in wing
Size: Wingspan – 9.83m/32ft 3in
Length – 8.36m/27ft 5in
Height – 3.15m/10ft 4in
Wing area – 30.01m^2/323sq ft
Weights: Empty – 1565kg/3450lb
Maximum take-off – 2155kg/4750lb
Performance: Maximum speed – 407kph/253mph
Ceiling – 10,060m/33,000ft
Range – 547km/340 miles
Climb – 6095m/20,000ft in 9 minutes, 30 seconds

Grumman Biplane fighters

The Grumman company's long association with the US Navy began in March 1931, when the Navy ordered a prototype two-seat biplane fighter, the XFF-1. The all-metal XFF-1 had a top speed of 314kph/195mph and was faster than the Navy's standard fighter of the time, the Boeing F4B-4. The Navy ordered the Grumman biplane and it entered service as the FF-1 from April 1933. Canadian licence-built versions, known as Goblins were supplied to the Royal Canadian Air Force, Nicaragua and Japan. Spanish Republican Forces also acquired 40 of them and the two-seaters were in action against Spanish Nationalist forces between 1936 and 1939, during the Spanish Civil War.

The FF-1 was certainly a winning design and Grumman unsurprisingly began to develop a lighter, single-seat version, which became the F2F-1. The single-seater was lighter than the FF1, had a top speed of 383kph/238mph and entered US Navy service during 1935, replacing the F4B. The F2F-1 remained in front-line service aboard USS *Lexington* until late September 1940, at which point it became an advanced trainer.

The F2F-1 had exhibited some inherent directional instability, which Grumman sought to eradicate in an improved design, the F3F. With a longer fuselage and wings, together with other aerodynamic refinements, the F3F-1 prototype first flew in March 1935 but crashed two days later, killing the pilot, when the engine and wings detached themselves in a test dive. Wing and engine fittings were strengthened on the second prototype which also crashed, on May 17, after the pilot was unable to recover from a flat spin. Remarkably, this crashed aircraft

ABOVE AND LEFT. **The Grumman F3F was in US Navy service from 1936 until 1941. The family resemblance to the later Wildcat monoplane is clear.**

was rebuilt and was back in the air after just three weeks, fitted with a small ventral fin beneath the tail to aid spin recovery.

The F3F-1 entered US Navy service aboard USS *Ranger* and USS *Saratoga* in 1936 and US Marine Corps unit VMF-211 was the last to retire the F3F, in October 1941.

Grumman F2F-1

First flight: October 18, 1933

Power: Pratt & Whitney 650hp R-1535-72 Twin Wasp Junior radial piston engine

Armament: Two 7.62mm/0.3in machine-guns

Size: Wingspan – 8.69m/28ft 6in
Length – 6.53m/21ft 5in
Height – 2.77m/9ft 1in
Wing area – 21.37m²/230sq ft

Weights: Empty – 1221kg/2691lb
Maximum take-off – 1745kg/3847lb

Performance: Maximum speed – 383kph/238mph
Ceiling – 8380m/27,500ft
Range – 1585km/985 miles
Climb – 939m/3080ft per minute

Grumman F4F Wildcat

If the Wildcat looks like a biplane missing a set of wings there is a good reason – it was originally conceived as a biplane but was redesigned as a monoplane, the F4F, in 1936. Its industrial appearance, due to the entirely riveted fuselage, masked an aircraft with excellent speed and manoeuvrability.

In early 1939 the French Aéronavale placed the first order for the type with Grumman and this was followed in August that year by an order from the US Navy. After France fell, aircraft destined for the Aéronavale were diverted to Britain, where the first machines for Britain's Fleet Air Arm arrived in

July 1940. The British named the F4F the "Martlet" and put the type into service almost immediately with No.804 Squadron in the Orkneys. In December 1940 two of these Martlets became the first US-built fighters in British World War II service to destroy a German aircraft. In September 1941 No.802 Squadron became the first FAA unit to go to sea with Martlets, aboard HMS *Audacity*, and on the 20th, two of the aircraft shot down a Focke-Wulf 200 that was shadowing their convoy. Martlets of the Royal Naval Fighter Unit saw action over the Western Desert and shot down an Italian Fiat G.50 on September 28, 1941.

In May 1942 over Madagascar, FAA Martlets saw action against Vichy French aircraft and in August that year, while escorting a convoy to Malta, they tackled Italian bombers over the Mediterranean. By now the Martlet/Wildcat was known as a formidable fighter aircraft. Pilots praised its hard-hitting firepower but knew it was a tricky aircraft to fly and to handle on the ground too.

When the USA entered World War II in December 1941 the F4F, by now known as the Wildcat, was the most widely used fighter on US aircraft carriers and also equipped many

LEFT: **Despite its origins in a biplane design, the F4F went on to be one of the most effective carrier fighters of World War II.** BELOW: **Impressed by the performance of the Wildcat prototype, the US Navy ordered 78 of the type in 1939.**

LEFT: **To survive the harsh environment of carrier operations, naval fighters have to be supremely rugged and the Wildcat was just that.** BELOW: **Royal Navy Wildcats, initially named Martlets, saw widespread action in World War II and destroyed many enemy aircraft.** BOTTOM: **British Fleet Air Arm Wildcats destroyed four Luftwaffe fighters over Norway in March 1945.**

land-based US Marine Corps units. This tough, hard-hitting and highly manoeuvrable aircraft was the US Navy's only carrier-borne fighter until the 1943 arrival of the Hellcat. Wildcats were central to some of the war's most remarkable heroic actions involving US Navy and USMC pilots.

USMC Wildcats operated extensively from land bases, one of which was Henderson Field on Guadalcanal and it was from here that the Americans mounted their first offensive action of the war in the Pacific. One USMC Wildcat pilot, Captain Joe Foss, a flight commander with Marine Fighting Squadron VMF-121, led his flight of eight Wildcats from Guadalcanal to 72 confirmed aerial victories in a matter of sixteen weeks. Foss himself shot down a total of 26 Japanese aircraft, including five in a single day, and was awarded the Congressional Medal of Honor.

Although in a straight fight Wildcats could not cope well with Japanese Zeros, the Grumman fighter's armour plating and self-sealing fuel tanks, together with its pilot's tenacity made it a potent adversary in a dogfight. US Navy Wildcats were phased out in favour of the Grumman Hellcat in late 1943 but Britain's Fleet Air Arm continued to operate the Wildcat to the end of the war. In March 1945 Wildcats (the British abandoned the name Martlet in January 1944) of No.882 Squadron destroyed four Messerschmitt Bf109s over Norway in what was the FAA's last wartime victory over German fighters.

Those Wildcats built by General Motors were designated FM-1 and -2.

Grumman FM-2 Wildcat

First flight: March 1943 (FM-2)

Power: Wright Cyclone 1350hp R-1820-56 nine-cylinder air-cooled radial engine

Armament: Six 12.7mm/0.5in machine-guns in outer wings, plus two underwing 113kg/250lb bombs or six 12.7cm/5in rockets

Size: Wingspan – 11.58m/38ft
Length – 8.8m/28ft 11in
Height – 3.5m/11ft 5in
Wing area – 24.16m²/260sq ft

Weights: Empty – 2226kg/4900lb
Maximum take-off – 3367kg/7412lb

Performance: Maximum speed – 534kph/332mph
Service ceiling – 10,576m/34,700ft
Range – 1,448km/900 miles
Climb – 610m/2000ft per minute

Grumman F6F Hellcat

The F6F Hellcat has been rightly described as a war-winning fighter. Developed from the F4F Wildcat, designed and produced in record time, the Hellcat's combat début in August 1943 swung the Pacific air power balance firmly in favour of the United States. From then on all the major Pacific air battles were dominated by the F6F. In its first big air battle, in the Kwajalein area on December 4, 1943, 91 Hellcats fought 50 Japanese A6M Zeros and destroyed 28 for the loss of only two. Powered by the Pratt and Whitney R-2800 Double Wasp engine, the robust Hellcat was credited with 75 per cent of all enemy aircraft destroyed by US Navy carrier pilots, with an overall F6F kills-to-losses ratio in excess of 19:1. The Hellcat was America's all-time top "ace-making" aircraft, with no less than 307 pilots credited with the destruction of five or more enemy aircraft while flying the Grumman fighter. US Navy pilot Lt Bill Hardy became an ace on the day of April 6, 1945, when in a single 70-minute sortie he engaged and destroyed five Japanese aircraft.

Effective at any altitude, the Hellcat's unusual features included backwards-retracting landing gear and a distinctive 31.13m^2/334sq ft wing, larger than that of any other major single-engined fighter of World War II. The outer sections of the folding wings each contained three 12.7mm/0.5in machine-guns, with 400 rounds each.

Nightfighter versions equipped with radar appeared in early 1944 and ensured that the Hellcats were an ever-present threat to their enemies. The Hellcat omnipresence in Pacific combat zones night or day came to be known as "The Big

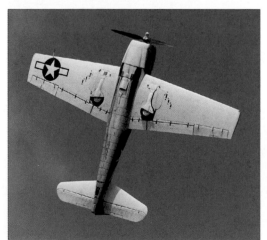

TOP: **The Hellcat turned the tide in favour of the USA in the Pacific air war during World War II.** ABOVE: **The XF6F-4, the Hellcat prototype.** LEFT: **During World War II the F6F was the single-engine fighter with the largest wing area.**

Blue Blanket". US Navy ace Lt Alex Vraciu destroyed 19 Japanese aircraft while flying Hellcats, including six in one spectacular eight-minute engagement, and later described the F6F Hellcat as "tough, hard-hitting, dependable – one hell of an airplane".

From April 1943 Britain's Fleet Air Arm received 252 F6F-3s under the Lend Lease programme. Initially renamed the "Gannet" in Royal Navy service, British F6Fs saw a lot of combat in actions off Norway, in the Mediterranean and the Far East, including the final assault on Japan. By late 1945 the Hellcat was virtually completely replaced in Royal Navy service, although a senior Fleet Air Arm officer is known to have had a personal F6F until 1953.

When the last aircraft rolled off the production line in November 1945 it made a total Hellcat production figure of 12,272, of which 11,000 were built in just two years. Swift production of the Hellcat has been attributed to the soundness of the original design, which required few engineering changes while production was underway.

Other nations that operated the Hellcat included France, whose Aéronavale used them in Indo-China, while the Argentine and Uruguayan navies used them until 1961.

Some US Navy Hellcats were converted into drones packed with explosives and in August 1952 six of these remotely controlled F6F-5Ks were directed on to North Korean targets.

ABOVE: **During the last two years of World War II the Hellcat was credited with 75 per cent of enemy aircraft shot down by US Navy pilots.** BELOW: **In all, the F6F destroyed over 5000 enemy aircraft.** BOTTOM: **US Navy ace Lt Alex Vraciu pictured with his personal Hellcat. This historic aircraft, also pictured below, is preserved in flying condition in the UK.**

Grumman F6F-5 Hellcat

First flight: June 26, 1942
Power: Pratt and Whitney 2000hp R-2800-10W 18-cylinder two-row air-cooled radial piston engine
Armament: Six 12.7mm/0.5in Browning machine-guns, plus provision for bombs up to 907kg/2000lb
Size: Wingspan – 13m/42ft 10in
    Length – 10.2m/33ft 7in
    Height – 3.96m/13ft
    Wing area – 31m^2/334sq ft
Weights: Empty – 4152kg/9153lb
    Maximum take-off – 6991kg/15,413lb
Performance: Maximum speed – 621kph/386mph
    Ceiling – 11,369m/37,300ft
    Range – 1674km/1040 miles on internal fuel
    Climb – 1039m/3410ft per minute

Grumman F8F Bearcat

The Grumman Bearcat was the last in the Grumman series of carrier-based fighters that had started back in 1931 with the Grumman FF. It was one of the fastest piston-engined aircraft ever and was built to a specification calling for a small, light fighter aircraft to be powered by the mighty R-2800 Double Wasp engine that had been used in the Hellcat and Tigercat.

The Bearcat was 20 per cent lighter than the Hellcat and had a 30 per cent greater rate of climb than its Grumman stablemate. These factors, together with its excellent manoeuvrability and good low-level performance made it an excellent fighter aircraft in all respects. It is worth noting that in comparative

trials the Bearcat's impressive performance allowed it to outmanoeuvre most of the early jet fighters. The first production aircraft (the F8F-1) were delivered in February 1945, a mere six months after the prototype test flight.

In May 1945 US Navy fighter squadron VF-19 became the first unit to equip with the Bearcat but the type arrived too late to see action in World War II. Production nevertheless continued until May 1949, by which time 24 US Navy squadrons were operating Bearcats. The F8F-1B version (of which 100 were built) was armed with four 20mm/0.78in cannon instead of the four 12.7mm/0.5in machine-guns of the F8F-1. Almost 300 examples of the F8F-2 were built with 20mm/0.5in cannon armament as standard. Small numbers of radar-equipped nightfighter and photo-reconnaissance versions were also made.

The Bearcat was phased out of front-line US Navy use by 1952 but around 250 were refurbished and sold as F8F-1Ds to the French Armée de l'Air, who used them in Indo-China. Many of these aircraft were later acquired by the air forces of both North and South Vietnam. The Royal Thai Air Force was also supplied with about 130 Bearcats.

TOP: **The Bearcat was the fastest piston-engined production aircraft ever built and was loved by its pilots.** ABOVE: **Too late for wartime service, the Bearcat remained in front-line US Navy service until the early 1950s.** LEFT: **Due to its high performance, the Bearcat has become a favourite of air racers and warbird collectors.**

Grumman F8F-1B Bearcat

First flight: August 21, 1944
Power: Pratt & Whitney 2100hp R-2800-34W Double Wasp 18-cylinder radial piston engine
Armament: Four 20mm/0.78in cannon, plus provision for two 454kg/1,000lb bombs or four 12.7cm/5in rockets under wings
Size: Wingspan – 10.92m/35ft 10in
Length – 8.61m/28ft 3in Height – 4.2m/13ft 10in
Wing area – 22.67m²/244sq ft
Weights: Empty – 3206kg/7070lb
Maximum take-off – 5873kg/12,947lb
Performance: Maximum speed – 677kph/421mph
Ceiling – 11,795m/38,700ft
Range – 1778km/1105 miles
Climb – 1395m/4570ft per minute

Hawker Fury

The Fury was loved by its pilots, who praised its light and sensitive controls and excellent rate of climb. This small biplane first flew in March 1931 and on entering Royal Air Force service in May that year, became the first RAF fighter to exceed 322kph/200mph. Displays of aerobatics by RAF Furies were for some years the highlight of the famous Hendon Air Pageants – on some occasions three Furies were literally tied together for a full aerobatic routine, demonstrating how stable and responsive the aircraft could be.

An improved performance version powered by the Kestrel VI engine entered RAF service in early 1937 as the Fury II – this was to serve as a stop gap while the Hurricane was developed. Although the Fury II could fly 10 per cent faster than the Mk I it had 10 per cent less range than the earlier model.

Furies were the main RAF fighters in the mid-1930s and some remained in the RAF front line until 1937, when they were replaced by Gladiators. When World War II broke out in September 1939, around 50 Fury IIs were still in service with training units.

Export versions were supplied to South Africa, Spain, Norway, Persia

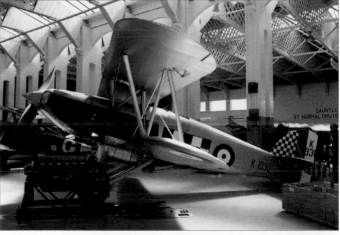

ABOVE: **This preserved Fury I is a regular at British air shows.** RIGHT: **The Fury was the first Royal Air Force fighter to exceed 322kph/200mph.** BELOW: **Furies were exported to a number of nations including Yugoslavia, who operated the machine pictured.**

(Iran), Portugal and Yugoslavia. Three squadrons of South African Furies saw action in East Africa early in World War II, while Yugoslav Furies were pitched against the Luftwaffe during the German invasion of April 1941. The Mk I examples supplied to Persia in 1933 were powered with Pratt and Whitney Hornet or Bristol Mercury radial engines and the RAF came up against some of these Furies during a revolt in 1941.

Hawker Fury II

First flight: March 25, 1931 (Fury I)
Power: Rolls-Royce 640hp Kestrel VI 12-cylinder V piston engine
Armament: Two synchronized forward-firing 7.7mm/0.303in machine-guns
Size: Wingspan – 9.14m/30ft
Length – 8.15m/26ft 9in
Height – 3.1m/10ft 2in
Wing area – 23.41m^2/252sq ft
Weights: Empty – 1245kg/2743lb
Maximum take-off – 1637kg/3609lb
Performance: Maximum speed – 359kph/223mph
Ceiling – 8990m/29,500ft
Range – 435km/270 miles
Climb – 3050m/10,000ft in 3.8 minutes

Hawker Hurricane

Comparison of the Hurricane and the earlier Hawker Fury's fuselages explains why the embryonic Hurricane was initially known as the Fury Monoplane. The aircraft that only became known as the Hurricane in June 1936 first flew in November 1935, retaining the metal tube construction with fabric covering used by Hawkers since the late 1920s, and not the more modern and complicated stressed-metal fuselage. War clouds were forming in Europe and it was important to get the RAF's first eight-gun monoplane fighter into production and into service as quickly as possible. Stressed-metal covered wings became standard after early Hurricane models appeared with fabric-covered wings.

When the Hurricane entered RAF service, replacing No.111 Squadron's Gloster Gauntlets at Northolt in December 1937, it became the first RAF aircraft able to exceed 482kph/ 300mph. In February 1938 a 111 Squadron Hurricane flew into the record books by making a nightflight from Edinburgh to RAF Northolt at a very impressive average speed of 656kph/408mph.

Hurricanes outnumbered Spitfires in RAF Fighter Command by about two to one when war broke out and so bore the brunt of early wartime fighter operations. Four squadrons operated in France and on October 30, 1939 a Hurricane of No.1 Squadron destroyed the first German aircraft of World War II, a Dornier Do 17.

It was, however, during the Battle of Britain in 1940 that the Hurricane earned its place in history, accounting for more enemy aircraft than all other defences, ground and air combined. In August of that historic year, Hurricane pilot

TOP: **Preserved in the UK, this Hurricane is painted as a nightfighter of No.87 Squadron, one of the longest serving RAF Hurricane nightfighter units.**
ABOVE: **The number of airworthy Hurricanes is growing.**

Flight Lt J.B. Nicholson of No.249 Squadron was awarded Fighter Command's only Victoria Cross for attacking a Luftwaffe Messerschmitt Me110 after his own aircraft had caught fire.

While the Battle of Britain raged, on August 2, 1940 Hurricanes of No.261 Squadron began their defence of Malta against Italian bombers. Hurricanes took on the Italians again, but this time over Britain, in November 1940, during a little-known episode of World War II. Italian bombers made their one and only en masse appearance over the UK and were badly mauled by the Hurricanes of Nos.46, 249 and 257 Squadrons. Seven out of ten Fiat BR.20 bombers were shot down, together with four Fiat CR.42 escort fighters.

The Mk II Hurricane reached RAF squadrons from September 1940 and differed from the Mk I by having a two-stage supercharged Merlin XX engine instead of the

ABOVE: **The world's only surviving Sea Hurricane is preserved in the UK.**

Merlin III. Armament on the Mk II varied between the eight machine-guns of the IIA to the 12 7.7mm/0.303in machine-guns of the IIB. The Mk IIC joined the squadrons in April 1941 and carried four 20mm/0.79in guns.

Nightfighter and navalized versions appeared later and ground-attack variants, some carrying two devastating 40mm/0.79in anti-tank guns (the Mk IID), were widely used in North Africa. Hurricanes operating in Burma became the leading RAF fighter against the Japanese. The last version to enter service was the Mk IV, which equipped the RAF's last Hurricane squadron, No.6, until January 1947. A total of 14,231 Hurricanes were built in Britain and Canada and a handful remain flying today.

In 1941 the Royal Navy began to use Hurricanes fitted with catapult and arrester gear. Known as Sea Hurricanes, they served with the Merchant Ship Fighter Unit and also the Fleet Air Arm from carriers. The former versions were carried on ships on rocket sleds and were launched when a threat appeared. When unable to recover to land or to a carrier the aircraft simply ditched in the sea.

As a fighter, the aircraft was extremely popular with pilots since it was fast, agile and, as celebrated Hurricane pilot Robert Stanford Tuck recalled, "The Hurricane was solid and could obviously stand up to a lot of punishment. It was steady as a rock and an excellent gun platform. Pilot visibility was better than the contemporary Spitfires as the nose sloped more steeply from the cockpit to the spinner and this of course made shooting rather easier".

Hawker Hurricane Mk I

First flight: November 6, 1935

Power: Rolls-Royce 1030hp Merlin III 12-cylinder liquid-cooled engine

Armament: Eight 7.7mm/0.303in Browning machine-guns with 334 rounds per gun

Size: Wingspan – 12.19m/40ft
Length – 9.57m/31ft 5in
Height – 4.m/13ft 1.5in
Wing area – 24m²/258sq ft

Weights: Empty – 2260kg/4982lb
Loaded – 2924kg/6447lb

Performance: Maximum speed – 511kph/318mph
Ceiling – 10,970m/36,000ft
Range – 740km/460 miles
Climb – 770m/2520ft per minute

TOP: **Turkey was one of the export customers for the Hurricane.** MIDDLE: **Though eclipsed by the Spitfire, the Hurricane was central to the British victory in the Battle of Britain.** BOTTOM: **A pre-war examination of a No.1 Squadron RAF aircraft.**

Hawker Tempest

The Tempest was developed from the Typhoon and differed from its predecessor mainly by its lengthened fuselage and a new thin-section laminar flow wing intended to improve on the Typhoon's disappointing climb and altitude performance. Five versions were planned to test various engine installations but only three ever saw service – the Mks II, V and VI. On the Mk II Tempest the radiator was moved from beneath the engine to the wing leading edges and fuel tankage moved from the wing to the longer fuselage. The first Tempest to fly, the Mk V, was a modified Typhoon which took to the air in September 1942.

The V was powered by a Napier Sabre II engine, while the Mk VI had the 2340hp Sabre V. Only the Tempest Mk V, retaining the Typhoon's distinctive chin radiator, saw wartime service, the first RAF Tempest wing being formed in April 1944. After initial train-busting and ground-attack duties, the Tempest V was used to tackle the V-1 flying bombs and excelled in the role. The Tempest V was the fastest fighter to be responsible for British air defence and destroyed 638 V-1s between June 13 and September 5, 1944.

Later, as part of the 2nd Tactical Air Force, Tempest Vs destroyed 20 Messerschmitt Me262s in air combat. Post-war, a number of Tempest Vs continued to serve as target tugs, and the Tempest VI was the RAF's standard Middle East fighter until the Vampire replaced them in 1949.

The Tempest II looked very different from the earlier Typhoon and was powered by a 2520hp Centaurus engine. It was designed for operations against the Japanese but the war ended before they could be deployed as part of the planned Tiger Force.

The Mk II first entered RAF service in November 1945 and the majority served overseas. Three Tempest II squadrons were based in Germany in 1946–8 and during the Berlin Airlift in 1948–9 Tempests of No.33 Squadron were based at Berlin's RAF Gatow to demonstrate the RAF's fighter potential in the area. No.33 later operated their Tempest IIs in the Far East and some saw action against Malayan terrorists in 1950–1.

ABOVE: **The Tempest's Typhoon origins are clear in this photograph of a Mk V – note the bubble canopy introduced in later Typhoons for improved pilot view.** BELOW: **Post-war, this Tempest V was used for target towing duties.**

Hawker Tempest V

First flight: September 1942

Power: Napier 2180-hp Sabre II 24-cylinder piston engine

Armament: Four 20mm/0.78in cannon in wings and provision for rocket-projectiles or 908kg/2000lb of bombs beneath wings

Size: Wingspan – 12.5m/41ft
Length – 10.26m/33ft 8in
Height – 4.9m/16ft 1in
Wing area – 28.06m²/302sq ft

Weights: Empty – 4082kg/9000lb
Maximum take-off – 6142kg/13,500lb

Performance: Maximum speed – 686kph/427mph
Ceiling – 11,125m/36,500ft
Range – 1191km/740 miles
Climb – 4575m/15,000ft in 5 minutes

Hawker Typhoon

The Typhoon was plagued with engine problems and structural weaknesses in its early days and failed to perform adequately for its intended role as a wartime interceptor. Nevertheless it went on to become an extremely effective fighter-bomber, accompanying the Allied advance through France and Holland in the later stages of World War II in 1944.

The Typhoon was born of a British Air Ministry specification for an interceptor designed to make the most of the new Rolls-Royce and Napier 24-cylinder 2000hp engines then under development. The Typhoon was paired with the Napier Sabre engine and flew for the first time in February 1940. Continued development and production problems delayed the Typhoon's delivery to the RAF until August 1941, when it became the RAF's first 643kph/400mph fighter. The price to pay for the high speed was

ABOVE: **A Typhoon IB of No.175 Squadron RAF is checked and armed for another D-Day period mission.**
BELOW LEFT: **This unusual trials Typhoon IB, built by Gloster Aircraft, is shown with a four-blade propeller.**
BELOW RIGHT: **A No.183 Squadron Typhoon IB – the "Tiffie" was the only RAF fighter with the speed to stop Fw190 hit-and-run raids on Britain.**

a low rate of climb and lacklustre performance at altitude, all due to the unreliable Sabre engine, which simply entered service before it was ready. A hazard unrelated to engine problems for early Typhoon pilots was a structural weakness in the tail, which cost the lives of a number of pilots – this problem was later rectified.

The whole Typhoon fleet was almost withdrawn from service, such was the effect of the combined problems, but these were fixed and a use was found for the Typhoon's high low-level speed. German Focke-Wulf 190s had been carrying out hit-and-run raids along Britain's south coast – the Typhoon with

its top speed of 664kph/412mph was the only RAF fighter that could catch them and destroyed four within days of being deployed.

From 1943, "Tiffies" went on the offensive, attacking targets in France and the Low Countries. When late in 1943 the Typhoons began carrying rocket projectiles, they proved to be truly devastating aircraft. The relentless day and night attacks by RAF Typhoon squadrons on German communications targets greatly aided the D-Day operations. The aircraft that was once almost scrapped from RAF service ultimately equipped no fewer than 26 squadrons of the 2nd Tactical Air Force.

Hawker Typhoon IB

First flight: May 27, 1941 (Production IA)
Power: Napier 2180hp Sabre IIA 24-cylinder sleeve-valve liquid-cooled piston engine
Armament: Four 20mm/0.78in cannon in outer wings and racks for eight rockets or two 227kg/500lb bombs
Size: Wingspan – 12.67m/41ft 7in
Length – 9.73m/31ft 11in
Height – 4.67m/15ft 4in
Wing area – 25.92m²/279sq ft
Weights: Empty – 3992kg/8800lb
Maximum take-off – 6010kg/13,250lb
Performance: Maximum speed – 664kph/412mph
Ceiling – 10,730m/35,200ft
Range – 821km/510 miles (with bombs)
Climb – 914m/3000ft per minute

Heinkel He162 Salamander

The He162 story shows what desperate means the German military conceived to stem the tide of the Allied advance in 1944. One solution was this small, cheap and easy-to-build jet fighter designed to attack the fleets of Allied bombers that pounded the Third Reich on a daily basis. The official requirement was issued on September 8, 1944 and the whole programme, not the aircraft, was given the name Salamander. Popularly known as the Volksjäger (people's fighter), it flew for the first time on December 6, 1944, incredibly only 38 days after detailed plans were passed to the factory. Total time from the start of design work to test flight was just over three months.

The light metal alloy streamlined fuselage had a moulded plywood nose and the one-piece wooden wing was tipped with metal. The He162 cockpit was modern-looking with an upward hinged canopy and an ejection seat. Maintenance was not judged to be an issue because damaged or unserviceable aircraft would be replaced by one of the many new ones in mass production.

The engine was top mounted to save design and construction time creating an aircraft around an engine, plus its intake and jet pipes. Fixed to the aircraft by three large bolts, the engine's location did not cause aerodynamic problems but did affect stability making the aircraft difficult to fly and fight in. An onboard two-stroke piston engine was used as a starter motor. During the first flight in December 1944 one of the main

TOP: **The He162 took to the air only 38 days after the design was handed to the factory.** ABOVE: **Planned mass production was expected to create 4000 examples of the Volksjäger (people's fighter) each month.**

undercarriage doors failed and broke away. The door was made of adhesive-bonded wood, as were the wings and fins. Investigation showed that the wood adhesive contained acid that was slowly eating into the wood of the aircraft. While a new adhesive was sourced for the production aircraft, the test flights had to continue and on December 10, 1944 the prototype crashed after the wing came apart in flight.

Production, fed by a network of sub-contractors including woodworkers and furniture makers, was expected to reach a peak of 4000 per month. Hundreds of factories were to take

part in the mass production of the Volksjäger. By February, about 100 He162s had been built but pilot training was not in step with aircraft production. Huge numbers of workers had been organized to build the He162 before the design was finished. Meanwhile Hitler Youth were being quickly trained in gliders as pilots for the new interceptor – their training was to be completed by flying the He162 in combat. Experienced fighter

TOP: **This captured He162, shown here with RAF markings, was shipped to Farnborough in Britain for evaluation – it crashed in November 1945.** ABOVE: **Only 200 were completed, but a further 800 incomplete examples were found when underground factories were captured by the Allies.** LEFT: **The type was equipped with an ejection seat – this example was a more aerodynamically refined He162A-2.**

pilots may have been able to manage the handful that the He162 certainly was, poorly trained Hitler Youth would have fared much worse.

In keeping with the breakneck speed of the programme, the first aircraft were delivered for operational evaluation and trials in January 1945. In February 1945 1/JG1 became the first unit to relinquish (some pilots reluctantly) their Fw190s, to begin conversion on the He162. One Gruppe (group) of three squadrons was formed on May 4, 1945 at Leck in Schleswig-Holstein but the airfield was captured by the British only four days later. Fuel shortages and general chaos had prevented the fighter from ever firing its twin 20mm/0.79in cannon in anger.

Although around 200 were completed, a further 800 were under production at underground factories when they were captured. Post-war, 11 Salamanders were taken to Britain for evaluation by the RAF.

Heinkel He162 Salamander

First flight: December 6, 1944
Power: BMW 800kg/1764lb thrust 0030A-1 turbojet
Armament: Two 20mm/0.78in cannon
Size: Wingspan – 7.2m/23ft 7.5in
Length – 9.05m/29ft 8.25in
Height – 2.55m/8ft 4.5in
Wing area – 11.2m²/120.56sq ft
Weights: Empty – 2050kg/4520lb
Maximum take-off – 2695kg/5941lb
Performance:
Maximum speed – 840kph/522mph (6000m)
Ceiling – 12,040m/39,500ft
Range – 695km/434 miles
Climb – 1280m/4200ft per minute

Heinkel He219

Heinkel's excellent nightfighter began as project P.1060 in 1940 as a high-speed multi-role aircraft. There was little interest in the design until late 1941, when RAF Bomber Command's raids began to have a strategic impact on the German war machine. Ernst Heinkel was then asked to produce his design as a nightfighter and so it first flew in November 1942. Among the design innovations were a tricycle undercarriage (the first operational Luftwaffe aircraft to have one) and ejection seats (the first anywhere in an operational aircraft) that accommodated the pilot and navigator in tandem but back to back.

The second prototype was evaluated in mock combat against other Luftwaffe types and was so successful that a production order was placed immediately.

The He219 Uhu (eagle-owl), equipped with radar that could find enemy bombers in the dark and a formidable armament with which to destroy them, was clearly a fearsome night-fighter and the Luftwaffe were keen to get it into service. So keen in fact that even the early prototypes were sent to form a trials unit at Venlo in Holland in April 1943. On the night of June 11, Major Werner Streib shot down five RAF Lancaster bombers in one sortie, thus proving the military value of dedicated nightfighter aircraft. During the first six night missions an incredible 20 RAF bombers were claimed as destroyed, among them six Mosquitoes. Despite this success, the He219 was never produced in adequate numbers, mainly because a bewildering profusion of sub-types appeared, with different armament and "black box" installations, to prove the aircraft's worth to sceptical officials. From November 1944 virtually the only aircraft being produced were jets and so the He219 only ever totally equipped one unit, 1/NJG 1, based at Venlo. Individual aircraft were attached to other units but the type was never used strategically. The Uhu was another fine German design that did not reach its potential due to the short-sightedness or sheer incompetence of the decision-makers within the Luftwaffe and government.

TOP: The He219 was an extremely effective nightfighter that wreaked havoc among RAF bombing raids. ABOVE: This He219A-7, an aircraft operated by 3/NJG (Nachtjagdgeschwader – nightfighter wing) 3, was evaluated after the war by the RAF. LEFT: One of many sub-types, the prototype A-5/R1.

Heinkel He219A-7/R2 Uhu

First flight: November 15, 1942
Power: Two Daimler-Benz 1800hp DB603E 12-cylinder engines
Armament: Four 20mm/0.78in cannon – two in underbelly "tray" and two in wing roots. Two 30mm/1.18in cannon, mounted to fire obliquely forward from rear of cockpit
Size: Wingspan – 18.5m/60ft 8.3in
Length – 16.34m/53ft 7.25in
Height – 4.1m/13ft 5.4in
Wing area – 44.5m²/478.99sq ft
Weights: Empty – 8345kg/18,398lb
Maximum take-off – 15,100kg/33,289lb
Performance: Maximum speed – 460kph/286mph
Ceiling – 9800m/32,150ft
Range – 1850km/1150 miles
Climb – 552m/1810ft per minute

LEFT: The I.A.R. 80 was a lesser-known fighter type that served for some years after World War II.

I.A.R. 80

First flight: April 1939
Power: I.A.R. 1025hp K14-1000A radial piston engine
Armament: Four 7.92mm/0.31in machine-guns
in wings
Size: Wingspan – 10.5m/34ft 5.25in
Length – 8.9m/29ft 2.5in Height – 3.6m/11ft 9.75in
Wing area – 15.97m²/171.9sq ft
Weights: Empty – 1780kg/3924lb
Maximum take-off – 2550kg/5622lb
Performance: Maximum speed – 550kph/342mph
Ceiling – 10,500m/34,450ft
Range – 940km/584 miles
Climb – 4500m/14,760ft in 5 minutes, 40 seconds

I.A.R. 80

The I.A.R. 80 was derived from the Polish-designed P.Z.L. P-24 fighter and was designed to replace the P-24. Development work was exclusively Romanian and began in 1938. The resulting fighter that first flew in April 1939 was tough and offered a drastically improved performance over the P-24. The front and rear of the two aircraft were almost identical. The significant difference was in the wholly new centre section. The bubble-type canopy was very advanced for the time and offered the pilot excellent visibility. Production was carried out on German authority and later models carried the German Mauser cannon. Strangely the type had a skid instead of a tailwheel.

About 250 were built in a number of versions and most served on the Eastern Front from May 1942. From 1943 all were based in Romania defending the country from US bomber attacks.

About half of all produced survived the war and served with the Romanian Air Force, this time under Soviet control, until they were replaced by Soviet fighters from 1949. A number were converted into two-seat dual control trainers and were in service until 1952.

LEFT: A Ju 88 nightfighter bristling with radar aerials. The Ju 88 was the most versatile combat aircraft in the wartime Luftwaffe inventory.

Junkers Ju 88G

First flight: December 21, 1936 (Ju 88 prototype)
Power: Two BMW 1700hp 801D-2 14-cylinder radials
Armament: Two 30mm/1.18in and up to six
20mm/0.78in cannon
Size: Wingspan – 20m/65ft 7in
Length – 14.54m/47ft 8in
Height – 4.85m/15ft 11in
Wing area – 54.5m/506.6sq ft
Weights: Empty – 9081kg/20,020lb
Maximum take-off – 14,690kg/32,385lb
Performance: Maximum speed – 573kph/356mph
Ceiling – 8840m/29,000ft
Range – 4 hours endurance
Climb – 504.78m/1655ft per minute

Junkers Ju 88

The Ju 88 is widely described as the "German Mosquito" because, like the de Havilland Mosquito, the Ju 88 was an extremely versatile design. It was first designed as a high-speed bomber but was then developed for dive-bomber, torpedo-bomber, close support, reconnaissance, heavy fighter and nightfighter roles. The Ju 88's speed, almost as good as fighters of the time, led to the C-series of heavy fighters and the first, the Ju 88C-0, made its maiden flight in July 1939. Large numbers of C-series fighters were eventually built, powered by Jumo 211 or BMW 801 engines, with solid noses housing a battery of cannon and machine-guns.

The Ju 88G was the definitive radar-equipped three-seat nightfighter, with typical armament of two 30mm/1.18in plus four to six 20mm/0.78in cannon all firing diagonally forward and upwards to destroy bombers with a short but deadly burst of fire from below.

Ju 88 nightfighters were one of the most effective German defences against enemy bombers.

Kawanishi N1K1-/K2-J

Land-based aircraft have often been turned into floatplanes, but in the case of the Kawanishi N1K1-J Shiden (violet lightning), it was uniquely a landplane derived from a floatplane fighter. Codenamed "George" by the Allies, it entered service during the last year of World War II, appearing throughout the Pacific from May 1944. In spite of production problems and shortages of parts caused by B-29 raids on the Japanese homeland, over 1400 were built and were formidable foes. Manoeuvrability was dramatically enhanced by unique automatic combat flaps that increased lift during extreme combat manoeuvres. The George proved to be one of the best all-round fighters in the Pacific theatre but lacked the high-altitude performance needed to counter the devastating B-29 raids.

Early versions had poor visibility due to the mid-mounted wing and inadequate landing gear and so the N1K2-J version known as the Shiden-Kai was produced. The main difference was the moving of the wing from mid to low position, which reduced the need for troublesome long landing gear. The prototype of this variant first flew in December 1943, and was soon adopted as the standard Japanese land-based fighter and fighter-bomber. The N1K2-J could be built in half the

LEFT: **The N1K1 Kyofu (mighty wind) floatplane fighter from which the "George" derived.**
BELOW: **The Shiden-Kai was an excellent fighter, but a number were used as kamikaze aircraft.**

Kawanishi N1K2-J

First flight: December 31, 1943
Power: Nakajima 1990hp NK9H Homare 21 radial piston engine
Armament: Four 20mm/0.78in cannon in wings plus two 250kg/551lb bombs under wings
Size: Wing span – 12m/39ft 4.5in
Length – 9.35m/30ft 8in
Height – 3.96m/13ft
Wing area – 23.5m²/252.96sq ft
Weights: Empty – 2657kg/5858lb
Maximum take-off – 4860kg/10,714lb
Performance: Maximum speed – 595kph/370mph
Ceiling – 10,760m/35,300ft
Range – 2335km/1451 miles with drop tanks
Climb – 1000m/3300ft per minute

time of the earlier version and became a truly outstanding fighter aircraft, which could hold its own against the best of Allied fighters.

Kawasaki Ki-45 Toryu

In 1937, the Imperial Japanese Army issued a requirement for its first long-range twin-engine fighter and Kawasaki's proposal was the Ki-45, which first flew in January 1939. Continued problems with engines

delayed production until September 1941, when the aircraft was designated Ki-45 Kai Toryu – kai was short for kaizo (modified) and Toryu means "dragon slayer". The two-seat Toryu finally entered service in August the following

year and first saw combat in October 1942. The fast and manoeuvrable Ki-45, codenamed "Nick" by the Allies, achieved a number of victories over USAAF B-24s – the aircraft was then modified for nightfighter duties when the American bombers began to operate at night. It proved so successful as a nightfighter that a specially developed nightfighter version (Kai-C) was produced, fitted with cannon that fired obliquely upward for attacks from below. On the night of June 15, 1944 alone, seven B-29s were claimed by Ki-45s.

In May 1944 four Ki-45s carried out the first kamikaze (divine wind) suicide attacks against Allied ships. More conventional anti-shipping and ground attack variants were also produced. Around 1700 Ki-45s were built.

TOP: **The Imperial Japanese Army's first long-range twin-engine fighter.** ABOVE: **The type was one of the most successful Japanese nightfighters.** LEFT: **Note the two obliquely firing cannon between the cockpits.**

Kawasaki Ki-45 Kai-C Toryu

First flight: January 1939
Power: Two Mitsubishi 1080hp Ha-102 14-cylinder two-row radial piston engines
Armament: Two 12.7mm/0.5in machine guns, installed at 30 degrees between cockpits, two 12.7mm/0.5in machine-guns and one 20mm/0.78in or 37mm/1.46in cannon in nose, plus one rear-firing 7.92mm/0.31in machine-gun
Size: Wingspan – 15.05m/49ft 4.5in
Length – 11m/36ft 1in Height – 3.7m/12ft 1.5in
Wing area – 32m²/344.46sq ft
Weights: Empty – 4000kg/8820lb
Maximum take-off – 5500kg/12,125lb
Performance: Maximum speed – 545kph/339mph
Ceiling – 10,000m/32,810ft
Range – 2000km/1243 miles
Climb – 700m/2300ft per minute

Kawasaki Ki-61 Hien

The Kawasaki Ki-61 Hien (swallow) fighter was a major departure in Japanese fighter aircraft design in World War II. While other Japanese fighters were designed with air-cooled radials, the Ki-61 used a licence-built Daimler-Benz 601A liquid-cooled in-line engine and was designed for speed. The Ki-61 was so radically different from other Japanese fighters that when the type was first encountered in combat in June 1943, the Allies thought it was a licence-built German or Italian fighter, the latter theory earning Hien the Allied codename of "Tony".

The very different nature of the design makes sense, given that from 1923 to 1933 Kawasaki Aircraft Engineering Company's head designer was Dr Richard Vogt, a German who returned to his homeland in 1933 for a similar role at Blohm und Voss during World War II. Kawasaki continued to be influenced by Vogt's design work long after he left.

The Hien was in constant use from its entry into service in August 1942 until the end of the war, but found itself increasingly outclassed. The Ki-100 was a "Tony" with a radial engine and proved to be an extremely good fighter.

ABOVE: **At one time the Ki-61 was thought to be a version of the Messerschmitt Bf109.** BELOW: **This captured "Tony" was taken for evaluation to the US Naval Air Station Patuxent River.** BOTTOM: **The Ki-61 was Japan's only in-line engined fighter in service during World War II.**

Kawasaki Ki-61-Ic Hien

First flight: December 1941

Power: Kawasaki 1175hp Ha-40 V12 liquid-cooled piston engine

Armament: Two 12.7mm/0.5in machine-guns on top of engine, plus two wing-mounted 20mm/0.78in cannon

Size: Wingspan – 12m/39ft 4.5in
Length – 8.95m/29ft 4.25in
Height – 3.7m/12ft 1.75in
Wing area – 20m²/215.29sq ft

Weights: Empty – 2630kg/5798lb
Maximum take-off – 3470kg/7650lb

Performance: Maximum speed – 560kph/348mph
Ceiling – 10,000m/32,810ft
Range – 1900km/1181 miles
Climb – 675m/2200ft per minute

Lavochkin LaGG-3 and La-5

The stopgap Lavochkin LaGG-3, built almost entirely of wood, was probably the greatest under-achiever of the early World War II fighters and was easily outclassed by the Messerschmitt Bf109 and Focke-Wulf 190. Even the few Italian Macchi 202s that served on the Russian Front outclassed the Lavochkins.

In 1941 development began on upgrading the powerplant of the LaGG-3's sound airframe by a shift from in-line V-12 engines to an M-82 14-cylinder, twin-row radial engine. Various changes were made to improve both performance and range, and the ever-present need for the use of strategically non-important materials was observed. The resulting aircraft, the La-5, was the first in a series of excellent radial-engined thoroughbred

fighters. The Lavochkin La-5FN, again constructed almost wholly of wood, became one of the best Soviet fighters of World War II. The Shvestov M-82 engine had a two-stage supercharger and gave the La-5FN a maximum speed of 648km/403mph. The fighter was responsive, could outperform any other Soviet fighter and, more importantly, almost all of its opponents. Armed with two 20mm/0.9in cannon, the La-5FN could deliver a small but deadly punch. After service with the Russians in World War II, the La-5FN went on to serve for a decade or so with various Soviet bloc countries, until being replaced by jets.

Further improved performance for the La-5 was, however, achieved by weight-saving and aerodynamic fine-tuning undertaken in late 1943, resulting in the high-altitude interceptor designated La-7. Over 5500 of these improved Lavochkins were built by 1946 and saw extensive wartime use.

TOP: **The LaGG-3's all-wooden construction was, among fighters, unique for its time.** ABOVE: **An La-5 of the 1st Czech Fighter Regiment, pictured in the Ukraine.** LEFT: **The higher flying La-7 was built in great quantities.**

Lavochkin La-5FN

First flight: January 1942

Power: Shvetsov 1330hp M-82A 14-cylinder two-row radial engine

Armament: Two 23mm/0.9in cannon, plus underwing bombs

Size: Wingspan – 9.8m/32ft 2in
Length – 8.46m/27ft 10.75in
Height – 2.84m/9ft 3in
Wing area – 17.5m^2/188.37sq ft

Weights: Empty – 2800kg/6173lb
Maximum take-off – 3360kg/7407lb

Performance: Maximum speed – 648kph/403mph
Ceiling – 9500m/31,170ft
Range – 765km/475 miles
Climb – 5000m/16,405ft in 4 minutes, 42 seconds

Lockheed P-38 Lightning

The P-38 Lightning's radical twin-boom, twin-engine configuration was Lockheed's answer to an exacting US Army Air Corps specification, in February 1937, for a high-performance long-range interceptor capable of flying at high altitude and high speed for at least an hour.

The P-38 was Lockheed's first purely military type and the prototype, the XP-38, first flew in January 1939. It made headlines almost immediately when it set a new record of 7 hours, 2 minutes for a transcontinental flight across America, even though at 6713kg/14,800lb it weighed more than most American light bombers of the time. From the outset the P-38 was designed as a hard-hitting fighter, being armed with a cannon and four machine-guns in the nose.

In spite of some official misgivings about its high cost and the sheer number of innovations incorporated into the P-38, it entered USAAC service in August 1941. The British had expressed interest in the P-38 but the American ban on the export of superchargers to Europe left the aircraft underpowered in the view of British test pilots. Aircraft were already on the production line earmarked for the RAF but these were diverted for US use when British interest waned. The British apparently named the P-38 "Lightning" and the name was already in widespread use.

Most early models were used for evaluation in the USA but during 1942–3 12 squadrons were equipped with P-38Es in the South West Pacific and the Aleutians. Even before that, an Iceland-based P-38E had claimed the first USAAF destruction of an enemy aircraft in World War II on December 7, 1941. A Focke-Wulf Condor was destroyed only hours after America's declaration of war.

TOP: **The radical twin-boom P-38 was a hard-hitting fighter capable of going deep into enemy territory.** ABOVE: **Regular P-38 combat missions were first flown from Africa.**

By this time the P-38's outstanding performance had unsurprisingly led to a reconnaissance version, known as the F-4, and later the F-5, armed only with cameras.

The P-38 came to be deployed extensively in the Pacific, Mediterranean and Europe where the P-38's speed, performance and firepower soon prompted the nickname "fork-tailed devil" from the Germans.

The J model of the P-38 had improved airscrews for better speed and climb at altitude and carried more fuel than earlier versions. With drop tanks, the P-38J had a range of around 3700km/2300 miles, enabling it to fly deep into the heart of enemy territory, engage in ten minutes of air combat and then make it back to the UK. Top speed of the P-38J was 666kph/414mph but in combat dives, pilots frequently exceeded 885kph/550mph. At that speed the aircraft's handling proved difficult and hydraulically assisted control systems were introduced, becoming one of the first examples of power-assisted controls in a combat aircraft.

Some P-38Js were modified to two-seaters equipped with a Norden bombsight, carried a bombardier and led formations of Lightning fighter-bombers on high-altitude precision bombing missions. As the P-47 and P-51 fighters appeared in huge numbers, the Lightnings in Europe were used more and more in the ground-attack and tactical bombing role.

However in the Pacific theatre, the Lightning equipped 27 USAAF squadrons and was credited with the destruction of more enemy aircraft than any other type. As a long-range fighter it was peerless. The top US ace of World War II, Major Richard Bong, earned all his 40 kills flying Lightnings in the Pacific. The most celebrated P-38 mission was probably the interception and destruction of the aircraft carrying Japan's Admiral Yamamoto. The P-38s responsible for this daring mission were from 339th Fighter Squadron on Guadalcanal, operating some 805km/500 miles from their base, using drop tanks to get the extra range. The 347th Fighter Group pilot credited with this remarkable feat was Lt Thomas G. Lanphier, who went on to become a Lockheed test pilot.

ABOVE: **In the Pacific Theatre the P-38 equipped 27 USAAF squadrons. The P-38 destroyed more enemy aircraft than any other Allied fighter.**

RIGHT: **The five-gun nose armament is clear on this aircraft painted as the aircraft of P-38 ace Jack Ilfrey.** BELOW: **The P-38's long range made it ideal for the war in the Pacific, where combats were fought over great distances.**

Lockheed P-38J Lightning

First flight: January 27, 1939

Power: Two Allison 1425hp V-1710-89 in-line piston engines

Armament: One 20mm/0.78in cannon, plus four 12.7mm/0.5in machine-guns in nose, up to 908kg/2000lb of bombs and ten 12.7cm/5in rocket projectiles

Size: Wingspan – 15.85m/52ft
Length – 11.52m/37ft 10in
Height – 2.99m/9ft 10in
Wing area – 30.42m²/327.5sq ft

Weights: Empty – 5707kg/12,580lb
Maximum take-off – 9798kg/21,600lb

Performance: Maximum speed – 666kph/414mph
Ceiling – 13,411m/44,000ft
Range – 3636km/2260 miles
Climb – 1524m/5000ft in 2 minutes

Macchi M.C.200 Saetta

The Saetta (lightning) was one of the principal fighters with which Italy joined World War II. It was developed in the mid-1930s in response to an Italian Air Force (Regia Aeronautica) requirement for a new single-seat fighter. The new fighter was part of a programme intended to re-equip the Regia Aeronautica following the end of Italy's military activity in East Africa. The prototype made its first flight in December 1937, and by the time of Italy's entry into World War II in June 1940 some 156 were in service. The M.C.200 was first employed against the British at Malta and eventually saw service in Greece, North Africa, Yugoslavia and the Soviet Union. Saettas were deployed against US forces in North Africa and in defence of Italy itself. A total of 1151 were built in all.

Macchi M.C.200

First flight: December 24, 1937
Power: FIAT 870hp A.74 RC38 double row, 14-cylinder, air cooled radial engine
Armament: Two 12.7mm/0.5in synchronized machine-guns
Size: Wingspan – 10.58m/34ft 8.5in
Length – 8.19m/26ft 10.25in
Height – 3.5m/11ft 5.75in
Wing area – 16.8m^2/180.84sq ft
Weights: Empty – 1895kg/4178lb
Maximum take-off – 2590kg/5710lb
Performance: Maximum speed – 502kph/312mph
Ceiling – 8900m/29,200ft
Range – 870km/540 miles with extra tanks
Climb – 3000m/9840ft in 3 minutes, 24 seconds

LEFT: **Early versions of the Saetta had a modern enclosed cockpit which was, by Italian pilot demand, deleted on later versions.** BELOW: **After the Italian Armistice of September 1943, a number of M.C.200s were flown to Allied airfields and were later flown with the Allies by the Italian Co-Belligerent Air Force.**

LEFT: **The C.202 was an excellent fighter.**

Macchi C.202 Folgore

First flight: August 10, 1940
Power: Alfa Romeo 1175hp RA.1000 RC 41-I
(licence-built DB-601A) inverted V-12 piston engine
Armament: Two 12.7mm/0.5in machine-guns in
engine cowling
Size: Wingspan – 10.58m/34ft 8.5in
Length – 8.85m/29ft 0.5in
Height – 3.04m/9ft 11.5in
Wing area – 16.8m²/180.84sq ft
Weights: Empty – 2350kg/5181lb
Maximum take-off – 3010kg/6636lb
Performance: Maximum speed 595kph/370mph
Ceiling – 11,500m/37,730ft
Range – 765km/475 miles
Climb – 3000m/9840ft in 2 minutes, 28 seconds

Macchi C.202 Folgore

This fighter, often neglected by historians, is said by many to have been the best Italian Air Force fighter of World War II. The Folgore (thunderbolt) was derived from the Macchi M.C.200 and married its airframe to the proven Daimler-Benz DB 601 liquid-cooled engine. No indigenous in-line engine of sufficient power was available when the war started and in early 1940 Macchi imported the German engine. Flight testing began in August 1940 and results were impressive – the Folgore was almost 97kph/60mph faster than the M.C.200.

By November 1941 the C.202 was deployed in Libya against RAF aircraft and was clearly superior to both the Curtiss P-40 and the Hawker Hurricane. In fact the Italian fighter outperformed all comers except the Spitfire and P-51 Mustang. When supplies of DB 601 engines ran out, Alfa Romeo built a copy under licence and by late 1942 Folgores outnumbered all other fighters in the Italian Air Force – the Regia Aeronautica. Folgore production reached about 1200 but only two survive.

The Germans also operated the C.202 in limited numbers.

LEFT: **After World War I, the many surplus Buzzards were sold around the world. Civilianized and floatplane versions were among the variants produced.**

Martinsyde F.4 Buzzard

First flight: May 1918
Power: Hispano-Suiza 300hp V-8 piston engine
Armament: Two forward-firing synchronized
7.7mm/0.303in machine-guns
Size: Wingspan 9.99m/32ft 9.5in
Length 7.77m/25ft 5.75in
Height 3.15m/10ft 4in
Wing area – 29.73m²/320sq ft
Weights: Empty – 776kg/1710lb
Maximum take-off – 1038kg/2289lb
Performance: Maximum speed – 233kph/145mph
Ceiling – 7620m/25,000ft
Range – 2 hours, 30 minutes endurance
Climb – 3050m/10,000ft in 7 minutes, 54 seconds

Martinsyde F.4 Buzzard

The Martinsyde F.4 single-seat biplane fighter was the ultimate model of the Martinsyde F series fighters and first flew in May 1918. The F.4 was really a production version of the fine F.3 that was thoroughly tested and even deployed on home defence duties by the Royal Flying Corps.

In tests carried out by the Royal Air Force the aircraft's performance and handling were so good that large-scale production was ordered immediately. A total of 1450 aircraft were ordered but due to delays in engine deliveries only a handful of aircraft were handed over to the Royal Air Force before the end of World War I at which point the order was cancelled. Martinsyde had however completed around 370 F.4s but as the F.4 was among the best fighters of the World War I period there was no shortage of customers for the excellent fighting aircraft. F.4s were widely exported to countries including Spain, Ireland, Japan, Latvia, the Soviet Union (100 aircraft), Portugal and Finland where they were used as trainers as late as 1939.

Messerschmitt Bf109

The Messerschmitt Bf109, the most famous German fighter of the World War II era, remained in production over a decade after the regime that spawned it was crushed. It first flew in September 1935, powered by a Rolls-Royce Kestrel engine and incorporating features of the Messerschmitt Bf108 four-seat touring aircraft. Messerschmitt 109Bs were first delivered to the Luftwaffe in 1937, to its "top guns" in Jagdgeschwader 132 "Richthofen". Later that year the 109 earned its spurs when it made its combat début with Germany's Condor Legion in the Spanish Civil War. This was invaluable, not only as combat experience for Germany's fighter pilots but also to help with developing and improving what was clearly already an exceptional fighter aircraft.

In November 1937 the 109 flew into the record books by setting a new world landplane speed record of 610.55kph/ 379.38mph. B, C and D versions all saw service but the type really came into its own with the definitive E model that appeared in late 1938 and was widely deployed at the outbreak of World War II, when the Luftwaffe had around 1000 of these fast and manoeuvrable fighters in service.

TOP AND ABOVE: **Two photographs of the very rare Messerschmitt Bf109G owned by the Royal Air Force Museum and returned to flying condition in the 1990s. Unfortunately the aircraft was damaged in a crash landing and will not fly again.**

The 109E was in action throughout the Blitzkrieg and in this first year of the war outclassed all the fighters it encountered, except the Spitfire. Like the famous Supermarine aircraft, the Messerschmitt 109 will be forever associated with the air fighting that took place in the Battle of Britain in 1940. In fact the 109's first action against the RAF had been on December 18, 1939, when 109Es attacked unescorted Vickers Wellington bombers on a daylight bombing mission over Wilhelmshaven.

Numerous versions of the 109E were in use during the Battle of Britain, including the E-4/B fighter-bomber. The 109 had two main advantages over the British Spitfires and Hurricanes. One was that the cannon armament carried by the Messerschmitt had a longer range and was more damaging

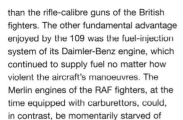

than the rifle-calibre guns of the British fighters. The other fundamental advantage enjoyed by the 109 was the fuel-injection system of its Daimler-Benz engine, which continued to supply fuel no matter how violent the aircraft's manoeuvres. The Merlin engines of the RAF fighters, at the time equipped with carburettors, could, in contrast, be momentarily starved of

TOP LEFT: **Incredibly, Spanish-built 109s (Buchons), powered by Rolls-Royce Merlins, were still being built in the mid-1950s.** TOP RIGHT: **The Bf109 was the principal fighter of the wartime Luftwaffe and destroyed more aircraft in combat than any other German fighter.** ABOVE: **Ten prototype Bf109s were built to prove the design in 1935–6 and the type entered Luftwaffe service in 1937.** BELOW: **One of the most widely produced fighter aircraft in history, the Bf109.**

fuel and cut out if the aircraft was pushed into a steep dive, thus generating negative gravity. RAF pilots soon developed the technique of rolling their aircraft over at the critical time and diving upside down so as not to lose the upper hand in what was often a kill or be killed air combat situation.

By early 1941 the "Emil", as the E model was widely known, had appeared in the Mediterranean theatre and tropicalized versions were serving in North Africa. After the success of the E model the 109F was developed and is considered by many to be the best version of all because of its high speed and excellent all-round performance. While in the West the 109F was able to outclass the Spitfire V, on the Eastern Front it spearheaded the attack on the USSR. At this stage in the 109 story it is worth making the point that throughout its life the 109 was fitted with a bewildering array of armament options, the F-model more than most.

After 1942 the G ("Gustav") became the standard model in Luftwaffe use and was numerically the most important version. Although well-armed, the Gustav needed great attention from the pilot and was particularly difficult to land satisfactorily. It served on all fronts in roles that included fighter-bomber, ground-attack and interceptor.

Post-war, the 109 remained in production, thanks to the Czech firm Avia who had an intact Bf109 factory. In 1948, Israel bought some 109s and used them in combat, while the Spanish Air Force also operated Spanish-built versions. In 1953, Spanish manufacturers began fitting Merlin engines to produce the Buchón (pigeon) and the last new-build 109 was test-flown in 1956. Total production exceeded 35,000.

Messerschmitt Bf109E-7

First flight: September 1935
Power: One Daimler-Benz 1200hp DB 601N liquid-cooled inverted-V 12-cylinder piston engine
Armament: One hub-firing 20mm/0.7in cannon and four 7.9mm/0.31in machine-guns, two in engine cowling and two in wings
Size: Wingspan 9.86m/32ft 4.5in
Length – 8.74m/28ft 8in   Height – 3.4m/11ft 2in
Wing area – 16.16m²/174sq ft
Weights: Empty – 2014kg/4440lb
Maximum take-off – 2767kg/6100lb
Performance: Maximum speed – 578kph/358mph
Ceiling – 11,125m/36,500ft
Range – 1094km/680 miles
Climb – 1006m/3300ft per minute

Messerschmitt Bf110

**Messerschmitt
Bf110G/R3 nightfighter**

First flight: May 12, 1936
Power: Two Daimler-Benz 1474hp DB 601B-1
inverted V-12 piston engines
Armament: Two 30mm/1.18in cannon and two
20mm/0.78in cannon in nose, plus two
7.92mm/0.31in machine-guns mounted
in rear cockpit
Size: Wingspan – 16.25m/53ft 3.75in
Length – 13.05m/42ft 9.75in
Height – 4.18m/13ft 8.5in
Wing area – 38.4m²/413.35sq ft
Weights: Empty – 5090kg/11,222lb
Maximum take-off – 9890kg/21,804lb
Performance: Maximum speed – 550kph/342mph
Ceiling – 8000m/26,245ft
Range – 2100km/1305 miles with drop tanks
Climb – 661m/2170ft per minute

The Bf110 was designed to a Luftwaffe specification for a heavy fighter that could also be used as a high-speed bomber and the prototype flew in 1936. It was intended to escort bombers deep into enemy territory and what it may have lacked in manoeuvrability,

it made up for with firepower. The 110 first saw action during the invasion of Poland and made its mark as a bomber-destroyer in December 1939, when it was used against a force of 22 RAF Wellington bombers and shot down nine. With its capability proven, production was stepped up and over 100 were produced each month during 1940. It was, however, during 1940 that the

Bf110 began to suffer heavy losses to more modern fighters such as the Spitfire and Hurricane. Although largely withdrawn as a day fighter, some persisted in this role against better aircraft until 1944, sustaining increasingly heavy losses. After a period of use on bombing and reconnaissance, the type found its niche during the winter of 1940–1 as a nightfighter defending Hitler's Reich.

At first the three-man crews had no special equipment for night operations and relied on their eyes alone to find enemy aircraft in the dark. Ground-controlled interception began from mid-1941, and the 110 began to take its toll of RAF bombers and was soon an aircraft to be feared. Airborne radar was used experimentally during 1941, effective up to a maximum distance of 3.5km/2.2 miles and capable of bringing the 110 to within 200m/655ft of a target. Front-line units received the radar from July 1942. By this time the standard version of the nightfighter was the Bf110F-4, with the usual armament of four 7.92mm/0.31in machine-guns and two 20mm/0.78in cannon. The usual means of attack was from below, the target bomber being raked across the belly and wing fuel

tanks with high explosive and incendiary ammunition as the Bf110 pilot pulled the aircraft up. In 1943 the armament was supplemented by upward-firing cannon, which meant the Bf110 only had to formate below the target aircraft to achieve a first-rate firing position.

These nightfighters continued to defend Germany right through to the end of the war and one pilot, Major Heinz-Wolfgang Schnaufer, claimed no less than 121 night kills while flying the Bf110.

LEFT: **This Bf110 nightfighter is preserved by the RAF Museum in Britain.** BELOW: **The Bf110 was a key aircraft in the Blitzkrieg.**

Messerschmitt Me410

On the basis of the Bf110's early successes, its manufacturers were asked to design a successor – this became the Me210. The aircraft was certainly a handful on its test flight and was essentially unstable, being prone to stalling and spinning. In spite of this it was ordered into production and 200 were built before it was abandoned in favour of a new production run of Bf110s.

The Me210 design was salvaged with a redesigned, longer, rear fuselage and automatic leading edge slats to counter the stall tendency. Fitted with more powerful engines than the original Me210, the new two-seat heavy fighter aircraft was designated Me410 and called Hornisse (Hornet).

The first Me410As reached front-line Luftwaffe units in January 1943, replacing Dornier Do 217s and Junkers Ju 88s. They were at first used as nightfighter-bombers over Britain and then as bomber-destroyers in the Mediterranean theatre. From Spring 1944 the Hornisse began to replace the Bf110 In bomber-destroyer (Zerstörer) units in defence of the Reich and also served as a nightfighter on tho Eastern Front.

The Me410A-1/U4 bomber-destroyer carried a 50mm/2in gun beneath the fuselage that weighed 900kg/1984lb and had a recoil effect of seven tons. Carrying 21 rounds, the effect of the weapon on enemy bombers would have been devastating whlle the effect on Me410 crews was at best startling and at worst terrifying.

The Me410 was no more effective than the Bf110 it was designed to replace but over 1100 were built before production ceased in September 1944.

TOP: **This excellent preserved example of an Me410 is part of the Royal Air Force Museum collection in Britain.** ABOVE: **The Hornisse was almost identical to the earlier Me210.** LEFT: **This Me410A-3 was captured in Italy and evaluated by the RAF while bearing the serial TF209.**

Messerschmitt Me410A-1/U2 Hornisse

First flight: Late 1942

Power: Two Daimler-Benz 1850hp 603A inverted V-12 in-line piston engines

Armament: Four 20mm/0.70in cannon and two 7.93mm/0.31in machine-guns, plus two 13mm/0.51in remotely controlled rear-firing barbettes

Size: Wingspan – 16.35m/53ft7.75in
Length – 12.48m/40ft 11.5in
Hcight – 4.28m/14ft 0.5in
Wing area – $36.2m^2$/389.67sq ft

Weights: Empty – 7518kg/16,574lb
Maximum take-off – 9650kg/21,276lb

Performance: Maximum speed – 625kph/388mph
Ceiling – 10,000m/32,180ft
Range – 1690km/1050 miles
Climb – 6700m/22,000ft in 10 minutes, 42 seconds

Messerschmitt Me163

When the German Komet first attacked USAAF bomber formations in July 1944 it struck fear into the Allies. This extremely high-performance rocket-powered fighter flew almost twice as fast as any Allied fighters and was a truly radical design. The very small and agile Komet was developed from designs originated by the brilliant Dr Alexander Lippisch, who joined the Messerschmitt company in 1939, having pioneered tailless gliders in the 1920s. The first step toward the revolutionary Me163 was an adaptation of the tailless all-wood DFS 194 research glider, powered by a Walter rocket motor. Fuel for the motor consisted of two hypergolic (spontaneously igniting) liquids, T-Stoff and Z-Stoff, which when mixed reacted violently, the resulting controlled explosion producing around 400kg/882lb of thrust. The rocket-powered glider was test flown at the secret Peenemünde research establishment in June 1940 and the pilot Heini Dittmar reported that the aircraft handled superbly. In later test flights the trailblazing prototype reached 547kph/340mph in level flight and amazed all with its steep climb capability.

The success of the test flights led to six Me163A prototypes, the first of which flew with rocket power in mid-1941. By now the Walter rocket motor had been developed to deliver 750kg/1653lb of thrust, pushing the Komet through the air at 885kph/550mph. One 163A, towed to 4000m/13,125ft before

ABOVE: **The revolutionary Komet was certainly the most futuristic form in the sky during World War II.**

the engine was fired, reached speeds of around 1003kph/ 623mph (greater than the world speed record of the time) before stability was affected. Minor design changes to the wing eradicated that problem, but others were experienced that plagued the Komet throughout its short service life. Its glider origins resulted in the Komet taking off from a wheeled "dolly", which was jettisoned once the aircraft was off the ground, while for landing the Komet landed on a sprung skid. The take-off and landing phases both held their own hazards for the Komet pilot due to the extremely dangerous nature of the fuels, but the percentage of landing accidents for the Komet, though high, was less than that of the Bf109.

The main production version was the Me163B, equipped with a more powerful rocket motor and armed with two 30mm/1.18in cannon in the roots of the swept wooden wings. The Komet first flew in anger on July 28, 1944, when six aircraft of 1/Jagdgeschwader 400 attacked a formation of USAAF Flying Fortresses heading for the Leuna-Merseburg oil refineries. The attack was ineffective as the pilots were not able to bring their guns to bear, mainly due to the very high closing speeds on the targets. At best the Komet pilot could

LEFT: **The Me163 was one of the first combat aircraft with swept wings.** BELOW: **The aircraft took off from a wheeled "dolly" and landed on the skid beneath the aircraft.**

fire his cannon for three seconds before his pass was over and, in addition, the guns only had 60 rounds each.

The preferred method of attack was to take-off when the enemy was known to be nearby, fly above it at very high speed then make a high speed gliding dive on the targets. The maximum period of powered flight was only 7.5 minutes and after the combat the Komet would then make an unpowered glide back to base for a risky landing. The bat like glider was an absurdly easy target on approach to landing as it could do nothing but land, even if under attack.

The Me163 was used to test an ingenious air-to-air weapon, the SG 500 Jagdfaust (Fighter fist) which consisted of five vertically firing tubes in each wing root. Each tube carried a single 50mm/ 1.97in shell and all ten would be fired as a salvo when triggered by the shadow of a bomber passing over the Komet, activating a photo-electric cell. All the Komet had to do was fly, top speed, under an enemy aircraft, and the system was proven on April 10, 1945, when a B-17 was destroyed in mid-air by a Jagdfaust-equipped Komet.

In late 1943, Japan negotiated manufacturing rights for the Me163 (as the Mitsubishi J8M1 for the Navy and the Mitsubishi Ki-200 for the Army) but one of the two submarines bringing the technical information to Japan was sunk. With incomplete drawings the Japanese still managed to produce prototypes, one of which flew before the end of the war.

Although around 300 entered service, the Komet never reached its potential and destroyed only nine Allied bombers. It was however by far the most futuristic aircraft in service during World War II.

Messerschmitt Me163B-1a Komet

First flight: June 23, 1943 (powered)

Power: Walter 1700kg/3748lb-thrust HWK 509A-1 rocket motor

Armament: Two 30mm/1.18in cannon

Size: Wingspan – 9.4m/30ft 7.3in
Length – 5.85m/19ft 2.3in
Height – 2.76m/9ft 0.6in
Wing area – 18.5m^2/199.1sq ft

Weights: Empty – 1900kg/4190lb
Maximum take-off – 4310kg/9502lb

Performance: Maximum speed – 960kph/596mph
Ceiling – 16,500m/54,000ft
Range – 100km/62 miles or 2 minutes, 30 seconds from top of powered climb
Climb – 5000m/16,400ft per minute

Messerschmitt Me262

The Me262 was the world's first operational jet aircraft and many Germans believed it was a war-winning aircraft. Design work began on the revolutionary aircraft in late 1938 and power was to be provided by ground-breaking gas turbines under development by BMW. The aircraft was ready before its engines and was test-flown with a single Jumo piston engine in the nose on April 18, 1941. The first test flight with the jet engines installed took place in March 1942. As a safety measure, the piston engine was retained in the nose

and the prototype took off under power of all three engines. The two jets seized shortly after take-off and the pilot was lucky to land the aircraft safely. The engines had to be redesigned and the test programme continued with the Me262 powered by two heavier Junkers turbojets. The development of this remarkable aircraft was not considered a top priority by the German High Command and the Messerschmitt company were more concerned with improvements of existing proven combat aircraft such as the Bf109 and Bf110. One of the greatest boosts to the Me262 programme came in May 1943 when legendary Luftwaffe ace General der Jagdflieger (fighter general) Adolf Galland flew the aircraft for the first time. He

ABOVE: **The trailblazing Me262 was the first operational jet aircraft and the Third Reich had high hopes for the futuristic fighter.** LEFT: **On July 25, 1944 the Me262 became the first jet to see combat.**

advocated the mass production of the aircraft as soon as possible but then the whole programme was delayed again by devastating August 1943 Allied bombing raids on the Regensburg factories housing the Me262 production lines. Messerschmitt then moved its jet development operation to Bavaria where a shortage of skilled labour delayed production again by several months. Hitler's oft-quoted ruling that the high-performance aircraft should also be used as a bomber was not the only reason that the 262 entered service late in the war – apart from enemy action, the unreliability and poor performance of the early jet engines were major factors.

And so it was not until July 1944 that the Me262, by now named Schwalbe (swallow), entered front-line service and on July 25 an Me262 became the first jet aircraft used in combat when it attacked a British photo-reconnaissance Mosquito flying over Munich. By late 1944 the Me262 was deployed in three forms – fighter-bomber, pure interceptor and an unarmed reconnaissance version. The first dedicated Me262 interceptor unit went into action for the first time on October 3, 1944. Although it arrived too late to make a real difference to the air war, the 262 was a deadly bomber-killer, equipped with 24 rockets and four 30mm/1.18in cannon. In combat with high-performance P-51 Mustangs, the Me262 sometimes came

LEFT: **Two-seat radar-equipped nightfighter versions were also developed.** BELOW: **Reliability problems plagued the pioneering jet fighter.**

off worse because of the inferior manoeuvrability compared to the piston-engined aircraft. It was however faster and better armed than the British Meteor jet fighter but the two trailblazing jets never met in air combat.

FAR LEFT: **The radical design of the Me262 is evident in this study.** LEFT: **A captured Me262A-1 shipped to Wright Field in the USA for evaluation**

As a fighter, the German jet scored heavily against Allied bomber formations, but although more than 1400 Me262s were produced by VE Day, less than 300 saw combat as hundreds were destroyed on the ground by Allied bombing. Most stayed firmly on the ground awaiting conversion to bombers or were unable to fly because of lack of fuel, spare parts or trained pilots. The German jet engines were unreliable and engine failures took their toll of the pioneer jet pilots. The under-carriage was prone to collapse and the guns regularly jammed making the pilots vulnerable in a dogfight.

The one period of concerted Me262 fighter activity came between March 18–21, 1945 when some 40 fighter sorties were flown daily against American bombers. It was however too little too late.

Although Germany never realized the potential of the 262, this revolutionary aircraft inspired British, American and Soviet designers and directly affected worldwide jet fighter design for years to come.

Messerschmitt Me262A-1a

First flight: July 18, 1942, solely on jet power
Power: Two Junkers 900kg/1984lb thrust Jumo 004B-1 turbojets
Armament: Four 30mm/1.18in cannon in nose plus up to 12 air to-air rockets under each wing
Size: Wingspan – 12.48m/40ft 11.5in
Length – 10.6m/34ft 9.5in
Height – 3.84m/12ft 7in
Wing area – 21.7m²/233.58sq ft
Weights: Empty – 3800kg/8378lb
Maximum take-off – 6400kg/14,110lb
Performance: Maximum speed – 870kph/540mph
Ceiling – 11450m/37,565ft
Range – 1050km/653 miles
Climb – 1200m/3937ft per minute

Mikoyan-Gurevich MiG-3

The MiG-3 interceptor was the third aircraft designed by Artem Mikoyan and Mikhail Gurevich and was developed from their MiG-1, which first flew in April 1940. The MiG-3 incorporated many improvements over the MiG-1, including a new propeller, a modified wing, greater

range, better armour and increased armament. The new MiG was first delivered to front-line units in April 1941 at the same time as the MiG-1, which remained in production despite its shortcomings. The Russians knew the MiG-1

was inadequate in many ways but any aircraft were better than none when facing the military might of the Third Reich.

Even the improved MiG-3 was no low-level fighter and was better suited to altitudes over 5000m/16,405ft. Although tricky to fly, the MiG-3's speed enabled it to give the Luftwaffe a real fight for air superiority over the Eastern Front.

Total production of the MiG-1 and -3 amounted to 3422 when MiG-3 production ceased in 1942. By 1942 the latest Luftwaffe fighters were generally getting the better of the long-nosed MiGs, so the type was progressively removed from front-line fighter units during the winter of 1942–3 and went on to be used mainly for armed reconnaissance and close support missions.

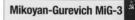

Mikoyan-Gurevich MiG-3

First flight: Late 1941
Power: Mikulin 1350hp AM-35A V-12 piston engine
Armament: One 12.7mm/0.5in and two 7.62mm/0.3in machine-guns in nose, plus up to 200kg/441lb of bombs and rockets under wings
Size: Wingspan – 10.2m/33ft 5in
  Length – 8.3m/27ft 1in
  Height – 3.5m/11ft 6in
  Wing area – 17.44m^2/187.73sq ft
Weights: Empty – 2595kg/5721lb
  Maximum take-off – 3350kg/7385lb
Performance: Maximum speed – 640kph/398mph
  Ceiling – 12,000m/39,370ft
  Range – 1195km/743 miles
  Climb – 1200m/3937ft per minute

LEFT: **The Soviet MiG-3 was a handful for its pilots, but did much to protect the USSR.**
BELOW: **A replica MiG-3 proudly displayed at a museum in Moscow, the city that the type was designed to protect above all else.**

Mitsubishi A5M

The 350kph/217mph top speed specified in a 1934 Imperial Japanese Navy fighter specification seemed to be a tall order at the time. To ease the designers' burden, the need to operate the new fighter from aircraft carriers was not even written into the specification. However, Mitsubishi's offering was the Ka 14, which, having flown in February 1935, showed a top speed of 450kph/280mph. It was designed with minimum drag in mind – the fuselage had a small cross-section, the aluminium skin was flush-riveted and the fixed undercarriage had streamlining spats. It was perhaps too complex a design and the inverted gull-wing that caused some handling headaches was replaced with a more conventional low wing. With this change and powered by a 585hp Kotobuki 2-KAI-1 engine, the type was ordered into production as the Navy Type 96 Carrier Fighter Model 1 (Mitsubishi A5M1) and began to enter service in early 1937. The subsequent A5M2a (basically the same aircraft powered by a 610hp KAI-3 engine) and A5M2b (with the 640hp Kotobuki 3 engine) became the most important Navy fighters during Japan's war with China. Until the A5M2a arrival in theatre, the Japanese were suffering heavy losses but after only a short time the A5M2a achieved total air superiority. Experience of air operations in China speeded up development of the A5M2b, which boasted the luxury of an enclosed cockpit and a three-bladed propeller driven by the more powerful engine. The greenhouse-style canopy was actually unpopular with pilots and was omitted on late-build A5M2bs. The A5M2s were so effective in China that all Chinese air units were withdrawn out of range of the Japanese fighters.

The final, best-known and most numerous production version was the A5M4, which was developed in response to the Chinese withdrawal – greater range was the most important consideration. The A5M4 looked identical to the late-production open-cockpit A5M2bs but was powered by the 710hp Nakajima Kotobuki 41 engine and carried a 160 litre/35.2 gallon drop tank. It entered service in China in 1938 and with its longer range greatly extended the area of Japanese air superiority while driving the less able Chinese air units even further away from the battle area.

ABOVE: **A5M4 of the 14th Kokutai, pictured in 1940.**

Codenamed "Claude" by the Allies, the A5M4 was in front-line use at the start of the Pacific War but it was soon withdrawn for second-line duties (including advanced fighter training) as it was no match for the newer Allied fighters. As the war in the Pacific approached its desperate end, remaining A5M4s were used in kamikaze (divine wind) attacks against Allied ships off the Japanese coast.

Mitsubishi A5M4	

First flight: February 4, 1935 (Ka-14)

Power: Nakajima 710hp Kotobuki 41 (Bristol Jupiter) nine-cylinder radial piston engine

Armament: Two 7.7mm/0.303in machine-guns firing on each side of upper cylinder of engine, plus two racks for two 30kg/66lb bombs under outer wings

Size: Wingspan – 11m/36ft 1in
Length – 7.55m/24ft 9.25in
Height – 3.2m/10ft 6in
Wing area – 17.8m^2/191.6sq ft

Weights: Empty – 1216kg/2681lb
Maximum take-off – 1707kg/3763lb

Performance: Maximum speed – 440kph/273mph
Ceiling – 10,000m/32,800ft
Range – 1200km/746 miles
Climb – 850m/2790ft per minute

Mitsubishi A6M Zero-Sen

Japan's most famous wartime aircraft and the first shipboard fighter capable of beating its land-based opponents had its origins in a 1937 Japanese Navy requirement for a new fighter with a maximum speed exceeding 499kph/310mph to replace the Mitsubishi A5M carrier fighter. The new aircraft had to climb to 3000m/9840ft in 3.5 minutes, and have manoeuvrability and range exceeding any existing fighter together with the impressive armament of two cannon and two machine-guns. Only Mitsubishi accepted the challenge and design work began under the direction of Jiro Horikoshi. The prototype was completed on March 16, 1939, first flew on April 1 and was accepted by the Navy on September 14, 1939 as the A6M1 Carrier Fighter. The chosen powerplant was the lightweight Mitsubishi Zuisei, later replaced by the more powerful Nakajima Sakae (Prosperity) 925hp radial which was only slightly larger and heavier than the original Zuisei. With its new-found power, the fighter amply exceeded the original performance requirements regarded as impossible only a few months earlier. At this time, production models of Navy aircraft were assigned type numbers based on the last number of the current Japanese year in which production began, and as 1940 was the year 2600 in the Japanese calendar, the A6M series was known as the Zero-Sen (Type 00 fighter).

ABOVE: **The A6M Zero-Sen – Japan's finest wartime fighter aircraft.** BELOW: **More Zero-Sens were produced than any other Japanese wartime aircraft.**

Even before the final acceptance of the A6M2 as a production fighter, the Japanese Navy requested that a number of machines be delivered for operational use in China to meet growing aerial resistance. So 15 A6M2s were delivered for service in China and first appeared over Chungking in August 1940 when the new Zeros shot down all the defending Chinese fighters. Washington were informed about the new high-performance Japanese fighter but no heed was taken and so its appearance over Pearl Harbor came as a complete surprise to the American forces. Its subsequent appearance in every major battle area in the opening days of the war seemed to indicate that Japan possessed almost unlimited supplies of the high-performance fighter. In fact in December 1941 the Japanese Navy had well over 400 Zero fighters. In 1941–2 the Zero certainly got the better of all opposing fighters whether it flew from carriers or had to operate over long distances from land bases. During a Japanese carrier-raid on Ceylon (now Sri Lanka), Zeros easily out-turned opposing RAF Hawker Hurricanes, aircraft which until then had been regarded as outstandingly manoeuvrable.

In mid-1942 the Allies eventually acquired an intact specimen and found that the Zero possessed many shortcomings. It was shipped to the USA where exhaustive tests revealed the fighter's faults and shattered the myth that surrounded it. The tables were turned when the Mitsubishi fighter finally came up against a new generation of US Navy and Army fighters, with powerful engines and heavy protection for their pilot and fuel tanks. Against them the Zero, still basically the design which had flown first in April 1939 offered minimal protection for pilot and fuel tanks and from 1943 the Zeros fell like flies. The installation of the 1560hp Kinsei engine brought the A6M8, the ultimate Zero, closer to the performance of Allied fighters but it was too late. The value of the fighter declined steadily and its lowest point was reached when it was selected as the first aircraft used intentionally as suicide attack (kamikaze or divine-wind) planes. The outstanding success of this form of attack led to the formation of dedicated Kamikaze units, and the bomb-carrying Zeros became the prime suicide attack bombers of the Navy.

More Zero-Sens were produced than any other wartime Japanese aircraft. Mitsubishi alone produced 3879 aircraft of this type, Nakajima built 6,215 which, together with the 844 trainer and floatplane variants produced by Sasebo, Hitachi and Nakajima, brought the grand total of A6M series aircraft to 10,938.

TOP LEFT: **The Zero was of great interest to Japan's enemies. A rare picture of an A6M2 in Chinese Nationalist markings – note the US serviceman by the tail.** TOP RIGHT: **This A6M3 in USAAF markings was assembled from five Zeros captured by the USA in December 1942.** ABOVE LEFT: **These captured Zeros pictured in 1946 were evaluated by the RAF in the Far East while flown by Japanese pilots.** ABOVE RIGHT: **An evaluation A6M3 in USAAF markings pictured over the USA on July 1, 1944.**

Mitsubishi A6M5 Zero-Sen

First flight: August 1943

Power: Nakajima 1130hp NK1C Sakae 21
14-cylinder two-row radial piston engine

Armament: Two 20mm/0.78in cannon in wing,
two 7.7mm/0.303in machine-guns in fuselage,
plus two 60kg/132lb bombs on underwing racks

Size: Wingspan – 11m/36ft 1in
Length 9.06m/29ft 9in Height – 2.98m/9ft 8in
Wing area – 21.3m²/229.28sq ft

Weights: Empty – 1876kg/4136lb
Maximum take-off – 2733kg/6025lb

Performance: Maximum speed – 570kph/354mph
Ceiling – 11,500m/37,500ft
Range – 1920km/1200 miles with drop tanks
Climb – 6000m/19,685ft in 7.05 minutes

LEFT: **This J2M had clearly seen better days.**

Mitsubishi J2M3 Raiden

First flight: March 20, 1942 (J2M1)
Power: Mitsubishi 1820hp MK4R-A Kasei 23a
14-cylinder two-row radial piston engine
Armament: Four 20mm/0.78in cannon,
plus two 60kg/132lb bombs
Size: Wingspan – 10.82m/35ft 5.25in
Length – 9.95m/32ft 7.75in Height – 3.95m/
12ft 11.5in Wing area – 20.05m^2/215.82sq ft
Weights: Empty – 2460kg/5423lb
Maximum take-off – 3945kg/8695lb
Performance: Maximum speed – 595kph/370mph
Ceiling – 11,700m/38,385ft
Range – 1055km/655 miles
Climb – 1170m/3838ft per minute

Mitsubishi J2M Raiden

The J2M, designed by the same team as the Zero, was the Japanese Navy's first interceptor, being designed to operate from shore bases to destroy enemy bombers. Breaking with the Japanese tradition of manoeuvrability above all else, the Raiden (thunderbolt) was built for speed and climb. Among the design points of interest were a streamlined nose, retractable tailwheel

and a laminar flow wing with "combat" flaps for improved agility. The small aerodynamic nose was achieved by connecting the propeller to the engine (which was set further back in the fuselage) by an extension shaft. Early J2M1 versions flew in March 1942 but proved troublesome and did not meet the Navy's requirements, consequently an improved Kasei 23a-engined J2M2

was ordered for production in October 1942. Continued technical difficulties meant the aircraft did not enter service until December 1943 and then as the improved J2M3 version with four wing-mounted cannon.

Codenamed "Jack" by the Allies, the Raiden played a key role in the defence of the Japanese homeland in the closing months of World War II.

LEFT: **A captured Ki-46 with US markings.**

Mitsubishi Ki-46-III Kai

First flight: October 1944
Power: Mitsubishi 1500hp Ha-112II piston engines
Armament: Two 20mm/0.78in cannon in nose and
one 37mm/1.46in oblique forward-firing cannon
in upper fuselage
Size: Wingspan – 14.7m/48ft 2.75in
Length – 11.48m/37ft 8.25in
Height – 3.88m/12ft 8.75in
Wing area – 32m^2/344.46sq ft
Weights: Empty – 3831kg/8446lb
Maximum take-off – 6228kg/13730lb
Performance: Maximum speed – 630kph/391mph
Ceiling – 10,500m/34,450ft
Range – 2000km/1243 miles
Climb – 600m/1970ft per minute

Mitsubishi Ki-46-III Kai

As Japan was forced on the defensive by the Allies, the Imperial Staff recognized the need for heavy fighter-interceptors to defend against Allied bombers. Since the very high-performance Ki-46 reconnaissance aircraft was some 83kph/53mph faster than the Army's standard twin-engine fighter (the Ki-45), the Ki-46 was selected for development as a stop-gap high-altitude interceptor. The development work, carried out by

the Army Aerotechnical Research Institute, began in June 1943.

Photographic equipment was removed from the nose and replaced by two forward-firing 20mm/0.78in cannon, complemented by an obliquely forward-firing 37mm/1.46in cannon in the upper fuselage. Around 200 interceptor versions were built.

The aircraft appeared from October 1944 and saw service in November,

but proved disappointing against B-29 daylight raids mainly due to its climb rate. When B-29 gunners found their mark, the Ki-46 was very vulnerable because of its lack of armour and self-sealing fuel tanks.

When the American bombers switched to night operations the Ki-46 proved to be even less effective as it was never fitted with radar for operational use.

Mitsubishi Ki-109

In 1943 the B-29 Superfortress was causing great concern among the Japanese military. The new super-bomber would have to be stopped and one of the means considered was a bomber hunter-killer developed from the fast and agile Mitsubishi Ki-67 heavy bomber. Initial plans called for a hunter version equipped with radar and a powerful searchlight that would have operated in concert with a killer version that would have destroyed the enemy aircraft. The scheme was then simplified to a large-calibre cannon-armed day interceptor.

The main offensive armament was a manually loaded 75mm/2.95in anti-aircraft cannon that could be fired out of range of the B-29's defending guns. The first prototype was completed in August 1944, two months after the dreaded B-29s carried out their first bombing raid on Japan.

Production versions had improved engines over the original bomber version and the sole defensive armament was a 12.7mm/0.5in machine-gun in the tail

TOP: **The Ki-109 was developed from the Ki-67 heavy bomber. Two versions were originally planned to work as a team – one radar-equipped hunter and a heavily armed killer. Only the armed version appeared.** ABOVE: **The Ki-109 differed from the Ki-67 pictured by mounting a 75mm/3in cannon in the nose.**

turret. Although it still lacked high-altitude performance, 22 examples of the highly manoeuvrable Ki-109s entered service, but by then the B-29s had switched to low-level night operations anyway.

Mitsubishi Ki-109

First flight: August 1944
Power: Two Mitsubishi 1900hp Ha-104 piston engines
Armament: One 75mm/2.95in cannon in nose and one 12.7mm/0.5in machine-gun in tail
Size: Wingspan – 22.5m/73ft 9.75in
Length – 17.95m/58ft 10.75in
Height – 5.8m/19ft 1in
Wing area – 65.85m^2/708.8sq ft
Weights: Empty – 7424kg/16367lb
Maximum take-off – 10,800kg/23,810lb
Performance: Maximum speed – 550kph/342mph
Ceiling – 9470m/31,070ft
Range – 2200km/1367 miles
Climb – 450m/1476ft per minute

Morane-Saulnier M.S.406

Morane-Saulnier built the 406 in response to a 1934 French Air Ministry requirement for a single-seat fighter. It first flew in August 1935 and was unusual for its Plymax construction – plywood with a light alloy sheet glued to the outside made up most of the aircraft except for the fabric-covered rear fuselage. Although the aircraft had a retractable undercarriage, it also had a tail-skid instead of a tailwheel.

The design was thoroughly tested by the M.S.405 series of pre-production aircraft, and in March 1938 Morane-Saulnier got an order for 1000 examples of the production M.S.406C-1, the

first of which flew in January 1939. Export orders were secured from China, Finland, Lithuania, Turkey, Poland and Yugoslavia. Swiss acquisition of two early examples led to the licence-built EFW D-3800 versions in that country.

Production problems with the 12Y engine meant that only 572 completed aircraft had been delivered to the French Air Force by the time war broke out. The brave French pilots soon found that their fighters, though only six years old as a design, were from an earlier age compared to the Messerschmitts that they had to fight. More than 400

ABOVE: **The M.S.406's fuselage is reminiscent of the Hawker Hurricane.** BELOW: **A row of M.S.406s of the Polish Air Force.**

M.S.406s were lost against 175 enemy aircraft in the Battle of France.

Although deliveries continued to the French Air Force and over 1000 had been delivered by the fall of France, only one group of the Vichy French Air Force operated the M.S.406 after the armistice.

Morane-Saulnier M.S.406

First flight: August 8, 1935
Power: Hispano-Suiza 860hp 12Y-31 V-12 liquid-cooled engine
Armament: One 20mm/0.78in cannon firing through propeller hub and two 7.5mm/0.295in machine-guns in wings
Size: Wingspan – 10.6m/34ft 9.75in
 Length – 8.16m/26ft 9.25in
 Height – 2.83m/9ft 3.75in
 Wing area – 16m²/172.23sq ft
Weights: Empty – 1900kg/4189lb
 Maximum take-off – 2470kg/5445lb
Performance: Maximum speed – 485kph/302mph
 Ceiling – 9400m/30,840ft
 Range – 800km/497 miles
 Climb – 850m/2789ft per minute

Morane-Saulnier Type N

The Type N, nicknamed "Bullet" by the Royal Flying Corps, was a neat little mid-wing monoplane that became the first French fighter aircraft – the British used the type due to the shortage of good British fighting scouts at the time. It first flew in July 1914, with the famous French pilot Roland Garros at the controls.

A huge metal propeller spinner, designed to streamline the front of the aircraft, earned the Type N its nickname but also caused engines to overheat because it so effectively deflected air around the aircraft instead of over the engine. As a result the spinner was often deleted from 1915 and in fact caused little loss of performance.

The N was armed with a fixed machine-gun, but without a synchronization gear, as the Allies had yet to develop it. Instead the N used metal bullet-deflectors on the propeller blades, an installation pioneered by Garros on a Type L. This technique was far from ideal as the impact of the bullets on the deflectors could still shatter the propeller or weaken the engine mount with disastrous results. There were also occasional ricochets of the bullets back at the pilot. With a high, for the time, landing speed, the Type N was a handful and required a skilful pilot at the controls.

The Type N was less popular than the earlier Morane-Saulnier Type L Parasol and as the Type N did not do well against the Fokker Eindecker, only 49 were built in 1917. In spite of that, the RFC Type Ns saw plenty of action as did those that flew with the French and the Russians.

At that point in aviation history, aircraft development proceeded so fast that most fighter planes were virtually obsolete by the time they reached the front-line squadrons.

Morane-Saulnier Type N

First flight: July 1914
Power: Le Rhône 110hp 9C rotary piston engine
Armament: One fixed forward-firing 7.7 or 8mm/0.303 or 0.315in machine-gun
Size: Wingspan – 8.3m/27ft 2.75in
   Length – 6.7m/21ft 11.75in
   Height – 2.5m/8ft 2.5in
   Wing area – 11m^2/118.41sq ft
Weights: Empty – 288kg/635lb
   Maximum take-off – 444kg/979lb
Performance: Maximum speed – 165kph/102.5mph
   Ceiling – 4000m/13,123ft
   Range – 225km/140 miles
   Climb – 250m/820ft per minute

LEFT: **Complete with huge spinner, the Type N experienced engine overheating problems.**
BELOW: **The earlier M.S Type L Parasol.**
BOTTOM: **With the spinner removed, the Type N experienced no further overheating problems.**

Nakajima Ki-27

The Nakajima Ki-27 was derived from a private venture all-metal stressed-skin aircraft called the PE designed by Nakajima in 1935. When the company was invited by the Imperial Japanese Army to tender a design for an advanced fighter, a revised PE was submitted as the Ki-27.

The prototype made its first flight in October 1936 and was accepted by the Army, after comparative trials with other prototypes, in December 1937. It was called the Army Type 97 Fighter Model A – the 97 refers to the year it went into service which was the Japanese year 2597. The Ki-27 was the Imperial Japanese Army's first monoplane fighter but it had fixed landing gear. The fighter was basic in many ways – it had a skid instead of a heavier tailwheel, no pilot armour or self-sealing fuel tanks, nor did it have a starter motor. This left the aircraft very light and incredibly manoeuvrable.

The Ki-27, codenamed "Nate" by the Allies, made its combat début over northern China in early 1938 and retained air superiority until the Chinese deployed the Polikarpov I-16. Nates later took part in the invasion of Burma, Malaya and the Philippines.

At the outbreak of the Pacific War most front-line Japanese fighter units were equipped with the Ki-27 and the type did prove to be initially very effective against the Allies, but once they were pitched against the more modern Western fighters, they were withdrawn to the Japanese mainland where they served until 1943. Nates did however continue in Japanese service in Manchuria until the end of World War II. Home-based examples were also used as advanced trainers and even as Kamikaze aircraft.

Nakajima Ki-27a

First flight: October 15, 1936
Power: Nakajima 710hp Ha-1b air-cooled radial piston engine
Armament: Two 7.7mm/0.303in machine-guns in nose
Size: Wingspan – 11.31m/37ft 1.5in
  Length – 7.53m/24ft 8.5in
  Height – 3.25m/10ft 8in
  Wing area – 18.55m²/199.68sq ft
Weights: Empty – 1110kg/2447lb
  Maximum take-off – 1790kg/3946lb
Performance: Maximum speed – 470kph/292mph
  Ceiling – 12,250m/40190ft
  Range – 635km/389 miles
  Climb – 900m/2953ft per minute

LEFT: **The first monoplane fighter of the Imperial Japanese Army, the Ki-27.** BELOW: **The Ki-27 was a very basic light fighter equipped with a tail skid in place of a tailwheel.**

Nakajima Ki-43 Hayabusa

In 1937, when the Japanese Imperial Army decided to acquire a fighter with a retractable undercarriage to succeed the Ki-27, it turned to the Nakajima company for a replacement, which emerged as the Ki-43 Hayabusa (peregrine falcon). Like the Ki-27 before it, lightness and manoeuvrability were central to the design of the Ki-43 so it had no pilot armour, self-sealing fuel tanks or starter motor. It was, however, disappointing in flight tests during early 1939

and development was abandoned until spring 1941, when combat flaps were added, thus increasing the wing area as required and creating a fighter that could turn inside the highly manoeuvrable Zero. This modified version, which could dogfight with the best of the Allies' fighters, went into service in June 1941 and proved very successful despite its light armament. Most of Japan's Army fighter aces built up their scores while flying the Ki-43.

After encounters with the newer Allied fighters, armour and self-sealing fuel tanks were added, together with a more powerful engine to produce the II version, a clipped-wing variant of which was widely produced. The Ki-43 was in action throughout the Pacific theatre

in World War II and in the final days was used in the defence of Tokyo and for kamikaze (divine wind) missions. Almost 6000 were built in all – this aeroplane, codenamed "Oscar" by the Allies, was deployed in greater numbers than any other Imperial Army fighter and was second only to the Navy's Zero in terms of sheer numbers in the Japanese inventory.

As an interesting post-war footnote, in late 1945 the French Armeé de l'Air flew captured Oscars painted in

ABOVE: **The Ki-43 was in service throughout the war in the Pacific.** LEFT: **A Ki-43-II captured by the Allies before the end of World War II, rebuilt for evaluation.**

French markings in the ground support role against Viet Minh forces in Indochina. Captured Hayabusas were also operated by the Indonesian People's Security Forces against the Dutch in the same period.

Nakajima Ki-43-II Hayabusa

First flight: January 1939

Power: Nakajima 1150hp Ha-115 air-cooled radial piston engine

Armament: Two 12.7mm/0.5in synchronized machine-guns, plus two 30kg/66lb or 250kg/551lb bombs

Size: Wingspan – 10.84m/35ft 6.75in
Length – 8.92m/29ft 3.3in
Height – 3.27m/10ft 8.75in
Wing area – 21.4m^2/230.4sq ft

Weights: Empty – 1910kg/4211lb
Maximum take-off – 2925kg/6450lb

Performance: Maximum speed – 530kph/329mph
Ceiling – 11,200m/36,750ft
Range – 1760km/1095 miles
Climb – 5000m/16,405ft in 5 minutes, 49 seconds

Nakajima Ki-44 Shoki

The Ki-44 was designed purely as an interceptor, so high speed and good climb were sought at the expense of manoeuvrability. The type first flew in August 1940 and when tested against an imported Messerschmitt Bf109E was shown to be superior in performance.

The Shoki (demon) did not enter production until mid-1942 and finally reached a production total of 1225. Virtually all were used in the defence of the Japanese home islands and in one defensive mission on February 19, 1945

a small number of Shokis attacked a force of 120 B-29s, destroying ten of the US bombers. The Allied codename for the Ki-44 was "Tojo".

TOP: **The Shoki was a good fighter, but high landing speeds demanded respect for the type from its pilots.** ABOVE: **The Allied codename for the Ki-44 was "Tojo".** LEFT: **Total production of the Ki-44 exceeded 1200.** BELOW: **The Ki-44 was an effective interceptor that could have wreaked havoc among enemy bomber formations, had it been deployed effectively in sufficient numbers.**

Nakajima Ki-44-IIb Shoki

First flight: August 1940
Power: Nakajima 1520hp Ha-109 radial piston engine
Armament: Four forward-firing 12.7mm/0.5in machine-guns
Size: Wingspan – 9.45m/31ft
　　　Length – 8.8m/28ft 10.5in
　　　Height – 3.25m/10ft 8in
　　　Wing area – 15m²/161.46sq ft
Weights: Empty – 2105kg/4641lb
　　　Maximum take-off – 2995kg/6603lb
Performance: Maximum speed – 605kph/376mph
　　　Ceiling – 11,200m/36,745ft
　　　Range – 1700km/1056 miles
　　　Climb – 1200m/3940ft per minute

Nakajima Ki-84 Hayate

ABOVE LEFT: **A Ki-84 of the 11th Sentai.** ABOVE: **The Ki-84 was a formidable fighter aircraft with an excellent performance.**

Introduced in mid-1944, the Nakajima Ki-84 Hayate (gale) was numerically the most important fighter that served with the Japanese Army Air Force during the last year of the war in the Pacific. If it had been available in larger numbers earlier in the war, the Hayate could have been a major obstacle for Allied aircraft to overcome. It was the equal of the most advanced Allied fighters including the P-51 and P-47 and in many cases had better climb and manoeuvrability. Japan was so desperate for Ki-84s in the last months of the war that underground factories were being built with a planned output of 200 aircraft per month.

The Ki-84 began in 1942 when the Nakajima Aeroplane Co. began to design a replacement for its Ki-43 Hayabusa. The JAAF wanted a high performance long-range fighter that could outperform those of the Allies.

The Ki-84 prototype flew for the first time in March 1943 and was quickly shown to be the best-performing Japanese fighter aircraft then available for production.

Service tests of the Ki-84 began in Japan under operational conditions in October 1943 and the type was accepted for production as the Army Type 4 Fighter Model 1A Hayate (gale) or Ki-84-Ia.

Production aircraft began to roll off the assembly lines in April 1944. In March 1944 the experimental squadron that was conducting the service test trials of the Ki-84 was disbanded, and its personnel transferred to the 22nd Sentai which was re-equipped with production Hayates and transferred to China in August 1944 for combat against the USAAF's 14th Air Force. The Ki-84-Ia swiftly established itself as a formidable foe that compared very well with the best Allied fighters of the time.

The Hayate exhibited an excellent performance and climb rate, and unlike most earlier Japanese fighters, it was well armoured for pilot protection.

The Ki-84 proved faster than the P-51D Mustang and the P-47D Thunderbolt at all but the highest altitudes while at medium height the Hayate was so fast that it was virtually uncatchable.

Fighter-bomber versions of the Ki-84 also proved to be formidable combat aircraft. On April 15, 1945 a flight of 11 Hayates made a surprise air attack on American airfields on Okinawa damaging or destroying many aircraft on the ground.

The Hayate did have some handling idiosyncrasies. Taxiing and ground handling were generally hazardous and on take-off, the considerable engine torque caused a swing to port once the tail came up.

Most Ki-84 defects were simply due to poor quality control in a country under siege. Later examples had progressively poorer performance and mechanical reliability – the metal of the landing gear struts inadequately hardened during manufacture, which made them likely to snap on landing. Production of the aircraft never reached the desired levels because the Nakajima factory was regularly bombed by US B-29 Superfortresses.

Nakajima Ki-84-Ia Hayate

First flight: March 1943
Power: Nakajima 1900hp Ha-45 radial piston engine
Armament: Two 12.7mm/0.5in machine-guns plus two 20mm/0.78in cannon and two underwing 250kg/551lb bombs
Size: Wingspan – 11.24m/36ft 10.5in
Length – 9.92m/32ft 6.5in
Height – 3.39m/11ft 1.5in
Wing area – $21m^2$/226sq ft
Weights: Empty – 2660kg/5864lb
Maximum take-off – 3890kg/8576lb
Performance: Maximum speed – 631kph/392mph
Ceiling – 10,500m/34,350ft
Range – 2168km/1347 miles
Climb – 1100m/3600ft per minute

ABOVE: **This Hayate was shipped to Wright Field in the USA for post-war evaluation by the USAAF.**

Nieuport fighting scouts

The Nieuport fighting scouts earned a fine reputation for both their designer Gustave Delage and the company that built them. The Nieuport XI was developed from the 1914 Bébé racer aircraft and retained the earlier aircraft's name as a nickname. By the summer of 1915 the first Bébés were in service in France and the Dardanelles with Britain's Royal Flying Corps and Royal Naval Air Service and were one of the first true fighters used by the British. In the hands of an experienced pilot, the tiny Nieuport XI had no problem outmanoeuvring an Eindecker and bringing it down. Powered by an 80hp Gnome or Le Rhône engine, the aircraft were much better than what was in use at the time. They were highly agile fighters with good rates of climb and speed but the chief problem lay in the fragility of the wing structure which could fail in flight.

They were armed with a single Hotchkiss or Lewis machine-gun mounted on the top wing but the Nieuport XI could also carry eight Le Prieur rockets for attacking balloons. In addition to French production, the Nieuport XI was also built in Russia, Spain and the Netherlands, as well as being copied by German designers.

Nieuport XI	
First flight: Early 1915	
Power: Le Rhône 80hp 9C rotary piston engine	
Armament: One 7.7mm/0.303in Lewis gun	
Size: Wingspan – 7.55m/24ft 9in	
Length – 5.8m/19ft 0.75in	
Height – 2.45m/8ft 0.5in	
Wing area – 13m²/139.94sq ft	
Weights: Empty – 350kg/772lb	
Maximum take-off – 480kg/1058lb	
Performance: Maximum speed – 155kph/97mph	
Ceiling – 4500m/14,765ft	
Range – 2 hours, 30 minutes endurance	
Climb – about 200m/660ft per minute	

ABOVE: The Nieuports were one of the most successful "families" of World War I aircraft. BELOW AND BOTTOM: The Nieuport XI was one of the earliest fighter aircraft used by Britain's RFC and RNAS. Though manoeuvrable, the type's wings were fragile.

The Nieuport XVII was one of the most famous fighter aircraft of World War I and was a significant improvement on the Bébé. The type first appeared with the French on the Western Front in May 1916, and was a direct development of the XI. It had a more powerful engine, larger wings and a stiffening of the entire structure. It first had the 110hp Le Rhône 9J rotary engine, and then was upgraded to the more powerful 130hp Clerget 9B. The XVII combined outstanding manoeuvrability with good speed and excellent climb, and influenced the design of many other aircraft – the German Siemens-Schuckert DI was, except for the tailplane, a direct copy of it.

Reloading of the top wing gun on this model was made easier by the Foster gun mount, a curved metal rail along which the gun could be pulled back and down – the pilot could then reach the magazine on top of the machine-gun but this was a difficult feat in anything but straight and level flight. Nevertheless many World War I Allied aces flew these aircraft, including René Fonck, Georges Guynemer, Charles Nungesser, Albert Ball and Billy Bishop.

The Nieuport 28 first flew in June 1917 and was the first fighter aircraft flown in combat by pilots of the American Expeditionary Forces (AEF) in World War I. Its second armed patrol with an AEF unit on April 14, 1918 resulted in two victories when Lts Alan Winslow and Douglas Campbell (the first American-trained ace) of the 94th Aero Squadron each downed an enemy aircraft. The 28 was very different to the earlier Nieuports and lost the familiar slim lower wing in favour of a lower wing almost as large as the top one.

By the time the Nieuport 28 was in service it had been overtaken in terms of performance by the SPAD, but American pilots maintained a good ratio of kills to losses while flying the Nieuport. The Nieuport was more manoeuvrable than the sturdier SPAD XIII that replaced it, but had a reputation for fragility and a tendency, in a dive, to shed the fabric covering its upper wing. Even so, many American aces of World War I, including Eddie Rickenbacker with 26 victories, flew the French-built Nieuport 28. Post-war, many Nieuport 28s continued to fly in air forces around the world.

Nieuport XVII

First flight: January 1916
Power: Le Rhône 120hp rotary piston engine
Armament: One 7.7mm/0.303in Lewis gun on flexible top wing mount plus one 7.7m/0.303in synchronized machine-gun
Size: Wingspan – 8.2m/26ft 10.75in
Length – 5.96m/19ft 7in
Height – 2.44m/8ft
Wing area – 14.75m²/158.77sq ft
Weights: Empty – 374kg/825lb
Maximum take-off – 560kg/1235lb
Performance: Maximum speed – 170kph/106mph
Ceiling – 5350m/17,550ft
Range – 250km/155 miles
Climb – 4000m/13,125ft in 19 minutes, 30 seconds

ABOVE: **Around 90 examples of the 120hp or 130hp engined Nieuport 27 were in service briefly with the RFC from mid-1917 to April 1918.** BELOW: **The ultimate Nieuport – the 28. As well as extensive wartime service, the type was also widely used post-World War I.**

Nieuport 28

First flight: June 14, 1917
Power: Gnome 160hp 9N rotary piston engine
Armament: Two fixed 7.7mm/0.303in machine-guns
Size: Wingspan – 8m/26ft 3in
Length – 6.2m/20ft 4in
Height – 2.48m/8ft 1.75in
Wing area – 20m²/215.29sq ft
Weights: Empty – 532kg/1172lb
Maximum take-off – 740kg/1631lb
Performance: Maximum speed – 195kph/121mph
Ceiling – 5200m/17,060ft
Range – 400km/248 miles
Climb – 5000m/16,405ft in 21 minutes, 15 seconds

North American P/F-51 Mustang

Considered to be one of the greatest US fighters ever, the first Mustangs were actually designed and built in the United States with Allison engines to a British specification for the Royal Air Force. Designed and built in the remarkably short time of 117 days, the new fighter was test flown in October 1940. The Mustang could outperform contemporary American fighters but the Allison's lack of power in the climb and at altitude led to the early Mustang's use in the European theatre being limited to armed tactical reconnaissance. In October 1942 RAF Mustangs attacked targets on the Dortmund-Ems canal and became the first British single-engined aircraft over Germany in World War II. The A-36 Invader was the dedicated dive-bomber version of the early Mustang and equipped the USAAF in Sicily, where it was used to devastating effect.

When in 1942 the Mustang airframe was matched with the proven Rolls-Royce Merlin, the "Cadillac of the skies" was born and the P-51 Mustang became one of the most successful fighter aircraft of all time. In October 1943, as a result of unacceptable losses, unescorted US daylight bomber

ABOVE: **With its long range, the P-51 Mustang enabled the resumption of US bombing missions deep in enemy territory.** BELOW: **This preserved P-51 is painted as the personal aircraft of US wartime ace Clarence "Bud" Anderson.**

missions deep into enemy Europe were suspended. No Allied fighter had the range to defend and escort the American bombers all the way to the target. The arrival of the Mustang, with its US-built Merlin engines and droppable wing tanks enabled the bombers to resume their daylight missions, safe in the knowledge that their "little buddies" could fly with them all the way to Berlin and back. Even at that range, the P-51's performance was superior to that of its Luftwaffe adversaries. The Mustang allowed the Allies to gain command of the daylight sky over Germany and as a result made a major contribution to the defeat of Nazi Germany.

The Mustang was a very comfortable long-range aircraft and pilot visibility was excellent. Cockpit ergonomics were well thought out, with everything readily to hand. It was so aerodynamically clean that it was capable of higher speeds than

Spitfires fitted with the same engine. Although manoeuvrable it demanded, however, great physical effort from the pilot to get the best from the aircraft at high speed.

The P-51D was produced in greater numbers than any other model but improvements continued to be made to the design, culminating in the P-51H, which was 454kg/1000lb lighter than the D model and was the fastest Allied piston-engined aircraft of the war.

Total production amounted to 15,586 and after World War II the Mustang was operated by at least 55 air forces, making it the world's most widely used fighter at the time. Licence-built versions were also produced in Australia in the late 1940s.

Always thought of as a World War II fighter, the P-51 was in action for many years after 1945. Mothballed USAF P/F-51s returned to service for the Korean War as fighter-bombers and also scored a number of air-to-air victories. South African and Australian Mustangs also served in the conflict until being replaced by jets.

Dutch P-51Ds and Ks were in combat in the Dutch East Indies in 1946 and following the withdrawal of Dutch forces the P-51s were given over to the embryonic Indonesian Air Force, who operated the type into the 1970s. The Israeli Air Force fielded Mustangs during the 1956 Arab-Israeli conflict and on January 15, 1962 Indonesian F-51Ds provided top cover for a failed attempt to invade Dutch New Guinea. Dutch Hawker Hunter F. Mk 4s were ready to engage the Mustangs when negotiations halted what could have been a remarkable air combat episode.

Such was the quality and longevity of the original design that the P-51 was put back into production in 1967 as a turboprop-powered counter-insurgency aircraft

TOP: **The Cadillac of the skies – looking every inch a thoroughbred.** ABOVE: **Where it all began – a Mustang I of No.2 Squadron RAF. Due to the low altitude power ratings of the Allison engines installed, the type was initially limited to armed tactical reconnaissance.** BELOW: **Drop tanks gave the Mustang even longer legs, and helped the type regain control of the sky over Europe from the Luftwaffe.**

North American P-51D Mustang

First flight: October 26, 1940
Power: Packard 1590hp V 1650-7 Merlin piston engine
Armament: Six 12.7mm/0.5in machine-guns and up to 454kg/1000lb of bombs or rockets in place of drop tanks
Size: Wingspan – 11.29m/37ft
Length – 9.85m/32ft 3in
Height – 4.16m/13ft 8in
Wing area – 21.83m^2/235sq ft
Weights: Empty – 3230kg/7125lb
Maximum take-off – 5262kg/11,600lb
Performance: Maximum speed – 703kph/437mph
Ceiling – 12,771m/41,900ft
Range – 3347km/2080 miles with drop tanks
Climb – 1060m/3475ft per minute

Northrop P/F–61 Black Widow

The large and heavily armed twin-engine twin-boom Black Widow was the first ever aircraft specifically designed as a nightfighter and was built to meet a specification issued in October 1940, following the early successes of RAF nightfighters against the Luftwaffe. In the nose it carried the then new radar equipment, which enabled its crew to locate enemy aircraft in total darkness and manoeuvre into an attacking position. The XP-61 was flight-tested in 1942 and delivery of production aircraft began in late 1943, following hold-ups due to technical challenges of both aircraft and radar that had to be overcome.

The P-61A flew its first operational intercept missions as a nightfighter in Europe in July 1944 and destroyed four German bombers in the type's first engagement. Black Widows were also credited with the destruction of nine V-1 flying bombs in Europe. Meanwhile in the Pacific, a Black Widow claimed its first kill on the night of July 6–7, 1944. As the P-61s became available, they replaced the stop-gap Douglas P-70s in all USAAF nightfighter squadrons.

Armament was carried below the nose and in a remotely controlled barbette at top centre of the fuselage – the latter was deleted early in production of the A model due to buffeting problems when pointed at right angles to the aircraft's centre line. The dorsal barbette was later reinstated during production of the B-model, which differed from the A model by being 20.3cm/8in longer and having the ability to carry four 726kg/1600lb bombs or 1136 litre/300 US gallon drop tanks. 200 P-61As were built, while B model production reached 450. After feedback about the P-61's combat performance, the P-61C was developed, powered by turbo-supercharged R-2800-73 engines with an emergency output of 2800hp apiece. As the take-off weight of the type increased to 18,144kg/40,000lb,

a recommended take-off run of 4.8km/3 miles was required.

A number of Black Widows continued to serve until 1950 in USAF service (by then designated F-51s) and in 1949 were the first aircraft of the embryonic US Air Defense Command, founded to defend the USA from Soviet air attack.

BELOW: **The P-61 Black Widow was the first ever purpose-designed nightfighter, and proved the value of the dedicated nightfighter aircraft.**

Northrop P-61B Black Widow

First flight: May 21, 1942 (XP-61)

Power: Two Pratt & Whitney 2000hp R-2800-65 Double Wasp 18-cylinder radial piston engines

Armament: Four 12.7mm/0.5in machine-guns in upper turret, four 20mm/0.78in cannons in belly, plus up to 2905kg/6400lb of bombs

Size: Wingspan – 20.11m/66ft 0.75in
   Length – 15.11m/49ft 7in
   Height – 4.47m/14ft 8in
   Wing area – 61.53m^2/662.36sq ft

Weights: Empty – 10,637kg/23,450lb
   Maximum take-off – 16,420kg/36,200lb

Performance: Maximum speed – 589kph/366mph
   Ceiling – 10,060m/33,000ft
   Range – 2172km/1350 miles
   Climb – 637m/2090ft per minute

Petlyakov Pe-3

Originally designed as a high altitude interceptor (designated VI-100), the Pe-2 became one of the most significant aircraft in the wartime Allied inventory. The prototype flew in mid-1939 and its high speed and high altitude capability would indeed have made it a very effective interceptor. However, early in 1940 the decision was taken to develop the type as a bomber as a priority over a high flying interceptor. It performed outstandingly as a tactical/dive-bomber and was very fast for the time. Two RAF Hurricane squadrons were sent to Russia in the autumn of 1941 to strengthen the Soviet defences, and when escorting the Pe-2 on bombing missions found it very hard to keep up.

When an early Pe-2 dive-bomber was modified as a multi-role fighter prototype it was given the designation Pe-3. It first flew in early 1941 and was structurally similar to the bomber version. The fighter had a two-man crew (as opposed to three for the bomber) and they sat back to back with the observer gunner facing backwards. Additional fuel was carried in the main bomb bay and the

small bomb bays in the rear of the two engine nacelles. Only 23 examples were built prior to the German invasion of Russia at which point production ceased.

The Pe-2 did however make it into production as a fighter in the summer of 1941. Every second aircraft on the Pe-2 production line was hastily modified to fighter configuration and were designated Pe-3bis. Armament consisted of two 20mm/0.78in cannon carried in the bomb bay. The bomber's nose armament of two 7.62mm/0.31in machine-guns were sometimes replaced by two harder-hitting 12.7mm/0.5in cannon, while the bomber's 12.7mm/0.5in cannon in the dorsal turret was retained. Front-line units had deliveries from August 1941 and those aircraft used in the nightfighter role were equipped with special equipment. Around 300 aircraft were built in all.

TOP: **The Pe-3 bristled with offensive armament.** ABOVE: **From mid-1941, every alternate Pe-2 on the production line was made as a fighter.**

Petlyakov Pe-3bis

First flight: December 22, 1939 (VI-100 prototype)

Power: Two Klimov 1260hp VK-105PF V12 piston engines

Armament: Two 20mm/0.78in cannon in bomb bay, two 7.62mm/0.31in machine-guns or two 12.7mm/0.5in cannon in nose, plus one 12.7mm/0.5in cannon in dorsal turret

Size: Wingspan – 17.16m/56ft 3.6in
Length – 12.6m/41ft 4.5in
Height – 3.42m/11ft 2.6in
Wing area – 40.5m^2/435.95sq ft

Weights: Empty – 5870kg/12,941lb
Maximum take-off – 8040kg/17,725lb

Performance: Maximum speed – 530kph/329mph
Ceiling – 8800m/28,700ft
Range – 1700km/1056 miles
Climb – 5000m/16,405ft in 10 minutes, 12 seconds

Pfalz D.III

The D.III appeared in mid-1917 and was built with the experience gained by Pfalz while producing LFG-Roland fighters. The D.III biplane fighter, the design of which owed much to the LFG-Roland D.I and D.II, was a competent, agile fighter aircraft that was also strong, easy to fly and popular with pilots. About 600 were built and supplied at least at first, only to Bavarian

fighter units in the German Air Force – this was no doubt due to the fact that the Pfalz factory was run by the Bavarian government. The excellent Pfalz D.XII was a development of the D.III and was, in 1918, accepted by the German High Command for mass production.

Among the refinements was the removal of the radiator from the top wing

ABOVE: **D.XIIs were in action on the Western Front from October 1918, but could do little to affect the final outcome of World War I.**

to the engine to prevent unfortunate pilots from being scalded by a punctured cooling system. Although the D.XII was powered by the same Mercedes engine as the D.III, it had a slightly higher top speed than the earlier mark.

ABOVE: **A Pfalz D.IIIa. By the end of 1917 some 275 were in action at the Front, but by April 1918 this number had risen to 433.**

Pfalz D.IIIa

First flight: Summer 1917

Power: Mercedes 180hp D.IIIa in-line piston engine

Armament: Two fixed 7.92mm/0.31in machine-guns

Size: Wingspan – 9.4m/30ft 10in
Length – 6.95m/22ft 9.5in
Height – 2.67m/8ft 9in
Wing area – 22.1m^2/237.89sq ft

Weights: Empty – 695kg/1532lb
Maximum take-off – 935kg/2061lb

Performance: Maximum speed – 165kph/103mph
Ceiling – 5180m/17,000ft
Range – 2 hours, 30 minutes endurance
Climb – 250m/820ft per minute

Polikarpov I-15

LEFT: The I-15 fought from Manchuria to Spain.

Developed from the earlier I-5 fighter, the agile little Polikarpov I-15 biplane actually replaced the monoplane I-16 in service in parts of the USSR. Having first flown during October 1933 in prototype TsKB-3 form, production of the I-15 Chaika (gull) began in 1934 and continued for three years.

The I-15 was used extensively by the Republicans during the Spanish Civil War (1936–9) and earned the nickname "Chato", meaning flat-nosed. The first I-15s arrived in Spain during October 1936 and during the subsequent combats earned a reputation as a tough opponent. In addition to the imported examples, Spanish government factories also licence-built some 287 examples and many fell into the hands of the Nationalists when the war ended in March 1939.

The improved I-15bis was tested in early 1937 and was distinguished by a longer cowling (covering a more powerful engine), and streamlining spats on the undercarriage legs. Over 2400 examples had been built by the time production ceased in early 1939. By then it had also seen action against the Japanese in Manchuria. In the Winter War of 1939–40, the I-15bis was extensively used against the Finns. The few examples of the improved version that made it to fight in Spain were nicknamed "Super Chatos" by the Spanish.

In 1937–8, the I-15bis was sent in quantity, with pilots, to help Chinese Nationalists fight the Japanese who were

LEFT: The I-15 fought from Manchuria to Spain.

invading. It was during these air battles that the tough biplane began to meet its match in some of the Japanese monoplanes. Nevertheless over 1000 I-15bis fighters were still in Soviet Air Force use in mid-1941 although most were used for ground attack. By late 1942 all were relegated to second-line duties.

Polikarpov I-15bis

First flight: October 1933 (prototype)
Power: M-25V 775hp radial piston engine
Armament: Four 7.62mm/0.3in machine-guns plus bombload of up to 150kg/331lb
Size: Wingspan – 10.2m/33ft 5.5in
　　Length – 6.27m/20ft 6.75in
　　Height – 2.19m/7ft 2.25in
　　Wing area – 22.53m²/242.52sq ft
Weights: Empty – 1320kg/2910lb
　　Maximum take-off – 1900kg/4189lb
Performance: Maximum speed – 370kph/230mph
　　Ceiling – 9500m/31,170ft
　　Range – 530km/329 miles
　　Climb – 765m/2500ft per minute

Polikarpov I-16

LEFT: The classic I-16 fighter was in the front line on at least four battle fronts.

The tiny I-16, reminiscent of the American Gee Bee racing aircraft, was one of the most important and innovative fighters of its time. With a wooden fuselage, it was also the first widely used low-wing cantilever monoplane with retractable landing gear. It first flew in December 1933, and in the mid-1930s this aircraft was one of the world's best fighters – it had a good top speed some 123kph/70mph faster than its contemporaries, and was well-armed and highly manoeuvrable. It remained in production until 1939 by which time a host of variants had been developed.

It was not until the Spanish Civil War that the I-16 came to the attention of the Western world. The Republicans were supplied with 278 I-16s from October 1935. Hispano-Suiza also licence-built the I-16 for the Republicans in Spain but after their surrender, others were produced for the Franco régime. Many of the I-16s that saw action in Spain were flown by volunteer Soviet pilots.

In 1937, Soviet I-16s also saw service in China against the Japanese. From 1938 the Chinese flew the type and by 1939, Soviet I-16s were locked in fierce air battles with the Japanese on the Manchurian border.

The 1939–40 Winter War with Finland saw the Soviet I-16s in action again but by the time of the German invasion of Russia, the I-16 was seriously outclassed. Though suffering large losses, the I-16 fought on in the battles of 1941 with the often desperate heroism displayed by the Soviet pilots – some

I-16s are known to have resorted to ramming enemy aircraft in attempts to stem the invasion. It was not until late 1943 that the I-16 was withdrawn from Soviet front-line service.

The I-16 was an excellent fighter for its time period, and fought on long after it should have been retired.

Polikarpov I-16 Type 24

First flight: December 31, 1933
Power: M 62 1000hp radial piston engine
Armament: Four 7.62mm/0.3in machine-guns – two in wings and two synchronized housed in forward fuselage
Size: Wingspan – 8.88m/29ft 1.5in
　　Length – 6.04m/19ft 9.75in
　　Height – 2.41m/7ft 10.75in
　　Wing area – 14.87m²/160sq ft
Weights: Empty – 1475kg/3252lb
　　Maximum take-off – 2060kg/4542lb
Performance: Maximum speed – 490kph/304mph
　　Ceiling – 9470m/31,070ft
　　Range – 600km/373 miles
　　Climb – 850m/2790ft per minute

LEFT: **The Potez 63.11 variant was a tactical reconnaissance/ground version of the series.**

Potez 631

First flight: April 25, 1936 (Potez 630)

Power: Two Hispano-Suiza 725hp 14AB 14-cylinder two row radials

Armament: Two forward-firing 20mm/0.78in cannon and a flexibly mounted 7.5mm/0.3in machine-gun in the rear cockpit plus four 7.5mm/0.3in machine-guns mounted under the wings

Size: Wingspan – 16m/52ft 6in
Length – 11.07m/36ft 10.5in
Height – 3.04m/9ft 11.6in
Wing area – 32.7m²/351.99sq ft

Weights: Empty – 2838kg/6256lb
Maximum take-off – 3760kg/8289lb

Performance: Maximum speed – 442kph/275mph
Ceiling – 10,000m/32,800ft
Range – 1200km/758 miles
Climb – 4000m/13,125ft in 5 minutes, 56 seconds

Potez 630/631

The three-seat Potez 630 was built to a demanding French air ministry specification for a twin-engine strategic fighter and first flew in April 1936. It was for its time a thoroughly modern design, powered by slim engines and boasting the far from standard retractable under-carriage. The first production version was the 630, all 80 of which were grounded for a time due to a series of catastrophic engine failures. Their generally poor performance soon took them into second-line training duties. The 631 however, powered by Gnome-Rhône engines was a great success and over 200 were built for both the Armée de l'Air and the French Navy. During the Battle of France, 631s flying in both day- and nightfighter units accounted for 29 Luftwaffe aircraft. After the fall of France, surviving 631s were for a time operated by Vichy forces but were later seized and passed on to Romania as trainers and target tugs.

LEFT: **The P.Z.L. P.11 was no match for the Luftwaffe fighters it faced in the Blitzkrieg.**

P.Z.L. P.11c

First flight: August 1931

Power: P.Z.L./Bristol Mercury 645hp VI.S2 radial piston engine

Armament: Two 7.7mm/0.303in machine-guns plus light bombs carried beneath wings

Size: Wingspan – 10.72m/35ft 2in
Length – 7.55m/24ft 9.25in Height – 2.85m/9ft 4.25in Wing area – 17.9m²/192.68sq ft

Weights: Empty – 1147kg/2529lb
Maximum take-off – 1630kg/3594lb

Performance: Maximum speed – 390kph/242mph
Ceiling – 8000m/26,245ft
Range – 700km/435 miles
Climb – 800m/2625ft per minute

P.Z.L. P.11

As the Germans prepared to invade Poland in September 1939, the bulk of the poorly organized fighter force that faced them was made up of around 160 P.11s. These aircraft were derived from the Polish-designed P.6 and P.7 fighters that first flew in 1930. Pilot forward view from the cockpit of the P.7 was compromised by the large radial engine that powered it. Smaller diameter engines were tested to improve the view and this together with other refinements led to the P.11 that was produced in three differently engined versions. The major variant was the P.11c powered by Skoda or P.Z.L-built Bristol Mercury radials and deliveries to the Polish Air Force were complete by late 1936.

When the Germans launched their invasion of Poland, the P.11 pilots fought well and made the most of their outmoded machines. Some sources claim that 114 of the P.11s were destroyed in the air battles that raged at the time of the invasion – although the defence failed, the P.11s did destroy 126 Luftwaffe aircraft. A more heavily armed version of the P.11 was tested but finished aircraft did not reach the Polish fighter squadrons before the German invasion.

Reggiane Re.2000 fighters

Development of the Re.2000 began in 1937 and was clearly influenced by the chunky radial-engined fighters being developed in the USA at the time. When the Re.2000 Falco I prototype flew in 1938, the Italian Air Force appeared to show little interest, but the Italian Navy

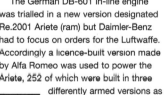

did order Serie II and Serie III versions for catapult launching and long-range missions respectively. The Hungarian Air Force also bought some Re.2000s and a few were manufactured in Hungary under licence – in Hungary the type was known as Hejja (hawk). Sweden also ordered 60 for the Swedish Air Force who operated the type until 1945.

The German DB-601 in-line engine was trialled in a new version designated Re.2001 Ariete (ram) but Daimler-Benz had to focus on orders for the Luftwaffe. Accordingly a licence-built version made by Alfa Romeo was used to power the Ariete, 252 of which were built in three differently armed versions as well as fighter-bomber and nightfighter variants.

Following the Re.2002 fighter-bomber version, the end of the Re.2000 line came with the Re.2005 Sagittario which many consider to be the best Italian fighter of World War II. Powered by an in-line engine, the test flight took place in September 1942, and when it entered production it was powered by a licence-built DB 605. Although only 48 Sagittarios were built before the Allies overran the factories, these fighters were widely used to defend Naples, Rome and Sicily. As the Allies closed in on Berlin, a few fanatical pilots and their Re.2005s even fought on over the city.

TOP: **The US design influence is clear on this study of an early Re.2000.** ABOVE: **A few Re.2000s were exported to Sweden and Hungary; the latter nation also undertook its own production of the type.**
LEFT: **Derivatives of the Re.2000 proved to be very potent fighter aircraft.**

Reggiane Re.2005 Sagittario

First flight: September 1942
Power: Fiat 1475hp RA.1050 RC.58 Tifone in-line piston engine
Armament: Three 20mm/0.78in cannon and two 12.7mm/0.5in machine-guns
Size: Wingspan – 11m/36ft 1in
Length – 8.73m/28ft 7.75in
Height – 3.15m/10ft 4in
Wing area – 20.4m²/219.59sq ft
Weights: Empty – 2600kg/5732lb
Maximum take-off – 3560kg/7848lb
Performance: Maximum speed – 630kph/391mph
Ceiling – 12,000m/39,370ft
Range – 1250km/777 miles
Climb – 1100m/3600ft per minute

Republic P-47 Thunderbolt

When the P-47 first flew in May 1941 it was the largest and heaviest single-seat piston fighter ever produced – it still is. Later versions, when fully loaded, weighed more than a loaded Luftwaffe Dornier Do 17 bomber. It was also produced in greater numbers than any other American fighter and was one of the outstanding US fighters of World War II.

Considerable technical difficulties were overcome in the development of the P-47 – making sure that the massive 3.7m/12ft-diameter propeller cleared the ground was a major concern, calling for very long landing gear which had to retract inwards to leave room for the heavy wing armament of eight 12.7mm/0.5in machine-guns. The deep fuselage was made to accommodate the large pipes and ducts that fed exhaust gas to the turbocharger in the rear fuselage or fed the high-pressure air back to the engine again. Among the cockpit innovations were cabin air-conditioning, variable gun-bay heating and electric fuel indicators.

The P-47B finally entered production in 1942 and Thunderbolts of the US Army Air Force began to arrive in Britain from early 1943 with the task of escorting Eighth Air Force B-17s and B-24s on hazardous daylight bombing raids over Europe. The first P-47 mission was in April 1943 and the "Jug" (short for juggernaut) excelled as a high-altitude escort fighter – in spite of its size it was agile and a favourite of pilots. P-47Cs introduced more powerful engines and provi-

TOP: **The mighty P-47 was a truly big aircraft – compare it to the slender Spitfire.** ABOVE: **This example, based at the Imperial War Museum Duxford in the UK, is a very popular participant in European air shows.**

sion for a belly tank – these auxiliary droppable fuel tanks were carried from March 1944, giving the Jugs the range to get them all the way to Berlin.

Thunderbolts were also formidable ground-attack aircraft and pilots were encouraged to indulge in train-busting for which the robustly constructed aircraft was ideally suited. It was a "get-you-home" aircraft that could absorb considerable damage. P-47s were also widely used by the UK-based US Ninth (tactical) Air Force, escorting their Havocs and Marauders.

The P-47D, produced from early 1943, was the definitive Thunderbolt and featured a host of improvements – a more powerful engine equipped for water injection emergency boost, a more efficient turbocharger, better pilot armour and multi-ply tyres to survive landings on the roughest of airstrips. The D model was also the first able to carry a 454kg/1000lb bomb under each wing as well as a belly tank – with three tanks the Jugs could go deep into enemy territory. Part way into D model production, the bubble canopy was introduced, replacing the old greenhouse type, and the removal of the "razorback" eradicated a blind spot to the rear. Unpainted aircraft were now also supplied from the factories, improving top speed slightly.

A special "hot-rod" version of the P-47D, the P-47M, was built in limited numbers and made its appearance in December 1944, to catch and destroy the V-1 flying bombs that Germany was launching against Allied targets. With a

ABOVE: **An early razorback version of the P-47 with the "greenhouse"-style canopy.**
LEFT: **A P-47 of the 78th Fighter Group, US Eighth Air Force, in World War II.**

top speed of 750kph/470mph, the P-47M had airbrakes fitted to the wings so that it could decelerate once it had caught enemy aircraft. The P-47M certainly scored victories over German Me262 and Arado 234 jets.

The long-range P-47N, the ultimate Thunderbolt, was virtually a complete redesign, with long-span wings containing fuel tanks. Produced from December 1944, it was intended for long-range operations in the Pacific and had square-tipped wings for better roll.

The Royal Air Force also used Thunderbolts from September 1944, but exclusively in the Far East against the Japanese. Sixteen RAF squadrons operated the type in both ground-attack and bomber escort missions but rarely had the opportunity to engage in a dogfight. Two RAF Thunderbolt squadrons continued in service in India until 1946 when the Tempest replaced it in Royal Air Force service.

By the end of World War II the P-47 had flown 546,000 missions and in Western Europe alone destroyed 3752 aircraft in air combat. The Jug was truly one of the greatest fighters ever and continued to equip air forces until the mid-1950s. A total of 15,660 P-47s were produced, of which 12,602 were D models.

LEFT: **The Thunderbolt was equally at home in the low-level ground attack role.** ABOVE: **Preparing for another mission, these "razorbacks" are pictured just after D-Day.**

Republic P-47D Thunderbolt

First flight: May 6, 1941 (XP-47B)
Power: Pratt & Whitney 2535hp R-2800-59 Double-Wasp eighteen-cylinder radial engine
Armament: Eight 12.7mm/0.5in machine-guns, plus provision for external load of bombs or rockets to maximum of 1134kg/2500lb
Size: Wingspan – 12.4m/40ft 9in
Length – 11.02m/36ft 1in Height – 4.47m/14ft 8in
Wing area – 27.87m²/300sq ft
Weights: Empty – 4513kg/9950lb
Maximum take-off – 7938kg/17,500lb
Performance: Maximum speed – 697kph/433mph
Ceiling – 12,495m/41,000ft
Range – 3060km/1900 miles with three drop tanks
Climb – 976m/3200ft per minute

Royal Aircraft Factory S.E.5a

The robust and long-lived S.E.5a was one of the few World War I aircraft to enjoy a lengthy production run, with over 5000 produced in all, compared to, for example, the mere 150 Sopwith Triplanes that entered service. The S.E.5a was developed from the S.E.5, designed to make maximum use of a new Hispano-Suiza engine that appeared in 1915. The unarmed prototype, made almost entirely of wood with a fabric covering, first flew in November 1916. Two versions of the engine (150hp and 200hp) were proposed for the aircraft and although early examples had the 150hp powerplant, the 200hp version soon became the standard engine.

The S.E.5 first entered service with the Royal Flying Corps' No.56 Squadron, but its operational use in France was delayed until April 1917 as a factory-fitted wrap-around windscreen was found to obscure the pilot's forward vision and had to be removed from all machines. About 60 of the 150hp S.E.5s were built but they were gradually replaced on the production line and in the squadrons by the 200hp-engined S.E.5a. Other improvements incorporated in the S.E.5a were shorter wings resulting from the rear spar being shortened for greater strength and a headrest and fairing behind the cockpit to improve pilot comfort and streamlining.

ABOVE: **The widely produced S.E.5a was a true classic fighter.** BELOW: **The air element of the American Expeditionary Force used the S.E.5a with great success.**

The S.E.5a reached front-line squadrons in France in 1917 and was soon found to be capable of outfighting most enemy aircraft. But by December that year, only five RFC squadrons were equipped with the S.E.5a, production delays being caused by the continued slow delivery of engines – literally hundreds of aircraft sat engineless. But when the S.E.5a finally reached the front line in quantity, the very capable fighter served extensively over the Western Front with British, Australian and American pilots of the US American Expeditionary Force. They were also deployed in Macedonia and on home defence duties in the UK. The S.E.5a, together with the Sopwith Camel which appeared a few months later, basically regained and maintained Allied air superiority until the end of the war.

The S.E.5a became the favoured mount of some of World War I's most successful Allied fighter pilots, including British flying ace Albert Ball, who initially described the S.E.5 as a "bloody awful machine". Other S.E.5 aces included Longton, Clayson, Shields, Maxwell, Mannock and McCudden.

LEFT: **Some of the Allies' highest scoring pilots owed their success to the performance of the S.E.5a.**

BELOW: **Victoria Cross recipient Captain Albert Ball pictured in the cockpit of a No.56 Squadron S.E.5a.**

By the time the war ended, 22 RFC and US Air Service units were flying the S.E.5a. Over 5000 had been built in just under 18 months by five companies – Austin, Bleriot & SPAD, Martinsyde, Vickers and Wolseley.

After World War I, hundreds of these fighters were passed on to air forces throughout the British Empire. The American Expeditionary Force had bought 38 S.E.5as in Britain during the war and the design was selected for US production. Wartime plans to licence-build 1000 examples of the S.E.5a in the USA for the US Air Service were scrapped after the Armistice. Only one Curtiss S.E.5a was completed in the USA but 56 more were completed in the 1922-3 period from components shipped from Britain. These were later converted for use as advanced trainers in the USA.

After the end of World War I the fighter was dropped from military inventories and hundreds were sold on to civilian operators. In 1921, one example went to Japan with the British aviation mission and is considered to have greatly influenced later single-seat fighter design in Japan. S.E.5as were also widely used to pioneer the advertising phenomenon of skywriting, spelling out company names in the air using trails of smoke.

LEFT: **Members of No.1 Squadron RAF and their S.E.5as pictured on July 3, 1918.**

Royal Aircraft Factory S.E.5a

First flight: November 22, 1916 (S.E.5)

Power: Wolseley 200hp Viper V-8 water-cooled engine

Armament: One synchronized 7.7mm/0.303in machine-gun, mounted off-centre on top of engine, plus another on a flexible mount in front of cockpit. Four 11.3kg/25lb bombs could be carried under the fuselage

Size: Wingspan – 8.12m/26ft 7.5in
Length – 6.38m/20ft 11in   Height – 2.9m/9ft 6in
Wing area – 22.67m^2/44sq ft

Weights: Empty – 649kg/1430lb
Maximum take-off – 880kg/1940lb

Performance: Maximum speed – 222kph/138mph
Ceiling – 5180m/17,000ft
Range – 2.5 hours endurance
Climb – 3050m/10,000ft in 13.25 minutes

ABOVE: **As well as their use on the Western Front, S.E.5as were also used defending Britain on home defence duties.**

Royal Aircraft Factory F.E. series

The Royal Aircraft Factory first started building the F.E.2 (F.E. stood for Fighter Experimental) in 1913. The F.E.2 was what was known as a pusher aircraft, that is the propeller was used to push from behind rather than pull from the front as in tractor aircraft.

The pusher arrangement was born, in the days before the invention of interrupter gear, of the need for a forward-firing gun

and the removal of the propeller, which tended to get in the way of the bullets. With no propeller in the way, the front seat was given to the gunner/observer while the pilot occupied the rear seat. Disadvantages of the pusher arrangement included the danger of anything flying out of the aircraft hitting the propeller, sometimes damaging or destroying it. Although the engine could protect the pilot if attacked from behind, in the event of a nose-down crash the engine and associated fuel tended to land on top of the two-man crew.

Early Fees, as they were known, had a 100hp engine which was soon replaced in the F.E.2b by a 120hp Beardmore engine. This was itself later supplanted by 160hp Beardmores which improved the aircraft's top speed and performance. The ultimate development of the Fee was the F.E.2d powered by a 250hp Rolls-Royce engine.

In combat the F.E.2b, along with the Airco D.H.2, kept the Fokkers at bay and it was an F.E.2b that shot down the German ace Max Immelmann in June 1916. This version was however soon outclassed by the latest German Albatros and Halberstadt fighting scouts

Royal Aircraft Factory F.E.2b

First flight: August 1913 (F.E.)
Power: Beardmore 120hp in-line piston engine
Armament: Up to two 7.7mm/0.303in machine-guns
Size: Wingspan – 14.55m/47ft 9in
    Length – 9.83m/32ft 3in
    Height – 3.85m/12ft 7.5in
    Wing area – 45.89m²/494sq ft
Weights: Empty – 904kg/1993lb
    Maximum take-off – 1347kg/2970lb
Performance: Maximum speed – 129kph/80mph
    Ceiling – 2745m/9000ft
    Range – 3 hours endurance
    Climb – 3050m/10,000ft in 51 minutes, 45 seconds

so the F.E.2d was brought to the Front in 1916. F.E.2bs did however serve until the end of the war on UK home defence against Zeppelins and Gotha bombers.

ABOVE: **This F.E.2b, serial A5666, is shown minus the usual nosewheel installation.** LEFT: **A rare air-to-air shot of a "Fee" in its element.**
BELOW: **An F.E.2d of No.20 Squadron, Royal Flying Corps, pictured in 1916.**

The single-seat F.E.8 pusher biplane was developed again because of the lack of an effective British interrupter gear and entered service on the Western Front in August 1916. Although lighter and more manoeuvrable than the F.E.2, the F.E.8 was no better as a fighter as the pilot had to deal with the machine-gun (which was prone to stoppages) while still flying the aircraft and looking for the enemy. Nine F.E.8s were effectively destroyed in a single engagement with a formation led by Baron von Richthofen and by mid-1917 all F.E.8s were withdrawn from front-line use.

Royal Aircraft Factory F.E.8

First flight: October 15, 1915
Power: Gnome Monosoupape 100hp rotary
    piston engine
Armament: One 7.7mm/0.303in machine-guns
Size: Wingspan – 9.6m/31ft 6in
    Length – 7.21m/23ft 8in
    Height – 2.79m/9ft 2in
    Wing area – 20.25m²/218sq ft
Weights: Empty – 406kg/895lb
    Maximum take-off – 610kg/1345lb
Performance: Maximum speed – 151kph/94mph
    Ceiling – 4420m/14,500ft
    Range – 2 hours, 30 minutes endurance
    Climb – 1830m/6000ft in 9 minutes, 28 seconds

Siemens-Schuckert D-series fighters

Throughout the history of aviation, good designs have both inspired competitors and been copied by enemies. The Siemens-Schuckert D-series of fighters began in 1916 with the D I that was an improved copy of the Nieuport XI. The arrival of the French fighter was a severe problem for Germany and, as no better aircraft was in the German design pipeline, they decided to copy it instead. Three German companies were ordered to produce improved copies of the Nieuport, and Siemens-Schuckert did the best job. Powered by a 110hp rotary engine and armed with one synchronized 7.9mm/0.31in machine-gun, the D I was otherwise identical to the French aircraft. During early tests in October 1916, the aircraft made an impressive climb to 5000m/16,405ft in 45 minutes. Although 150 aircraft were ordered, engine production problems delayed their delivery and by mid-1917 only 95 had been completed. By then other aircraft with better performance were available and so, when the D I finally made it to the Western Front, it was used mainly for training.

The Siemens-Schuckert D III with its circular section fuselage was built around the new 160hp Siemens-Halske Sh III rotary engine. The D III was derived from D II prototypes that first flew in June 1917. Just like the D I, engine development had delayed the D II programme and unreliability was initially a problem on the D III. However, when the engine's teething problems were resolved, the D III proved to have great potential as an interceptor due its good rate of climb. Unfortunately its level speed was not high enough for it to be a viable modern fighter, so the type was used to trial aerodynamic refinements which led to the D IV fighter version. The D IV had the same impressive climb as

ABOVE. **With its origins in a Nieuport XI copy, the D-series evolved into some worthwhile fighter types.**
LEFT: **A number of D-Series replicas fly in the USA.**

the D III and all round performance was improved. The first of around 60 D IVs to see service reached front-line units in August 1918 but it was a case of too little too late to make a difference. Strangely, production of the D IV was allowed to continue after the Armistice until mid-1919.

Siemens-Schuckert D III

First flight: October 1917
Power: Siemens-Halske 160hp Sh III rotary piston engine
Armament: Two fixed forward-firing 7.92mm/0.31in machine-guns
Size: Wingspan – 8.43m/27ft 7.75in
 Length – 5.7m/18ft 8.5in
 Height – 2.8m/9ft 2.25in
 Wing area – 18.9m²/203.44sq ft
Weights: Empty – 534kg/1177lb
 Maximum take-off – 725kg/1598lb
Performance: Maximum speed – 180kph/112mph
 Ceiling – 8000m/26,245ft
 Range – 2 hours endurance
 Climb – 5000m/16,400ft in 13 minutes

Sopwith Camel

The Camel, arguably the best-known aircraft of the World War I period, is now credited with the destruction of around 3000 enemy aircraft, making it by far the most effective fighter of the War. It evolved from the Sopwith Pup (which it replaced in service) and Triplane but was much more of a handful than its Sopwith stablemates. It was extremely sensitive on the controls and its forward-placed centre of gravity (due to the concentration of the engine, armament, pilot and fuel in the front 2.17m/7ft of the fuselage) made it very easy to turn. It earned a reputation for weeding out the less able student pilots in the most final of ways but in skilled hands the Camel was an excellent fighter and virtually unbeatable. Like the Pup, the Sopwith Biplane F.1 became better known by its nickname, in this case the Camel, and the official designation is largely forgotten.

The prototype, powered by a 110hp Clerget 9Z engine, first flew at Brooklands in February 1917 and was followed by the F.1/3 pre-production model. First deliveries were to the RNAS No.4 (Naval) Squadron at Dunkirk, who received their new fighter in June 1917. The first Camel air victory occurred on June 4, when Flight Commander A.M. Shook sent a German aircraft down into the sea – on the next day Shook attacked 15 enemy aircraft and probably destroyed two of them. The RFC's first Camel victory was achieved by Captain C. Collett on June 27.

TOP AND ABOVE: **Though replicas, these two aircraft salute World War I's most effective fighter aircraft, the Sopwith Camel.**

One manoeuvre unique to the Camel was an incredibly quick starboard turn, assisted by the torque of the big rotary engine. So fast was the right turn that pilots were able to use it to great advantage in combat, sometimes choosing to make three-quarter right turns in place of the slower quarter turn to the left. It was risky, however, as during the sharp right turns, the nose tried to go violently downwards and a left turn brought a tendency to climb, all due to the torque of the engine. Camels were built equipped with a variety of engines, including the Clerget 9B, Bentley BR1, Gnome Monosoupape and Le Rhône 9J.

In the Battle of Cambrai in March 1918, Captain J.L. Trollope of No.43 Squadron used his Camel to shoot down six enemy aircraft in one day, March 24. Later that year Camels were in the thick of what many historians believe to be the greatest dogfight of World War I. On the morning of November 4, 1918 Camels of Nos.65 and 204 Squadrons attacked 40 Fokker D. VIIs. The pilots of No.65 claimed eight

LEFT: **One of the very early Sopwith-built Camel F.1s, serial N6332.** ABOVE: **Major William Barker V.C., D.S.O., M.C., at one time commander of No.28 Squadron, with his personal Camel.**

RIGHT: **Credited with the destruction of around 3000 aircraft – the Camel. Note the Sopwith branding and address on the tail of this Camel.** BELOW: **A portrait of Major William Barker's Camel. Barker scored the first "kill" on the Italian Front, flying in the famous Sopwith fighter.**

destroyed, six out of control and one driven down while the pilots of 204 claimed two destroyed and five out of control. Perhaps the most famous single Camel victory is, however, that of Canadian Camel pilot Roy Brown, who was credited with the death of Manfred von Richthofen, the "Red Baron", on April 21, 1918.

Camels were also operated against the Austro-Hungarians on the Italian Front, and Major William Barker scored the first British victory in that theatre while flying a Camel on November 29, 1917.

By the end of 1917 over 1000 Camels were delivered and work began on sub-variants. Camels that went to sea on the early aircraft carriers had a removable tail for easy stowage. Those specially designed for shipboard use were designated 2F.1 Camel and were the last type of Camel built. Many stayed in use after the war. A ground-attack version with downward-firing Lewis guns was developed – called the TF.1 (trench fighter), it did not go into production.

Nightfighter Camels on home defence duties in the UK were powered by the Le Rhône engine and were armed with two

Lewis guns above the upper wing, in place of the usual twin-Vickers that fired through the propeller arc. They were widely used against the German Gotha bombers. As part of experiments to provide British airships with their own fighter defence, Camels were experimentally launched from a cradle beneath airship R.23.

In addition to the RFC, RNAS and RAF, Camels were also operated by Belgium, Canada, Greece and the air element of the American Expeditionary Force. The Slavo British Aviation Group also operated Camels in Russia in 1918. Total Camel production was around 5500.

Sopwith F.1 Camel

First flight: February 26, 1917

Power: Clerget 130hp 9-cylinder air-cooled rotary piston engine

Armament: Two 7.7mm/0.303in synchronized Vickers machine-guns on nose, plus four 11.35kg/25lb bombs carried below fuselage

Size: Wingspan – 8.53m/28ft
Length – 5.72m/18ft 9in
Height – 2.6m/8ft 6in
Wing area – 21.46m²/231sq ft

Weights: Empty – 421kg/929lb
Maximum take-off – 659kg/1453lb

Performance: Maximum speed – 188kph/117mph
Ceiling – 5790m/19,000ft
Range – 2 hours, 30 minutes endurance
Climb – 3050m/10,000ft in 10 minutes, 35 seconds

LEFT: **The well-armed Sopwith Dolphin.**

Sopwith 5F.1 Dolphin

First flight: May 22, 1917
Power: Hispano-Suiza 200hp piston engine
Armament: Two forward-firing synchronized
7.7mm/0.303in machine-guns plus one or two
machine-guns mounted in front of the cockpit,
fixed to fire obliquely forward
Size: Wingspan – 9.91m/32ft 6in
Length – 6.78m/22ft 3in Height – 2.59m/8ft 6in
Wing area – 24.46m²/263sq ft
Weights: Empty – 671kg/1480lb
Maximum take-off – 911kg/2008lb
Performance: Maximum speed – 180kph/112mph
Ceiling – 6095m/20,000ft
Range – 315km/195 miles
Climb – 260m/855ft per minute

Sopwith Dolphin

By the time the Dolphin first flew in May 1917, Sopwith had produced an impressive line of fighting aircraft, each benefiting from the experiences gained producing earlier models. With the Dolphin, prime design considerations were armament and pilot view from the cockpit. The pilot's all-round view was indeed excellent as his head poked through a gap in the centre section of the top wing which was mounted very close to the deep section fuselage.

The Dolphin Mk I entered service in 1917 and of the 1532 Dolphins produced a small number were also Mk II and Mk IIIs powered by different engines.

Dolphins were apparently not very popular with some pilots – their protruding head was vulnerable in nose-over landing incidents and the unusual back-staggered wing created odd stalling characteristics. Pilots' concerns for their safety led to the addition of a crash pylon above the top wing centre section, to prevent the aircraft slamming on to the top wing. Some pilots ran up impressive tallies of victories in Dolphins, including a Captain Gillett of No.79 Squadron who destroyed 14 enemy aircraft and three balloons.

LEFT: **The Pup was an excellent dogfighter.**

Sopwith Pup

First flight: February 1916
Power: Le Rhône 80hp rotary engine
Armament: One forward-firing synchronized Vickers
7.7mm/0.303 machine-gun, plus up to four
11.3kg/25lb bombs on external racks
Size: Wingspan – 8.08m/26ft 6in
Length – 6.04m/19ft 3.75in Height – 2.87m/9ft 5in
Wing area – 23.6m²/254sq ft
Weights: Empty – 357kg/787 lb
Maximum take-off – 556kg/1225 lb
Performance: Maximum speed – 180kph/112mph
Ceiling – 5335m/17,500ft
Range – 3 hours endurance
Climb – 4911m/16,100ft in 35 minutes

Sopwith Pup

The Pup was the Allies' best answer to the Fokker Scourge and from late 1916 helped them turn the tide on the Western Front. Originally known as the Admiralty Type 9901, it retained the interplane struts (between the upper and lower wing) used on the Sopwith 1½-Strutter, but as its wings were 20 per cent smaller, the nickname of "Pup" was given and eventually kept as the official name. The Pup was manoeuvrable and a fine dogfighter. It entered Royal Naval Air Service (RNAS) and Royal Flying Corps service in 1916, soon earning a reputation as a formidable foe. It was responsive even at high altitude, and fully aerobatic up to 4575m/15,000ft. No.8 (Naval) Squadron accounted for 20 enemy aircraft with the Pup within little over two months in late 1916.

Production of this potent fighter exceeded 1770. Examples powered by the 100hp Gnome Monosoupape rotary engine were used for home defence in Britain, the larger engine markedly improving the Pup's performance.

RNAS Pup's were used to pioneer the use of aircraft from Royal Navy ships – one flown on August 2, 1917 became the first aircraft to land on a ship underway.

Sopwith Snipe

The Sopwith Snipe was the last significant aircraft produced by Thomas Sopwith during World War I. Designed and developed by Herbert Smith in late 1917, the Snipe was an improved version of the Sopwith Camel with a new engine, the 230hp Bentley rotary, which enabled it to fly faster and higher than its predecessor.

The Snipe was, by 1918, considered to be the best Allied fighter plane on the Western Front and was praised by pilots for its speed, strength and agility. The view from the cockpit was much better than that of the Camel which was particularly important on nightflying. Almost 500 Snipes were built in 1918 and eventually 1567 were delivered to the Royal Air Force.

The Snipe introduced a number of innovations including electric cockpit heating and pilot oxygen. Although the Snipe reached the front line only eight weeks before the end of the war, its few encounters with the enemy showed its clear superiority. On October 27, 1918 Major William Barker, in a Snipe of No.201 Squadron RAF, came upon no fewer than 60 Fokker D. VIIs, 15 of which attacked him repeatedly. He took them all on single-handed, destroyed four and probably two others before he crash-landed his bullet-ridden Snipe weak from loss of blood from wounds sustained in his epic aerial battle against seemingly overwhelming odds. Barker was awarded the Victoria Cross for his action.

Sopwith Snipe

First flight: September 1917
Power: Bentley 230hp B.R.2 rotary piston engine
Armament: Two forward-firing synchronized 7.7mm/0.303in machine-guns
Size: Wingspan – 9.17m/30ft 1in
Length – 6.02m/19ft 9in
Height – 2.67m/8ft 9in
Wing area – 25.08m^2/270sq ft
Weights: Empty – 595kg/1312lb
Maximum take-off – 916kg/2020lb
Performance: Maximum speed – 195kph/121mph
Ceiling – 5945m/19,500ft
Range – 3 hours endurance
Climb – 460m/1500ft per minute

After the war the Snipe remained the most important fighter in the RAF, and up until 1923 it constituted Britain's only fighter defence, remaining in service until 1927.

Sopwith Triplane

Following the success of the Sopwith Pup, the Sopwith Triplane was designed and built in 1916 and combined what were thought at the time to be the prime performance requirements for a fighter – high rate of climb and excellent manoeuvrability. In what was

really a daring experiment the new aircraft was built using a fuselage and tail unit similar to that of the Sopwith Pup, a more powerful engine and the all-important extra wing. Although it could not outmanoeuvre the earlier Pup, the Triplane could outclimb any other aircraft, friendly and hostile.

After its first flight in May 1916, the prototype was sent to France immediately for combat trials and became the first triplane fighter on the Western Front. Within only 15 minutes of its arrival in France, it was sent up to attack a German aircraft. Observers were amazed at the Triplane's ability to get to 3660m/12,000ft in only 13 minutes.

The enthusiastic response of its first pilots got the Sopwith rushed into production for service with the Royal Naval Air Service, who flew it with devastating effect between February and July 1917. The all-Canadian "B" Flight (nicknamed "Black Flight") of No.10 Squadron RNAS alone notched up 87 kills in Triplanes in less than 12 weeks. German pilots actively avoided flights of Triplanes. Such was the impact of the Tripehound, as the Sopwith came to be affectionately known, that the German High Command offered a substantial prize for an aircraft of equal capability. Anthony Fokker had set about designing his own triplane before a captured example

TOP: **In a climb, no contemporary fighter could match the performance of the "Tripehound".** ABOVE: **The Royal Naval Air Service was a very effective user of the Triplane.** LEFT: **The Triplane was so impressive in action that the Germans were desperate to develop their own equivalent, which resulted in the Fokker Dr.I Triplane.**

could be examined. It is hard to believe that this small fighter, of which only 140 examples were built, had the upper hand over enemy fighters for so long.

Sopwith Triplane

First flight: May 28, 1916
Power: Clerget 130hp rotary piston engine
Armament: One or two forward-firing synchronized 7.7mm/0.303in Vickers machine-guns
Size: Wingspan – 8.08m/26ft 6in
Length – 5.74m/18ft 10in Height – 3.2m/10ft 6in
Wing area – 21.46m²/231sq ft
Weights: Empty – 499kg/1101lb
Maximum take-off – 699kg/1541lb
Performance: Maximum speed – 188kph/117mph
Ceiling – 6250m/20,500ft
Range – 2 hours, 45 minutes
Climb – 366m/1200ft per minute

SPAD S.XIII

First flight: April 4, 1917
Power: Hispano-Suiza 220hp 8Be piston engine
Armament: Two forward-firing synchronized
  7.7mm/0.303 machine-guns
Size: Wingspan – 8.1m/26ft 6.75in
  Length – 6.3m/20ft 8in
  Height – 2.35m/7ft 8.5in
  Wing area – 20.2m2/217.44sq ft
Weights: Empty – 601kg/1326lb
  Maximum take-off – 845kg/1863lb
Performance: Maximum speed – 215kph/134mph
  Ceiling – 6650m/21,815ft
  Range – 2 hours endurance
  Climb – 2000m/6500ft in 4 minutes, 40 seconds

SPAD S. series fighters

The SPAD (Société Pour l'Aviation et ses Dérivés) S.VII, the French company's first really successful military aircraft, took to the air for the first time in April 1916. It showed such promise that it was put into production immediately. The S.VII was an immediate success, mainly because of its sturdy construction, which permitted it to dive at high speeds without disintegrating. Two engine types were used to power the S.VII – the 150hp Hispano-Suiza 8Aa and the 100hp 8Ac.

By September 1916 it began to appear at the Front in both French and British (Royal Flying Corps and Royal Naval Air Service) fighter squadrons. The sought-after fighter was also operated by the Belgians, the Italians and the Russians. The famed Escadrille Lafayette, made up of American pilots, was operating the SPAD VII in February 1918 at the time it transferred from the French forces to the Air Service of the American Expeditionary Force (AEF) and became the 103rd Aero Squadron. More than 6,000 SPAD S.VIIs were built, of which 189 were purchased by the AEF.

The success of the S.VII inevitably led to developments of the aircraft, such as the S.XIII, designed in 1916 to counter the twin-gun German fighters. It had an increased wingspan and a more powerful engine, plus other aerodynamic refinements. The highly successful S.XIII doubled the firepower of the earlier S.VII by mounting two 7.7mm/0.303in machine-guns. French test pilots enthused about the aircraft and the French government ordered more than 2000 – in the end almost 8500 were built. It began to enter service with French units on the Western Front late in May 1917, replacing S.VIIs and Nieuports, and became the mount of the French aces Nungesser, Fonck and Guynemer.

The Royal Flying Corps operated the S.XIII as did the air forces of Italy and Belgium. The US Air Service also began operating the S.XIII in March 1918, and by the end of the war in November 1918 it had acquired 893. Throughout 1917 and into 1918 the S.XIII held its own against German aircraft, but during the summer of 1918 it was outclassed by the new Fokker D. VII. Nevertheless, at the war's end,

TOP LEFT: **The French "Cicognes" Group de Chasse 12 were famed for the flying stork insignia carried on their aircraft.** ABOVE: **The SPAD S.XIII, a replica in this example, was a great fighter aircraft.** BELOW: **Another distinctive scheme, the famous "hat in the hoop" insignia on this replica SPAD S. XIII was sported by aircraft of the 94th Squadron, US Air Service. This aircraft is painted as the personal aircraft of American ace Eddie Rickenbacker.**

outstanding orders for more than 10,000 examples were cancelled, such had been the demand for this excellent fighter aircraft.

Supermarine Spitfire

The Spitfire is perhaps the most famous combat aircraft of all time, and some would say the most beautiful. Spitfires first entered Royal Air Force service at RAF Duxford in August 1938 and it was on October 16, 1939 that a Spitfire of No.603 Squadron claimed the first German aircraft, a Heinkel He111, to be destroyed over Britain in World War II.

The Spitfire Mk I is the model inevitably associated with Britain's Finest Hour, but by the time the Mark Is were battling to keep the Germans from invading Britain, the Spitfire had undergone a series of modifications that made it quite different to the aircraft that first entered RAF service in 1938. At the start of the Battle of Britain, Fighter Command could field a total of 19 Spitfire squadrons. Although some Mk IIs reached squadron service during the battle, it is the Mk I Spitfire that will forever be considered the Spitfire that won the Battle of Britain. During 1941 the Spitfire Mk I was relegated from the front line but its work was done – the Spitfire had earned a special place in the nation's heart and it had already become a legend.

The Spitfire Mk V began to reach RAF squadrons in February 1941 and swiftly became Fighter Command's primary weapon. Six thousand Mk Vs entered service between 1941 and 1943 and the type equipped more than 140 RAF squadrons, as well as nine overseas air forces, including the USAAF in Europe. Throughout 1941 the Mk V took part in fighter sweeps over occupied Europe, its range boosted by drop tanks. In 1942

TOP: **R.J. Mitchell's classic design, the Supermarine Spitfire, is surely the most famous of all fighters and has earned itself a special place in history, not just for what it achieved but also for what it represented.** ABOVE: **This Mk IX, MH434, is operated in the UK by the Old Flying Machine Company and has delighted crowds at air shows for decades.**

Mk Vs were used in support of the Dieppe landings, fought in the North African campaign, defended Malta, took part in Operation Torch and were supplied to the USSR. In 1943 they even moved as far afield as Australia to defend against attack by Japanese aircraft.

When the Spitfire Mk IX was introduced in June 1942, it offered the RAF a much-needed counter to the deadly Focke-Wulf 190. With its armament of two 20mm/0.788in cannon, four .303 machine-guns and up to 2540kg/1000lb of bombs or rockets, the Spitfire Mk IX was indeed a potent fighting machine.

ADOVE: **The first of many – these early No.19 Squadron machines are shown with two blade propellers and unusual pre-war squadron numbers painted on the tails.** BELOW: **MB882, a late production Mk XII, in classic pose. Note the clipped wings, changing the distinctive "Spit" wing shape for better handling at low altitude.**

ABOVE: **This Mk V, preserved in the UK by the Shuttleworth Collection, was operated by No.310 (Czechoslovakian) Squadron during World War II and is seen in its wartime scheme.**
LEFT: **An excellent wartime photograph of a Spitfire preparing to depart for another sortie.**

The Mk IX went on to equip around 100 RAF and Commonwealth fighter squadrons and later had the distinction of destroying several Me262 jets.

Designed to operate at high altitude, the Spitfire Mk XIV entered RAF service in January 1944 with 610 (City of Chester) Squadron. With a top speed of almost 724kph/450mph, it was capable of catching and destroying the V-1 flying bombs that were then menacing Britain. By the end of the war, the Mk XIV had accounted for more than 300 "doodlebugs". Compared to the early Merlin-engined Spitfire, the Mk XIV with its new fin and larger rudder was almost 1m/3ft longer and weighed up to 1224kg/2700lb more. In October 1944 a Mk XIV claimed a Messerschmitt Me262 jet fighter, the first to be shot down by an Allied aircraft, and in December of that year RAF Spitfire Mk XIVs carried out the heaviest fighter-bomber attack of World War II on V-2 rocket sites. A total of 957 Spitfire Mk XIVs were built, and the later Mk XVIII was directly developed from this powerful fighting machine.

Post-war, the Spitfire was widely used by many air forces but the last operational sortie of an RAF Spitfire was by a PR.19 of No.81 Squadron in Malaya on April 1, 1954. In all, over 20,000 Spitfires and Seafires (the naval version) were built by the time production ceased in 1949.

Supermarine Spitfire Mk Va

First flight: March 5, 1936
Power: Rolls-Royce 1478hp Merlin 45 liquid cooled V 12 engine
Armament: Eight 7.7m/0.303in machine-guns
Size: Wingspan – 11.23m/36ft 10in
Length – 9.12m/29ft 11in
Height – 3.02m/9ft 11in
Wing area – 22.48m²/242sq ft
Weights: Empty – 2267kg/4998lb
Maximum take-off – 2911kg/6417lb
Performance: Maximum speed – 594kph/369mph
Ceiling – 11,125m/36,500ft
Range – 1827km/1135 miles
Climb – 6100m/20,000ft in 7 minutes, 30 seconds

Vickers F.B.5

The Vickers F.B.5, nicknamed "Gun Bus", was directly developed from one of the world's first combat aircraft, the Vickers Destroyer, and was designed to meet a late 1912 British Admiralty specification for a machine-gun armed fighting aeroplane. It was the first British aircraft to mount a machine-gun. The two-seat F.B.5 was, like the F.E.2, a pusher aircraft, that is the propeller was used to push from behind rather than pull from the front. With no propeller in the way, the front seat was given to the gunner/observer while the pilot occupied the rear seat.

Although the first of these planes arrived on the Western Front in February 1915 it was not until July 25, 1915 that No.11 Squadron, Royal Flying Corps, arrived in France. No.11 was the world's first squadron formed for fighting duties and it was equipped throughout with one aircraft type – the Vickers F.B.5.

This slow but strong machine fought well but F.B.5 crews were wise to keep

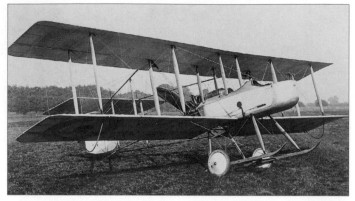

ABOVE: **The relatively slow F.B.5 could be vulnerable. This No.18 Squadron RFC "Gun Bus" was shot down on December 29, 1915 by anti-aircraft fire.** BELOW: **An F.B.5 replica pictured at the Royal Air Force Museum in Britain.**

away from the faster and better-armed Fokker E. Combat reports of the time regularly state that enemy aircraft simply got away due to their better speed.

After a few months of combat the F.B.5 was withdrawn from front-line duties and was used for training purposes back in Britain.

Vickers F.B.5

First flight: October 1914 (production F.B.5)
Power: Gnome Monosoupape 100hp rotary engine
Armament: One 7.7mm/0.303in machine-gun aimed from front cockpit
Size: Wingspan – 11.13m/36ft 6in
Length – 8.2m/27ft 2in Height – 3.51m/11ft 6in
Wing area – 35.5m^2/382sq ft
Weights: Empty – 553kg/1220lb
Maximum take-off – 930kg/2050lb
Performance: Maximum speed – 113kph/70mph
Ceiling – 2745m/9000ft
Range – 386km/240 miles
Climb – 122m/400ft per minute

Westland Whirlwind

The Whirlwind was the Royal Air Force's first single-seat twin-engine fighter and was designed to provide the RAF with a high-performance long-range escort-nightfighter. It was ahead of its time in many ways – the engine radiators were housed in the leading edges of the slim wings, pilot visibility was excellent thanks to the clear bubble hood and the armament housed in the nose was devastating. The Whirlwinds' shape was dominated by the two large engine nacelles, and entry into service was delayed by development troubles with the Peregrine engines they contained.

Whirlwinds first entered front-line Royal Air Force service with No.263 Squadron in December 1940 and it was used on offensive sweeps from June 1941. The aircraft proved to be unpopular with Fighter Command chiefs because it was underpowered and its Peregrine engines, the only ones used in the RAF, had constant servicing problems. Operational flexibility was further limited by the Whirlwind's high landing speed of 129kph/80mph, which required it to operate from long runways.

TOP: **Ahead of its time, the Whirlwind was only operated by two Royal Air Force units.** ABOVE: **Note the hard-hitting armament of four cannon in the nose of this aircraft being prepared for a cross-channel fighter-bomber mission.** RIGHT: **Only 112 Whirlwinds were produced for the RAF.**

Nevertheless, the Whirlwinds of No.263 escorted RAF bombers on daylight raids, the most famous being the Blenheim raid on Cologne in August 1941.

The second Whirlwind unit, No.137 Squadron, used Whirlwinds modified as fighter-bombers (Mark IAs) on low-level cross-Channel missions. By December 1943, both squadrons were re-equipped with other types, and in June 1944 the Whirlwind was declared obsolete.

Westland Whirlwind I

First flight: October 11, 1938
Power: Two Rolls-Royce 885hp Peregrine liquid-cooled piston engines
Armament: Four 20mm/0.78in cannon in nose
Size: Wingspan – 13.72m/45ft Length – 9.98m/32ft 9in
Height – 3.52m/11ft 7in
Wing area – 23.23m²/250sq ft
Weights: Empty – 3556kg/7840lb
Maximum take-off – 4658kg/10,270lb
Performance: Maximum speed – 580kph/360mph
Ceiling – 9144m/30,000ft
Range – Approx. 1290km/800 miles
Climb – 915m/3000ft per minute

Vought F4U Corsair

The Corsair was undoubtedly one of the greatest ever fighters. Designers Igor Sikorsky and Rex Beisel employed the largest propeller and most powerful engine ever fitted to a fighter aircraft, the latter a 2000hp Pratt and Whitney R-2800 Double Wasp. It was no surprise when, in 1940, the prototype Corsair exceeded 640kph/400mph, the first American combat aircraft to do so. It was equipped with a variety of armament over its long career but the Corsair was originally designed to carry two wing and two fuselage guns. Six 12.7mm/0.5in Browning machine-guns became standard, carried in the outer section of the foldable wings. Cannon and rockets were later added to the weapon options.

Ironically, as one of the fastest and most powerful fighters of World War II, the Corsair was originally rejected by the US Navy, who considered it unsuitable for carrier operations. Poor cockpit visibility and a tendency to bounce on landing meant that when, in February 1943 over Guadalcanal, the US Marines got the first chance to use the formidable fighter in action, it was as a land-based rather than carrier-based aircraft. It swiftly established itself as an excellent combat aircraft and the first Allied fighter able to take on the Japanese Zero on equal terms. The Corps was so impressed by the Corsair that all Marine squadrons re-equipped with the type within six months of its début. Marine Corsair pilot Major Gregory "Pappy" Boyington became the Corps' highest scoring pilot, ending the war with a total of 28 victories.

TOP: **The distinctive gull-wing of the Corsair is evident in this photograph of a preserved example.** ABOVE: **Initial US Navy reservations led to the type being considered unsuitable for operation from US carriers.**

By the end of the year the mighty bent-wing fighter, operating purely from land, had accounted for over 500 Japanese aircraft. It was nicknamed "Whistling Death" by Japanese troops, who came to fear the noise made by air rushing through the diving Corsair's cooler vents heralding a deadly attack. By the end of World War II, the Corsair's total tally had increased to 2140 enemy aircraft destroyed in air combat, with over 64,000 air combat and ground attack missions recorded.

The Corsair's first use as a carrier fighter was with Britain's Fleet Air Arm, who had each of the aircraft's distinctive gull-wings clipped by around 20cm/8in to allow its stowage in the below-deck hangars on Royal Navy carriers. This début, in April 1944, was an attack on the German battleship *Tirpitz*. The Corsair became the principal aircraft of the FAA in the Pacific and almost 2000 were supplied to the Royal Navy and the Royal New Zealand Air Force.

"In dogfights the Corsair could out-turn most contemporary aircraft and in a dive, she could out-run anything," said Keith Quilter, FAA Corsair pilot.

The Corsair's outstanding performance led to extensive post-war use, notably in Korea, where they flew 80 per cent of all US Navy and Marine close-support missions in the conflict's first year, 1950. Nightfighter versions were particularly successful during the conflict, and during daytime combats the Corsairs even engaged and destroyed MiG 15s.

When production ceased in 1952, over 12,500 had been built, giving the Corsair one of the longest US fighter production runs in history. The late F2G version was powered by the 3000hp Pratt and Whitney R-4350 Wasp Major engine, which was 50 per cent more powerful than the Corsair's original powerplant.

The Corsair continued to serve in the front line for a number of years, and French naval pilots operated Corsairs from land bases during the anti-guerrilla war against the Viet Minh in Indochina from 1952 to 1954.

The Corsair was built in a number of versions, from the F4U-1 to the F4U-7. The designation differed when aircraft were produced by other manufacturers – Brewster (F3A) and Goodyear (FG, F2G).

BELOW: The space-saving effect of wing folding and the location of the six wing-mounted guns can be seen in this photograph.

TOP: **The Corsair's designers utilized the most powerful engine available.** LEFT: **Fleet Air Arm Corsairs first went into action in April 1944.**

ABOVE: **Royal Navy versions of the Vought fighter had to be slightly clipped for Fleet Air Arm carrier use.**

Vought F4U Corsair

First flight: May 29, 1940
Power: Pratt and Whitney 2000 hp R-2800-8 18-cylinder Double Wasp two-row air-cooled radial engine
Armament: Six 12.7mm/0.5in machine-guns with total of 2350 rounds – C model had four M2 cannon
Size: Wingspan – 12.5 m/41ft
  Length – 10.15m/33ft 4in
  Height – 4.9m/16ft 1in
  Wing area – 29.17 m^2/314sq ft
Weights: Empty – 4074kg/8982lb
  Loaded – 6350kg/14,000lb
Performance: Maximum speed – 671kph/417mph
  Ceiling – 11,247m/36,900ft
  Range – 1633km/1015 miles
  Climb – 951m/3120ft per minute

Yakovlev wartime fighters

The Ya-26 fighter, made mostly of wood, was first flown in March 1939, having been designed to meet a Soviet requirement for a standard Soviet fighter. When it entered production it was as the I-26 but it was then redesignated the Yak-1. Production had barely begun when Germany invaded in June 1941. Designed to be as simple to manufacture as possible, the Yak was surprisingly agile and fast for its time. The Yak-1 had considerably closed the fighter gap that existed at the beginning of Russo-German hostilities and was able to hold its own to some degree with the Bf109. Total production was 8721.

Development was ongoing and the Yak-3 was a further development of a Yak-1 variant now referred to as the Yak-1M. First flown in late 1943, the Yak-3 proved to be an extremely capable dogfighter with outstanding manoeuvrability and a very high rate of climb. When it reached operational units in July 1944, the Luftwaffe knew it had met its match. On July 14, 1944 a force of 18 Yak-3s met 30 German fighters and destroyed 15 Luftwaffe aircraft for the loss of only one of their own. As the more powerful 1700hp VK-107 engine became available, Yakovlev installed a small number into existing airframes and the Yak-3 achieved ultimate capability with a top speed of 720kph/447mph.

TOP, ABOVE RIGHT AND ABOVE: **The Yak-3 was an excellent fighter aircraft that could give a very good account of itself against any enemy aircraft of the time. Since the end of the Cold War, more Yak-3s have been rebuilt to fly for customers in the West.**

Yakovlev Yak-3

First flight: Late 1943
Power: Klimov 1300hp VK-105PF-2 piston engine
Armament: One 20mm/0.78in cannon firing through the propeller hub, plus two synchronized 12.7mm/0.5in machine-guns
Size: Wingspan – 9.2m/30ft 2.25in
　　　Length – 8.49m/27ft 10.25in
　　　Height – 2.42m/7ft 11.25in
　　　Wing area – 14.83m²/159.63sq ft
Weights: Empty – 2105kg/4641lb
　　　Maximum take-off – 2660kg/5864lb
Performance: Maximum speed – 655kph/407mph
　　　Ceiling – 10,700m/35,105ft
　　　Range – 900km/559 miles
　　　Climb – 1300m/4265ft per minute

ABOVE: **Yak-7Bs of the Red Air Force. The B model was built in great numbers, with a total of around 5000 reaching front-line units.** RIGHT: **A Yak-3 of an unknown Soviet fighter regiment.** BELOW RIGHT: **Before it took delivery of Yak-9s, the Free French Normandie-Niemen Group were equipped with Yak-3s.**

The Yak-7 was designed as a dual control fighter trainer and displayed such excellent flying qualities (better than the Yak-1 fighter) that a single-seat fighter version was ordered into production and over 5000 were built in all.

The Yak-9 was designed in parallel with the Yak-3 and was a development of an experimental Yak-7. Production of the Yak-9 began in October 1942 and differed from the earlier Yak by having light metal alloy spars in the wings.

The type became a significant factor in the air battles over Stalingrad where it met and outclassed the Messerschmitt Bf109G. The Free French Normandie-Niemen Group that flew with the Soviet Air Force and Free Polish squadrons were both equipped with the Yak-9. By mid-1943, the aircraft was incorporating more and more aluminium to save weight and increase strength. Fitted with increasingly more powerful versions of the VK-105 engine, the various variants include the standard Yak-9M, the long-range Yak-9D. The very long-range Yak-9DD was used to escort USAAF bombers and some even flew from the Ukraine to southern Italy to aid partisans.

The final major variant of the Yak-9 was the all-metal Yak-9U, first flown in December 1943, that entered service in the latter half of 1944. At first the Yak-9U was fitted with the VK-105PF-2 engine but the VK-107A engine was introduced later giving a maximum speed of 698kph/434mph. Even the early -9Us were able to outfly any fighters the Germans cared to field. The Yak-9 remained in production well into 1946 and was the most numerous of all the wartime Yak fighters with 16,769 built. When the Korean War began in 1950, the post-war cannon-armed Yak-9P was the most advanced fighter in the North Korean Air Force inventory.

Total production of the wartime Yak fighter series was in excess of 37,000.

Yakovlev Yak-9U

First flight: Late 1943
Power: Klimov 1650hp VK-107A in-line piston engine
Armament: One 20mm/0.78in cannon firing through hub plus two 12.7mm/0.5in machine-guns and two 100kg/220lb bombs under wings
Size: Wingspan – 9.77m/32ft 0.75in
Length – 8.55m/28ft 0.5in
Height – 2.96m/9ft 8.5in
Wing area – 17.25m²/185.68sq ft
Weights: Empty – 2716kg/5988lb
Maximum take-off – 3098kg/6830lb
Performance: Maximum speed – 698kph/434mph
Ceiling – 11,900m/39,040ft
Range – 870km/541 miles
Climb – 1500m/4920ft per minute

A–Z of Modern Fighter Aircraft

1945 to the Present Day

By the end of World War II, piston-engined fighters had been developed as far as they could go. Although many remained in service for some years, jet fighters were clearly the way ahead and effectively rendered the piston fighter obsolete. After limited use towards the end of World War II, jets were within a decade regularly flying at supersonic speeds, if only in dives. Wartime German aerodynamic research and experiments revolutionized post-war fighter design, and as swept-wing fighters began to appear, supersonic flight became routine. Many of the fighters featured in the following pages were conceived in the Cold War to tackle fleets of enemy bombers carrying deadly nuclear cargoes. These sophisticated fighters were sometimes bigger than World War II bombers and weighed more than 20 times as much as World War I fighters. Some were never used in anger, possibly serving to deter their enemy from attack, while others have been used many times in conventional wars around the globe.

New ideas for fighter configurations, new materials and construction techniques, and even more complex on-board systems will shape the fighter aircraft of the future.

LEFT: **Lockheed P-80A Shooting Star, the first US jet fighter in military service.**

LEFT: **The US design influence on the Ching-kuo is clear in this photograph.**

AIDC Ching-kuo

First flight: May 28, 1989
Power: Two International Turbofan Engine Company 4269kg/9400lb afterburning-thrust TFE1042-70 turbofans
Armament: One 20mm/0.78in cannon, plus six hardpoints for a variety of AAMs, anti-ship missiles and bombs
Size: Wingspan – 8.53m/28ft
Length – 13.26m/43ft 6in
Height – 4.65m/15ft 3in
Wing area – 24.3m²/261.1sq ft
Weights: Empty – 6485kg/14,300lb
Maximum take-off – 12,245kg/27,000lb
Performance: Maximum speed – 1295kph/804mph
Ceiling – 16,470m/54,000ft
Range – Approx. 965km/600 miles
Climb – 15,250m/50,000ft per minute

AIDC Ching-kuo

Also known as the Indigenous Defensive Fighter (IDF), the Ching-kuo (named after the late President Chiang Ching-kuo) was built in Taiwan with major technical help from US companies, notably General Dynamics. The aircraft bears more than a passing resemblance to the F-16 and is essentially a smaller version of the famous General Dynamics fighter. Development began after a 1982 arms embargo by the USA was imposed (to improve relations with China), prohibiting the import by Taiwan of US fighter aircraft. It did not however prohibit technical help, which is why the Ching-kuo is an F-20A Tigershark nose married to the body, wings and fin of an F-16.

Taiwan wanted the IDF to replace ageing F-5 and F-104 Starfighter fighters – the IDF accelerates faster than the F-104 and can turn inside an F-5. The prototype first flew in May 1989, deliveries to the Republic of China Air Force began in January 1994 and the last of 130 examples was delivered in January 2000.

Armstrong Whitworth Meteor nightfighters

LEFT: **The NF.11 was the first Meteor nightfighter, and was built until 1954.**

Armstrong Whitworth Meteor NF.11

First flight: May 31, 1950
Power: Two Rolls-Royce 1588kg/3500lb static-thrust Derwent 8 turbojet engines
Armament: Four 20mm/0.78in cannon mounted in wings
Size: Wingspan – 13.11m/43ft
Length – 14.78m/48ft 6in Height – 4.24m/13ft 11in
Wing area – 34.75m²/374sq ft
Weights: Empty – 5451kg/12,091lb
Maximum take-off – 9088kg/20,035lb
Performance: Maximum speed – 933kph/580mph
Ceiling – 12,192m/40,000ft
Range – 1480km/920 miles
Climb – 9144m/30,000ft in 11 minutes, 12 seconds

Wartime Mosquitos were Britain's nightfighter defence from the end of the war until Meteor (and Vampire) nightfighters entered service in 1951.

The Meteor NF.11 was built as a stop-gap while delays of the all-weather Javelin dragged on. The NF.11 was basically a Meteor Mk 7 trainer with the new AI Mk 10 radar in an enlarged nose. The rear cockpit's dual-controls were replaced by navigator/radar operator equipment and displays. Cannon were moved from the nose out to the long span wing. The Meteor 8's tail completed the composite nightfighter which first flew in May 1950. Derwent 8s were the chosen powerplant and 335 NF.11s were produced up to 1954. The tropicalized version of the Mk 11 was the Mk 13, 40 of which were built – they only served with two RAF units in the Middle East and six were later sold on to Egypt.

The Mk 12 had improved American APS-21 radar and first flew in April 1953 powered by Derwent 9s – altogether 97 of these were built.

The Meteor NF.14 was the last of the line and can be identified by its clear vision two-piece canopy – the aircraft was also some 43.2cm/17in longer than previous NF marks. It was an NF.14 of No.60 Squadron in Singapore that flew the RAF's last Meteor sortie in 1961.

Armstrong Whitworth built a total of 547 Meteor nightfighters.

Armstrong Whitworth (Hawker) Sea Hawk

The Sea Hawk is remarkable for two reasons – it was the first standard jet fighter of Britain's Fleet Air Arm and it remained in front-line service long after swept-wing fighters equipped navies elsewhere. Also, the aircraft's layout was unusual in that the single jet engine jet pipe was bifurcated (split) to feed two exhaust ducts, one at each trailing-edge wing root. The leading-edge wing roots incorporated the two corresponding air intakes.

The first incarnation of the Sea Hawk was the Hawker P.1040, which flew in September 1947 and was proposed as a new fighter for both the Royal Navy and the RAF. Only the Navy placed orders for the Sea Hawk and after building just 35 production Sea Hawk fighters, Hawkers transferred production to Armstrong Whitworth, hence the

occasional confusion over the Sea Hawk manufacturer's identity. As a design the Sea Hawk certainly looked right, coming from the same team that designed the Hurricane and, later, the Hunter.

The first Royal Navy Sea Hawk squadron, No.806, formed in March 1953, carrying its distinctive ace of diamonds logo on its Sea Hawk Mk 1s. In February the following year, 806 embarked on HMS *Eagle*. The most widely-used Sea Hawk version was the Mk 3 fighter-bomber, capable of carrying considerable amounts of ordnance under its wings. This change in usage was due to the realization that the Sea Hawk's performance could not match that of potential enemies in air-to-air combat. That said, the Fleet Air Arm's Sea Hawks did see action in the ground-attack role during the 1956 Suez Crisis, with Sea Venoms as fighter escort. The type continued in front-line FAA service until 1960, but some continued in second-line roles until 1969.

Some ex-Royal Navy aircraft were supplied to the Royal Australian and Canadian navies but the biggest export customers were the West German naval air arm, Holland and the Indian Navy.

ABOVE: **The Sea Hawk was the Royal Navy's first standard jet fighter.** LEFT: **Fleet Air Arm Sea Hawks saw action during the Suez Crisis of 1956.**

Dutch aircraft were equipped to carry an early version of the Sidewinder air-to-air missile until their phasing-out in 1964. German Sea Hawks operated exclusively from land bases in the air defence role until the mid-1960s. The Indian Navy's Sea Hawks saw action in the war with Pakistan in 1971 and continued to be flown, remarkably, into the mid-1980s, when they were replaced by Sea Harriers.

Armstrong Whitworth (Hawker) Sea Hawk F. Mk 1

First flight: September 2, 1947 (P.1040)
Power: Rolls-Royce 2268kg/5000lb thrust Nene 101 turbojet
Armament: Four 20mm/0.78in Hispano cannon beneath cockpit floor
Size: Wingspan – 11.89m/39ft
  Length – 12.08m/39ft 8in
  Height – 2.79m/8ft 8in
  Wing area – 25.83m²/278sq ft
Weights: Empty – 4173kg/9200lb
  Maximum take-off – 7355kg/16,200lb
Performance: Maximum speed – 901kph/560mph
  Ceiling – 13,176m/43,200ft
  Range – 1191km/740 miles
  Climb – 10,675m/35,000ft in 12 minutes, 5 seconds

Atlas/Denel Cheetah

The multi-role Cheetah was developed in response to a 1977 United Nations arms embargo against South Africa. At the time, the South Africans were hoping to import combat aircraft to replace their ageing 1960s Mirage IIIs but instead looked to develop and improve the existing airframes. State-owned Atlas already had experience of assembling imported Mirage F1 kits. Arguably the most comprehensive upgrade of the Mirage III achieved anywhere, the result was one of the world's most capable combat aircraft. Though never officially disclosed, the updates were undertaken with the assistance of IAI of Israel who had upgraded their own Mirages to Kfir standard.

Nearly 50 per cent of the airframe was replaced, canard foreplanes, new avionics and weapons systems were added, and more powerful engines were installed in two-seaters.

The first Cheetah unveiled in 1986 was the Cheetah D attack aircraft,

a two-seat upgraded version of the Mirage IIIDZ two-seater. Single-seat Cheetah fighters, declared operational in 1987, were designated EZ and kept the old Mirage SNECMA Atar 9C engine but this version led to the Cheetah C fighter, considered by many to be the ultimate Mirage upgrade. Developed in great secrecy, news of the C model only reached the outside world in the early 1995. With a powerful radar, state-of-the-art cockpit avionics and advanced self-defence systems, the Cheetah C's main armament is indigenous South African air-to-air missiles.

TOP: **The Cheetah is one of the world's most capable combat aircraft.** ABOVE: **The two-seat attack D version was developed from the Mirage IIIDZ.** BELOW: **The Cheetah is the ultimate Mirage III development.**

Atlas/Denel Cheetah EZ

First flight: Believed to be 1986
Power: SNECMA 6209kg/13,670lb thrust Atar 9C turbojet
Armament: One 30mm/1.18in cannon plus V3B Kukri, V3C Darter, Python and Shafrir air-to-air missiles as well as bombs/rockets
Size: Wingspan – 8.22m/26ft 11in
Length – 15.5m/51ft
Height – 4.5m/14ft 9in
Wing area – 34.8m²/374.6sq ft
Weights: Empty – 6608kg/14,550lb
Maximum take-off – 13,700kg/30,200lb
Performance: Maximum speed – 2338kph/1452mph
Ceiling – 17,000m/55,777ft
Range and climb data are not published but likely to be similar to Mirage IIIE, i.e. 1200km/745 miles and 7930m/26,000ft in 3 minutes

Avro Canada CF-100 Canuck

The CF-100 was the first combat aircraft of indigenous Canadian design and had its maiden flight in January 1950. This large and impressive Interceptor was designed very quickly for the Royal Canadian Air Force (RCAF) to operate at night, in all weathers and with great range to protect the vast expanses of Canadian airspace.

The first true fighter version, the Mk 3, entered RCAF service in 1952, armed with eight machine-guns housed in a "belly" pack beneath the rear cockpit. The Mk 4 had a more powerful engine and was armed with wingtip pods, each containing 29 Mighty Mouse air-to-air rockets that could be fired by an on-board computer. Having steered the aircraft on a collision course with

the target using the radar housed in the nose, the computer could then fire the rockets at the optimum range. Additional rockets or guns could be carried in the belly.

In 1957 the joint Canadian/US North American Air Defense Command (NORAD) was established and the RCAF Canucks joined the USAF F-86s, F-89s and F-94s, ranged to protect North America against Soviet incursion from the north. The Canuck's short take-off run allowed it to fly from small airstrips and its good climb rate meant it could reach incoming Soviet aircraft very quickly if needed.

The ultimate CF-100, the Mk 5, had even more powerful engines and a 1.83m/6ft increase in wingspan for better high-altitude performance. Fifty-three of this final version were also supplied to Belgium, where they comprised the 1st All-Weather Interception Wing. These excellent and underrated fighters protected Canadian skies through to 1981.

ABOVE: **A Mk 4B of No.445 Squadron, Royal Canadian Air Force.** LEFT: **The underrated CF-100 was a key Cold War fighter.** BELOW: **This Mk 4 is preserved in the UK by the Imperial War Museum at Duxford.**

Avro Canada CF-100 Canuck Mk 5

First flight: January 19, 1950
Power: Two Orenda 14 3300kg/7275lb thrust turbojets
Armament: 58 Mighty Mouse 70mm/2.75in unguided air-to-air rockets, carried in two wingtip pods, 29 in each
Size: Wingspan – 17.7m/58ft
 Length – 16.5m/54ft 1in
 Height – 4.72m/15ft 7in
 Wing area – 54.8m^2/591sq ft
Weights: Empty 10,478kg/23,100lb
 Maximum take-off – 16,783kg/37,000lb
Performance: Maximum speed – 1046kph/650mph
 Ceiling – 16,460m/54,000ft
 Range – 1046km/650 miles
 Climb – 9144m/30,000ft in 5 minutes

BAE Systems Harrier/Sea Harrier

The Harrier is among the best examples of British innovation in the field of aircraft design. This truly remarkable aircraft, constantly improved and updated since its first hovering flight in October 1960, is still the only single-engined vertical or short take-off and landing (V/STOL) in service. It enables military planners to wield air power without the need for airfields.

During the Cold War it was obvious that the West's military airfields would have been attacked very early in any offensive. Dispersal of aircraft and equipment was one option of

response – the other was the Harrier, with its ability to operate from any small piece of flat ground. The Harrier is equally at home operating from a supermarket car park or woodland clearing as it is from conventional airfields. The fact that an aircraft can take off vertically with no need for forward movement still leaves spectators stunned over four decades after the prototype carried out its first uncertain and tethered hover.

The Harrier can take off and land vertically by the pilot selecting an 80-degree nozzle angle and applying full power. At 15–30m/50–100ft altitude, the nozzles are gradually directed

ABOVE: **Two Royal Navy Sea Harrier FRS. Mk 1s. Developed from the land-based Harrier, the naval versions of the type have been a great success.** LEFT: **Although it has an air-to-air combat facility, the Harrier GR.7 is a versatile all-weather ground-attack aircraft.**

rearwards until conventional wingborne flight is achieved. The key to the Harrier's vertical take-off lies with the vectored thrust from the aircraft's Pegasus engine, directed by four jet nozzles controlled by a selector lever next to the throttle in the cockpit. The nozzles swivel as one, directing thrust from directly to the rear to just forward of vertical. While hovering or flying at very low speeds, the aircraft is controlled in all planes of movement by reaction control jets located in the nose, wing and tail. These jets are operated by the Harrier's conventional rudder pedals and control column.

The Harrier's agility is legendary and it is able to make very tight turns by using the nozzles. In air combat the nozzles can be used to decelerate the aircraft rapidly so that an enemy aircraft, previously on the Harrier's tail, shoots by, unable to stop – it becomes the Harrier's prey instead.

The Harrier GR.1 first entered squadron service with the RAF in October 1969 and many were subsequently upgraded to GR.3 standard, with more powerful engines and a tail warning radar to alert pilots to hostile missiles locking on to their aircraft. Early in the Harrier's operational life, the US Marine Corps expressed an interest in the aircraft, leading to more than a hundred being built as the AV-8A by McDonnell Douglas in the USA. The USMC continue to operate Harriers today with the AV-8B variant, which is roughly equivalent to the GR.7 in current RAF service. The other customer for the early Harrier was the Spanish Navy, who ordered the US-built AV-8A and who subsequently sold some of the aircraft on to the Thai Navy in 1996. Manufacture of new AV-8Bs and GR.7s stopped in late 1997, when AV-8Bs were supplied to the Italian Navy. Many existing aircraft are, however, being upgraded to Harrier II Plus standard, allowing the Harrier to carry more weaponry over a greater distance. Improved radar and compatibility with the AMRAAM air-to-air missile can be part of the upgrade.

The Harrier's V/STOL capability was not lost on naval strategists and in February 1963 an early version of the Harrier landed on HMS *Ark Royal* at sea. The Royal Navy ordered a maritime version in 1975 and the Sea Harrier FRS. Mk 1 flew for the first time in August 1978. This aircraft was similar to the GR.3 but had a completely redesigned front fuselage, different avionics and was powered by a special version of the Pegasus engine (104), with improved corrosion resistance. Examples of this version were exported to the Indian Navy as FRS.51s. The Sea Harriers are true fighter aircraft, while the Harriers are close air support aircraft.

The Sea Harrier FA.2 was a mid-life upgrade of the FRS.1, with changes to the airframe, armament, avionics, radar and cockpit. The FA.2 was the first European fighter to be equipped with the AIM-120 AMRAAM air-to-air missile. The Royal Navy's FA.2s made their combat début in August 1994 over Bosnia, operated by No.899 Squadron from the deck of HMS *Invincible*. Early versions of the Sea Harrier, however, had already been in action with the FAA 12 years earlier. In 1982 Britain's Task Force sailed south on its 12,872km/8000 mile journey to retake the Falkland Islands but it faced serious opposition from Argentine forces. Against considerable odds, the combined Harrier force of RAF and Fleet Air Arm pilots and machines flew a total of 1850 missions and destroyed 32 Argentine aircraft, 23 of them in air combat, including high-performance Daggers.

Two-seat trainer versions of all marks have been produced.

ABOVE: **Sea Harrier FA.2s pictured on the deck of Britain's HMS *Illustrious* in 1995.** LEFT: **The Harrier can provide versatile and flexible air power from small unexpected locations.**

ABOVE: **Harriers are still flying more than 40 years after the prototype first took to the sky.** BELOW LEFT: **The distinctive nose of the FA.2 houses the advanced Blue Vixen radar.**

BAE Systems Sea Harrier FA.2

First flight: September 19, 1988

Power: Rolls-Royce 9765kg/21,500lb-thrust Pegasus 106 turbofan

Armament: Four AIM-120 air-to-air missiles or two AIM-120s and four AIM-9 Sidewinders. Two 30mm/1.18in Aden cannon can also be carried on underfuselage stations, as well as up to 2270kg/5000lb of bombs, rockets and anti-ship missiles

Size: Wingspan – 7.7m/25ft 3in
Length – 14.17m/46ft 6in
Height – 3.71m/12ft 2in
Wing area – 18.7m²/201sq ft

Weights: Empty – 6374kg/14,052lb
Maximum take-off – 11,880kg/26,200lb

Performance Maximum speed – 1185kph/736mph
Ceiling – 15,555m/51,000ft
Range – 1300km/800 miles
Climb – 15,240m/50,000ft per minute at VTOL weight

McDonnell Douglas/Boeing F-15

The F-15 Eagle, designed to succeed the legendary F-4 Phantom, is an all-weather, highly manoeuvrable fighter originally designed to gain and maintain US Air Force air superiority in aerial combat. It is probably the most capable multi-role fighter in service today. Between entering service in 1974 and 2000, the F-15 has achieved an unprecedented air combat record with 100.5 victories for zero losses.

The first F-15A flight was made in July 1972, and the first flight of the two-seat F-15B trainer followed in July 1973. The first USAF Eagle (an F-15B) was delivered to the Air Force in November 1974. The first Eagle destined for a front-line combat squadron was delivered in January 1976, and some squadrons were combat-ready by the end of the year.

The Eagle's air superiority is achieved through a mixture of incredible manoeuvrability and acceleration, range, weapons and avionics. It can penetrate enemy defence and outperform and outfight any current enemy aircraft. The F-15 has electronic systems and weaponry to detect, acquire, track and attack enemy aircraft while operating in friendly or enemy-controlled airspace. The weapons and flight control systems are designed so one person can safely and effectively perform air-to-air combat.

The F-15's superior manoeuvrability and acceleration are achieved through high engine thrust-to-weight ratio and low wing loading. Low wing loading (the ratio of aircraft weight to its wing area) is a vital factor in manoeuvrability and, combined with the high thrust-to-weight ratio, enables the aircraft to turn tightly without losing airspeed.

The F-15's avionics system sets it apart from other fighter aircraft. It includes a Head-Up Display, advanced radar, ultra-high frequency communications, and an instrument landing system for automatic landings. The Eagle also has an internally mounted, tactical electronic-warfare system, "identification friend or foe" system, electronic countermeasures set and a central digital computer system.

The Head-Up Display projects on the windscreen all essential flight information gathered by the integrated avionics system. This display, visible in any light condition, provides the pilot with information necessary to track and destroy an enemy aircraft without having to look down at cockpit instruments.

ABOVE: **An F-15E – this two-seat Strike Eagle was based in the UK at RAF Lakenheath.** BELOW: **The F-15 is a world-class fighter with a remarkable combat record. The USAF will operate F-15s for some years to come.**

LEFT: Widely deployed in Europe during the Cold War, the F-15 actually first saw combat in Israeli service in 1977. BELOW: F-15As of the 21st Tactical Fighter Wing based at Elmendorf AFB, Alaska, helped protect North America from an attack over the North Pole.

The F-15's versatile pulse-Doppler radar can look up at high-flying targets and down at low-flying targets, detect and track aircraft and small high-speed targets at distances beyond visual range down to close range and at altitudes down to treetop level. The radar feeds target information into the central computer for effective weapons delivery. For close-in dogfights, the radar automatically acquires enemy aircraft, and this information is projected on the Head-Up Display. The F-15's electronic warfare system provides both threat warning and automatic countermeasures against selected threats.

The single-seat F-15C and two-seat F-15D models entered the USAF inventory from 1977. Among the improvements were 900kg/2000lb of additional internal fuel and provision for "conformal" fuel tanks that fit flush with the fuselage.

The F-15E Strike Eagle, first flight July 1980, is a two-seat, dual-role fighter for all-weather, air-to-air and deep interdiction missions – the rear cockpit is reserved for the weapons systems officer. It can fight its way to a target over long ranges, destroy ground targets and fight its way out. Its engines incorporate advanced digital technology for improved-performance acceleration – from a standstill to maximum afterburner takes less than four seconds.

The F-15's combat début came not with the USAF but with export customer Israel who shot down four Syrian MiG-21s in June 1977. Unconfirmed numbers of Syrian fighters were also shot down by Israeli F-15s in 1982. USAF F-15C, D and E models were in action during the Gulf War where they proved their superior combat capability with a confirmed 36 air-to-air victories. Saudi F-15s also downed Iraqi aircraft in combat. In the 1999 Balkans conflict, USAF F-15s destroyed four Serb MiG-29s.

More than 1500 F-15s have been produced for the USA and international customers Israel, Japan and Saudi Arabia. The F-15I Thunder, a model designed for Israel, has been built in the USA, the first of 25 Thunders arriving in Israel in January 1998.

LEFT: F-15s proved their worth during the Gulf War. Here a Royal Saudi Air Force F-15C is seen refuelling from a USAF tanker.

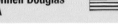

McDonnell Douglas F-15A

First flight: July 27, 1972

Power: Two Pratt & Whitney 11340kg/25000lb afterburning thrust F100-PW-100 turbofans

Armament: One 20mm/0.78in cannon, four AIM-7 Sparrow and four AIM-9 Sidewinder AAMs plus up to 7267kg/16,000lb of other weaponry on five hardpoints

Size: Wingspan – 13.04m/42ft 9.5in
Length – 19.44m/63ft 9.5in
Height – 5.64m/18ft 6in
Wing area – 56.48m²/608sq ft

Weights: Empty – 12,247kg/27,000lb
Maximum take-off – 25,402kg/56,000lb

Performance: Maximum speed – 2655kph/1650mph
Ceiling – 19,200m/63,000ft
Range – 966km/600 miles
Climb – 15,250m/50,000ft per minute

Boeing/McDonnell Douglas/Northrop F/A-18 Hornet

The twin-engine Hornet was developed for the US Navy from the YF-17 project that Northrop had proposed for the US Air Force. As the company had no experience building carrier-borne aircraft, it teamed up with McDonnell Douglas (now Boeing) to develop the F-17. Two versions, ground attack and fighter, were originally proposed but the two roles were combined in the very capable F/A-18, the first of which flew in 1978. With its excellent fighter and self-defence capabilities, the F/A-18 was intended to increase strike mission survivability and supplement the F-14 Tomcat in US Navy fleet air defence.

The F/A-18's advanced radar and avionics systems allow its pilots to shift from fighter to strike mode on the same mission by the flip of a switch, a facility used routinely by Hornets in Operation Desert Storm in 1991 – they fought their way to a target by defeating opposing aircraft and then attacking ground targets. This "force multiplier" capability gives more flexibility in employing tactical aircraft in a rapidly changing battle scenario.

ABOVE: **The remarkable F/A-18 is, at the flip of a switch, a fighter or a strike aircraft. The type was proven in combat during the Gulf War.** LEFT: **The Hornet was originally intended to support the F-14 in defending the US Fleet in the air.**

In addition to air superiority, fighter escort and forward air control missions, the F/A-18 is equally capable in the air-defence suppression, reconnaissance, close air support and strike mission roles. Designed to be reliable and easily maintainable, survivability was another key consideration and was proven by taking direct hits from surface-to-air missiles, recovering successfully, being repaired quickly and flying again the next day.

The F/A-18 Hornet was built in single- and two-seat versions. Although the two-seater is a conversion trainer, it is also combat capable and has a surprisingly similar performance to the single-seat version although with reduced range. The F/A-18A and C are single-seat aircraft while the F/A-18B and D are two-seaters. The B model is used primarily for training, while the D model is the current US Navy aircraft for attack, tactical air control, forward air control and reconnaissance squadrons.

In November 1989, the first F/A-18s equipped with night strike capability were delivered, and since 1991 F/A-18s have been delivered with F404-GE-402 enhanced-performance engines that produce up to 20 per cent more thrust than the previous F404 engines. From May 1994, the Hornet has been equipped with upgraded radar – the APG-73, which substantially increases the speed and memory capacity of the radar's processors. These upgrades and improvements help the Hornet maintain its advantage over potential enemies and keep it among the most advanced and capable combat aircraft in the world.

Apart from the US Navy and Marine Corps, the F/A-18 is also in service with the air forces of Canada, Australia, Spain, Kuwait, Finland, Switzerland and Malaysia.

ABOVE: **The twin fins canted at 30 degrees are a prime recognition feature of the F/A-18.** LEFT: **A US Marine Corps F/A-18D. This versatile version is equipped for improved weapons delivery and has better radar and more effective armament.**

Canada was the first international customer for the F/A-18, and its fleet of 138 CF-18 Hornets is the largest outside the United States. The CF-18s have an unusual element to their paint scheme in that a "fake" cockpit is painted on the underside of the fuselage directly beneath the real cockpit. This is intended to confuse an enemy fighter, if only for a split second, about the orientation of the CF-18 in close air combat. That moment's hesitation can mean the difference between kill or be killed in a dogfight situation.

The manufacturers have devised a life extension programme that will keep the Hornet in the front line until 2019.

The F/A-18E/F Super Hornet was devised to build on the great success of the Hornet and, having been test flown in November 1995, entered service for evaluation with US Navy squadron VFA-122 in November 1999. It was approved for US Navy service and the first Super Hornet fleet deployment was scheduled for 2002. Export versions were expected to be available in 2005. The Super Hornet is 25 per cent larger than its predecessor but has 42 per cent fewer parts. Both the single-seat E and two-seat F models offer increased range, greater endurance, more payload-carrying ability and more powerful engines in the form of the F414-GE-400, an advanced derivative of the Hornet's current F404 engine family that produces 35 per cent more thrust.

Structural changes to the airframe increase internal fuel capacity by 1633kg/3600lb which extends the Hornet's mission radius by up to 40 per cent. The fuselage is 86.3cm/34in longer and the wing is 25 per cent larger with an extra 9.3m²/100sq ft of surface area. There are two additional weapons stations, bringing the total to 11.

In the words of its manufacturers "The Super Hornet is an adverse-weather, day and night, multi-mission strike fighter whose survivability improvements over its predecessor make it harder to find, and if found, harder to hit, and if hit, harder to disable".

ABOVE: **US Marine Corps F/A-18 Hornets of VFA-25, pictured on the deck of USS *Independence* in 1991.**

Boeing/McDonnell Douglas/Northrop F/A-18C Hornet

First flight: November 18, 1978
Power: Two General Electric 7267kg/16,000lb thrust F404-GE-400 turbofans
Armament: One 20mm/0.78in cannon, nine hard points carrying up to 7031kg/15,500lb of weapons including AIM-7, AIM-120 AMRAAM, AIM-9 air-to-air missiles or other guided weapons, bombs and rockets
Size: Wingspan – 11.43m/37ft 6in
Length – 17.07m/56ft
Height – 4.66m/15ft 3in
Wing area – 37.2m²/400sq ft
Weights: Empty – 10,455kg/23,050lb
Maximum take-off – 25,400kg/56,000lb
Performance: Maximum speed – 1915kph/1189mph
Ceiling – 15,250m/50,000ft
Range – 3336km/2027 miles
Climb – 13,725m/45,000ft per minute

British Aircraft Corporation/English Electric Lightning

When the very high-performance Lightning joined front-line squadrons in 1960, it gave the RAF an interceptor capable of a performance way beyond any of its predecessors. During a lengthy development and testing programme, the Lightning became the first aircraft to exceed the speed of sound in level flight over the UK. With a top speed of around 2.5 times the speed of sound and a climb rate that few fighters have ever equalled, the Lightning was the fastest British fighter ever.

Design work for the aircraft began in 1947, when English Electric were awarded a study contract for a supersonic research aircraft. Extensive research into swept-wing fighters had been carried out in German wind tunnels during World War II, and the English Electric designers looked carefully at the data. The fruit of the study was the P.1A, which first flew in August 1954 and soon exceeded Mach 1, the speed of sound. The aerodynamics of the aircraft were considered to be so complex that Britain's first transonic wind tunnel was constructed to help with development. A scaled-down flying test bed was also built by Short Brothers to test the various swept-wing and tailplane configurations.

ABOVE: **XS897, a Lightning F.6 of No.56 Squadron, pictured in 1975. Note the phoenix and flames unit badge on the tail and the 1930s era chequerboard design by the roundel.** BELOW: **Range was always an issue with the Lightning – this F.3 has overwing ferry tanks as well as a large ventral fuel tank.**

The design was eventually refined and became the P.1B, powered by Avon turbojets, the two engines mounted one above the other with the nose acting as one large air intake. In November 1958, fitted with afterburning Avons, the P.1B topped Mach 2 for the first time. The Lightning, as it was then

LEFT: **Demonstrating the Lightning's unusual outboard retraction of the undercarriage, this aircraft has its burners lit and is preparing to go vertical.** BELOW: **This F.6, XS928, was based at RAF Binbrook for the last years of its RAF service.** BOTTOM: **The Lightning was the last all-British-built fighter in RAF service.**

called, was cleared for service shortly afterwards. The first RAF unit to receive the new Lightning was No.74 Squadron, based at Coltishall.

The Lightning was a relatively complicated aircraft compared to its predecessors, but it did give the RAF an all-weather fighter that could have held its own with any other fighters of the time. The radar, housed in the cone at the entrance to the air intake, could search above and below the horizon, take the aircraft to within firing range of a target and then automatically loose off two Firestreak or Red Top air-to-air missiles. Thus the Lightning was the RAF's first single-seat fighter integrated weapons system, as opposed to a simple gun platform.

Modifications to the Lightning throughout its service life improved its performance and it remained a viable air defence weapon until its retirement. When the F. Mk 1A was introduced it included an inflight refuelling capability, giving the Lightning the ability to transit over long distances such as the North Sea. The Lightning Mk 6 had a new wing that improved the aircraft's performance to the point where the fuel load could be doubled without significantly affecting performance.

A two-seat version, the T. Mk 5, was developed as a trainer and first flew in March 1962, accommodating the instructor and pupil side by side with duplicated instruments and controls. The change to the forward fuselage profile did nothing to slow the version down, as it was still capable of achieving Mach 2.3. Tornado F.3s finally replaced the last RAF Lightnings in 1988.

Saudi Arabia and Kuwait both operated export versions of the F. Mk 6, which served in the multi-role fighter and ground-attack roles. In 1969, Saudi Lightning F.53s flew ground-attack missions against targets in Yemen.

The Lightning was the last solely UK-designed fighter to enter RAF service and is considered by many to be the peak of UK fighter development.

BAC Lightning F. Mk 6

First flight: April 4, 1957 (P.1B)

Power: Two Rolls-Royce 7420kg/16,360lb-thrust Avon 301 afterburning turbojets

Armament: Two Red Top or Firestreak infra-red homing air-to-air missiles or two batteries of 22 50mm/2in unguided rockets. Twin 30mm/1.18in Aden cannon can also be carried in a ventral pack

Size: Wingspan – 10.62m/34ft 10in
Length – 16.84m/55ft 3in, including probe
Height – 5.97m/19ft 7in
Wing area – 42.97m^2/458.5sq ft

Weights: Empty – 12,717kg/28,041lb
Maximum take-off – 19,047kg/42,000lb

Performance: Maximum speed – 2112kph/1320mph
Ceiling – 16,770m/55,000ft
Range – 1290km/800 miles
Climb – 15,240m/50,000ft per minute

Convair F-102 Delta Dagger

In 1950 the US Air Force invited designs for a fighter that could exceed the performance of known Soviet bombers, but this aircraft would be ground-breaking because it was going to be just one part of a weapon package built around the Hughes Electronic Control System. The successful proposal came from Convair and led to the first fighter to be developed as part of an integrated weapons system, the F-102, and ultimately the F-106. Convair's design had an unorthodox delta (triangular) wing, which was, it turned out, a little ahead of its time. The company had some experience of deltas already, having produced the experimental XF-92 research aircraft inspired by the German wartime deltas of Dr Alexander Lippisch.

Development delays with the proposed Wright J67 engine and the various electronic "black boxes" forced the USAF to ask Convair to develop an interim version of the proposed new fighter, which was then designated F-102. The original design progressed to become the F-106. Far from being a spin-off or a poor relation, the F-102 became a very able combat aircraft and was the first fighter armed only with missiles, the AIM-4 and AIM-26 Falcon.

The F-102's development was far from painless – during its maiden flight in October 1953 it became apparent that the aircraft was incapable of exceeding the speed of sound in level flight, which had been a basic requirement from the

USAF. The design team had literally to go back to the drawing board to overcome the high levels of transonic drag. The fuselage was lengthened by 1.21m/4ft, the air intakes and the fin were made bigger and the wing was modified too. By then the Pratt and Whitney J57 engine had been chosen, to help

TOP: **The F-102 came about as an interim version of the F-106 but was a potent fighter in its own right.**
ABOVE: **A total of 875 F-102s were delivered to the US Air Force.**

the aircraft punch through the sound barrier. Test flights beginning in December 1954 showed the modifications had worked and the design could indeed fly faster than Mach 1. The first production version flew in June 1955, and the F-102 finally entered USAF service in April 1956, three years later than planned. In doing so it became the first supersonic delta-winged aircraft to reach operational status.

By 1958, 26 squadrons of F-102s equipped the USAF's Air Defense Command but this was the peak. The 102 was always seen as an interim aircraft by the USAF, plugging the gap while the F-106 was developed. The F-102 did, however, continue in the front line with the USAF in Europe, Alaska and the Pacific for some years and was the main fighter equipment of the Air National Guard through to the early 1970s. The last Air Defense Command unit to operate the F-102 was the 57th Fighter Interception Squadron, based at Keflavik in Iceland, who finally relinquished their machines in April 1973.

In the F-102 cockpit the pilot had two control columns to handle – one managed the aircraft's movements, while the other was used to control the impressive on-board radar, which could pick up an enemy aircraft and direct the aircraft to the target. Pilots then had to choose their weapons from between small unguided rockets, carried within the doors of the weapons bay, or Falcon air-to-air missiles, one of which could have been nuclear-tipped. The Falcons were stored in the aircraft's internal weapons bay until the pilot or the fire control system extended them for firing.

Exported models of ex-USAF Delta Daggers were supplied to the air forces of Greece and Turkey in the early 1970s. Around 200 ex-USAF F-102s also became pilotless target aircraft, helping the USAF's "top guns" perfect their weapon skills in the air and not in the classroom.

TOP: **This F-102A served with the 82nd Fighter Interception Squadron on Okinawa, Japan, and bears a typical camouflage scheme of the era.** ABOVE: **With its internal missile bays open, this F-102 shows some of the armament that made the Delta Dagger such a potent interceptor.**

Convair F-102A Delta Dagger

First flight: October 24, 1953

Power: Pratt and Whitney 5307kg/11,700lb (7802kg/17,200lb afterburning) thrust J57P-23 turbojet

Armament: Three AIM-4C Falcon infra-red homing air-to-air missiles and one AIM-26A Nuclear Falcon or three AIM-4A semi-active radar homing and three AIM-4C infra-red air-to-air missiles

Size: Wingspan – 11.62m/38ft 1.5in
Length – 20.84m/68ft 5in
Height – 6.46m/21ft 2.5in
Wing area – 61.45m²/661.5sq ft

Weights: Empty – 8630kg/19,050lb
Maximum take-off – 14,288kg/31,500lb

Performance: Maximum speed – 1328kph/825mph
Ceiling – 16,460m/54,000ft
Range – 2173km/1350 miles
Climb – 5304m/17,400ft per minute

Convair F-106 Delta Dart

Initially designated F-102B, the F-106 was conceived as the ultimate interceptor. Delayed engine and electronic development for what became the F-106 forced the development of the interim F-102. While the F-102 was developed, the USAF refined its requirements for the new super-fighter – it had to intercept enemy aircraft in all weathers up to 21,335m/70,000ft and be capable of Mach 2 interceptions up to 10,670m/35,000ft. Prototype flights between December 1956 and February 1957 were disappointing and the USAF almost scrapped the whole programme. Instead they reduced the order from

1000 aircraft to 350 to save spiralling costs. Engine and avionics improvements brought the F-106 up to an acceptable standard and the type entered operational service as the F-106A in October 1959. Production ceased in December 1960 but the F-106 remained in front-line service for more than 20 years thanks to constant updating programmes – it was finally phased out of Air National Guard service in 1988.

The F-106's Hughes MA-1 fire control system essentially managed all interceptions from radar-lock to missile firing while the pilot simply acted as a

systems supervisor. Among the weaponry were two devastating Genie nuclear-tipped air-to-air missiles carried in an internal bomb-bay, which the computer would instruct the pilot to arm just prior to firing.

From 1973 F-106s were equipped with a multi-barrel "Gatling-gun" rotary cannon, reflecting the realization that fighters might once again need to tackle an enemy in close combat and not just from a stand-off position using long-range missiles. Pilots say the F-106 was a delight to fly and at its peak the F-106 equipped 13 US Air Defense Command squadrons.

TOP: **A fine air-to-air photograph of a New Jersey Air National Guard F-106A. The bump on the fuselage forward of the windscreen is a retractable infra-red detector.** ABOVE: **This F-106 is believed to have been used by NASA for some unmanned drone missions after its retirement from USAF Air Defense Command.**

Convair F-106A Delta Dart

First flight: December 26, 1956

Power: Pratt & Whitney 11,113kg/24,500lb afterburning-thrust P-17 turbojet engine

Armament: One 20mm/0.78in cannon, four Falcon AAMs, plus two Genie unguided nuclear rockets

Size: Wingspan – 11.67m/38ft 2.5in
Length – 21.55m/70ft 8.75in
Height – 6.18m/20ft 3.3in
Wing area – 64.8m²/697.8sq ft

Weights: Empty – 10,800kg/23,814lb
Maximum take-off – 17,350kg/38,250lb

Performance: Maximum speed – 2393kph/1487mph
Ceiling – 17,680m/58,000ft
Range – 3138km/1950 miles with external tanks
Climb – 9144m/30,000ft per minute

Dassault Mystère/Super Mystère

LEFT: **Unusually, the Mystère IVs that joined the Armée de l'Air in 1955 were funded by the USA under a NATO Assistance Programme.**
BELOW: **A Super Mystère B2 of an Armée de l'Air "Tiger squadron" – not a usual paint scheme.**

Developed from the Dassault Ouragan, France's first jet fighter, the Mystère was essentially an Ouragan with swept wing and tail surfaces, and first flew in 1951.

The production version, the Mystère II, was one of the first swept-wing aircraft in production in Western Europe and entered Armée de l'Air service between 1954 and 1956, powered by the SNECMA Atar, the first French turbojet engine to be used in military aircraft. A Mystère IIA was the first French aircraft to break Mach 1 in controlled flight (in a dive), on October 28, 1952. The Armée de l'Air ordered 150 Mystère IICs and the last was delivered in 1957, by which time the type was already being relegated to advanced training duties. Even as the Mystère was becoming operational, the better Mystère IV was already flying. Mystère IIs remained in use as advanced trainers until 1963.

The Mystère IV was a new aircraft, having few common parts with the Mark II and had a new oval-section fuselage, thinner wings with greater sweep, and new tail surfaces. The first prototype was flown in September 1952, powered by an Hispano-built Rolls-Royce Tay 250 turbojet engine, as were the first 50 production examples – later examples were powered by the Hispano-Suiza Verdon. The production contract for 225 Mystère IVAs for the Armée de l'Air was paid for by the United States as part of the NATO Military Assistance Program. The first production Mystère IVA flew in late May 1954 and the type entered

service with the Armée de l'Air the following year. The Mystère IVA remained a first-line fighter with the Armée de l'Air until the early 1960s but continued to serve as an operational trainer until 1980.

Sixty Verdon-powered Mystère IVAs ordered by the French were sold on to Israel and the first batch of 24 arrived in April 1956, just in time for the war in October. In the hands of skilled Israeli pilots, they proved more than a match for Egyptian MIG-15s. The Indian Air Force also bought 110 all-new production Verdon-powered Mystère IVAs. First delivered in 1957, they were used in the close-support role during the 1965 Indo-Pakistan War.

The ultimate Mystère was the Super Mystère, which like the Mystère IV was largely a new aircraft. It was bigger and heavier than previous Mystères and was the first European production aircraft capable of transonic flight. The first prototype flew in March 1955 and had wings with a 45-degree sweepback and an F-100-like oval air intake. The prototype exceeded Mach 1 in level flight the day after it first took to the air. A total of 180 Super Mystère B2s were built for the Armée de l'Air, and the last was delivered in 1959. They were relegated to the attack role once the Mirage III was available and remained in French service

until late 1977. In 1958, 36 Super Mystères bought by the French were sold on to the Israelis who used them to counter the MiG-19s favoured by Arab nations. In the early 1970s, the Israelis upgraded surviving Super Mystères by retrofitting a non-afterburning Pratt & Whitney J52-P8A turbojet engine and 12 of these uprated Super Mystères were sold to Honduras, who operated them until 1989, when the operational career of the Mystère series came to an end.

Dassault Mystère IVA

First flight: February 23, 1951 (Mystère prototype)
Power: Hispano-Suiza 3500kg/7716lb-thrust Verdon 350 turbojet engine
Armament: Two 30mm/1.18in cannon, plus two 454kg/1000lb bombs or 12 rockets
Size: Wingspan 11.12m/36ft 6in
 Length – 12.85m/42ft 2in
 Height – 4.6m/15ft 1in
 Wing area – 32m^2/344.46sq ft
Weights: Empty – 5886kg/12,950lb
 Maximum take-off – 9500kg/20,944kg
Performance: Maximum speed – 1120kph/696mph
 Ceiling – 15,000m/49,200ft
 Range – 912km/570 miles
 Climb – 2700m/8860ft per minute

Dassault-Breguet Mirage 2000

In December 1975 Dassault got the green light to proceed with what became the Mirage 2000 programme to develop a replacement for the Mirage F.1. With this design, Dassault revisited the delta wing shape of the Mirage III series and brought greatly improved manoeuvrability and handling thanks to fly-by-wire systems and a much greater knowledge of aerodynamics. Although the Mirage 2000 looks very similar to the Mirage III series, it is an entirely new aircraft. The prototype first flew in March 1978 and service deliveries began in 1983. For its secondary ground-attack role, the Mirage 2000 carries laser guided missiles, rockets and bombs.

The last of 136 single-seat Mirage 2000Cs were delivered to the Armée de l'Air in 1998 but foreign orders for this very capable fighter were secured some years before. Abu Dhabi, Greece, Egypt, Peru and India all operate export 2000 models.

There is a two-seat version of this aircraft, the 2000N, which has nuclear stand-off capability. The Mirage 2000D, derived from the Mirage 2000N operated by the French Air Force, is a two-seater air-to-ground attack aircraft that carries air-to-ground high precision weapons which can be fired at a safe distance, by day or by night. Its navigation and attack systems enable it to fly in any weather conditions, hugging the terrain at a very low altitude.

A modernized multi-role version, the Mirage 2000-5, was also offered from 1997, featuring improved more powerful

ABOVE: **The Mirage 2000 is a fine example of a very good aircraft being developed into a series of specialist variants.** BELOW: **The aircraft's M53-P2 turbofan generates 9917kg/21,835lb of afterburning thrust.**

radar, more powerful engine and compatibility with the Matra Mica air-to-air missile. The Mirage 2000-5 is a single-seater or two-seater fighter and differs from its predecessors mainly in its avionics and its new multiple target air-to-ground and air-to-air firing procedures. The aircraft has Hands On Throttle and Stick control, a Head-Up Display and five cathode ray tube multi-function Advanced Pilot Systems Interface (APSI) displays. The combined head-up/head-level display presents data relating to flight control, navigation, target engagement and weapon firing. The Taiwan Republic of China Air Force operates 60 Mirage 2000-5s while Qatar took delivery of 12 in 1997 having sold its Mirage 1s to Spain to finance the purchase.

Mirage 2000 has nine hardpoints for carrying weapon system payloads, five on the fuselage and two on each wing. The single-seat version is also armed with two internally mounted high-firing rate 30mm/1.18in guns. Air-to-air weapons include the MICA multi-target air-to-air intercept and combat missiles and the Matra Magic 2 missiles. The aircraft can carry four MICA missiles, two Magic missiles and three drop tanks simultaneously. The Mirage 2000-5 can fire the Super 530D missile or the Sky Flash air-to-air missile as an alternative to the MICA.

The Mirage 2000 is equipped with a multi-mode doppler radar which provides multi-targeting capability in the air defence role, and the radar also has a look down/shoot down mode of operation. The radar can simultaneously detect up to 24 targets and carry out track-while-scan on the eight highest priority threats, an invaluable tool for a pilot.

Armée de l'Air Mirage 2000Cs served as part of the UN peacekeeping force over Bosnia and Kosovo.

TOP: **A single-seat Mirage 2000C fighter is seen here armed with Matra Magic and Matra Super 530S air-to-air missiles.** ABOVE: **The Mirage 2000 is an incredibly agile aircraft which always thrills crowds.** BELOW: **The stork emblem on the tail of this two-seat Mirage 2000B identifies it as an aircraft of Escadron de Chasse 1/2 Cigognes.**

Dassault-Breguet Mirage 2000C

First flight: March 10, 1978

Power: SNECMA 9917kg/21,835lb afterburning thrust M53-P2 turbofan

Armament: Two 30mm/1.18in cannon, nine hardpoints capable of carrying 6300kg/13,890lb of weaponry including Super 530D, 530F, 550 Magic, Magic 2 AAMs, bombs and rockets

Size: Wingspan – 9.13m/29ft 11in
Length – 14.36m/47ft 1in Height – 5.2m/17ft
Wing area – 41m²/441.4 sq ft

Weights: Empty – 7500kg/16,534lb
Maximum take-off – 17,000kg/37,480lb

Performance: Maximum speed – 2338kph/1452mph
Ceiling – 16,470m/54,000ft
Range – 1850km/1149 miles
Climb – 17,080m/56,000ft per minute

Dassault Etendard and Super Etendard

Dassault's private venture Etendard (standard) was designed to meet the needs of both French national and NATO programmes for new light fighters, reflecting air combat experiences during the Korean War. Dassault clearly adhered to the proven Super Mystère layout, although slightly scaled down, but various versions did not get beyond the prototype stage. Then the Etendard IV drew the attention of the French Navy as a multi-role carrier-based fighter, leading to the development of the Etendard IVM specifically for the Navy – it was the first naval aircraft developed by Dassault.

The Etendard IVM made its maiden flight in May 1958 and between 1961 and 1965, the French Navy took delivery of 69 Etendard IVMs that served on the French carriers *Foch* and

Clemenceau, as well as 21 reconnaissance Etendard IVPs. The Etendard IVMs continued to serve in the French Navy until July 1991, by which time they had logged 180,000 flying hours and made 25,300 carrier landings.

The search for an Etendard replacement led to Dassault proposing the Super Etendard, an updated and much improved aircraft based on the Etendard IVM but a 90 per cent new design. Designed for strike and interception duties, it featured the more powerful Atar 8K-50 engine and a strengthened structure to withstand higher-speed operations. The weapons system was improved through the installation of a modern navigation and combat management system centred on a Thomson multi-mode radar. The wing had a new leading edge and revised flaps which, with the newer engine, eased take-off with greater weight than the Etendard.

The aircraft prototype made its maiden flight on October 28, 1974 and the first of 71 production aircraft were delivered from mid-1978, again for service on the aircraft carriers *Foch* and *Clemenceau*. 100 Super Etendards were planned for the Navy but spiralling costs called for a reduction of the order. Armed with two 30mm/1.18in cannon, the Super Etendard could carry a variety of weaponry on its five hard points, including two Matra Magic air-to-air missiles, four pods of 18 68mm/2.68in

ABOVE: **The Etendard was designed to reflect the experiences of air combat during the Korean War.** BELOW: **The Etendard IVP reconnaissance version was in Aeronavale service for almost three decades.**

LEFT: **The Super Etendard was developed from the Etendard but was a 90 per cent new aircraft.**
BELOW: **This Aeronavale Super Etendard was photographed at Boscombe Down in 1992.**
BOTTOM: **Thanks to a programme of upgrades, French Super Etendards will remain in service until 2008, by which time the Rafale will have replaced the type.**

rockets, a variety of bombs or two Exocet anti-ship missiles. A number were also modified to carry the Aérospatiale ASMP nuclear stand-off bomb.

The Argentine Navy's use of the Super Etendard/Exocet combination during the Falklands War of 1982 proved devastating against British ships – Argentina had ordered 14 Super Etendards from Dassault in 1979 but only five had been delivered from 1981. These five strike fighters, with pilots unwilling to engage the agile British Harriers in air combat, were nevertheless a very potent element of the Argentine inventory.

A handful of Super Etendards were supplied to Iraq in October 1983 as the Iraqis were desperate to cripple Iran by attacking tankers in the Persian Gulf with Exocets. Around 50 ships were attacked in the Gulf in 1984, the majority of the actions apparently carried out by Iraqi Super Etendards.

Production of the Super Etendard ended in 1983 but from 1992 a programme of structural and avionics upgrading was undertaken to extend the service life of the "fleet" until 2008.

ABOVE: **The Etendard IVP had a fixed refuelling probe and cameras in the nose. It could also carry a "buddy pack" and act as an inflight refuelling tanker.**

Dassault Super Etendard

First flight: October 28, 1974
Power: SNECMA 5000kg/11,025lb afterburning thrust Atar 8K-50 turbojet engine
Armament: Two 30mm/1.18in cannon, plus 2100kg/4630lb of weapons, including Matra Magic air-to-air missiles, AM39 Exocet ASMs, bombs and rockets
Size: Wingspan – 9.6m/31ft 6in
Length – 14.31m/46ft 11.5in
Height – 3.86m/12ft 8in
Wing area – 28.4m^2/305.71sq ft
Weights: Empty – 6500kg/14,330lb
Maximum take-off – 12,000kg/26,455lb
Performance: Maximum speed – 1205kph/749mph
Ceiling – 13,700m/44,950ft
Range – 650km/404 miles
Climb – 6000m/19,685ft per minute

Dassault Mirage F1

The swept-wing F1 multi-role fighter was developed as a successor to the excellent Mirage III and first flew just before Christmas in 1966. The first customer for the single-seat F1 was the French Armée de l'Air, who received the first of 100 F1Cs in May 1973. Later deliveries to the same service were of the F1C-200 version, which had a fixed probe for inflight refuelling. The F1 could carry a large offensive/defensive payload, handled well at low altitude and had a very impressive climb rate – all essential for truly great fighters. The aircraft's very good short take-off and landing performance (it could take-off and land within 500–800m/1640–2625ft) was produced by the wing's high lift system of leading-edge droops and large flaps.

The Mirage F1's turn-around time between missions was impressive, due to its onboard self-starter and a high-pressure refuelling system which filled all onboard tanks within six minutes. The F1 could be airborne within two minutes, courtesy of a special self-propelled ground vehicle that kept the aircraft's systems "alive", cooled or heated as required, and

ready to go. The ingenious vehicle also carried a cockpit sunshade on a telescopic arm so the pilot could sit at readiness in the cockpit for hours in the highest of temperatures. As soon as the aircraft started to taxi, the umbilicals were automatically ejected and the aircraft was on its own.

TOP: **A quarter of a century after it first flew, the Mirage F1 is still a very effective fighter in a number of air force inventories.** ABOVE: **This French Air Force F1 sports a very striking squadron anniversary paint scheme.**

The F1's Thomson-CSF Cyrano IV radar, housed in the glass-reinforced plastic nose, enabled the F1 pilot to intercept targets at all altitudes, even those flying at low level. A fire-control computer could then fire the appropriate weapons automatically, if required.

Although production of the F1 ceased in 1989, the F1 continues to be a key aircraft in French air defence strategy and upgrades of the popular jet will undoubtedly keep it in service with other air forces well beyond 2010.

France has exported the F1 to Ecuador, Greece, Jordan, Morocco, Spain, South Africa, Libya and Iraq. The last country, however, fielded the type without success during the Gulf War. The F1A was also built under licence by Atlas Aircraft in South Africa.

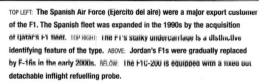

TOP LEFT: **The Spanish Air Force (Ejercito del aire) were a major export customer of the F1. The Spanish fleet was expanded in the 1990s by the acquisition of Qatar's F1 fleet.** TOP RIGHT: **The F1's stalky undercarriage is a distinctive identifying feature of the type.** ABOVE: **Jordan's F1s were gradually replaced by F-16s in the early 2000s.** BELOW: **The F1C-200 is equipped with a fixed but detachable inflight refuelling probe.**

Dassault Mirage F1

First flight: December 23, 1966
Power: One SNECMA 49kN/11,025lb
(70.2kg/15,785lb afterburning)
Atar 9K-50 turbojet engine
Armament: Two 30mm/1.17in DEFA 553 cannons in fuselage and up to 4000kg/8818lb of other weapons, including AIM-9 Sidewinder or Magic air-to-air missiles on wingtips or R.530 or Super 530F radar-guided air-to-air missiles on underwing or centreline hardpoints
Size: Wingspan – 8.4m/27ft 7in, excluding wingtip missiles
Length – 15.3m/50ft 3in Height – 4.5m/14ft 9in
Wing area – 25m²/269.1sq ft
Weights: Empty – 7400kg/16,315lb
Maximum loaded – 16,200kg/35,715lb
Performance: Maximum speed – 2338kph/1452mph
Ceiling – 20,008m/65,600ft
Range – 900km/560 miles with full weapon load, unrefuelled
Climb – 12,789m/41,931ft per minute

Dassault Mirage III family

The delta-wing Mirage III is certainly one of the greatest ever combat aircraft and was produced in greater numbers than any other European fighter. The success of this aircraft brought France to the forefront of the military aircraft industry. It started as a Dassault private venture project and first flew in November 1956, having benefited from the testing of the small Mirage I experimental delta aircraft. After some refinements to the wing design, in October 1958 it became the first western European aircraft to reach Mach 2 in level flight. The aircraft's capability soon caught the attention of the French Armée de l'Air, who quickly ordered the high-performance aircraft as a new fighter for their inventory.

Foreign air forces were also very interested in the Mirage III and orders from Israel and South Africa followed in late 1960. By now the first production aircraft, the Mirage IIIC single-seat air defence fighter, was coming off the production line for the Armée de l'Air and the first were delivered in July 1961. Equipped with the Cyrano AI radar, the Mirage IIIC was armed with two 30mm/1.18in cannon and air-to-air missiles. Some of Israel's IIICs, well used in combat, were sold to Argentina in 1982, a country which already operated that type.

The Mirage IIIE was a long-range fighter-bomber version powered by the SNECMA Atar 9C turbojet. While the IIIC was a dedicated interceptor, the IIIE was designed and equipped for both air defence and all-weather ground attack and French

versions were equipped to carry a nuclear bomb. It was widely exported and was also built under licence in Australia and Switzerland. Although France has retired its Mirage IIIs, many air forces still operate the type, having upgraded it in many ways – Swiss and Brazilian IIIs, for example, have acquired canard wings to enhance their handling.

It was the IIIE that spawned the Mirage 5 ground-attack fighter, basically a simplified version of the IIIE, designed as

ABOVE: **The Belgian Air Force operated over 70 Mirages – a Mirage 5 is here seen nearing the end of its landing roll with braking parachute deployed.**
BELOW: **This 1966 photograph features an Armée de l'Air Mirage IIIC of Escadre de Chasse 3/2 "Alsace". The fin of this early paint scheme IIIC carries the Alsace coat of arms.**

a daytime clear weather ground-attack fighter in response to an Israeli Air Force request. The need for sophisticated radar was considered to be not so great in the Middle East and when the Israeli Mirage 5 first flew in May 1967 it was minus the Cyrano radar. The delivery to Israel was stopped for political reasons by President de Gaulle and the aircraft instead served as the Mirage 5F in the Armée de l'Air. Israel then decided to go it alone and developed their Mirage III into the Kfir.

Some 450 Mirage 5s were, however, exported to other nations and more advanced avionics were offered later. Belgium built their own Mirage 5s and upgraded them in the 1990s to keep them flying until 2005.

The Mirage 50 multi-mission fighter was created by installing the more powerful Atar 9K-50 engine in a Mirage 5 airframe. It first flew in April 1979 and boasted Head-Up Displays and a more advanced radar than the Mirage III. Chile and Venezuela both ordered Mirage 50s. Dassault offers the Mirage 50M upgrade for existing Mirage IIIs and 5s but several operator nations have undertaken local upgrade programmes with improved avionics and the addition of canard foreplanes.

In the 1967 and 1973 Arab-Israeli wars, the Israeli Mirage IIIs outclassed Arab-flown MiGs and generated lots of export sales, but Mirage pilots admit that the type did not have a great sustained turn capability due to the aerodynamic idiosyncrasies of the delta wing. Indeed three Mirages were shot down by Iraqi Hunters during the Six Day War of 1967. Nevertheless, the Mirage III series gave many air forces their first fighters capable of flying at twice the speed of sound and many upgraded examples around the world will be flying until at least 2005.

TOP: **The Swiss Air Force operated fighter and reconnaissance versions of the Mirage III.** ABOVE: **The Mirage III was undoubtedly one of the finest fighting aircraft ever built.**

ABOVE: **Two-seat trainer versions were supplied to most Mirage III/5 export customers.**

Dassault Mirage IIIC

First flight: November 18, 1956

Power: SNECMA 6000kg/13,228lb afterburning thrust Atar 9C turbojet engine

Armament: Two 30mm/1.18in cannon, plus two Sidewinder air-to-air missiles and one Matra R.530 air-to-air missile

Size: Wingspan – 8.22m/27ft
Length – 14.75m/48ft 5in
Height – 4.5m/14ft 9in
Wing area – 35m²/375sq ft

Weights: Empty – 6575kg/14,495lb
Maximum take-off – 12,700kg/27,998lb

Performance: Maximum speed – 2112kph/1320mph
Ceiling – 20,000m/65,615ft
Range – 1610km/1000 miles
Climb – 5000m/16,400ft per minute

Dassault Rafale

ABOVE: **The Rafale is a twin-engined highly advanced fighter. The two-seat Rafale B can be a trainer or multi-role combat aircraft.** LEFT: **The Rafale's delta wing is complemented by small canards forward of the leading edge, resulting in outstanding agility.**

Even as Mirage 2000 was entering service in the early 1980s, a successor was already being sought to be the prime French Air Force fighter. After France withdrew from what became the Eurofighter programme, attention was then focused on Dassault's Avion de Combat Experimentale (ACX) which first flew on July 4, 1986 and was later designated Rafale A.

This demonstrator aircraft was used to test the basic design including the airframe, powerplant and the fly-by-wire system.

Directly derived from the slightly (3 per cent) larger Rafale A demonstrator, production Rafales appeared in three versions – the single-seat air defence Rafale C, the two-seater trainer/multi-role Rafale B and the single-seat Rafale M fighter for the Navy. The three versions were fitted with the same engines (the SNECMA M88-2), navigation/attack system, aircraft management system and flight control systems. The cockpit had Hands On Throttle

and Stick (HOTAS) controls, a wide-angle Head-up Display (HUD), two multi-function display (MFD) monitors showing all flight and instrument information, and a helmet-mounted weapons sight. Voice recognition is planned to feature in future versions so the pilot will be able to issue orders to the aircraft simply by using his or her voice.

All three versions had the same 213kph/132mph approach speed and take-off/landing run of less than 400m/1312ft made possible by complementing the delta wing with canard foreplanes, which together optimize aerodynamic efficiency and stability control without impeding the pilot's visibility. The materials employed and the shapes that make up the aircraft were both carefully selected to minimize the aircraft's electro-magnetic and infra-red signature to make it as "stealthy" as possible. Carbon and Kevlar composites, superplastic-formed diffusion-bonded titanium and aluminium-lithium alloys have all been used in this aircraft.

The first production aircraft, Rafale B1, flew in December 1998 with a total of up to 234 aircraft to be delivered to the

French Air Force from 1998 to 2005. The total programme for the French Air Force and Navy is set at 294 aircraft.

The single-seat Rafale C (first flight May 19, 1991) is an air defence fighter with fully integrated weapons and navigation systems. Making full use of the latest technology, it is capable of outstanding performance on multiple air-to-air targets.

The two-seat multi-role Rafale B first took to the air on April 30, 1993 and retained most of the elements of the single-seater version, including its weapons and navigation system. The Rafale B could undertake an operational mission with just a pilot as crew or with a pilot and a weapons system operator. In Armée de l'Air service the B model is intended to replace the popular ground-attack Jaguar and can carry up to 8000kg/17,637lb of weaponry – in the air-to-air role this will include up to eight Matra Mica AAM missiles.

The Rafale M was ordered to replace the French Navy's ageing fleet of F-8 Crusaders, and is a single-seat fighter strengthened for seaborne use with a toughened undercarriage, arrester hook and catapult points for deck launches. This navalized Rafale first flew in December 1991. The first flight of a production Rafale M took place in July 1999, and on the same day a Rafale M prototype landed on France's nuclear-powered aircraft carrier Charles de Gaulle. The Navy's first Rafale unit of 12 aircraft was scheduled to embark on the carrier in 2002, the first of a total of 60 aircraft planned for the French Navy.

The first Rafale produced for the French Air Force, a two-seater, was handed over in December 1999.

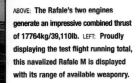

ABOVE: **The Rafale's two engines generate an impressive combined thrust of 17764kg/39,110lb.** LEFT: **Proudly displaying the test flight running total, this navalized Rafale M is displayed with its range of available weaponry.**

RIGHT: **An early Rafale pictured the year after the type's test flight.** BELOW: **The Rafale was designed to be central to the French fighter force. Until the type is ready to equip the French Air Force and Navy, existing types such as the Mirage F1 and Mirage 2000 will continue to serve.**

Dassault Rafale C

First flight: May 19, 1991

Power: Two SNECMA 8882kg/19,555lb afterburning thrust M88-2 augmented turbofans

Armament: One 30mm/1.18in cannon, maximum of 14 hardpoints carrying a weapons load of up to 6000kg/13,228lb including eight Matra Mica AAMs, ASMP stand-off nuclear missile and other munitions

Size: Wingspan – 10.9m/35ft 9in
Length – 15.3m/50ft 2in
Height – 5.34m/17ft 6in
Wing area – 46m^2/495.1sq ft

Weights: Empty – 9060kg/19,973lb
Maximum take-off – 21,500kg/47,399lb

Performance: Maximum speed – 2125kph/1320mph
Ceiling – 20,000m/65,620ft
Range – 1850km/1150 miles with maximum weapon load
Climb – not published

LEFT: **Royal Navy Sea Hornet F.20s of No.728 Squadron, Fleet Air Arm.** BELOW: **Designed for combat in the Pacific Theatre, the Hornet arrived before the end of World War II. The photograph shows PX210, the first production Hornet F.1.**

de Havilland Hornet

Following the success of the Mosquito, the de Havilland design team turned their thoughts to a scaled-down single-seat Mosquito capable of taking on Japanese fighters in the Pacific. Very long range was a major feature of the design that came to be known as the Hornet and streamlining was seen as one way of achieving that. Rolls-Royce were involved from the outset and were responsible for developing Merlin engines with a

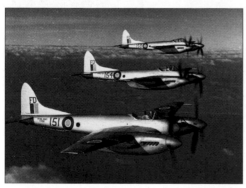

reduced frontal area to lessen the drag on the aircraft. Although inspired by the Mosquito, the Hornet was a completely new aircraft – the main similarity between the two types was the plywood-balsa-plywood technique for building the wooden fuselage. The Hornet wing also differed from that of the Mosquito in that it was made

of wood and metal – the Hornet was the first aircraft in which wood was cemented to metal using the pioneering Redux adhesive.

Geoffrey de Havilland Jr took the Hornet into the air for the first time in July 1944. Although the first production aircraft were delivered to the RAF in April 1945, the type did not see action in World War II. In fact the first RAF Hornet squadron, No.64, was not formed until May 1946. Hornets defended UK air space until replaced by Meteor 8s in 1951, but from 1949 they were switched from interceptor to intruder duties.

Most RAF Hornets joined the Far East Air Force in early 1951 for action in Malaya. Equipped with rocket projectiles or bombs, the Hornets proved very effective against terrorist targets in the jungle. The Hornets of No.45 Squadron became the last piston-engined fighters in RAF service and were finally replaced by Vampires in 1955.

A naval version was considered from the start and the production Sea Hornet had folding wings, arrester hook, plus naval radio and radar, as well as landing gear modified for deck landings. Sea Hornets appeared in day and two-seat

nightfighter versions, the latter version proving to be considerably slower. The Fleet Air Arm's No.801 Squadron operated Sea Hornet F.20s from the carrier HMS *Implacable* between 1949 and 1951.

ABOVE: **The engines dominated the Hornet from any perspective – a Hornet F.3 of the RAF Linton-on-Ouse Station Flight.** LEFT: **The Hornet/ Sea Hornet pioneered the use of Redux adhesive in construction – Royal Navy Sea Hornet F.20s.**

de Havilland Hornet F. Mk 3

First flight: July 28, 1944 (prototype)

Power: Two Rolls-Royce 2030hp Merlin 130/131 in-line piston engines

Armament: Four 20mm/0.78in cannon in nose, plus provision for up to 908kg/2000lb of underwing bombs or rockets

Size: Wingspan – 13.73m/45ft
Length – 11.18m/36ft 8in
Height – 4.32m/14ft2in
Wing area – 33.54m²/361sq ft

Weights: Empty – 5850kg/12,880lb
Maximum take-off – 9493kg/20,900lb

Performance: Maximum speed – 759kph/472mph
Ceiling – 10,675m/35,000ft
Range – 4827km/3000 miles
Climb – 1220m/4000ft per minute

de Havilland Sea Vixen

The Sea Venom's successor in Royal Navy service was the impressive de Havilland Sea Vixen, which, when it first appeared in the early 1950s, was a match for any land-based fighter of the time. It gave the Royal Navy its first swept-wing two-seat all-weather fighter and was developed from the D.H.110 that was designed to meet Royal Navy and Royal Air Force requirements. Although it followed the Vampire/Venom-type twin-boom configuration, this was a

totally modern aircraft. Development delays following the high-profile and tragic 1952 crash of the prototype at Farnborough kept the Sea Vixen from entering Royal Navy Fleet Air Arm service until 1958. The aircraft became operational the following year and was

the mainstay of carrier-borne fighter squadrons for a decade. It was the first British interceptor to dispense with guns and was armed only with air-to-air missiles and rockets.

The Sea Vixen FAW. Mk 1 had a hinged radome, power-folding wings and a steerable nosewheel. The novel nose arrangement had the pilot's cockpit off-set to the port side to provide sufficient working space for a radar operator below and behind on the starboard side.

The FAW. Mk 2 was an improved version, either upgraded from Mk 1 standard or built from new. More fuel was carried in the forward sections of the tail-booms, which were extended forward of the wings, and armament for this model was four Red Top air-to-air missiles in place of the Firestreaks carried by the FAW. Mk 1.

Despite the Sea Vixen's late entry into service, the aircraft gave the Royal Navy a formidable all-weather interception and surface-attack capability until the type was finally retired in 1972.

TOP LEFT: **This weary FAW. Mk 2 shows the extent of wing folding on the type.** ABOVE LEFT: **The Sea Vixen pilot's cockpit sat offset to the port side to make room for the fellow crew member.**

TOP: **The very capable Sea Vixen was the first British fighter to be armed exclusively with rockets and air-to-air missiles.** ABOVE: **An excellent photograph of a Royal Navy Sea Vixen buzzing the island of British aircraft carrier HMS Hermes, June 1961.**

de Havilland Sea Vixen FAW. Mk 2

First flight: September 26, 1951 (D.H.110)
Power: Two Rolls-Royce 5094kg/11,230lb-thrust Avon 208 turbojet engines
Armament: Four Red Top infra-red homing air-to-air missiles, plus two retractable nose pods with 28 51mm/2in rocket projectiles
Size: Wingspan – 15.54m/51ft
Length – 16.94m/55ft 7in
Height – 3.28m/10ft 9in
Wing area – 60.2m²/648sq ft
Weights: Empty – 9979kg/22,000lb
Maximum take-off – 16,793kg/37,000lb
Performance: Maximum speed 1110kph/690mph
Ceiling – 14,640m/48,000ft
Range – 1287km/800 miles
Climb – 12,200m/40,000ft in 8.5 minutes

de Havilland Vampire

The Vampire was Britain's first single-jet fighter and was probably the first aircraft whose designers thought the advent of the jet engine called for a rethink of aircraft layout. While many early jets were just modified ex-propeller-driven airframes, the de Havilland company produced instead a radical twin-boom design to accommodate the new form of propulsion – the jet engine.

The Vampire first flew in September 1943 with Geoffrey de Havilland at the controls, only 16 months after detailed design work began. It arrived too late to see action in World War II but joined RAF squadrons in 1946, becoming the second jet aircraft in Royal Air Force service. When the prototype jet fighter first took to the air it was powered by an engine with 1226kg/2700lb thrust, a far cry from, for example, the 6097kg/13,490lb-thrust Eurojet turbofans that power today's Eurofighter.

In the early post-war years, the Vampires of RAF Fighter Command played a key part in the first-line air defence of the UK, until they were replaced in this role by the Meteor 8 in 1951. By then the Vampire was in widespread use with the RAF's Middle East and Far East Air Forces until it was replaced by the de Havilland Venom, the second of de Havilland's distinctive twin-boom designs.

ABOVE: **LZ551 was an English Electric-built prototype equipped with an arrester hook for deck trials.**

In December 1945 the world's first deck landing by jet was made by the prototype Sea Vampire, which was the first jet aircraft to go into service with any navy. This version was a modified Vampire F.B.5, strengthened to cope with the extra strain put on airframes during arrester-hook landings. It served in the Royal Navy as a much-needed trainer for the Fleet Air Arm's first generation of jet pilots.

Vampires continued to fly in air forces around the world until the mid-1970s and even into the early 1980s, in the cases of the Dominican Republic and, most famously, Switzerland.

In the early 1950s more than 430 Vampires were licence-built by SNCASE at Marseilles (and named the Mistral) giving France's aviation industry a much-needed post-war shot in the arm. Meanwhile Macchi built 80 in Italy and Switzerland produced 178.

Vampire NF. Mk 10 nightfighters also provided valuable service for the RAF. A total of 95 machines were built and some were later refurbished for sale to the Indian Air Force in the mid-1950s. Privately owned versions continue to fly.

de Havilland Vampire F.I

First flight: September 20, 1943
Power: de Havilland 1408kg/3100lb-thrust Goblin 1 turbojet
Armament: Four 20mm/0.78in cannon in nose
Size: Wingspan – 12.2m/40ft
 Length – 9.37m/30ft 9in Height – 2.69m/8ft 10in
 Wing area – 24.35m²/262sq ft
Weights: Empty – 2894kg/6372lb
 Maximum take-off – 4760kg/10,480lb
Performance: Maximum speed – 868kph/540mph
 Ceiling – 12,500m/41,000ft
 Range – 1175km/730 miles
 Climb – 1312m/4300ft per minute

ABOVE: **Britain's first single-engine jet fighter, the Vampire, joined RAF squadrons in 1946. The twin-boom layout was a response to the revolutionary new form of propulsion, the jet engine.** RIGHT: **Vampire F.B.9s of No.8 Squadron RAF pictured over Kenya. The F.B.9 was a special version produced for use in tropical climates and had, among other innovations, much needed cockpit air-conditioning.**

Douglas F4D Skyray

German wartime aerodynamics experiments led the post-war US Navy to consider the use of a delta wing for a carrier-borne fighter. In 1947, the Douglas Corporation proposed the delta-winged XF4D-1 and, following US Navy approval, the prototype first flew in January 1951. The F4D's capabilities were evident when, on October 3, 1953, the second prototype set a new world air speed record of 1211.7kph/752.9mph.

Deliveries to the US Navy began in April 1956 and 17 front-line US Navy/USMC units, plus three reserve units, were eventually equipped with the Skyray.

The F4D-1 had an incredible climb rate for the time and on May 22 and 23, 1958 the Skyray piloted by Major Edward LeFaivre of the US Marine Corps broke five world records for time-to-altitude. This feat led to one US Navy unit, VFAW-3, based at Naval Air Station North Island in California, being part of North American Air Defense Command tasked with defending the USA against expected fleets of Soviet bombers.

This unusual aircraft was finally retired in the late 1960s, having been redesignated F-6A in 1962.

TOP: **This F4D is preserved at the Museum of Naval Aviation at Pensacola, Florida, in the United States.**
ABOVE: **The Skyray was a record-breaker and set a number of records for speed and time-to-altitude.**
BELOW: **Directly influenced by German wartime delta wing research, the Skyray entered US Navy service over a decade after the end of World War II.**

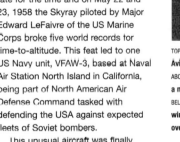

Douglas F4D Skyray

First flight: January 23, 1951
Power: Pratt & Whitney 6577kg/14,500lb afterburning thrust J57-P-8B turbojet engine
Armament: Four 20mm/0.78in cannon, plus up to 1814kg/4000lb of fuel or ordnance on six underwing hardpoints
Size: Wingspan – 10.21m/33ft 6in
Length – 13.93m/45ft 8.25in
Height – 3.96m/13ft
Wing area – 51.75m^2/557sq ft
Weights: Empty – 7268kg/16,024lb
Maximum take-off – 11,340kg/25,000lb
Performance: Maximum speed – 1162kph/722mph
Ceiling – 16,765m/55,000ft
Range – 1931km/1200 miles
Climb – 5580m/18,300ft per minute

Eurofighter Typhoon

In the modern world, few nations can "go it alone" and develop a new high-performance fighter aircraft. So in 1983 Britain, France, Germany, Italy and Spain issued a joint requirement for a highly agile single-seat fighter with a secondary ground attack capability. The French withdrew in 1985 to pursue their own indigenous design but the other nations continued with what became Eurofighter.

Development work was split between UK and Germany (33 per cent each), Italy (21 per cent) and Spain (13 per cent). Germany threatened to withdraw from the programme in 1992 unless spiralling costs were pegged. A lower specification Eurofighter was proposed, accepted by all partners, and the programme continued.

Eurofighter first flew in Germany in March 1994 and is optimized for air-dominance performance with high instantaneous and sustained turn rates. Special emphasis has been placed on

low wing loading, high thrust-to-weight ratio, excellent all round vision and ease of handling. The use of stealth technology is incorporated throughout the aircraft's basic design and it only needs a 700m/2300ft runway.

Eurofighter's high performance is matched by excellent all round vision and by sophisticated attack, identification and defence systems which include long-range radar, Infra-Red Search and Track, advanced medium and short-range air-to-air missiles and a comprehensive electronic warfare suite to enhance weapons system effectiveness and survivability. As well as the expected chaff and flare dispensers, towed decoys are carried in wingtip pods.

Eurofighter is aerodynamically unstable to provide extremely high levels of agility, reduced drag and enhanced lift. The unstable design cannot be flown by conventional means and the pilot controls the aircraft via a computerized "fly-by-wire" system. The pilot has an advanced cockpit dominated by a wide-angle Head-Up Display and three colour monitors displaying all instrument information and flight data, as well as a helmet-mounted sight for weapon aiming. Direct voice input allows the pilot to control aspects of the flight just by talking to the aircraft.

The Eurojet EJ200 turbofan combines high thrust with low fuel consumption and strength.

ABOVE: **The Eurofighter Typhoon is an excellent example of multi-national industry co-operation. The result is a very high-performance fighter that will equip a number of key European air arms for decades to come.** LEFT: **The Eurofighter Typhoon's two turbofans generate a combined thrust of 18396kg/40,500lb, comparable to that of the F-14 Tomcat. An unladen Eurofighter is, however, half the weight of an empty F-14.**

British Eurofighters will be assembled by BAE Systems from components manufactured by companies in the partner nations. In the other nations the respective partner companies will have their own assembly lines in Munich, Turin and Madrid.

Eurofighter Typhoon

First flight: March 27, 1994
Power: Two EJ200 9198kg/20,250lb afterburning thrust turbofans
Armament: One 27mm/1.05in cannon plus 13 hardpoints carrying up to 6500kg/14,330lb of ordnance including short- and medium-range AAMs plus a range of stand-off weapons, bombs, rockets
Size: Wingspan – 10.95m/35ft 11in
Length – 15.96m/52ft 4in
Height – 5.28m/17ft 7in
Wing area – 50m²/538.2sq ft
Weights: Empty – 9990kg/22,043lb
Maximum take-off – 21,000kg /46,297lb
Performance: Maximum speed – 2020kph/1255mph
Ceiling – 16,775m/55,000ft
Range – 1390km/863 miles
Climb – 10,670m/35,000ft in 2 minutes, 30 seconds

Fiat/Aeritalia G91

In response to a 1953 NATO specification for a light strike fighter with rough field capability that was still capable of 0.92 Mach, Fiat proposed the F-86 Sabre-inspired G91. Despite the loss of the prototype on its first flight (August 9, 1956), an accident which would cause

the French to refuse to purchase the aircraft, the G91 entered production for the Italian Air Force. While the design was intended for use by all the NATO countries, only Italy and Germany initially acquired the design.

The Italian Air Force and the Luftwaffe took delivery of the G91R single-seat tactical reconnaissance/ground attack fighter version in the early 1960s. Dornier undertook some production in Germany historically making the G91 the first jet combat aircraft built in Germany since World War II. Some G91s were later transferred to the Portuguese Air Force in 1965.

The G91Y twin-engined fighter, first seen as a development of the G91R, was really a totally new design capable of carrying much greater military loads over much longer distances. Powered by two General Electric jet engines, the G91Y first flew in December 1966 and deliveries to the Regia Aeronautica took place between 1971–5.

ABOVE: **A G91R of the Portuguese Air Force's Escuadra 121 "Tigres".** Portugal operated around 40 of the type. LEFT: **Resembling a late mark F-86 Sabre, the G91 was a straightforward design said by pilots to be easy to handle in the air.**

Fiat G91R

First flight: August 9, 1956
Power: Fiat/Bristol 2268kg/5000lb thrust Orpheus 803 turbojet
Armament: Four 12.7mm/0.5in machine-guns, plus four underwing pylons for a variety of tactical nuclear weapons, iron bombs, air-to-air missiles and other ordnance
Size: Wingspan – 8.56m/28ft 1in
Length – 10.3m/33ft 9.25in
Height – 4m/13ft 1.25in
Wing area – 16.42m²/176.74sq ft
Weights: Empty – 3100kg/6838lb
Maximum take-off – 5500kg/12,125lb
Performance: Maximum speed – 1075kph/668mph
Ceiling 13,100m/42,978ft
Range – 630km/392 miles
Climb – 1827m/5990ft per minute

ABOVE: **The G91T two-seat trainer was developed to give pilots experience of flight at transonic speeds. The pre-unification Federal German Air Force took delivery of 66 trainer versions, 22 built under licence in Germany and the rest by Fiat in Italy.**

Folland/Hawker Siddeley Gnat

Best known as a jet trainer, the Gnat actually began life as a private-venture single-seat fighter, the Midge, which first took to the air in August 1954. While fighters around the world were getting more complex and heavier, the Gnat was designed by W.E.W. Petter as a lightweight jet fighter, making use of the smaller jet engines then available.

Although the British government ordered six Gnats for development flying, the Gnat failed to be adopted as an RAF fighter. By mid-1957 the Gnat's potential

as a two-seat trainer was recognized by the RAF, leading to orders for a total of 105 two-seat Gnat trainers for the RAF.

India had, however, been impressed by the Gnat as a fighter and had licence-built 213 of them by 1973. In the Indo-Pakistan war of 1971 the Indian Gnats proved most effective in close combat; then in 1974 Hindustan Aircraft Ltd signed an agreement to produce the Gnat II or Ajit (unconquerable). Finland also operated Gnat fighters between 1958 and 1972.

TOP: **The Gnat is best known as a mount of the world-famous RAF Red Arrows aerobatic team.**
ABOVE: **Indian licence-built Gnats saw action against Pakistan in the early 1970s.** BELOW: **Where it all began – the private-venture Midge that first flew in 1954.**

Folland Gnat 1

First flight: July 18, 1955
Power: Bristol 2050kg/4520lb-thrust Orpheus 701 turbojet engine
Armament: Two 30mm/1.18in Aden cannon, plus underwing hardpoints for 454kg/1000lb bomb load
Size: Wingspan – 6.75m/22ft 2in
Length – 9.06m/29ft 9in
Height – 2.69m/8ft 10in
Wing area – 16.26m²/175sq ft
Weights: Empty – 2200kg/4850lb
Maximum take-off – 4030kg/8885lb
Performance: Maximum speed – 1150kph/714mph
Ceiling – 15,250m/50,000ft plus
Range – 1900km/1180 miles
Climb – 6096m/20,000ft per minute

Gloster Javelin

**Gloster Javelin
F(AW). Mk 1**

First flight: November 26, 1951
Power: Two Armstrong Siddeley 3629kg/8000lb-thrust
 Sapphire ASSa.6 turbojet engines
Armament: Two 30mm/1.18in cannon in each wing
Size: Wingspan – 15.85m/52ft
 Length – 17.15m/56ft 3in
 Height – 4.88m/16ft
 Wing area – 86.12m²/927sq ft
Weights: Empty – 10,886kg/24,000lb
 Maximum take-off – 14,324kg/31,580lb
Performance: Maximum speed – 1141kph/709mph
 Ceiling – 16,000m/52,500ft
 Range – 1530km/950 miles with drop tanks
 Climb – 15,250m/50,000ft (Mk 9) in 9.25 minutes

The Javelin was the first British combat aircraft designed for the all-weather day and night role and was the first twin-engined delta-wing jet in service anywhere.

The design team began work on the Javelin in 1948 and the type first flew on November 26, 1951. After competitive trials with the de Havilland 110 (which led to the Sea Vixen) in July 1952 Britain's Air Ministry chose the Javelin to equip the RAF's all-weather fighter units. Following the loss of three prototypes in accidents and after much redesign, production finally got under way in 1954.

The Javelin was designed to have the very high performance and long endurance that would enable it to intercept high-speed, high-altitude Soviet bombers. With state-of-the-art electronics and radar, the two-seat Javelin was able to operate day or night in all weather conditions. The Javelin's large delta wing provided good high-altitude performance, while the massive swept vertical tail fin carried a delta tailplane on top which helped keep the aircraft's landing angle-of-attack within safe limits for night and all-weather landings.

When the Mk 1 Javelins entered RAF service in 1956, they were the first of 427 of a type that ultimately appeared in nine versions.

The Mk 2 entered service in August 1957 and had uprated engines (3770kg/8300lb, compared to the 3702kg/8150lb-thrust of the Mk 1) and an improved Westinghouse radar. Next came the T.3 dual control trainer, which had no radar but was armed with 30mm/1.18in guns.

Fifty examples of the pilot-friendly Mk 4 were built and with its all-moving tailplane it was much easier to fly. An extra 1137 litres/250 US gallons of internal tankage in a modified wing was the principal performance improvement on the Mk 5 while the Mk 6 was simply a Mk 5 equipped with American radar.

The Javelin FAW.7 was a major redesign and was produced in greater numbers (142) than the other versions. It boasted the much more powerful 4996kg/11,000lb-thrust Sapphire 203 engines and much-needed missile armament of four Firestreak infra-red homing air-to-air missiles in place of two of the 30mm/1.18in guns. This model entered front-line service in July 1958.

The Mk 8 had afterburners that increased thrust to 6082kg/13,390lb and the final variant was the Mk 9. This ultimate Javelin was a conversion of existing Mk 7s to Mk 8 standard and an inflight refuelling (IFR) probe. Four No.23 Squadron Javelins demonstrated the usefulness of IFR by flying non-stop to Singapore in 1960. FAW.9s were first delivered to No.25 Squadron at Waterbeach in December 1959.

Javelins were the last aircraft built by the famous Gloster company, and their last product was withdrawn from service in June 1967. At its peak, the Javelin equipped 14 Royal Air Force squadrons.

BELOW: **The Javelin was the world's first twin-engined delta jet fighter in service.**

Grumman F7F Tigercat

In 1941 Grumman began design work on a hard-hitting high-performance twin-engine fighter to operate from the Midway class of US aircraft carriers – the Tigercat. As the Tigercat developed it was apparent that it was going to be heavier and faster than all previous US carrier aircraft. It was also unusual in that it had a tricycle undercarriage,

although it retained the usual arrester hook and folding wings for carrier operations. Even before the prototype flew in December 1943, the US Marine Corps had placed an order for 500 of the F7F-1 version. They wanted to use the Tigercat primarily as a land-based fighter in close support of Marines on the ground. Although deliveries began in April 1944, the big fighter arrived too late to be cleared for use in World War II.

Wartime production had diversified to deliver the F7F-2N nightfighter, which differed from the F7F-1 by the removal of a fuel tank to make way for a radar operator cockpit and the removal of nose armament for the fitting of the radar.

An improved fighter-bomber version was also developed, the F7F-3, and had different engines for more power at altitude, a slightly larger fin and bigger fuel tanks.

Tigercat production continued after the war's end with F7F-3N and F7F-4N nightfighters, both having lengthened noses to house the latest radar and a few of these aircraft were strengthened and equipped for carrier operations. Some F7F-3s were modified for electronic and photographic reconnaissance missions.

Although it missed action in World War II, the Tigercat did see combat with the Marine Corps over Korea. USMC fighter unit VMF(N)-513 was based in Japan when the Korean War broke out. Equipped with Tigercat nightfighters, they went into action immediately as night-intruders and performed valuable service.

The US Marines were the only operators of the Tigercat.

TOP: **The fast and heavy F7F was only used by the US Marines.** ABOVE: **Despite its vintage, the high-performance Tigercat is a popular "warbird", and a number are preserved by collectors in the USA and Europe.** LEFT: **Too late for World War II, the F7F was widely used in the Korean War.**

Grumman F7F-3N

First flight: December 1943 (F7F-1)
Power: Two Pratt & Whitney 2100hp R-2800-34W Double Wasp radial piston engines
Armament: Four 20mm/0.78in cannon in wing roots
Size: Wingspan – 15.7m/51ft 6in
  Length – 13.8m/45ft 4in
  Height – 5.06m/16ft 7in
  Wing area – 42.27m^2/455sq ft
Weights: Empty – 7379kg/16,270lb
  Maximum take-off – 11,666kg/25,720lb
Performance: Maximum speed – 700kph/435mph
  Ceiling – 12,414m/40,700ft
  Range – 1609km/1000 miles
  Climb – 1380m/4530ft per minute

Grumman F9F Cougar

Grumman, aware of wartime German swept-wing research, had considered a swept-wing version of the F9F in December 1945. In March 1950 the company sought official approval for a swept-wing version of the Panther – Grumman was given the green light for this logical and speedy development of an already successful programme.

Having been granted a contract in March 1951, Grumman tested the first swept-wing aircraft of the F9F family on September 20, 1951. It was different enough from the Panther to warrant the new name F9F-6 Cougar – in fact only the forward fuselage was retained from the original straight-winged aircraft. The wings had 35 degrees sweep and the wingtip fuel tanks were deleted – power was provided by the J48-8 engine with water/alcohol injection giving a thrust of 3289kg/7250lb. The Cougar entered US Navy service in late 1952.

The F9F-7 version, powered by the 2880kg/6350lb J33 engine, reached a production total of 168. The final Cougar version, the F9F-8 with its bigger wing, first flew in December 1953 and in

January 1954 exceeded the speed of sound in a shallow dive – 662 were built. This version was equipped to carry early Sidewinder missiles.

Many Cougars and Panthers were converted for use as target drones, and two-seat trainer versions of the Cougar were still flying in US Navy service in the mid-1970s.

ABOVE: **Two-seat conversion of Cougars flew on with the US Navy in the mid-1970s.**

BELOW: **Benefiting from wartime German swept-wing research, the Cougar was a swept-wing version of the Panther.**

Grumman F9F-8 Cougar

First flight: September 20, 1951 (F9F-6)

Power: Pratt & Whitney 3266kg/7200lb thrust J48-P-8A turbojet

Armament: Two 20mm/0.78in cannon plus 908kg/2000lb of underwing weapons

Size: Wingspan – 10.52m/34ft 6in
Length – 13.54m/44ft 5in, including probe
Height – 3.73m/12ft 3in
Wing area – 31.31m^2/337sq ft

Weights: Empty – 5382kg/11,866lb
Maximum take-off – 11,232kg/24,763lb

Performance: Maximum speed – 1041kph/647mph
Ceiling – 15,240m/50,000ft
Range – 1610km/1000 miles
Climb – 1860m/6100ft

Grumman F9F Panther

LEFT: **The folded wings of this F9F-2 betray its origins as a naval fighter.** BELOW: **In the Korean War the Panther flew 78,000 missions.** BOTTOM: **The Panther could carry up to 908kg/2000lb of bombs and rockets beneath its wings.**

The Panther was the US Navy's most widely used jet fighter of the Korean War.

Although it was mainly used in the ground-attack role, it did notch up some air combat successes against North Korean MiGs. On July 3, 1950 a Panther of US Navy unit VF-51 aboard USS *Valley Forge* scored the Navy's first aerial kill of the Korean War when it downed a Yak-9. By the end of the war the F9F had flown 78,000 combat missions.

Grumman's first jet fighter for the US Navy had its origins in the last days of World War II, when the US Navy Fighter Branch drew up a requirement for an all-weather/night radar-equipped carrier-borne fighter. As originally planned, Grumman's proposed XF9F-1 was powered by no less than four jet engines positioned in the wings. The high number of engines was dictated by the low power output of early turbojets. As many engines as this called for a wingspan of almost 17m/55.7ft, which worried Grumman – they knew that their twin-engine Tigercat had already proved somewhat large for carrier operations.

As better powerplants were available, the design was refined and when the prototype flew on November 24, 1947 it was powered by a lone Rolls-Royce Nene engine. The Panther's distinctive 454 litre/120 US gallon wingtip fuel tanks were first tested in February 1948 and were adopted as standard to extend the aircraft's range.

This straight-wing model, now called F9F-2, went into production and was equipping US naval units by May 1949, having completed carrier trials two months earlier.

The most produced Panther was the F9F-5, which featured water injection and the J48 engine of 3175kg/7000lb thrust. A total of 616 of this version were built and delivered between November 1950 and January 1953. Panthers continued in US Navy service until 1958, and in 1966 one batch was reconditioned as fighters for the Argentine Navy. Total Panther production was 1382.

Grumman F9F-2B Panther

First flight: November 24, 1947
Power: Pratt & Whitney 2586kg/5700lb-thrust J42-P-8 turbojet engine (licence-built Rolls-Royce Nene)
Armament: Four 20mm/0.78in cannon, plus underwing weapon load of up to 908kg/2000lb
Size: Wingspan – 11.58m/37ft 11.75in
  Length – 11.35m/37ft 3in
  Height – 3.45m/11ft 4in
  Wing area – 23.22m²/250sq ft
Weights: Empty – 4533kg/9993lb
  Maximum take-off – 8842kg/19,494lb
Performance: Maximum speed – 877kph/545mph
  Ceiling – 13,600m/44,600ft
  Range – 2177km/1353 miles
  Climb – 1567m/5140ft per minute

Grumman F11F Tiger

TOP: **Pleasant to fly and well armed, the F11F was popular with pilots.**
AROVE: **Like the Folland Gnat, the F11F was a diminutive fighter and the type was easy to operate from carriers.** BELOW: **Continued engine problems plagued the Tiger's short US Navy career.**

While the Grumman Cougar was making its first flight, Grumman designers were already hard at work on a successor derived from the Cougar/Panther family. In the end, a totally new design was undertaken, with high performance in combat a major requirement. The resulting aircraft was the smallest and lightest airplane that could be designed for the dayfighter mission. The reduced size had another advantage – only the wingtips needed to be folded for carrier handling and storage, thus eliminating the need for complex heavy wing-folding gear.

The prototype flew in July 1954 but the overall performance was not enough of an improvement over that of the Cougar – supersonic speed was the goal. The engine manufacturers Wright proposed that an afterburner version of the J-65 (which was a licence-built British Sapphire engine) could be developed and a complete redesign of the aft fuselage and tail surfaces followed. During the long and troubled development period that followed, the aircraft got a new designation – the F11F.

The afterburner problems continued and a de-rated engine was fitted to bring the aircraft into service. As a result, the expected performance was never achieved and production was limited to only 201 aircraft.

The Tiger entered US Navy service in March 1957. Easy to maintain and having pleasant flying qualities, it continued to be plagued by many engine problems. The last US Navy Tigers were phased out by April 1961, after only four years of service and were replaced by F-8 Crusaders.

Grumman F11F-1

First flight: July 30, 1954
Power: Wright 3379kg/7450lb-thrust J65-W-18 turbojet engine
Armament: Four 20mm/0.78in cannon and four Sidewinder air-to-air missiles under wings
Size: Wingspan – 9.64m/31ft 7.5in
Length – 14.31m/46ft 11.25in
Height – 4.03m/13ft 2.75in
Wing area – 23.23m²/250sq ft
Weights: Empty – 6091kg/13,428lb
Maximum take-off – 10,052kg/22,160lb
Performance: Maximum speed – 1207kph/750mph
Ceiling – 12,770m/41,900ft
Range – 2044km/1270 miles
Climb – 1565m/5130ft per minute

189

Grumman F-14 Tomcat

Despite its age, the swing-wing, twin-engine Grumman F-14 Tomcat is still one of the world's most potent interceptors. Its primary missions, in all weathers, are air superiority, fleet air defence and, more recently, precision strikes against ground targets. Continued developments and improvements have maintained its capabilities to the extent that it is still a potent threat and an effective deterrent to any hostile aircraft foolish enough to threaten US Navy aircraft carrier groups. Its mix of air-to-air weapons is unmatched by any other interceptor type, and its radar is the most capable long-range airborne interception radar carried by any fighter today. With its mix of weapons, it can attack any target at any altitude from ranges between only a few hundred feet to over 160km/100 miles away. It is already a classic fighter.

The F-14 had its beginnings in the early 1960s when Grumman collaborated with General Dynamics on the abortive F-111B, the carrier-based escort fighter version of the F-111. Even before the F-111B cancellation took place, Grumman began work on a company-funded project known as Design 303, a carrier-borne aircraft for the air superiority, escort fighter and deck-launched interception role.

Having flown for the first time on December 21, 1970, the first two US Navy F-14 squadrons were formed in 1972 and

ABOVE: **Wings sweeping back for high-speed flight – the F-14 is over three decades old but is still one of the finest interceptors in service today.**

went to sea in 1974, making the Tomcat the first variable geometry carrier-borne aircraft in service. Its variable-geometry wings are designed for both speed and greater stability. In full forward-sweep position, the wings provide the lift needed for slow-speed flight, especially needed during carrier landings. In swept-back position, the wings blend into the aircraft, giving the F-14 a dart-like configuration for high-speed, supersonic flight. Only a handful of swing-wing types are in service.

The F-14 Tomcat was designed to carry a million dollar missile, the AIM-54 Phoenix, and is the only aircraft that is armed with the AIM-54. With a range of over 200km/120 miles the AIM-54 gives the Tomcat a very long-range punch. Enemy aircraft can be engaged before the Tomcat even appears on their radar screens. Less expensive Sidewinders are also carried for close air fighting.

The F-14B, introduced in November 1987, incorporated new General Electric F-110 engines. A 1995 upgrade program was initiated to incorporate new digital avionics and weapons system improvements to strengthen the F-14s multi-mission capability. The vastly improved F-14D, delivered from 1990,

was a major upgrade with F-110 engines, new APG-71 radar system, Airborne Self Protection Jammer (ASPJ), Joint Tactical Information Distribution System (JTIDS) and Infra-Red Search and Track (IRST). Additionally, all F-14 variants were given precision strike capability using the LANTIRN (Low Altitude Navigation and Targeting Infra-Red for Night) targeting system, night vision compatibility, new defensive countermeasures systems and a new digital flight control system. LANTIRN pods, placed on an external point beneath the right wing, allow the F-14 to drop laser-guided bombs under the cover of darkness. The improved F-14B and F-14D have been built and deployed by the US Navy in modest numbers.

The Tomcat first got to prove itself in combat on August 19, 1981 when two F-14s from the USS *Nimitz* were "intercepted" by two Libyan Sukhoi Su-22 fighter-bombers. The Libyan jets apparently attacked the F-14s and were destroyed with ease. Again on January 4, 1989, two Libyan MiG-23 "Floggers" were engaged by two F-14s and shot down.

Tomcats also saw combat during Operation Desert Storm in 1991, providing top cover protection for bombers and other aircraft, and performing TARPS (Tactical Air Reconnaissance Pod System) missions – the F-14, equipped with TARPS, is the US Navy's only manned tactical reconnaissance platform.

In late 1995, the F-14 Tomcat was used in the bomber role against targets in Bosnia. Nicknamed "Bombcats", the F-14s dropped "smart" bombs while other aircraft illuminated the targets with lasers.

A total of 79 of the type were even exported to Iran before the downfall of the Shah in 1979 and a number were still in service in 2000, having been without the benefit of US technical back-up since 1980.

TOP: **The F-14 earned a much broader audience when it starred in the Hollywood film** *Top Gun.* MIDDLE: **A Tomcat of USS** *George Washington.* **Note the port of the single 20mm/0.788in cannon low down on the nose just ahead of the cockpit.** ABOVE: **This F-14 of US Navy fighter squadron VF-142 was based on the US Navy carrier USS** *Dwight D. Eisenhower.*

ABOVE: **On the deck of the USS** *Nimitz,* **this F-14 is about to be moved and prepared for take-off. The F-14 will continue to protect US Navy carrier groups and project American Air Power for the foreseeable future.**

Grumman F-14 Tomcat

First flight: December 21, 1970
Power: Two Pratt & Whitney 9480kg/20,900lb afterburning thrust TF30-P-412A turbofans
Armament: One 20mm/0.78in cannon plus six AIM-7F Sparrow and four AIM-9 Sidewinder AAMs, or six AIM-54A Phoenix long-range AAMs and two AIM-9s, or a variety of air-to-surface weapons up to 6575kg/14,500lb
Size: Wingspan – 19.55m/64ft 1.5in, unswept
Length – 19.1m/62ft 8in
Height – 4.88m/16ft
Wing area – 52.49m²/565sq ft
Weights: Empty – 18,036kg/39,762lb
Maximum take-off – 31,945kg/70,426lb
Performance: Maximum speed – 2486kph/1545mph
Ceiling – 18,290m/60,000ft
Range – 725km/450 miles
Climb – 18,290m/60,000ft in 2 minutes, 6 seconds

Hawker Hunter

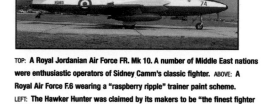

TOP: **A Royal Jordanian Air Force FR. Mk 10. A number of Middle East nations were enthusiastic operators of Sidney Camm's classic fighter.** ABOVE: **A Royal Air Force F.6 wearing a "raspberry ripple" trainer paint scheme.** LEFT: **The Hawker Hunter was claimed by its makers to be "the finest fighter in the world". In addition to its use by the RAF and Royal Navy, Hunters were exported to at least 19 other nations.**

The Hunter, the longest-serving British jet fighter aircraft, was designed to replace the Gloster Meteor in RAF service. Ultimately over 1000 Hunters were built for the RAF in five versions. The prototype flew in July 1951 powered by a 2948kg/6500lb thrust Avon 100 series turbojet and was supersonic in a shallow dive. The Hunter prototype WB188 appeared at the 1951 Farnborough SBAC show, and in April 1952 test pilot Neville Duke took the Hunter through the much-publicized "sound barrier" for the first time.

The first production F. Mk 1 flew on May 16, 1953, but this and a further 22 early production aircraft were used for development purposes. The Hunter F.1 entered RAF service with 43 Squadron in July 1954, replacing their Meteor F.8s, providing the RAF with its long-awaited first transonic fighter. The interceptor capabilities of the Mk 1 were however drastically limited as cannon firing in this mark was restricted to altitudes below 9150m/30,000ft because exhaust gas from the guns caused the engine to flame out. Also, spent cartridge links being ejected by the guns and tumbling along the lower fuselage caused damage or could have even been ingested into the air intakes, so bulbous link collectors were fitted from the F.4 onwards, and were retro-fitted to earlier marks too.

While the F. Mk 1 and the F. Mk 4 that succeeded it were Avon powered, a parallel series of Hunters with the Armstrong Siddeley Sapphire turbojet was developed – the F. Mk 2 and F. Mk 5. The F.2 equipped the RAF's No.257 Squadron from September 1954 and was only produced in limited numbers, despite it not having the flame-out problem of the Mk 1. Both variants were however short-range interceptors and Hawkers

looked at ways to give the Hunter longer legs. The F.4 entered service with 111 Squadron in June 1955, replacing their F.1s. The new model, powered by Avon 115s instead of the problematic Avon 113s of the Mk 1, carried more fuel in strengthened wings which allowed carriage of bombs, rockets and drop tanks.

The Sapphire-powered F.5, otherwise similar to the Mk 4, entered service with 263 Squadron in April 1955 and was the first variant to see active service, being deployed against ground targets in Egypt during the Suez campaign.

Next came the Hunter F. Mk 6 with the 4536kg/10,000lb thrust Avon 203 engine that bestowed a much improved performance and an impressive climb. Although it was only transonic in a dive, the F.6 was built in greater numbers than any other version. Early examples of this high-powered Hunter had a tendency to pitch-up at high speeds, and this was cured by extending the leading edges of the outer portion of the wing, giving the saw-toothed look. F.6s could also scramble more quickly as they used an AVPIN starter system, enabling quicker engine start-up than the cartridge-started early variants. The Hunter F. Mk 6 entered front-line service in October 1956. With better performance at altitude, the Hunter was now able to hold its own with most contemporary fighters but this was shortlived. Britain's V-bombers could climb

beyond its reach and the new American fighters could outperform it. The arrival of the very high-performance Lightning in RAF service spelt the end for the Hunter as an interceptor and the last Fighter Command F.6s were replaced in April 1963. From then on the Hunter's role in the RAF was primarily ground attack, and so the next variant was the FGA.9 which served until 1970 when it was replaced by a mixture of Buccaneers, Phantoms and Harriers. Hunters continued to be used as weapons trainers in the RAF into the 1980s.

The Hunter was of course a major export success and was used by at least 19 foreign air forces. In addition, licence production was carried out in Holland and Belgium. Sweden, Singapore, Denmark and Switzerland all operated Hunters; the latter nation proved to be a long-lived Hunter operator, flying theirs from 1958 until 1995. India made extensive use of the Hunter from 1957 to the early 1980s, and was the first export customer of the type. Participating in the 1965 and 1971 conflicts with Pakistan, the Indian Hunters proved to be a formidable ground attack aircraft and took part in air-to-air combat with Pakistani Sabres and even an F-104. In the 1971 IndoPak war, eight Sabres were claimed by Indian Hunters in air-to-air combat.

In the Middle East, Hunters were operated by Abu Dhabi, Qatar, Saudi Arabia and Kuwait. Jordan operated Hunters from 1958 until 1974, and their aircraft were the first Arab aircraft to attack Israeli territory in the Six Day War. The Lebanon and Zimbabwe were still operating front-line Hunters in early 2000.

ABOVE: **At its peak use, over 1000 Hunters were in service with the RAF.** LEFT: **The Royal Navy used the two-seat Hunters for training pilots of transonic fighter types such as the Scimitar and Sea Vixen.**

ABOVE: **Early problems with gun firing were eliminated by simple modifications.** LEFT: **The first of the many – WB188 was the prototype P.1067 that first flew in July 1951. The basic design changed little for production versions.** BELOW: **An F.6, XF515, in the markings of No.43 Squadron RAF, "The Fighting Cocks". Note the unit insignia on the forward fuselage.**

Hawker Hunter F. Mk 6

First flight: July 20, 1951 (prototype)

Power: Rolls-Royce 4542kg/10,000lb thrust Avon 203

Armament: Four fixed 30mm/1.18in cannon in removable pack. Provision under wings for two 454kg/1000lb bombs, 5cm/2in or 7.62cm/3in multiple rocket batteries

Size: Wingspan – 10.2m/33ft 8in
Length – 14m/45ft 11in Height – 4.01m/13ft 2in
Wing area – 31.6m^2/340sq ft

Weights: Empty – 5795kg/12,760lb
Maximum take-off – 8062kg/17,750lb

Performance: Maximum speed – 1150kph/715mph
Ceiling – 15,707m/51,500ft
Range – 2960km/1840 miles
Climb – 13,725m/45,000ft in 7.5 minutes

Hawker Sea Fury/Fury

The Fury was designed as a lighter, smaller version of the Hawker Tempest to a joint British Air Ministry and Admiralty wartime specification. The land-based Fury first flew in September 1944 but at the war's end RAF interest in the ultimate Hawker piston-engined fighter ceased. Development of the Sea Fury did, however, continue, following the version's test flight in February 1945. This aircraft was essentially a navalized land plane, complete with non-folding wings. The second prototype Sea Fury was a fully navalized aircraft, with folding wings and arrester hook and was powered by a Bristol Centaurus XV.

The production version, the Sea Fury Mk X, began to replace Fleet Air Arm Supermarine Seafires from August 1947. Meanwhile trials with external stores and rocket-assisted take-off equipment led to the Sea Fury FB. Mk 11. It was this aircraft that represented the ultimate development of British piston-engined fighters and the FB.11 proved to be an extremely capable combat aircraft. FAA Sea Furies were among the few British aircraft types that saw combat during the Korean War (1950–3), where they were mainly used in the ground-attack role, operating from HMS *Theseus*, HMS *Ocean*, HMS *Glory* and HMAS *Sydney*. Korea was the first true jet versus jet war but the Sea Fury is known to have destroyed more Communist aircraft than any other non-US type and even shot down a number of North Korean MiGs.

ABOVE: **SR661 was a prototype of the Mk X production version intended to replace Seafires in Fleet Air Arm service.** BELOW: **Certainly the ultimate British piston fighter and considered by some to be the best single-engine piston-powered fighter ever, the Hawker Sea Fury was a very capable fighting aircraft. The example pictured is an FB.11.**

While flying the piston-engined Sea Fury off HMS *Ocean*, Royal Navy Lt Peter Carmichael destroyed a MiG-15 jet and earned himself a place in the history books. "At dawn on August 9, 1952 I was leading a section of four aircraft on a patrol near Chinnampo. We were flying at 1068m/3500ft, looking for rail targets when my Number Two called out, 'MiGs five o'clock – coming in!' Eight came at us from the sun. One came at me head on and I saw his tracer coming over. I managed to fire a burst and then he flashed past. I looked over my shoulder and saw an aircraft going down. When all

LEFT: **The Iraqi Air Force operated a number of land-based Furies in the late 1940s and early 1950s while Pakistan had a number of the type in use into the 1970s.**

my section called in, I knew I'd bagged a MiG! I believe the Sea Fury is the finest single-seat piston fighter ever built".

The Sea Fury, the last piston-engined fighter in RN front-line service, continued flying with Royal Navy Volunteer Reserve units until 1957 and was replaced in FAA service by the Sea Hawk.

Although the RAF rejected the Fury design, a little-known contract with Iraq saw 55 land-based Furies and five two-seat trainers delivered to the Iraqi Air Force between 1948 and 1955. The IAF are known to have used the aircraft in a counter-insurgency role. Pakistan also received Furies and used them in action against India until 1973.

Sea Furies were also exported to Egypt, Burma, Canada, Australia and the Netherlands, where a number were also licence-built by Fokker. At the time of the Cuban Missile Crisis in 1962, Cuba's fighter defence centred on 15 FB.11s, which had been imported in the Batista period.

After their military service a number of these high-performance piston aircraft were snapped up for air racing in the United States, where they set world record speeds.

ABOVE: **The Royal Netherlands Navy was the only other European operator of the Sea Fury. Twenty-two aircraft were exported from the UK while a further 210 were built in Holland by Fokker.** BELOW: **The Royal Australian Navy's HMAS Sydney took its Sea Furies into combat during the Korean War.**

Hawker Sea Fury FB.11

First flight: September 1, 1944
Power: Bristol 2480hp Centaurus 18 two-row sleeve-valve radial engine
Armament: Four 20mm/0.78in cannon in outer wings, plus underwing provision for up to 907kg/2000lb of bombs or rockets
Size: Wingspan – 11.69m/38ft 4.75in, spread 4.9m/16ft 1in, folded
Length – 10.56m/34ft 8in
Height – 4.81m/15ft 10in
Wing area – 26.01m²/280sq ft
Weights: Empty – 4090kg/8977lb
Maximum take-off – 5669kg/12,500lb
Performance: Maximum speed – 740kph/460mph
Ceiling – 11,000m/36,000ft
Range – 1223km/760 miles
Climb – 1320m/4320ft per minute

LEFT: **The Marut shows what the Third Reich may have been capable of producing.**

Hindustan HF-24 Marut

First flight: June 17, 1961
Power: Two HAL/Rolls-Royce 2200kg/4850lb-thrust Orpheus Mk 703 turbojet engines
Armament: Four 30mm/1.18in cannon, plus retractable pack of 50 68mm/2.68in rockets in belly, plus hardpoints to carry a variety of weapons
Size: Wingspan – 9m/29ft 6.25in
Length – 15.87m/52ft 0.75in
Height – 3.6m/11ft 9.75in
Wing area – 28m²/301.4sq ft
Weights: Empty – 6195kg/13,658lb
Maximum take-off – 10,908kg/24,048lb
Performance: Maximum speed – 1112kph/691mph
Ceiling – 12,200m/40,000ft
Range – 1000km/620 miles
Climb – 12,200m/40,000ft in 9 minutes 20 seconds

Hindustan HF-24 Marut

The Marut (spirit of the tempest) was the first fruit of the Indian Air Staff's desire for their country to be self-reliant in combat aircraft production. In mid-1950s India, however, there was little expertise in jet aircraft design so the famous Focke-Wulf designer Kurt Tank was invited to create a team (that ultimately included 18 German engineers) to work on the project in India. Design work began in 1957 with

the aim of building a Mach-2 capable all-weather multi-role aircraft.

The prototype first flew in June 1961, powered by two Rolls-Royce Bristol Orpheus 703 turbojets and the production aircraft had Indian licence-built Orpheus engines. The Marut finally entered service in April 1967 and was the first supersonic fighter built by a non-superpower.

By late 1975 about 100 aircraft had been delivered and had seen action

in the 1971 war against Pakistan, on some occasions dogfighting with enemy F-86 Sabres.

The Marut did not meet expectations as a fighter, but it served the Indian Air Force well until mid-1990.

LEFT: **The Kfir, the ultimate Mirage development.**

IAI Kfir-C7

First flight: October 19, 1970 (Kfir prototype)
Power: IAI/General Electric 8112kg/17,860lb after-burning thrust licence-built J79-JIE turbojet engine
Armament: Two 30mm/1.18in cannon, five underfuselage and two underwing hardpoints for AIM-9 Sidewinder, Python or Shafir air-to-air missiles or anti-radar missiles and bombs
Size: Wingspan – 8.22m/27ft
Length – 15.65m/51ft 4in
Height – 4.55m/14ft 11in
Wing area – 34.8m²/374.6sq ft
Weights: Empty –7285kg/16,060lb
Maximum take-off – 16,500kg/36,375lb
Performance: Maximum speed – Mach 2.3/2440kph/1515mph
Ceiling – 17,690m/58,000ft
Range – 882km/548 miles
Climb – 13,989m/45,866ft per minute

Israel Aircraft Industries Kfir

The original Kfir (lion cub) prototype that first flew on October 19, 1970 combined a French-built Mirage III airframe with the licence-built GE-J79 afterburning turbojet of the F-4 Phantom II. By the time the Kfir reached production in 1974–5, the airframe was a version of the Israeli-built Mirage 5 (Nesher), equipped with Israeli-built electronics. Only 27 Kfir-C1s were built and 25 were later sold on to the US

Navy and Marine Corps for use as "aggressor" aircraft, designated F-21A.

The first of 185 Kfir-C2s entered service in 1976, having first flown in 1974. It sported a canard mounted on the air-intakes. Virtually all C1s were upgraded to C2 standard.

The Kfir-C7 was introduced in 1983 and is an improved upgraded version of the C2, with a more powerful engine and improved performance. It can also

carry "smart" weapons, has a sophisticated cockpit and is equipped for inflight refuelling.

The Kfir, widely considered to be the most potent development of the Mirage, is expected to be phased out of IAF service in the early 2000s.

Lavochkin La-11

This aircraft was among the last Soviet piston-engined fighters produced and emerged into a world of jet aircraft. Developed from the earlier Lavochkin La-9, the La-11 was designed to escort Soviet bombers on their long missions. Although it had the same engine and the wing was similar to that of the La-9, other changes were

incorporated. Auxiliary fuel tanks were added to the wingtips and the earlier aircraft's distinctive underbelly oil cooler was built into the engine cowling. Armament was reduced from four to three 23mm/0.9in cannon.

The new aircraft first flew in late 1944 and remained in production until 1951 by which time 1182 examples had been

built. Both the North Korean and Chinese air forces were supplied with La-11s and the type was used in combat during the Korean War (1950–3). By the end of that conflict, the La-11 was being phased out as a fighter by all operating air arms but a number carried on in second-line training duties into the 1960s.

TOP: **The La-11 was the end of the line for Soviet piston-engined fighters, and saw action in the Korean War.** ABOVE: **This example crash-landed in Sweden during World War II.**

Lavochkin La-11

First flight: late 1944
Power: Shvetsov 1870hp ASh-82FNV radial piston engine
Armament: Three 23mm/0.9in cannon
Size: Wingspan – 9.95m/32ft 7.75in
  Length – 8.6m/28ft 2.5in
  Height – 2.95m/9ft 8in
  Wing area – 17.7m^2/190.53sq ft
Weights: Empty – 2770kg/6107lb
  Maximum take-off – 3995kg/8807lb
Performance: Maximum speed – 690kph/429mph
  Ceiling – 10,250m/33,630ft
  Range – 750km/466 miles
  Climb – 5000m/16,405ft in 6 minutes, 35 seconds

Lockheed F-80 Shooting Star

Lockheed began design work on a jet fighter as early as 1941 but abandoned it due to lack of the right powerplant. Work restarted in earnest in June 1943, when the British de Havilland Goblin jet engine (1361kg/3000lb thrust) became available. The first prototype was built and ready to fly in only 143 days but its maiden flight was delayed due to an engine

ABOVE: Too late for action in World War II, the Lockheed P-80 (later F-80) was the USA's first jet fighter. BELOW LEFT: The two-seater trainer version, the T-33, still flies with air forces around the world, and many are also in private hands.

The sleek low-winged P-80 entered USAAF service in February 1945 and the first Shooting Stars, pre-production models, arrived in Italy before the end of World War II. By the end of the war a total of 45 had been delivered to the USAAF but they did not see service. The first unit solely to operate the P-80 was the 412th Fighter Group established at March Field in November 1945.

Post-war the P-80 was selected to re-equip pursuit (fighter) units of the USAAF and was the first jet fighter to be entrusted with the task of defending the USA, until being superseded by the F-86 Sabre.

In 1948, a wing of P-80As were deployed to Fürstenfeldbrück during the Berlin Airlift, in reaction to Yak-3s and La-5FNs buzzing Allied transport aircraft. As the USAF's first jet fighter, its deployment demonstrated the gravity with which the West viewed the situation. Also in 1948, the USAF (an independent service from September 1947, formerly USAAF) changed the designation of its pursuit aircraft to fighters and the P-80 became the F-80.

The last P-80A was built in December 1946 and was replaced on the production line by the much improved P-80B, which was some 454kg/1000lb heavier and powered by a better engine.

When the Korean War broke out in 1950 the F-80 was the principal USAF fighter in the theatre and ultimately the 8th,

failure and the XP-80 finally took to the sky in January 1944. Later prototypes and the first P-80As were powered by a General Electric engine developed from Frank Whittle's W.1 turbojet. Early tests flights saw the aircraft attain speeds of 805kph/500mph, considerably faster than the piston-engined fighters in service at the time and the 660kph/410mph of the Gloster Meteor Mk 1.

35th, 49th and 51st Fighter Groups all flew Shooting Stars in Korea. On June 27, 1950 the first jet fighter combat involving US fighters saw four F-80s shoot down four North Korean Air Force Ilyushin Il-10 Shturmoviks.

By now the F-80C, the definitive fighter version of the Shooting Star, was in service and among other improvements offered the pilot the reassurance of an ejection seat. It was also the first USAF aircraft equipped with an explosive canopy remover. Produced in greater numbers than any other version, many earlier models were at least partly upgraded to "C" standard.

The first jet against jet air combat came on November 8, 1950, when four MiGs were seen to fly into Korean air space and were challenged by F-80Cs of the 51st Fighter-Interceptor Wing. Even though all but one of his guns jammed, Lt Russell J. Brown attacked and destroyed one of the MiGs in mid-air. In spite of this and other air combat successes, the F-80 was replaced by F-84s and F-86s during the conflict, as it had become outclassed, but it continued to serve in the fighter-bomber role.

Although the Shooting Star broke much new ground with the US Air Force, it was not widely exported, the only customers being in South America – Ecuador, Chile, Brazil, Uruguay, Colombia and Peru.

The trainer version, the two-seat T-33, was, however, widely exported and continues to serve in air arms half a century after the single-seat P-80 fighter first flew. The T-33 version was created by extending the fuselage to accommodate the two seats in tandem. Between 1040 and 1959 Lockheed built 5691 T-33s and they served with the air forces of nearly 00 countries.

Lockheed F-80C Shooting Star

First flight: January 8, 1944 (XP-80)

Power: Allison 2449kg/5,400lb-thrust J33-A-35 turbojet engine

Armament: Six 12.7mm/0.5in machine-guns, plus two 454kg/1000lb bombs and eight underwing rockets

Size: Wingspan – 11.81m/38ft 9in
Length – 10.49m/34ft 5in
Height – 3.43m/11ft 3in
Wing area – 22.07m^2/237.6sq ft

Weights: Empty – 3819kg/8420lb
Maximum take-off – 7646kg/16,856lb

Performance: Maximum speed – 956kph/594mph
Ceiling – 14,265m/46,800ft
Range – 1328km/825 miles
Climb – 1524m/5000ft per minute

TOP: **Deployed to Europe during the Berlin Airlift, the Shooting Star first fired its guns in combat during the Korean War, where it was able to hold its own for a time against the MiG-15.** ABOVE: **Tasked with defending the USA, P-80s protected their country until the arrival of the much more able F-86 Sabres.**

LEFT: **Hastily produced to defend the USA against Soviet bombers, the F-94 was derived from the T-33.** BELOW: **A battery of 48 unguided missiles gave the F-94 a powerful punch intended to knock enemy bombers from the sky.**

Lockheed F-94

When the USSR exploded its first atomic bomb in 1949, the USA quickly began to develop a range of interceptors that could tackle the expected Soviet bomber fleets. Some were to be developed for the USAF's Air Defense Command over the long term while others, such as the F-94, were rushed into production as stop-gaps.

The tandem-seat F-94 was one of the earliest radar-equipped jet fighters and eventually made up more than 24 squadrons of the fledgling US Air Defense Command, founded on 21 March 1946 to defend the USA. Based on the T-33, the F-94 was fitted with radar, carried a rear-seat observer and was armed with only four 12.7mm/0.5in machine-guns.

The prototype YF-94 first flew in April 1949 and the first production aircraft were in squadron service by the end of that year, such was the urgency to counter the perceived Soviet threat. The ADC F-94s were kept on three-minute alert for the interception of enemy bombers. With 427kg/940lb of radar kit on board, it needed an afterburner to lift off. Once airborne, the F-94 had a performance on a par with the F-80 but no better.

A total of 853 F-94s were built, and A and B models saw action in Korea,

particularly on night missions, although because of their secret radar, they were initially forbidden to overfly enemy territory. When regulations were relaxed, the F-94 began to score victories over the enemy at night and solely by use of instruments.

Named Starfire in the C variant only, the F-94C had a more powerful engine (and in turn a higher top speed), thinner wing, swept tailplane, longer fuselage and a new airborne interception radar. Armament was beefed up to 24 Mighty Mouse rockets and a further 24 housed in wing launchers. These rockets were unguided and were simply intended to destroy bombers by filling the sky with "lead". As the new generation of interceptors came into service, the F-94 was gradually retired and the type ended its brief but useful career equipping National Guard Units in the mid-1950s.

ABOVE: **This aircraft, 48-356, was the YF-94A prototype, having already served as the T-33 prototype in 1948. It is preserved in the USA at a United States Air Force base.**

Lockheed F-94

First flight: April 16, 1949 (YF-94)

Power: Pratt & Whitney 3969kg/8750lb afterburning thrust J48-P-5 turbojet engine

Armament: 24 69.85mm/2.75in Mighty Mouse air-to-air rocket projectiles, plus a further 24 housed in wing launchers

Size: Wingspan – 12.93m/42ft 5in
Length – 13.56m/44ft 6in
Height – 4.55m/14ft 11in
Wing area – 31.4m^2/338sq ft

Weights: Empty – 5761kg/12,700lb
Maximum take-off – 10,977kg/24,200lb

Performance: Maximum speed – 941kph/585mph
Ceiling – 15,665m/51,400ft
Range – 1930km/1200 miles
Climb – 2430m/7980ft per minute

Lockheed F-104 Starfighter

The F-104 was designed by Lockheed based on the experiences of American pilots in the Korean War – high performance was the overriding feature of this aircraft, which was frequently described as a missile with a man in it. The short wing had a maximum thickness of 10.16cm/4in and had a leading edge so sharp that when the F-104 was on the ground, it had to have a safety covering for the protection of ground crews. The Starfighter, once nicknamed "Widowmaker" because of the large number of fatal crashes of the type, found greater use with foreign air forces than with the US Air Force.

Development problems delayed the type's entry into USAF service by two years, and deliveries began in January 1958. The F-104 was the first operational fighter capable of sustained speeds above twice the speed of sound and became the first aircraft ever to hold the world speed and altitude records simultaneously. On May 7, 1958 Major Howard C. Johnson reached an altitude of 27,830m/91,243ft, and on May 16, Captain Walter W. Irwin reached a speed of 2259.3kph/1404.19mph.

On December 14, 1959, an F-104C Starfighter boosted the world's altitude record to 31,534m/103,389ft, becoming the first aircraft to take-off under its own power and exceed the 30,480m/ 100,000ft barrier.

The F-104G that first flew in October 1960 was an all-new version designed for the Luftwaffe as a fighter-bomber and was the most successful mark.

The US Air Force used only about one-third of the F-104s built, with most going to or being built in Canada, West Germany, Italy, Japan, Belgium, Denmark, Greece, Norway, Spain, Taiwan, Jordan, Pakistan and Turkey. In the USA, the last Air National Guard Starfighters were retired in 1975.

In 1997–8, the Italian Air Force extended the life of their licence-built F-104s to keep them flying half a century after the prototype had its maiden flight.

RIGHT: **The F-104G was a multi-role fighter-bomber version designed to meet a Luftwaffe requirement.** BELOW: **Clearly illustrating its nickname, the sleek lines of the F-104 fuselage were very missile-like. It was the "hot ship" of its time.**

Lockheed F-104G Starfighter

First flight: March 4, 1954 (XF-104)
Power: General Electric 7076kg/15,600lb afterburning thrust J79-GE-11A turbojet engine
Armament: One 20mm/0.78in six barrel cannon, wingtip-mounted Sidewinder air-to-air missiles and up to 1814kg/4000lb of external stores
Size: Wingspan – 6.36m/21ft 9in, excluding wingtip missiles
Length – 16.66m/54ft 8in
Height – 4.09m/13ft 5in
Wing area – 18.22m²/196.1sq ft
Weights: Empty – 6348kg/13,995lb
Maximum take-off – 13,170kg/29,035lb
Performance: Maximum speed – 1845kph/1146mph
Ceiling – 15,240m/50,000ft
Range – 1740km/1081 miles
Climb – 14,640m/48,000ft per minute

General Dynamics/Lockheed Martin F-16 Fighting Falcon

The F-16 Fighting Falcon, with its origins in the 1972 USAF Lightweight Fighter Program, is one of the best combat aircraft in service today. It is highly manoeuvrable and has proven itself in air-to-air combat and air-to-surface attack. It is a relatively low-cost, high-performance weapons system used by the USAF and a number of other nations.

The single-seat F-16A first flew in December 1976 and became operational with the USAF in January 1979. The F-16B, a two-seat model, has tandem cockpits with a bubble canopy extended to cover the second cockpit. Space for the second cockpit was created by reducing the forward fuselage fuel tank size and reduction of avionics growth space. During training, the forward cockpit is used by a student pilot with an instructor pilot in the rear cockpit.

All F-16s delivered since November 1981 have built-in structural and wiring provisions and systems architecture that permit expansion of the multi-role flexibility to perform precision strike, night attack and beyond-visual-range interception missions. This improvement programme led to the F-16C and F-16D aircraft, which are the single- and two-seat equivalents of the F-16A/B, and incorporate the latest cockpit control and display technology. All active USAF units and many Air National Guard and Air Force Reserve units have converted to the F-16C/D.

The F-16 was also licence-built by Belgium, Denmark, the Netherlands and Norway – who needed to replace their F-104 Starfighters. Final airframe assembly lines were located in Belgium and the Netherlands, and these European F-16s are

assembled from components manufactured in the four client countries as well as in the USA. Belgium also provided final assembly of the F100 engine used in the European F-16s. The programme increased the supply and availability of repair parts in Europe and thus improved the Europe-based F-16's combat readiness. Turkey also had an F-16 production line.

In the air combat role, the F-16's manoeuvrability and combat radius exceed that of all potential threat fighter aircraft. It can locate targets in all-weather conditions and detect low-flying aircraft in radar ground clutter. In an air-to-surface role, the F-16 can fly more than 860km/500 miles, deliver its weapons with superior accuracy while defending itself against enemy aircraft, and then return to base. The

TOP: **This early F-16 caused a stir when it visited the UK in the late 1970s. The type was a quantum leap in fighter design.** ABOVE: **The highly manoeuvrable fly-by-wire F-16 is always a favourite at air shows.**

aircraft's all-weather capability allows it to deliver ordnance accurately during non-visual bombing conditions.

In designing the F-16, advanced aerospace science and proven reliable systems from other aircraft such as the F-15 and F-111 were selected. These were combined to simplify the design process and reduce the aircraft's size, purchase price, maintenance costs and weight. The light weight of the fuselage is achieved without reducing its strength – with a full load of internal fuel, the F-16 can withstand up to 9G, which exceeds the capability of other current fighter aircraft. The cockpit and its bubble canopy give the pilot unobstructed

ABOVE: **F-16s will be in service for many years to come.** FAR LEFT: **The USAF Thunderbirds aerobatic team were a great advertisement for the type.** LEFT: **An excellent photograph of an F-16C Fighting Falcon, showing the cockpit area and to its right the exit nozzle of the internal cannon.**

forward and upward vision, and greatly improved vision over the side and to the rear while the seat-back angle was expanded from the normal 13 degrees to 30 degrees, increasing pilot comfort and gravity force tolerance. The pilot has excellent flight control of the F-16 through its fly-by-wire system, where electrical wires relay commands, replacing the usual cables and linkage controls. For easy and accurate control of the aircraft during high G-force combat manoeuvres, a side-stick controller is used instead of the conventional centre-mounted control column. Hand pressure on the side-stick controller sends electrical signals to actuators of flight control surfaces such as ailerons and rudder.

Avionics systems include a highly accurate inertial navigation system in which a computer provides steering information to the pilot. The plane has UHF and VHF radios, plus an instrument (automatic) landing system. It also has a warning system and electronic countermeasure pods to be used against airborne or surface electronic threats.

USAF F-16Cs and Ds were deployed to the Persian Gulf during 1991 in support of Operation Desert Storm, where more sorties were flown than with any other aircraft. These versatile fighters were used to attack airfields, military production facilities, Scud missile sites and a variety of other targets.

In February 1994, Italy-based USAF F-16s, deployed to help NATO keep the peace in Bosnia, engaged and destroyed Serb bombers attacking targets in central Bosnia. Turkish licence-built F-16s also enforced the No Fly Zone over Bosnia. Other F-16 operators include Bahrain, Egypt, Greece, Indonesia, Israel, Pakistan, South Korea, Portugal, Singapore, Taiwan, Thailand and Venezuela. The 4000th F-16 was delivered in May 2000 and production and upgrades will undoubtedly keep the F-16 in the front line for many years to come.

ABOVE: **Belgium was one of the European nations who engaged in a licence-build F-16 programme.**

General Dynamics/ Lockheed Martin F-16A

First flight: January 20, 1974 (YF-16)

Power: Pratt & Whitney 10,824kg/23,830lb afterburning thrust F100-PW-100 turbofan engine

Armament: One 20mm/0.78in cannon, nine hard points to carry up to 5435kg/12,000lb of air-to-air missiles, bombs and rockets

Size: Wingspan – 10m/32ft 10in, including wingtip air-to-air missiles
Length – 15.03m/49ft 4in
Height – 5.01m/16ft 5in
Wing area – 28.9m²/300sq ft

Weights: Empty – 6607kg/14,567lb
Maximum take-off – 14,968kg/33,000lb

Performance: Maximum speed – 2125kph/1320mph
Ceiling – 15,250m/50,000ft plus
Range – 580km/360 miles
Climb – 15,250m/50,000ft per minute

Lockheed Martin/Boeing F-22 Raptor

The advanced air superiority F-22 Raptor fighter was developed in response to a 1983 United States Air Force request for designs of an Advanced Tactical Fighter – a next generation, air superiority fighter. The designs of current front-line US fighter aircraft are decades old and with so much new technology now available, the US military are keen that replacement aircraft incorporate as many new developments in performance and function as possible.

The Lockheed proposal, the YF-22A, was rolled out on August 29, 1990, and first flew on September 29 having been unofficially named Lightning II, after the famous Lockheed fighter of World War II. More stealthy than the F-15, the YF-22A design was more optimized for manoeuvrability, featuring design elements such as vertical thrust vectoring engine exhausts.

The YF-22 was declared the winner of the competition in April 1991 – the first true F-22 impressive prototype was rolled out on April 9, 1997 and its first flight was on September 7, 1997. Flight tests demonstrate that the F-22 combines good handling characteristics with very high manoeuvrability and the

ABOVE: **The second F-22, pictured here on its first flight on June 29, 1998. The Raptor is considered by many to be the world's most advanced fighter.**

test program is expected to continue through 2003, with operational introduction of the Raptor scheduled for 2005.

The heart of the F-22's electronic capability is the APG-77 radar system which is able to detect an enemy aircraft's radar from distances up to 460km/286 miles. It will then acquire the enemy aircraft as a target it can kill at distances of up to 220km/136 miles – the F-22 radar signal will be very difficult to detect and the stealthy F-22 will be virtually invisible to radar.

If the enemy does manage to detect the signal, they must then get a radar lock on the F-22 to launch an attack – the F-22 radar can also analyze the enemy's radar and send out a jamming burst. Between dealing with active threats, the radar system collects information from the combat area, locates electronic systems, classifies them, and alerts the pilot to possible threats or high-priority targets. The F-22's avionics were designed to enable a lone pilot to undertake missions that normally require a two-man crew.

As a safety measure, the aircraft's eight internal fuel tanks are flooded with nitrogen to reduce the danger of fire from fuel fumes. The gas is produced by an on-board nitrogen generation system from air.

Ground crews can monitor the status of the aircraft systems through a laptop computer that can list faults, undertake diagnosis and even check the oil level.

The F-22 is constructed mainly from composites and titanium alloys. Radar absorbent materials are used to minimize the aircraft's radar signature, and the aircraft's shape is intended to make it less conspicuous to radar. The aircraft's frameless canopy is also designed to reduce radar reflections.

The cockpit control layout is based on high-intensity monitor displays, plus a holographic Head-Up Display (HUD). The cockpit also features HOTAS controls so the pilot can issue commands to the systems without releasing the flight controls.

The Pratt & Whitney F-119-PW-100 engine is very advanced but has been designed for ease of maintenance so that all components can be removed or replaced with one of six standard tools. The engine includes vertical thrust vectoring

exhaust nozzles to improve the Raptor's manoeuvrability in low-speed combat and are automatically directed by the F-22's flight control system. The exhaust does not emit visible smoke during normal operations. The engine's supersonic cruise capability allows, without the use of afterburner, rapid location to a combat area, fast exit from the target area as a means of defence and higher launch velocities for munitions.

Despite some official doubts about the need for an advanced fighter that is estimated to cost at least $70 million a unit, the USAF plans to field 339 Raptors. The first squadron will be operational by 2005.

Lockheed Martin/ Boeing F-22 Raptor

First flight: September 29, 1990 (YF-22)
Power: Two Pratt & Whitney 16,095kg/35,438lb afterburning thrust F119-100 turbofans
Armament: One 20mm/0.78in cannon, four AIM-9 Sidewinders carried in side weapons bays. Ventral weapons bay can carry four AIM-120 AAMs or six AIM-120s. Additional ordnance can be carried on four underwing hardpoints
Size: Wingspan – 13.56m/44ft
Length – 18.92m/62ft 1in
Height – 5m/16ft 5in
Wing area – 78m²/840sq ft
Weights: Empty – 14,395kg/31,760lb
Maximum take-off – 27,216kg/60,000lb
Performance: Maximum speed – Mach 2
Ceiling – 15,250m/50,000ft
Range and climb data not published

LEFT: A US Navy F2H-2 Banshee – note the straight wings.

McDonnell F2H-3 Banshee

First flight: January 11, 1947
Power: Two Westinghouse 1474kg/3250lb thrust J34-WE-34 turbojets
Armament: Four 20mm/0.78in cannon plus underwing racks for 454kg/1000lb of bombs
Size: Wingspan – 12.73m/41ft 9in
Length – 14.68m/48ft 2in
Height – 4.42m/14ft 6in
Wing area – 27.31m^2/294sq ft
Weights: Empty – 5980kg/13,183lb
Maximum take-off – 11,437kg/25,214lb
Performance: Maximum speed – 933kph/580mph
Ceiling – 14,205m.46,600ft
Range – 1883km/1170 miles
Climb – 2743m/9000ft per minute

McDonnell F2H Banshee

The F2H Banshee, though similar in design and appearance to the company's earlier FH-1 Phantom, was larger and had more powerful twin Westinghouse J34 engines which gave about twice the power of the J30 engines in the FH-1.

Designed to meet the US Navy's exacting requirements for carrier operations, while also satisfying the requirement for high speed and increased rates of climb, the F2H Banshee first flew in January 1947. It became the Navy's standard long-range all-weather fighter and entered US Navy service in 1948 as their second carrier jet fighter, after the FH-1. They served with distinction with the US Navy in Korea in 1950–3 but by the end of the conflict they had been superseded

by more advanced designs. That said, Banshees remained in service with US Navy reserve units until the mid-1960s.

The Royal Canadian Navy acquired 39 ex-US Navy Banshees between 1955 and 1958. A total of 805 F2H Banshees were made.

McDonnell F3H Demon

LEFT: The F3H was planned to be the world's first missile-only fighter.

McDonnell F3H-2 Demon

First flight: August 7, 1951 (XF3H-1)
Power: Allison 6350kg/14,000lb afterburning thrust J71-A-2E turbojet
Armament: Four 20mm/0.78in cannon and four AIM-7C Sparrow AAMs
Size: Wingspan – 10.77m/35ft 4in
Length – 17.96m/58ft 11in
Height – 4.44m/14ft 7in
Wing area – 48.22m^2/519sq ft
Weights: Empty – 10,039kg/22,133lb
Maximum take-off – 15377kg/33,900lb
Performance: Maximum speed – 1041kph/647mph
Ceiling – 13,000m/42,650ft
Range – 2205km/1370 miles
Climb – 3660m/12,000ft per minute

The F3H Demon was the first swept-wing jet fighter aircraft built by McDonnell Aircraft and also the first aircraft designed to be armed only with missiles rather than guns. The carrier-based, transonic, all-weather Demon fighter was designed with the philosophy that carrier-based fighters need not be inferior to land-based fighters. However, the planned powerplant, the new J40 turbojet, failed to meet its expectations and left early Demons (F3H-1N) under-powered. Production delays were also

caused by the Navy's desire for the Demon to be an all-weather nightfighter. And so, although the prototype had flown in August 1951, the radar-equipped Demon did not enter service until March 1956 as the F3H-2N and then with the Allison J71 turbojet as the powerplant.

By the time production ceased in 1959, 519 Demons had been built including the definitive Demon fighter-bomber (F3H-2). At its peak US Navy use, the Demon equipped 11 squadrons.

McDonnell F-101 Voodoo

Developed from the XF-88 prototype interceptor that first flew in 1948, the F-101 Voodoo was conceived as a long-range escort fighter for USAF Strategic Air Command B-36s. The F-101 was never going to have the range to stay with the intercontinental bombers but with the still impressive range of over 2414km/1500 miles, the Voodoo went on to a lengthy career as an interceptor and the first USAF supersonic reconnaissance aircraft. The prototype F-101A first flew in September 1954, and after entering USAF service in 1957 the F-101 was used in a number of speed and endurance record attempts, which were intended to show the Soviets just how fast and far USAF fighters could go. On November 27, 1957, four RF-101As (reconnaissance

versions) took off from California and after refuelling in flight, two of the aircraft landed at McGuire Air Force Base, New Jersey, while the other two turned around and landed back at March Air Force Base in California on the other side of the continental United States. Meanwhile, Major Adrian Drew, flying an F-101A at Edwards Air Force Base, set a new absolute speed record of 1942.97kph/1207.34mph. All these record-breaking flights earned the Voodoo the nickname "One-Oh-Wonder".

The two-seat all-weather F-101B first flew in 1957. In service it had a Hughes fire-control system and was armed with six Falcon air-to-air missiles, or two Genie nuclear-tipped air-to-air missiles and four Falcons.

Fifty-six surplus Voodoos were transferred to the Royal Canadian Air Force in 1961 as CF-101Bs. A decade later these were replaced by more capable ex-USAF aircraft that continued in RCAF service until 1985. USAF and

RCAF Voodoos guarded the polar approaches to North America against Soviet bombers.

The last US Air Force F-101 was retired in 1971, while the last Air National Guard F-101s were retired in 1983. Reconnaissance versions of the Voodoo were also supplied to the Chinese Nationalist Air Force.

McDonnell F-101B Voodoo

First flight: September 29, 1954 (F-101A)
Power: Two Pratt & Whitney 6749kg/14,880lb afterburning thrust J57-P-55 turbojet engines
Armament: Two MB-1 Genie nuclear-tipped air-to-air missiles and four Falcon air-to-air missiles or six Falcon air-to-air missiles
Size: Wingspan – 12.09m/39ft 8in
  Length – 20.54m/67ft 4.75in
  Height – 5.49m/18ft
  Wing area – 34.19m²/368sq ft
Weights: Empty – 13,141kg/28,970lb
  Maximum take-off – 23,768kg/52,400lb
Performance: Maximum speed – 1965kph/1221mph
  Ceiling – 16,705m/54,800ft
  Range – 2494km/1550 miles
  Climb – 11,133m/36,500ft per minute

ABOVE LEFT: **The F-101 Voodoo set a number of speed and endurance records.** BELOW: **The RF-101 was the first USAF supersonic reconnaissance platform.**

McDonnell Douglas F-4 Phantom II

One of the world's greatest ever combat aircraft, the two-seat Phantom was designed to meet a US Navy requirement for a fleet defence fighter to replace the F3H Demon and counter the threat from long-range Soviet bombers. When the F-4 proved faster than their F-104 Starfighter, the United States Air Force ordered the Phantom too.

The F-4 was first used by the United States Navy as an interceptor but was soon employed by the US Marine Corps (USMC) in the ground support role. Its outstanding versatility made it the first US multi-service aircraft flying concurrently with the US Air Force, Navy and Marine Corps. The Phantom excelled in air superiority, close air support, interception, air defence suppression, long-range strike, fleet defence, attack and reconnaissance.

The sophisticated F-4 was, without direction from surface-based radar, able to detect and destroy a target beyond visual range (BVR). In the Vietnam and Gulf Wars alone, the F-4 was credited with 280 air-to-air victories.

Capable of flying at twice the speed of sound with ease, the Phantom was loved by its crews, who considered it a workhorse that could be relied on, that could do the job and get them home safely. F-4s have also set world records for altitude (30,040m/98,556ft on December 6, 1959), speed (2585kph/1606mph on November 22, 1961) and a low-altitude

TOP: **The F-4 Phantom, a truly classic combat aircraft, served US forces until 1996.** ABOVE: **Britain's Royal Navy operated the F-4 from its carriers from 1968.**

speed record of 1452kph/902mph that stood for 16 years. Phantom production ran from 1958 to 1979, resulting in a total of 5195 aircraft. 5057 were made in St Louis, Missouri, in the USA while a further 138 were built under licence by the Mitsubishi Aircraft Co. in Japan. F-4 production peaked in 1967, when the McDonnell plant was producing 72 Phantoms per month.

The US Air Force had 2874 F-4s, while the US Navy and USMC operated 1264. A number of refurbished ex-US forces aircraft were operated by other nations, including the UK, who bought a squadron of mothballed ex-US Navy F-4Js to complement the RAF's F-4Ms.

LEFT: **The Royal Air Force operated F-4s from 1968 until 1992, including some ex-Royal Navy examples.**

Regularly updated with the addition of state-of-the-art weaponry and radar, the Phantom served with 11 nations around the globe – Australia, Egypt, Germany, Greece, Iran, Israel, Japan, South Korea, Spain, Turkey and the UK. Britain's Royal Navy and Royal Air Force both operated Phantoms from 1968 and the last RAF Phantoms were retired in January 1992. The Phantom retired from US military forces in 1996, by which time the type had flown more than 27,350,000km (around 17 million miles) in the nation's service. In May 1998, when the aircraft was celebrating 40 years in the air, the Phantom was still flying in defence of eight nations – Egypt, Germany, Greece, Israel, Japan, South Korea, Spain and Turkey.

Israel, Japan, Germany, Turkey, Greece, South Korea and Egypt have undertaken or plan to upgrade their F-4s and keep them flying until 2015, nearly 60 years after the Phantom's first flight on May 27, 1958.

LEFT: **This German Air Force F-4 is typical of the many examples bought by foreign air arms.** BELOW LEFT: **This fine study of an RAF F-4 shows the impressive weapon load that made the Phantom such a formidable fighter.**

McDonnell Douglas Phantom FGR.2 (F-4M)

First flight: February 17, 1967

Power: Two Rolls-Royce 9305kg/20,515lb afterburning thrust Spey 202 turbofans

Armament: Fighter role – Four Sky Flash or Sparrow medium-range air-to-air guided missiles, four AIM-9 Sidewinder short-range air-to-air missiles and a 20mm/0.79in rotary cannon

Size: Wingspan – 11.68m/38ft 4in
Length – 17.73m/58ft 2in
Height – 4.95m/16ft 3in
Wing area – 49.25m²/530sq ft

Weights: Empty 14,080kg/31,000lb
Maximum take-off – 26,300kg/58,000lb

Performance: Maximum speed – 2230kph/1386mph
Ceiling – 18,300m/60,000ft
Range – 2815km/1750 miles
Climb – 9760m/32,000ft per minute

Mikoyan-Gurevich MiG-15

This formidable fighter was designed in the USSR with the benefit of swept-wing research captured from the Germans at the end of World War II. The RD-45 engine, an illegally copied Rolls-Royce Nene turbojet, was far more advanced than contemporary Russian engines and produced a performance that could outclass virtually all NATO's fighters of the time. The MiG-15 was developed for the Project S requirement for an interceptor designed to shoot down heavy bombers and was armed with one 37mm/1.45in cannon and two 23mm/0.9in cannon – German experience in World War II found that cannons larger than 20mm/0.79in were needed to bring down four-engine bombers.

The MiG-15 first flew in December 1947 but it only came to the attention of the West during the Korean War. On November 1, 1950 some USAF P-51 Mustang pilots reported coming under fire from six swept-wing jet fighters that had flown across the Yalu river from Manchuria – the Mikoyan-Gurevich MiG-15 was now in the Korean War and gave the United Nations forces a wake-up call.

After the first combat encounters with Western fighters, the MiG-15bis (improved) version appeared. Its VK-1 engine had 454kg/1000lb more thrust than the RD-45 of the earlier version, was lighter and could carry a greater fuel load. The Russian jets were starting to enjoy relatively easy victories against USAF B-29 bombers, which had previously operated in relative safety. Flying from Chinese bases immune from UN attack, the MiGs were used to defend North Korean installations and represented a major threat to UN air superiority in the north where they created the very dangerous "MiG Alley". UN aircraft could fly freely across the battlefields but faced deadly opposition when they neared areas in range of the MiG bases. The MiGs forced the B-29s to move their operations to night-time.

The USAF was quick to respond to the MiG threat by deploying the F-86A Sabre, the most modern USAF fighter available. Even so, the MiG had a better rate of climb, a tighter turning circle and a much better ceiling than the early three-cannon Sabre. The Sabre's armament of six 12.7mm/0.5in machine-guns was no match for the MiGs, although the Sabre was a steadier gun platform.

The first MiG versus Sabre dogfight took place on December 17, 1950, when four F-86s came upon four MiGs at an altitude of 7620m/25,000ft. Leader of the F-86 section, Lt Colonel Bruce H. Hinton, fired 1500 rounds of ammunition and set fire to one of the MiGs, causing it to crash.

During the Korean War, the NATO Allies were so desperate to examine a MiG at close quarters that they offered a $100,000 reward for any pilot who would defect and bring his MiG-15 with him. When a North Korean pilot, Lt Ro Kun Suk, did defect in September 1953 he was not aware of the prize but was given it anyway.

BELOW: **Developed with captured wartime German data, the MiG-15 is a classic jet fighter aircraft.**

LEFT: **Operating from Chinese bases during the Korean War, the MiG-15s were immune to UN attack on the ground.** BELOW: **The arrival of the MiG-15 in the sky over Korea came as an unpleasant surprise to the West.**

Codenamed "Fagot" by NATO, the MiG-15 became standard equipment with Warsaw Pact air forces until the late 1960s, when it was relegated to training duties. At least 3000 single-seat MiG-15s were built in the former Soviet Union and in Czechoslovakia (as the S-102 and S-103) and Poland (as the LIM1 and 2). In addition, from 1949 over 5000 two-seat MiG-15UTIs (known as the CS-102 and LIM-3 in Czechoslovakia and Poland respectively) were built for operational conversion or training and a number remain in service at the time of writing. More than half a century after it first flew, the MiG-15 is still earning its keep.

RIGHT: **Fifty years after it first took to the air, the MiG-15 remained in service with some air arms in 2000.** BELOW: **Two preserved Korean War adversaries – the MiG-15 in the background and the F-86 Sabre in the foreground.**

MiG-15bis

First flight: December 30, 1947
Power: Klimov 2700kg/5952lb VK-1 turbojet
Armament: One 37mm/1.45in cannon
and two 23mm/0.9in cannon
Size: Wingspan – 10.08m/33ft 0.75in
Length – 10.86m/35ft 7.5in
Height – 3.7m/12ft 1.75in
Wing area – 20.6m²/221.74sq ft
Weights: Empty – 3681kg/8115lb
Maximum take-off – 6045kg/13,327lb
Performance: Maximum speed – 1075kph/668mph
Ceiling – 15,500m/50,855ft
Range – 1860km/1156 miles
Climb – 3500m/11,480ft per minute

Mikoyan-Gurevich MiG-17

Design of the MiG-17, initially an improved version of the MiG-15, began in 1949 and the aircraft flew long before the MiG-15's guns were fired in anger over Korea. The development work was particularly focused on the MiG-15's poor handling at high speed and the MiG-17, a completely revised design, introduced longer more swept wings and a taller tail with a greater sweep of the horizontal surfaces.

The prototype MiG-17 first flew in 1950 and production of what NATO codenamed "Fresco-A" began in August 1951. Deliveries began in 1952 but were too late to take part in the Korean War, although in reality the first MiG-17s were not much of an improvement over the MiG-15s.

The F model (NATO codename "Fresco-C") of the MiG-17 had an afterburning engine developed from the illegally copied Rolls-Royce Nene that powered the MiG-15. This represented the first major improvement over the -15, so much so that production began in early 1953 while manufacture of the single-seat MiG-15 was stopped. The MiG-17 could carry no more fuel than the MiG-15 internally but its afterburning engine demanded rather more fuel, consequently MiG-17Fs were rarely seen without two 400 litre/88 gallon drop tanks.

Most -17s produced were F models, the only other versions produced in quantity being night/all-weather fighters developed from the earlier unsuccessful MiG-17P. The first was the MiG-17PF codenamed "Fresco-D" by NATO and equipped with search and ranging radar. In 1956 the MiG-17PFU

TOP: **Designed to replace the MiG-15, early MiG-17s had a minimal performance edge over their earlier cousin.** ABOVE: **MiG-17s remained in service as trainers into the third millennium AD.**

became the first missile-armed fighter in Soviet service, equipped with four ARS-212 (later known as AA-1) "Alkali" air-to-air missiles in place of guns. These missiles were "beam-riding", in that they were guided to a target by a radar beam aimed by the launch target.

The MiG-17 was only produced for five years in the USSR but in that time over 6000 were built, of which some 5000 were MiG-17Fs. The Fresco remained one of the most numerous fighters in Soviet service well into the 1960s and many remained in service as trainers as late as 2000.

At least 9000 MiG-17s were built, the majority of them in the USSR but with production also undertaken in Poland, where around 1000 were built as the LIM-5P. A dedicated ground-attack version known as the LIM-5M was developed in Poland, equipped for bomb-carrying and rocket-assisted take-off. China also licence-produced the MiG-17, as the J-5, well into the 1970s. Two-seat versions of the MiG-17 were only built in China as the Soviet Union believed the two-seat MIG-15 to be a perfectly adequate trainer for the MiG-17 and MiG-19. The Chinese two-seat MiG-17 was made by Chengdu (1060 built between 1966 and 1986) and designated JJ-5. The export JJ-5 was known as the FT-5.

Some Warsaw Pact nations went on to use the type in the ground-attack role, armed with bombs and rockets and the type was supplied to many other nations.

MiG-17s saw action in the Congo and in the Nigerian civil war while the Syrians also made extensive use of the MiG fighter. Perhaps the best-known combat use of the MIG-17 is, however, its actions with North Vietnam from 1965 to 1973. The Soviet fighter was a major thorn in the side of the US Air Force and Navy, whose supersonic fighters were expected to rule the skies over Vietnam. The much lighter and more agile MiG-17 could out-turn any US jet fighter and its guns were more reliable and effective than missiles in close combat. The MiG-17 gave US pilots in Vietnam a kill-to-loss ratio about four times worse than in Korea and directly led to a far-reaching evaluation of US fighter aircraft design and tactics, from which the F-16 was one result.

Often eclipsed by earlier and later MiG designs, the MiG-17 was certainly one of the greatest fighters.

ABOVE: **A number of MiG-17s are kept in flying condition by private collectors in the USA.**

ABOVE: **A preserved example at Titusville, Florida.** BELOW: **This MiG-17 has the tell-tale air intake fairing which housed the aircraft's Izumrud radar equipment.**

Mikoyan-Gurevich MiG-17F

First flight: January 1950

Power: Klimov 3380kg/7452lb thrust VK-1F afterburning turbojet

Armament: One 37mm/1.46in cannon, two or three 23mm/0.9in cannon plus up to 500kg/1102lb of weapons under wings

Size: Wingspan – 9.63m/31ft 7.25in
Length – 11.26m/36ft 11.25in
Height – 3.8m/12ft 5.5in
Wing area – 22.6m^2/243.27sq ft

Weights: Empty – 3930kg/8664lb
Maximum take-off – 6075kg/13,393lb

Performance: Maximum speed – 1145kph/711mph
Ceiling – 16,600m/54,460ft
Range – 1980km/1230 miles with external fuel
Climb – 5000m/16,405ft in 2 minutes, 36 seconds

Mikoyan-Gurevich MiG-19

Like the MiG-17, design of the MiG-19 was underway long before the Korean War (1950–3). Reportedly on a direct order from Stalin, the MiG design bureau sought to create an all-new supersonic fighter and not just a development of an existing type. The resulting aircraft, capable of supersonic speed in level flight, was a truly great fighter.

The MiG-19, Russia's first supersonic fighter, first flew, powered by two Mikulin AM-5 turbojets (the first Soviet-designed

turbojets to be mass-produced), in September 1953 and entered service as the MiG-19P. The type was withdrawn, however, after a series of accidents due to stability problems. The redesigned

MiG-19S had an all-moving tailplane (which aided stability at all speeds) and was powered by Tumansky RD-9B turbojets, which were essentially renamed but more powerful AM-5s. Air for the engines was drawn in through what appeared to be a single nose intake but was actually split to allow each engine to draw in air through its own intake. This reduced the potential damage caused by bird strike or ingestion of foreign objects on the ground.

The -19S was delivered from mid-1955 and when production ceased in 1959, about 2500 had been built. Among the variants were the all-weather radar-equipped MiG-19PF and the MiG-19PM, armed with missiles in place of guns. NATO codenamed the MiG-19 as "Farmer".

Soviet-built aircraft were supplied to Poland and Czechoslovakia, where they were known as the LIM-7 and S-105

respectively. MiG-19s were also licence-built by the Chinese, who recognized the exceptional fighter capability of the MiG-19 and built twice as many as the USSR from 1961. Under the designation Shenyang J-6, China exported to Albania, Bangladesh, Egypt, Kampuchea (Cambodia), Pakistan, Tanzania and Vietnam. Pakistan's J-6s saw extensive combat in its war against India and J-6s were also encountered over Vietnam by US fighters.

LEFT: **This example of a MiG-19, preserved in a Russian museum, was an all-new supersonic fighter from the MiG bureau.** BELOW: **The MiG-19 was the Soviet Union's first fighter capable of supersonic flight.**

Mikoyan-Gurevich MiG-19SF

First flight: September 18, 1953
Power: Two Tumansky 3300kg/7275lb afterburning thrust turbojets
Armament: Three 30mm/1.18in cannon, plus up to 500kg/1102lb of weapons under the wings
Size: Wingspan – 9.2m/30ft 2.25in
Length – 12.6m/41ft 4in
Height – 3.88m/12ft 8.75in
Wing area – 25m^2/269.11sq ft
Weights: Empty – 5760kg/12,699lb
Maximum take-off – 9100kg/20,062lb
Performance: Maximum speed – 1450kph/901mph
Ceiling – 17,900m/58,725ft
Range – 2200km/1367 miles with drop tanks
Climb – 6900m/22,640ft per minute

Mikoyan-Gurevich MiG-21

The MiG-21, originally designed as a short-range high-performance fighter, has, because of its hard-hitting armament and simple cost-effectiveness, become the most widely used fighter aircraft in the world. Experiences from the air war over Korea influenced the design of the delta-winged MiG-21, which was developed from a series of prototypes that flew in the mid-1950s.

The first MiG-21s (codenamed "Fishbed" by NATO) reached front-line units in the winter of 1957–8, initially armed with only two 30mm/1.18in cannon. The MiG-21F was the first major production version and was exported to the Soviet Union's Warsaw Pact allies as well as to Finland. Large numbers were

also sold to Arab air forces, who used them against the Israeli Air Force in the Arab-Israeli War (1973). The MiG-21 was popular with pilots because it handled well, was highly manoeuvrable and could fly at twice the speed of sound.

Licensed production was also undertaken in Czechoslovakia and India, while China undertook major unlicensed production, having reverse-engineered (copied) examples they had acquired legitimately. Main shortcomings were limited range and endurance but the -F model came with a centreline 490 litre/108 gallon drop tank, giving the MiG longer legs. 1960 saw the development of the MiG-21PF with a redesigned nose to accommodate the new R1L radar in a moveable conical centrebody in the middle of the nose air intake. This model also introduced the more powerful R-11F2-300 engine for improved performance. Throughout its service life the -21 has been improved

and upgraded, and in 2000 Romania's Aerostar were still offering upgraded MiG-21 Lancers for air defence duties, having upgraded Romanian Air Force MiG-21s. Romania was just one of many countries still operating the MiG-21 almost 50 years after the prototype first flew.

ABOVE: **This MiG-21, airbrakes deployed, is a Czech Air Force machine.** LEFT: **A MiG-21MF of the Slovak Air Force.**

Mikoyan-Gurevich MiG-21bis

First flight: Late 1957 (Production MiG-21F)
Power: Tumansky 7500kg/16,535lb afterburning thrust R-25 turbojet engine
Armament: One twin-barrel 23mm/0.9in cannon in underbelly pack and underwing provision for 1500kg/3307lb of weapons, including AA-2 or AA-8 air-to-air missiles and rocket pods
Size: Wingspan – 7.15m/23ft 5.5in
Length – 15.76m/51ft 8.5in
Height – 4.1m/13ft 5.5in
Wing area – 23m^2/247sq ft
Weights: Empty – 5200kg/11,465lb
Maximum take-off – 7960kg/17,550lb
Performance: Maximum speed – 2230kph/1385mph
Ceiling – 18,000m/59,050ft
Range – 1160km/720 miles
Climb – 17,680m/58,000ft per minute

Mikoyan-Gurevich MiG-23/-27

The disappointing range of the MiG-21 led to a 1965 requirement for a replacement fighter with considerably better endurance. An enlarged MiG-21 and the all-new Ye-23-11/1 were proposed, the latter becoming the prototype MiG-23, which first appeared at the 1967 Aviation Day flypast. Like the MiG-21 before it, the new aircraft was planned in two versions – an interceptor for use with the Soviet Union's PVO air defence forces, and a ground-attack version (the MiG-27) to serve with the USSR's tactical air forces, Frontal Aviation.

The -23 differed from previous production MiG jets by switching the air intake from a centre nose inlet to side inlets, which allowed the search radar to be accommodated in a large nose-cone. The MiG-23MF, known as "Flogger-B" by NATO, was the first production variant, entering Soviet service in 1973 and other Warsaw Pact air arms soon after.

The MiG-23 was not only the USSR's first production aircraft with a variable-geometry "swing-wing", it was also the first swing-wing fighter anywhere. It and the MiG-27 have three sweep positions – minimum (16 degrees) for take-off, low-speed flight and landing; middle (45 degrees) for cruising, and maximum (72 degrees) for high-performance flight.

The MiG-27 ("Flogger-D") fighter-bomber/attack version, can be distinguished from the MiG-23 by its different nose, which slopes away sharply from the cockpit for better pilot view, earning the nickname "ducknose" from its crews. Due to the aircraft's role as a battlefield attack aircraft, the pilot of the -27 is protected from small arms fire by armour on the side of the cockpit. Terrain-avoidance radar relieves the pilot of some of the high workload associated with low-level operations.

Among the operators of the MiG-23/-27 were Poland, Hungary, Bulgaria, East Germany, Romania and Czechoslovakia. Downgraded MiG-23s were exported outside the Warsaw Pact nations to Libya, Syria, Egypt, Ethiopia, India, Cuba, Algeria, Iraq, Afghanistan and North Korea. India's Hindustan Aeronautics produced MiG-27Ms for the Indian Air Force until 1997, finally bringing Flogger production to a close after nearly three decades, with around 4000 aircraft built. MiG-23s and -27s are, however, likely to remain potent aircraft for Russia and many of the nations listed for years to come.

In the late 1980s the US Air Force acquired some ex-Egyptian Air Force MiG-23s for realistic air-combat training of American and NATO pilots.

TOP: **Having "lit the fires", the pilot of this Czech Air Force MiG-23 prepares to accelerate away.**

ABOVE: **More than three decades after it first flew, the MiG-23 is still an effective interceptor.**

Mikoyan-Gurevich MiG-23MF

First flight: 1966
Power: Tumansky 12,500kg/27,550lb afterburning thrust R-29 turbojet engine
Armament: One 23mm/0.9in cannon in belly pod, plus five pylons for air-to-air missiles and rockets
Size: Wingspan – 14.25m/46ft 9in, spread
Length – 16.8m/55ft 1.5in
Height – 4.35m/14ft 4in
Wing area – 28m²/301.4sq ft
Weights: Empty – 11,300kg/24,912lb
Maximum take-off – 18,500kg/40,785lb
Performance: Maximum speed – 2500kph/1550mph
Ceiling – 18,600m/61,025ft
Range – 1300km/808 miles
Climb – 15,240m/50,000ft per minute

Mikoyan-Gurevich MiG-25

Mikoyan-Gurevich MiG-25P

First flight: March 6, 1964 (Ye-155R-1 prototype)
Power: Two Tumansky 11,000kg/24,250lb
afterburning thrust R-31 turbojet engines
Armament: External pylons for four air-to-air missiles,
typically four AA-6 "Acrid" air-to-air missiles
or two AA-7 "Apex" with two AA-8 "Aphid"
air-to-air missiles
Size: Wingspan – 13.95m/45ft 9in
Length – 23.82m/78ft 1.75in
Height – 6.1m/20ft
Wing area – 56.83m²/611.7sq ft
Weights: Empty – 20,000kg/44,090lb
Maximum take off – 36,200kg/79,800lb
Performance: Maximum speed – 2975kph/1848mph
Ceiling – 24,385m/80,000ft
Range – 1125km/700 miles
Climb – 15,240m/50,000ft per minute

The MiG-25 was developed in the early 1960s to counter the threat posed to the Soviet Union by the remarkable US B-70 Valkyrie Mach 3 bomber. Although the B-70 never entered service, the MiG-25 (NATO codename "Foxbat") did and it remains the world's fastest fighter aircraft, capable of Mach 2.8 and up to Mach 3 (3200kph/2000 mph) for short periods. The West was first publicly aware of the Foxbat in April 1965, when it was announced that the prototype had set a new speed record in a 1000km/620 mile closed circuit. The prototype of the reconnaissance version had actually first flown in March 1964. The type subsequently set a number of other records, including an absolute world altitude record of 37,650m/123,524ft.

The high-speed flight environment is a hostile one and aircraft have to be made of special materials to withstand the high temperatures experienced in these operations – the MiG-25 airframe is made of nickel steel and has titanium wing and tail unit leading-edges to withstand the heat generated during very high speed flight. The MiG-25 is no dogfighter, uses a lot of fuel quickly and needs a very long take-off and landing but it was after all a highly specialized aircraft designed for a very specific purpose – to get very high very quickly.

The interceptor version, MiG-25P, went into production first and entered service in 1970. The later MiG-25PD had look-down/shoot-down radar, more powerful engines and an infra-red search and track capability. Although the B-70 threat never materialized, the MiG-25 did, however, have another high-speed high-altitude target, the USAF SR-71 Blackbird, and it was soon stationed along the eastern and western borders of the USSR to keep the Blackbird at bay. Intercepts were directed by ground control until the powerful on-board radar could lock on to the target. Four of the world's largest, long-range missiles, the AA-6 "Acrid", could then be fired from up to 80km/50 miles away. These missiles, some 6m/19.5ft long, were specially developed to

kill the B-70 and were fitted with either infra-red or radar homing heads.

The reconnaissance MiG-25RB Foxbat entered service about the same time as the interceptor. Four aircraft were stationed in Egypt in 1971 to spy on Israeli positions and were completely immune to the Israeli F-4 Phantoms far below.

Export versions were supplied to Algeria, India, Libya, Syria and Iraq – the only confirmed Iraqi air-to-air victory of the Gulf War of 1991 was scored by a MiG-25 over a US Navy F/A-18 Hornet.

ABOVE: **The MiG-25 was developed into the MiG-31.**
BELOW: **The MiG-25 is made largely of nickel steel and titanium.**

Mikoyan-Gurevich MiG-29

Over 1200 examples of this very capable, incredibly agile fighter have been built and the type has been exported widely. The MiG-29 was developed in the early 1970s as a high-performance, highly manoeuvrable lightweight fighter to outperform the best the West could offer. The prototype took to the air for the first time in 1977 but it

was a further seven years before the type entered service – ultimately 460 were in Russian service and the rest were exported.

Codenamed "Fulcrum" by NATO, the aircraft has been exported to Bulgaria, Germany, Cuba, Romania, Poland, Slovakia, Peru, Syria, Hungary, Iraq, India, Iran, North Korea, Malaysia and Moldova amongst others. It is not

widely known, but the USA acquired 21 MiG-29s in 1997 from Moldova after Iran had expressed interest in the high-performance fighters. In a unique accord between the USA and Moldova, the aircraft were shipped to the USA to prevent them being acquired by rogue states.

The radar can track ten targets up to 245km/152 miles away and enables look-down-shoot-down capability, while the pilot's helmet-mounted sight allows him or her to direct air-to-air missiles wherever the pilot looks.

The MiG is also designed for rough-field operations – special doors seal off the main air intakes to protect against foreign object ingestion during start up and taxiing. Air is drawn in via louvres in the wingroots instead and as the aircraft takes off the inlet doors open.

The Russians have begun to upgrade some MiG-29s to MiG-29SMT standard by increasing the range and payload,

Mikoyan-Gurevich MiG-29

First flight: October 7, 1977

Power: Two Klimov 8312kg/18,300lb afterburning thrust RD-33 turbojet engines

Armament: One 30mm/1.18in cannon, six underwing hardpoints carrying 3000kg/6615lb of weapons, including six AAMs or rockets and bombs

Size: Wingspan – 11.36m/37ft 3in
Length – 14.87m/48ft
Height – 4.73m/15ft 6in
Wing area – 38m²/409sq ft

Weights: Empty – 10,900kg/24,030lb
Maximum take-off 18,500kg/40,785lb

Performance: Maximum speed – 2445kph/1518mph
Ceiling – 18,013m/59,060ft
Range – 3000km/1863 miles
Climb – 19,825m/65,000ft per minute

new computer screens replacing cockpit instruments, as well as improved radar and inflight refuelling capability.

Daimler Chrysler Aerospace modified a number of Polish MiGs for NATO compatibility after that nation joined NATO in 1999, just as they did the East German MiG-29s after German reunification in 1990.

A navalized version, the MiG-29K, was developed but has so far not been produced.

LEFT: **Although it was designed in the early 1970s, the MiG-29 remains a very potent fighter in service around the world.** BELOW: **A fine air-to-air photograph of a Czech Air Force MiG-29.**

Mikoyan-Gurevich MiG-31

Codenamed "Foxhound" by NATO, the very large MiG-31 was developed from the MiG-25, and replaced the Tu-128 as the main Soviet long-range interceptor. The MiG-31 and its two-man crew was designed to counter low-flying strike aircraft and cruise missiles and is able to engage targets from a considerable distance. Equipped with the long-range AA-9 air-to-air missiles, it is a most effective protector of Russian airspace.

Development began in the 1970s and the prototype MiG-31 (the Ye-155MP) first flew in 1975. The first of around 300 MiG-31s were delivered to the Soviet Air Force from 1979.

Although the Foxhound was inspired by the MiG-25, it is a new all-weather, all-altitude aircraft. Its airframe is composed of nickel steel, light alloy and titanium to cope with the rigours associated with its high performance. The aircraft's sophisticated "Flash Dance" radar, said to be the most powerful fitted to any of the world's fighters, can scan almost 200km/124 miles ahead as well as behind and below. Managed by the back-seater, it can track up to ten targets at once and simultaneously engage four of them having established which present the greatest threat.

Later models had an in-flight refuelling capability which greatly

LEFT: Derived from the formidable MiG-25, the MiG-31 is equipped with a very powerful radar.

Mikoyan-Gurevich MiG-31

First flight: September 16, 1975 (Ye 155)
Power: Two Aviadvigatel 15,520kg/34,170lb afterburning thrust D-30F6 turbofan engines
Armament: One 23mm/0.9in cannon, four AA-9 "Amos" long-range air-to-air missiles under fuselage, two AA-6 "Acrid" air-to-air missiles and four AA-8 "Aphid" air-to-air missiles on underwing hardpoints
Size: Wingspan – 13.464m/44ft 2in
Length – 22.7m/74ft 5in
Height – 6.15m/20ft 2in
Wing area – 61.6m²/663sq ft
Weights: Empty – 21,825kg/48,115lb
Maximum take-off – 46,200kg/101,850lb
Performance: Maximum speed – 3000kph/1863mph
Ceiling – 20,618m/67,600ft
Range – 720km/447 miles at Mach 2.3 with full armament load
Climb – 10,000m/32,810ft in 7 minutes, 54 seconds

extended the aircraft's endurance and on-board digital datalinks, allowing aircraft to exchange data about targets and tactical situations.

Mitsubishi F-2

The Mitsubishi F-2, formerly known as the FS-X, was developed in Japan with the help of the former General Dynamics (now Lockheed Martin) and the similarities between the F-2 and the F-16 are obvious. The type first flew in October 1995 and initial production versions were supplied to the Japan Air Self-Defence Force in 2000. Japan has ordered 130 F-2s to replace the JASDF's Mitsubishi F-1s.

The programme has, however, been dogged by technical problems and by the time the F-2 entered service, each aircraft had cost four times more than a basic F-16.

The Japanese FS-X project was originally intended to produce an indigenous fighter aircraft but in 1987, after considerable US pressure, the F-16 was chosen as the basis of the new aircraft. The F-2 wing is 25 per cent larger than that of the F-16 and an enlarged radome houses a Japanese-designed radar. The fuselage is longer than the F-16 and the fly-by-wire system

LEFT: The F-2's family connections with the F-16 are clear.

Mitsubishi F-2

First flight: October 1995
Power: General Electric 13,444kg/29,600lb afterburning thrust F110-GE-129 turbofan engine
Armament: One 20mm/0.70in cannon, plus AIM-9L Sidewinders/Mitsubishi AAM-3 air-to-air missiles on wingtips plus underwing hardpoints for weaponry including AIM-7M Sparrow air-to-air missiles
Size: Wingspan – 11.13m/36ft 6in
Length – 15.52m/50ft 10in
Height – 4.96m/16ft 4in
Wing area – 34.8m²/375sq ft
Weights: Empty – 9525kg/21,000lb
Maximum take-off – 22,100kg/48,722lb
Performance: Maximum speed – Mach 2
Ceiling – 15,250m/50,000ft
Range – 830km/515 miles
Climb – not published

is all-Japanese due to US reluctance to provide their fly-by-wire software.

The F-2 will initially serve in ground-attack/maritime strike roles but an air defence version is planned to replace Japan's ageing F-4 Phantom fleet.

North American F-86 Sabre

The North American Aviation Company's first jet design was begun in 1944, but following the capture of German research at the end of World War II, the XP-86 was redesigned to incorporate swept-tail surfaces and a swept wing, which would allow supersonic speeds. The prototype of the Sabre flew in 1947 and the aircraft entered service with the US Air Force in 1949. It proved faster than expected: in 1948 an early production F-86 exceeded the speed of sound in a shallow dive, though the aircraft could not achieve this in level flight.

On November 1, 1950, some USAF Mustang pilots on a mission over Korea reported coming under fire by six swept-wing jet fighters that had flown across the Yalu river from Manchuria – the Russian-built Mikoyan-Gurevich MiG-15 was in the Korean War. The USAF were quick to respond to the MiG threat and on 8 November ordered the F-86 Sabre-equipped 4th Fighter Group from the USA to Korea. The F-86A was the most modern USAF fighter available but the Sabre's armament of six 12.7mm/0.5in machine-guns was no real match for the two 23mm/1.09in and one 37mm/1.46in cannon

ABOVE: **North American made full use of wartime German swept-wing research to produce the F-86.** LEFT: **The F-86, the USAF's most modern fighter, was sent to Korea to deal with the MiG-15 threat.**

of the MiG. USAF pilot training and tactics were, however, much better and the Sabre was able to give as much as it got.

The first MiG v. Sabre dogfight took place in December 1950, when four USAF F-86 Sabres came upon four MiGs at an altitude of 7620m/25,000ft. Leader of the F-86 group was Lt Colonel Bruce H. Hinton. He fired on the enemy jets and set fire to one of the MiGs, causing it to crash. On December 22, eight Sabres took on 15 MiGs and in the dogfights that followed from 9145m/30,000ft down to 305m/1000ft, the USAF fighter pilots destroyed no fewer than six of the MiGs. By the end of the Korean War, USAF F-86 Sabres had achieved 757 victories for 103 losses in combat.

The F-86D, virtually a complete redesign on the early Sabres, was an all-weather version fitted with the Hughes fire control system and was essentially a bomber-destroyer. The collision-course radar would take the jet to the target on autopilot and at the right moment the system would extend a box from the belly and unleash 24 70mm/2.75in unguided Mighty Mouse high explosive rockets.

The F-86E was produced from late 1950 and had an "all-flying" tail that was adjustable in flight. Canadian-built versions of the F-86E were supplied to the Royal Canadian Air Force, the RAF and the new Luftwaffe. The RAF received 460 Sabres, all of them flown to the UK in the space of 12

days in December 1952. Britain's Sabres were a much-needed stop-gap while the UK brought its own swept-wing fighters into service and enabled RAF squadrons based in West Germany, the Cold War front line, to provide a totally robust and modern fighter defence against Soviet would-be attackers. In December 1953, No.66 Squadron at Linton-on-Ouse became the first swept-wing unit of RAF Fighter Command when they swapped Meteor F.8s for F-86s. The RAF's Sabres based in West Germany were all replaced by Hunters by the end of May 1956.

Some of the Canadian-built Sabres were later passed on to Italy and Greece under NATO terms to ensure those countries' air forces were well-equipped. Italy's Fiat also licence-built the all-weather F-86K for Italy, France, West Germany, the Netherlands and Norway. For most NATO pilots, the Sabre gave them their first experience of high-speed jet flight. The very capable Sabre, so widely deployed throughout NATO, must have had some deterrence value against the USSR.

Australia's Commonwealth Aircraft Corporation also licence built the F-86 (as the Sabre Mk 30, 31 and 32) for the Royal Australian Air Force.

The Sabre remained in production until 1957. The US Navy version, known as the FJ-0 Fury, entered service in 1952. Total Sabre and Fury production amounted to over 9500 aircraft. A number of preserved examples continue to fly.

TOP: The all-weather D model was essentially an all-new Sabre. ABOVE: USAF F-86Ds were deployed for all-weather UK air defence between late 1953 and mid-1958. BELOW: The Sabre gave many NATO fighter pilots their first high-speed jet experience.

North American F-86D Sabre

First flight: October 1, 1947 (XP-86)
Power: General Electric 3402kg/7500lb afterburning thrust J47-GE-17B turbojet engine
Armament: 24 70mm/2.75in unguided Mighty Mouse high-explosive rockets
Size: Wingspan – 11.3m/37ft 1in
Length – 12.29m/40ft 4in
Height – 4.57m/15ft
Wing area – 26.76m^2/288sq ft
Weights: Empty – 5656kg/12,470lb
Maximum take-off – 7756kg/17,100lb
Performance: Maximum speed – 1138kph/707mph
Ceiling – 16,640m/54,600ft
Range – 1344km/835 miles
Climb – 3660m/12,000ft per minute

North American F-82 Twin Mustang

It would be easy to say that this aircraft looks as if it were made of left-over parts at the North American factory but despite its name, this aircraft was not simply two P-51s joined by a new centre wing. The F-82 (originally P-82) was conceived by North American in World War II as a dedicated long-range escort fighter for war in the Pacific. The vast distances between islands in the Pacific

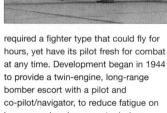

required a fighter type that could fly for hours, yet have its pilot fresh for combat at any time. Development began in 1944 to provide a twin-engine, long-range bomber escort with a pilot and co-pilot/navigator, to reduce fatigue on long-range bomber escort missions.

The Twin Mustang was certainly produced quickly by using the existing P-51 powerplant and some common components including the two modified P-51H fuselages which, combined in a twin-boom configuration, carried the two pilots in separate cockpits. Deliveries of what was the last propeller-driven dayfighter acquired in quantity by the Air Force did not begin until early 1946, but although the Twin Mustang arrived too late for World War II, it had useful post-war Air Force service as an escort fighter and, most importantly, a nightfighter.

Radar-equipped F-82F and Gs were used extensively by Air Defense Command as replacements for the P-61 night-fighter and nine F-82Fs and five F-82Gs were converted as F-82H winterized interceptors for Alaska.

The F-82 had a very successful combat career in the Korean War. Japan-based F-82s were among the first

North American F-82G Twin Mustang

First flight: July 6, 1945
Power: Two Allison 1600hp V-1710-143/145 V-12 piston engines
Armament: Six wing-mounted 12.7mm/0.5in machine-guns, plus up to four 454kg/1000lb bombs under wings
Size: Wingspan – 15.62m/51ft 3in
Length – 12.93m/42ft 5in
Height – 4.22m/13ft 10in
Wing area – 37.9m^2/408sq ft
Weights: Empty – 7256kg/15,997lb
Maximum take-off – 11,608kg/25,951lb
Performance: Maximum speed – 742kph/461mph
Ceiling – 11,855m/38,900ft
Range – 3605km/2240 miles
Climb – 1150m/3770ft per minute

USAF aircraft to operate over Korea and the first three North Korean aircraft destroyed by US forces were shot down by all-weather F-82G interceptors on June 27, 1950. The type flew 1868 sorties in the Korean War before being withdrawn in February 1952.

LEFT: **Developed in World War II, the F-82 saw extensive action in Korea.** BELOW: **The unbelievable but effective configuration of the Twin Mustang – an unusual but potent fighter.**

North American F-100 Super Sabre

The Super Sabre was the world's first supersonic combat aircraft and was developed by North American from 1949 as a successor to the company's highly successful F-86 Sabre. The goal was an aircraft that could exceed Mach 1 in level flight and the F-100 was developed very quickly.

In May 1953 one of the prototypes exceeded the speed of sound on its first flight giving a taste of the performance to come. On October 29, 1953 the first production aircraft set a new world speed record of 1215kph/755mph. Although the first F-100s were delivered to the USAF in 1953, a series of catastrophic

inflight failures delayed the F-100A's entry into service for another year. After the wings and fin were reworked to eradicate stability problems, 200 F-100As gave sterling service in the USAF.

The improved and more powerful F-100C and D fighter-bombers reached the Cold War front lines in 1956–7. The C model had in-flight refuelling capability to extend the already impressive range

and a more powerful engine. The F-100D was built in greater numbers than any other version and carried ECM equipment as well as a low-altitude bombing system for "tossing" nuclear weapons. Two-seat and reconnaissance versions were also produced. By the time production stopped in 1959 almost 2300 Super Sabres had been built.

From 1966–71 in the Vietnam War USAF F-100s saw extensive service in

the fighter, reconnaissance and ground-attack roles, flying more missions than the P-51 had in World War II.

Super Sabres retired from USAF service in 1972 but they remained in use with Air National Guard units until 1980. F-100s were supplied to Denmark, France, Taiwan and Turkey, the latter nation finally retiring the type in the mid-1980s.

TOP: **The F-100 was first delivered to the US Air Force in 1953.** ABOVE: **Extensively used in the Vietnam War, the Super Sabre flew many varied types of mission.** LEFT: **USAF F-100s were deployed to Europe in the late 1950s.**

North American F-100D Super Sabre

First flight: March 24, 1953
Power: Pratt and Whitney 7711kg/17,000lb afterburning-thrust J 57-P21 turbojet
Armament: Four 20mm/0.78in cannon plus six underwing load points for up to 3402kg/7500lb of weapons
Size: Wingspan – 11.81m/38ft 9in
Length – 15.09m/49ft 6in
Height – 4.95m/16ft 3in
Wing area – 35.77m^2/385sq ft
Weights: Empty – 9525kg/21,000lb
Maximum take-off – 15,800kg/34,832lb
Performance: Maximum speed – 1390kph/864mph
Ceiling – 13,716m/45,000ft
Range – 3210km/1995 miles with external drop tanks
Climb – 4877m/16,000ft per minute

Northrop F-5 series

The Northrop F-5 Freedom Fighter is a versatile, low cost, easy to maintain, lightweight supersonic fighter that first flew in 1959. More than 2000 of the 2700 aircraft built were widely exported to over 30 countries friendly to the USA. Deliveries to USAF Tactical Air Command for instructing foreign pilots began in April 1964 and pilots from Iran and South Korea were the first to be trained. A two-place combat-trainer

version, the F-5B, first flew in February 1964, and in 1966–7 a US Air Force squadron of F-5s flew combat missions in South-east Asia for operational evaluation purposes.

Canada and Spain undertook licence production of the F-5 – many Freedom Fighters remain in service with air forces around the world.

The improved F-5E Tiger II appeared in 1972 with more powerful J85 engines which required a wider fuselage. It had much better avionics and an air-to-air fire control radar system as well as a computerized gunsight. Like the F-5 before it, the F-5E attracted interest from foreign air forces, and some 20 foreign air arms had acquired Tiger IIs by the mid-1980s. Although the F-5 may lack all-weather capability, it is relatively cheap, easy to operate, robust and very agile. The first flight of the F-5E was on August 11, 1972 and the first USAF unit to receive the aircraft was the 425th TFS, responsible for training foreign pilots in the F-5 aircraft. Perhaps the best-known use of the Tiger II was as an aggressor aircraft for the USAF. US aggressor pilots were trained in Soviet tactics and used the F5-Es to provide a realistic "enemy" for USAF pilots training in aerial combat skills. Eventually, aggressor squadrons were used to help train pilots of friendly foreign nations. The F-5F was the two-seat combat trainer version of the F-5E. Taiwan, South Korea and Switzerland all produced the Tiger II under licence. Although F-5E production ceased in 1987, the manufacturers have offered

TOP: **This Norwegian Air Force F-5A sports a special scheme for a meet of Tiger squadrons.** ABOVE: **The Swiss Air Force was one of 20 foreign air arms that bought the F-5E.** BELOW LEFT: **This two-seat USAF F-5F shows how much ordnance could be carried by the type.**

a host of update options which should keep the Tiger II in the front line well beyond 2010.

The ultimate development of the F-5 was the F-20 Tigershark with, among other improvements, 80 per cent greater engine power. The USAF declined the aircraft and this effectively doomed the F-20's export potential.

Northrop F-5E Tiger II

First flight: July 30, 1959 (N-156F F-5 prototype)
Power: Two General Electric 2268kg/5000lb afterburning thrust J85-GE21 turbojets
Armament: Two 20mm/0.78in cannon in nose, two AIM-9 Sidewinder AAMs on wingtip launchers plus up to 3175kg/7000lb of mixed ordnance
Size: Wingspan – 8.13m/26ft 8in
    Length – 14.45m/47ft 4.75in
    Height – 4.06m/13ft 4in
    Wing area – 17.28m^2/186sq ft
Weights: Empty – 4410kg/9723lb
    Maximum take-off – 11,214kg/24,722lb
Performance: Maximum speed – 1734kph/1083mph
    Ceiling – 15,790m/51,800ft
    Range – 2483km/1543 miles with drop tanks
    Climb – 8754m/28,700ft per minute

Northrop F-89 Scorpion

The F-89 was an all-weather jet fighter-interceptor designed to replace the P-61 Black Widow and F-82 Twin Mustang. It first flew in August 1948 and had a conventional layout but included what was for the time an unusual design feature called decelerons, a control surface that could operate as a speed brake to allow crews to get into firing position behind a target. While the pilot controlled the aircraft, the back-seat "observer" managed the

radar. The F-89 picked up the unofficial nickname "Stanley Steamer" because of the oversize main landing gear wheels that appeared to be more at home on a locomotive than a fighter.

The definitive F-89 Scorpion, and one version that was built in greater numbers than any other, was the D model, which carried 104 Mighty Mouse 70mm/2.75in unguided rockets in two enormous pods, one on each wingtip. This version also carried the APG-40 radar, which could detect target aircraft up to 80km/50 miles away. The impressive Hughes E-6 fire-control system could then instruct the autopilot on course corrections and even fire the F-89's rockets automatically when in range.

A total of 350 F-89Ds were converted to F-89Js under Project Ding Dong, which saw the aircraft equipped to carry the AIR-2A Genie, an unguided nuclear-tipped air-to-air missile. On July 19, 1957, a Genie was launched from an F-89J, marking the first and only time in history that an air-to-air rocket with a nuclear warhead was launched and detonated. Called Operation Plumb Bob, this test took place at 6100m/20,000ft over Nevada. The rocket was fired at a point approximately 4270m/14,000ft from the F-89 and the Genie covered this distance in 4.5 seconds.

The F-89 was withdrawn from active service in 1959 after protecting the USA, and especially the frozen north, for almost a decade. The last examples of the Air National Guard F-89s were retired from service in July 1969.

Northrop F-89D Scorpion	
First flight: August 16, 1948	
Power: Two Allison 3266kg/7200lb afterburning thrust J-35-A-35 turbojet engines	
Armament: 104 Mighty Mouse 70mm/2.75in unguided rockets in wingtip pods or 27 rockets and three Falcon missiles	
Size: Wingspan – 18.18m/59ft 8in	
Length – 16.41m/53ft 10in	
Height – 5.36m/17ft 7in	
Wing area – 52.21m²/562sq ft	
Weights: Empty – 11,428kg/25,194lb	
Maximum take-off – 19,160kg/42,241lb	
Performance: Maximum speed – 1024kph/636mph	
Ceiling – 14,995m/49,200ft	
Range – 4184km/2600 miles	
Climb – 1600m/5250ft per minute	

LEFT. Note the F-89's twin turbojets almost "bolted on" beneath the fuselage. ABOVE: The F-89 was a large fighter. It protected the USA from Soviet bombers coming from the north. BELOW: As a design the F-89 didn't really break new ground, but it earned its keep as a Cold War all-weather interceptor for over ten years.

Panavia Tornado ADV

The Tornado was produced by a three-nation (UK, West Germany and Italy) consortium, each of which assumed responsibility for the manufacture of specific aircraft sections. The resulting aircraft was a technological, political and administrative triumph, given the problems that had to be overcome. Each nation assembled its own air force's aircraft, and power for all was provided by Rolls-Royce-designed Turbo-Union engines. The strike Tornado was developed and entered service first, while the fighter version was sought as a replacement for the RAF's F-4 Phantoms and Lightnings. The resulting aircraft is an interceptor with a better rate of acceleration than either of these two classic jets. While it cannot manoeuvre as well as the F-16, the Tornado was not designed for manoeuvre. It was made to defend the UK Air Defence Region, a vast area stretching from the south-west approaches up to Iceland, including all of the UK, most of the North Sea, and much of the eastern Atlantic. The Tornado interceptor will be central to the UK's air defence for some years to come.

TOP: **The RAF's Tornado ADV is ideally suited to its primary role of defending the enormous UK Air Defence Region.** ABOVE: **Only the RAF and the Italian and Saudi Arabian air forces operate the ADV.**

The Tornado ADV (Air Defence Variant) was designed to an RAF requirement for an interceptor that could perform unrefuelled combat air patrols 563km/350 miles from base, in all weathers and at all altitudes in a hostile electronic warfare environment. In simple terms the main mission envisaged for the Tornado interceptor was to loiter far out over the ocean, beyond the range of land-based radar, waiting to attack Soviet bombers as they approached from over the Arctic.

Although there is 80 per cent commonality between the airframes, the ADV differs from the strike Tornado in having a 1.36m/4ft 7in longer fuselage. Its sophisticated GEC-Marconi Foxhunter radar can track up to 20 targets while scanning a search area up to 165km/100 miles distant. The chosen armament was the Sky Flash AAM and to achieve the required performance the missiles are carried in tandem semi-recessed pairs under the fuselage centreline.

The Tornado is one of a handful of combat aircraft with variable-geometry or "swing" wings. The wings can move automatically from the swept to the spread position and two interim settings to maximize the aircraft's aerodynamic performance as required at take-off, landing and in high-speed flight.

It has excellent short take-off capability which, together with its on-board Auxiliary Power Unit, makes the ADV well suited for operation from basic forward airfields.

The prototype ADV, the F.2, first flew in 1979 and the first F.2s were delivered to the RAF in November 1984. Due to delays in the development of the Foxhunter radar the aircraft only carried ballast in the nose, and subsequently a version of the radar that did not fully meet RAF standards, until 1989 when the full-specification radar was installed.

Early in production, from the 19th on the production line, all were produced as F. Mk.3s, featuring the RB199 Mk 104 engines, improved afterburners, larger drop-tanks, fully automatic wing-sweep control and provision for four Sidewinders in addition to the four Sky Flash missiles. The F.3 was also 35.5cm/14in longer than the F.2 to accommodate the new engines, carried 891 litres/200 gallons more internal fuel and an inflight refuelling probe was fitted on the port side as standard. However, on September 24, 1987 an F.3 flew direct from Canada to the BAE Systems plant at Warton in the UK without the need to refuel in flight, showing just how long the ADV's legs are.

During the 1980s the RAF Tornado F.3s also assumed the role of an AWACS aircraft as part of the RAF's Mixed Fighter Force plan. Using the Tornado's radar, the navigator was able to direct Hawk trainers towards bogeys, armed with AIM-9 Sidewinder missiles.

Although only Britain wanted the Tornado interceptor version, in 1995 Italy began leasing 24 F.3s from Britain while awaiting delivery of the Eurofighter. These aircraft were modified to carry the Italian Alenia Aspide AAM.

Saudi Arabia is the only export customer and Saudi F.3s, together with RAF ADVs, flew combat patrols throughout the Gulf War (1991) but without seeing action. RAF F.3s subsequently flew as part of the UN Operations Deny Flight/Decisive Edge over Bosnia-Herzegovina, policing the no-fly zone.

In 2000, the RAF F.3s were modified to carry the AMRAAM and ASRAAM missiles and were equipped with the Joint Tactical Information Distribution System (JTIDS), to enable the aircraft to engage multiple targets beyond visual range (BVR).

TOP: **Wings extended to generate maximum lift at take-off, the Tornado is one of the world's few swing-wing aircraft.** ABOVE: **The Tornado fighter variant will defend the UK for years to come.**

BELOW: **Although RAF Tornado fighters were deployed during the Gulf War, they did not see action.**

Panavia Tornado ADV/F.3

First flight: October 27, 1979

Power: Two Turbo Union 4808kg/10,600lb (7292kg/16,075lb afterburning)-thrust RB199-34R Mk 104 turbofans

Armament: One 27mm/1.05in cannon, four Sky Flash AAMs, plus four AIM-9 Sidewinder AAMs. Italian Air Force F.3 carry Alenia Aspide AAMs instead of Sky Flash

Size: Wingspan – 13.91m/45ft 8in, spread 8.60m/28ft 3in, swept
Length – 18.68m/61ft 4in
Height – 5.95m/19ft6in
Wing area – 26.6m²/286.3sq ft, at 25 degrees sweepback

Weights: Empty – 14,500kg/31,970lb
Maximum take-off – 27,896kg/61,700lb

Performance: Maximum speed – 2381kph/1480mph
Ceiling – 21,335m/70,000ft
Range – 1853km/1150 miles intercept radius
Climb – 12,200m/40,000ft per minute

Republic F-84 Thunderjet/Thunderstreak

The F-84 aircraft was the USAF's first post-war fighter, and production began in June 1947. It was also the first US Air Force jet fighter capable of carrying a tactical nuclear weapon and the last USAF subsonic straight-wing fighter-bomber to enter service.

F-84s became the standard fighter-escort for USAF Strategic Air Command's bomber force and pioneered the use of aerial refuelling for fighters. During August 1953 F-84Gs, refuelled in mid-air by Strategic Air Command KC-97 tankers, were flown

7216km/4485 miles non-stop from Turner Air Force Base in Georgia, USA, to RAF Lakenheath in the UK, to demonstrate the USAF's long-range fighter-escort capability. Codenamed Operation "Longstride", this was at that point the longest non-stop mass movement of fighter-bombers in history and the greatest distance ever flown non-stop by single-engine jet fighters. F-84s had also been used in two different programmes to provide protection for B-36 Peacemaker bombers.

USAF Thunderjets saw much combat in the Korean War and entered service there in December 1950. Initially assigned to escort B-29 bombers, they were later increasingly used for ground operations. Devastating F-84 raids on dams on May 13 and 16, 1953 caused the loss of all electrical power to North Korea. During that conflict, F-84 pilots flew 86,408 missions, dropped 15,370 tonnes/50,427 tons of bombs, and managed to shoot down or damage 105 North Korean MiG-15 fighters.

The first swept-wing model, the F-84F Thunderstreak, originally designated YF-84A, was first flown on June 3, 1950 and became the only USAF production fighter derived from a straight-wing aircraft.

Under the Mutual Defense Assistance Program, some 2000 F-84s were supplied to many European air forces to bring NATO up to strength during some of the darkest days of the Cold War.

In the USA, the last straight-wing F-84s were retired from the US Air National Guard in 1957 and the last ANG F-84Fs were retired in 1971.

ABOVE: **Designed during World War II, the original straight-wing F-84 entered USAF service in 1947.**
LEFT: **The addition of swept wings in the F model extended the operational life of the F-84 – these are Royal Netherlands Air Force examples.**

Republic F-84F Thunderstreak

First flight: June 3, 1950 (YF-84A)
Power: Wright 15,917kg/7220lb-thrust J65-W-3 turbojet engine
Armament: Six 12.7mm/0.5in machine-guns, plus up to 2722kg/6000lb of external ordnance
Size: Wingspan – 10.24m/33ft 7.25in
Length – 13.23m/43ft 4.75in
Height – 4.39m/14ft 4.75in
Wing area – 30.19m²/325sq ft
Weights: Empty – 6273kg/13,830lb
Maximum take-off – 12,701kg/28,000lb
Performance: Maximum speed – 1118kph/695mph
Ceiling – 14,020m/46,000ft
Range – 1384km/860 miles
Climb – 2257m/7400ft per minute

Republic F-105 Thunderchief

Republic F-105D Thunderchief

First flight: June 9, 1959
Power: Pratt & Whitney 11113kg/24,500lb afterburning thrust J75-P-19W turbojet
Armament: AIM-9 Sidewinder AAM, one 20mm/0.78in cannon plus up to 6359kg/14,000lb of bombs, mines and air-to-surface missiles
Size: Wingspan – 10.59m/34ft 9in
Length – 19.61m/64ft 4in
Height – 5.97m/19ft 7in
Wing area – 35.77m²/385sq ft
Weights: Empty – 12,474kg/27,500lb
Maximum take-off – 23,967kg/52,838lb
Performance: Maximum speed – 2237kph/1390mph
Ceiling – 12,560m/41,200ft
Range – 1480km/920 miles
Climb – 10,485m/34,400ft per minute

The Republic F-105 Thunderchief is remembered as an outstanding combat aircraft which formed the backbone of United States Air Force tactical air power during the 1950s and 1960s. The F-105 was conceived in 1951 as a Republic private venture high-performance all-weather fighter-bomber to replace the F-84. The USAF,

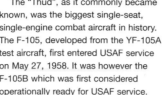

impressed by the design, ordered two prototypes, the first flying in October 1955. Pure fighters were becoming rarer by this time and so from the outset the F-105 was designed to carry up to 5443kg/12,000lb of mixed, possibly nuclear, ordnance, with 3629kg/8000lb of it carried in an internal weapons bay.

The "Thud", as it commonly became known, was the biggest single-seat, single-engine combat aircraft in history. The F-105, developed from the YF-105A test aircraft, first entered USAF service on May 27, 1958. It was however the F-105B which was first considered operationally ready for USAF service.

The United States Air Force in Europe first received the F-105D on May 12, 1961. The first model of the Thunderchief family to possess genuine all-weather capability, the F-105D was at the time the most sophisticated and complex type to be found in Tactical Air Command's inventory. In appearance the model of the Thunderchief was similar to the earlier F-105B, but possessed a larger nose radome. This contained a radar which permitted the F-105D to perform visual or blind

attacks with a variety of ordnance ranging from air-to-air missiles to conventional "iron" bombs.

F-105 Thunderchief's service in Vietnam was truly impressive, the type seeing action throughout the conflict but half of the 833 F-105s built were destroyed over Vietnam.

LEFT: **Before the F-84 was even in service, Republic were already working on a successor and came up with the excellent F-105.**
BELOW: **The two-seat fighter-bomber version, the F-105F, first flew in 1963.**

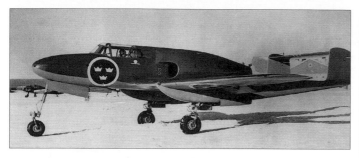

LEFT: **The Saab-21 had its origins as a propeller-driven aircraft.**

Saab J21RB

First flight: March 10, 1947
Power: de Havilland 1500kg/3307lb-thrust Goblin 3 turbojet
Armament: One 20mm/0.78in cannon and two 13.2mm/0.53in machine-guns mounted in nose, plus two further machine-guns in wings. Provision for ventral gun pack of eight more 13.2mm machine-guns
Size: Wingspan – 11.6m/38ft 0.75in
Length – 10.45m/34ft 3.5in
Height – 2.95m/9ft 8in
Wing area – 22.2m²/238.97sq ft
Weights: Empty – 3200kg/7055lb
Maximum take-off – 4990kg/11,001lb
Performance: Maximum speed – 800kph/497mph
Ceiling – 12,000m/39,370ft
Range – 720km/447 miles
Climb – 1400m/4600ft per minute

Saab-21

Development of the Saab-21 began in 1941 in response to a need for a Swedish-built fighter/attack aircraft to replace the various obsolete US and Italian fighters then in service with the Swedish Air Force. The resulting Saab-21 has a special place in the history books because it is the only aircraft ever to have seen front-line service propelled by piston and, later, jet power. The Daimler Benz piston-engined version, the J21A, entered service in June 1945, the only pusher-engined fighter to do so in World War II. It was fitted with an early ejection seat to meet the problem of vacating the cockpit unassisted with a snarling propeller blade some 4.58m/15ft behind.

After some problems with adapting the aircraft, the jet-engined J21RA entered service in 1949, with a top speed increase of 160kph/100mph.

Ground-attack versions were produced of both powered types but the Saab-21 is fondly remembered by its pilots for being an excellent fighter, being manoeuvrable, tough and a steady gun platform.

LEFT: **The name of "Tunnan" meaning "barrel" fitted the J29 perfectly.**

Saab J29F

First flight: September 1, 1948 (prototype)
Power: Flygmotor 2800kg/6173lb RM2B afterburning turbojet
Armament: Four 20mm/0.78in cannon and two RB24 Sidewinder AAMs
Size: Wingspan – 11m/36ft 1in
Length – 10.13m/33ft 2.75in
Height – 3.73m/12ft 3.75in
Wing area – 24m²/258.34sq ft
Weights: Empty – 4300kg/9480lb
Maximum take-off – 8000kg/17,637lb
Performance: Maximum speed – 1060kph/658mph
Ceiling – 15,500m/50,855ft
Range – 2700km/1678 miles
Climb – 3600m/11,810ft per minute

Saab J29 Tunnan

Wartime German swept-wing research directly influenced the design of Saab's second jet fighter, which came to be named "Tunnan" (barrel) because of its shape. As Saab had no direct swept-wing experience the proposed wing for the J29 was first tested on a Saab Safir aircraft. The test worked well and the first J29 prototype, powered by a Flygmotor licence-built de Havilland Ghost, took to the air on September 1, 1948. Tunnens began to enter service in 1951 and remained in production until 1956. The J29B had larger fuel tanks, while the E model introduced an afterburner and the J29F incorporated all previous improvements. Ground-attack and reconnaissance versions were also developed.

From 1958 the J29 was gradually replaced in Swedish Air Force units by the J32 Lansen, but in 1960 Sweden committed J29s to the UN air component that provided air cover for UN troops in the Belgian Congo. From 1961, Austria took delivery of 30 former Swedish Air Force J29Fs.

Saab J35 Draken

The remarkable Draken (dragon) was an aircraft ahead of its time and it could, if it had not been for Sweden's strict export policies, have equipped many air forces around the world. It was designed to satisfy a demanding 1949 Swedish Air Force requirement for an advanced high-performance interceptor, capable of tackling transonic-speed bombers. The specification called for speed 50 per cent greater than new fighters elsewhere, and the ability to operate from roads and other dispersed non-airfield locations. The solution was a futuristic double delta wing that gave strength with low weight and delivered all-round performance, while being able to accommodate fuel, weapons and other equipment. Before the Draken flew, its unique double delta wing was tested on a 70 per cent-scale research aircraft, which proved the viability of the design. The Draken first took to the air in October 1955 and the production version, the J35A, began to reach front-line units of the Swedish Air Force in 1960.

Among its features was a tricycle undercarriage complemented by two retractable tailwheels, deployed to permit a tail-down landing to gain the full aerodynamic braking effect of the wing. This landing technique, coupled with the use of a braking parachute, allowed the Draken to land in 610m/2000ft.

Improved versions appeared throughout the Draken's long operational life, including the J35B, with collision-course radar and increased armament, and the J35D with more powerful engines and improved avionics. The J35F had avionics that were even more advanced, an Aden cannon and the ability to carry Falcon air-to-air missiles instead of Sidewinders. The J35J upgrade of 66 J35Fs produced the ultimate Draken, to keep the type viable until the Gripen was ready to replace it from 1993. Few fighter aircraft remained as capable as the Draken for so long a period.

Reconnaissance versions (with a nose containing five cameras) and training versions were built among the total production run of 606 aircraft. Drakens were also exported to Denmark, Finland and Austria.

TOP: **The Draken was a front-line fighter for over three decades.** ABOVE: **The Draken's double delta-wing planform was very advanced in its day.**

Saab J35F Draken

First flight: October 25, 1955

Power: Volvo 7830kg/17,262lb afterburning Volvo Flygmotor RM6C (licence-built R-R Avon 300) turbojet

Armament: One 30mm/1.18in cannon in right wing, two RB 27 and two 28 Falcon missiles, plus up to 1000kg/2205lb of bombs or rockets

Size: Wingspan – 9.4m/30ft 10in
Length – 15.35m/50ft 4.3in
Height – 3.89m/12ft 9in
Wing area – 49.2m²/529.6sq ft

Weights: Empty – 7425kg/16,369lb
Maximum take-off – 12,700kg/27,998lb

Performance: Maximum speed – 2125kph/1320mph
Ceiling – 20,000m/65,615ft
Range – 960km/597 miles with external tanks
Climb – 12,000m/39,370ft per minute

Saab Gripen

This lightweight multi-role fighter is probably the most advanced and capable single-seat fighter in service today. Designed to replace the Swedish Air Force's Viggen and Draken, the Gripen (griffin) first flew in December 1988 and employs the latest advances in aerodynamics, materials and engine technology. From the outset the designers have striven to integrate pilot and machine. The Gripen pilot receives information through an air-to-air Tactical Information Data Link System that permits real-time exchange of data within, and between, tactical air groups. Overall situational awareness is thus maximized, enabling pilots to use their aircraft weapon systems to best effect.

Cockpit ergonomics were exhaustively researched to allow the pilot the maximum amount of time for tactical operation of the aircraft. The cockpit is dominated by three large colour Multi-Function Displays and a wide-angle Head-Up Display – these four displays are the principal flight instruments. The displays are even fitted with light sensors for computer-controlled brightness.

Power is provided by a single Swedish licence-built General Electric F404-GE-400 turbofan engine, which can push the Gripen along at speeds of up to Mach 2, or, crucially, Mach 1 at any altitude. Some 20 per cent by weight of the airframe is made from carbon fibre composites. The Gripen's advanced aerodynamic configuration employs a delta wing and canard foreplanes for short-field operations and to ensure optimum agility at all altitudes, even when fully armed. This manoeuvrability is optimized by the aircraft's fly-by-wire system and the Gripen could probably outmanoeuvre all other current fighters. In these days of stealth, the Gripen has a surprisingly low radar and infra-red signature, improving its air combat survivability chances.

Central to the Gripen's targeting system is the long-range Ericsson PS-05/A multi-mode pulse-Doppler radar, which can track multiple targets simultaneously and provide rapid assessment information to the pilot. This system enables the Gripen to perform equally well in the fighter and the air-to-surface attack role. This truly remarkable aircraft's multi-role

ABOVE: A fighter for the 21st century, the Gripen is perhaps the most advanced fighter in service today.

TOP: The Gripen can operate from 800m/2626ft strips, which is short for such a potent combat aircraft. ABOVE: The Mach 2-capable Gripen is a much sought-after "ride" by today's fighter pilots.

capability can be realized by the push of a button, effectively changing the Gripen's mission in mid-air.

The aircraft's flexibility is further enhanced by its ability to operate from dispersed sites, including ordinary roads and it can land and take-off from 800m/2625ft strips. An on-board auxiliary power unit allows rapid reaction times even in dispersed locations.

Considerable emphasis has been placed on maximizing component reliability and ease of access for maintenance. Fast turn-round times and in-built test equipment keeps the Gripen's time off-line to a minimum. This results in low life-cycle costs and high availability – this "force multiplier" effect has not been lost on some of the countries expressing interest in export Gripens.

The first of around 200 Gripens began operational service with the Swedish Air Force in June 1997 and the aircraft has also been ordered by the South African Air Force. The Gripen is generally acknowledged as one of the ultimate modern fighters.

Saab JAS 39A Gripen

First flight: December 9, 1988

Power: Volvo Aero Corporation/General Electric 8210kg/18,100lb afterburning thrust RM-12 turbojet

Armament: One internally mounted 27mm/1.06in cannon, one Sidewinder on each wingtip, plus five hardpoints for Sky Flash or Sidewinder AAMs, rockets or bombs

Size: Wingspan – 8.4m/27ft 6in, including wingtip launchers
Length – 14.1m/46ft 3in
Height – 4.5m/14ft 9in
Wing area – 30m²/323 sq ft

Weights: Empty – 6622kg/14,600lb
Maximum take-off – 13,989kg/30,800lb

Performance: Maximum speed – 2126kph/1321mph
Ceiling, range and climb data not published

Saab Viggen

The multi-role Viggen (thunderbolt) was designed to replace the Draken and continued Sweden's desire to remain independent of the East or West for their supply of combat aircraft. The Viggen was, for some time, the most advanced combat aircraft produced in Europe and appeared in fighter, strike and reconnaissance versions. In December 1961 the

Swedish government approved development of Aircraft System 37 which evolved into the Viggen. The basic platform was to be the AJ 37 attack aircraft, to be followed by the S 37 reconnaissance version and finally the all-weather JA 37 fighter.

Design of this ground-breaking aircraft began as far back as 1952 and by 1954 it had grown its distinctive canard wings just to the rear of the cockpit. The canards, working with the wing control surfaces, help generate additional lift during the crucial stages of landing and take-off to reduce the speeds and landing runs required to the minimum. In fact one of the essential requirements of the original specification was that the aircraft could operate from 500m/1640ft runways. Landing

distance is reduced by several means – the Head-Up Display doubles as a precision landing aid, making it possible to aim just 30m/98ft in from the threshold, and the thrust reverser is interconnected with the nose gear, so that it can be selected in the air and will operate as soon as the nose is lowered.

In order to keep the aircraft as small and light as possible, it was decided to install a state-of-the-art navigational computer instead of a human navigator. The aircraft looks a lot heavier than it actually is thanks to the use of honeycomb panels in the aircraft. It is however very strong and is stressed to stand 12G in the tight turns made possible by vast wing area.

The chosen engine for the Viggen, the Pratt & Whitney JT8D-22 designed for the Boeing 727, was licence-built by Volvo in Sweden as the RM8A together with a locally designed afterburner. The fighter version however required that the engine was redesigned, at great cost, to better suit the demands of the fighter mission. The new engine, the RM8B, gave greater thrust at all altitudes and in extreme manoeuvres. The prototype first flew in February 8, 1967 and was described by the test pilot Eric Dahlstrom as being "as simple to fly as a sportsplane". In April 1968 the Swedish Government authorized Viggen production, with the first aircraft being delivered in July 1971.

LEFT: **A JA 37 Viggen, the all-weather Viggen interceptor.** BELOW: **The SF 37 Viggen reconnaissance version carries the night reconnaissance pod on the left under-fuselage pylon.**

LEFT: **The SF 37 reconnaissance version has cameras in the distinctively shaped nose.** BELOW: **The Viggen was a very advanced design, far ahead of other European types of the time.**

The aircraft was designed for simple maintenance from the outset so that conscripts with little training could turn the aircraft around quickly in readiness for its next mission. Refuelling and re-arming by seven ground personnel, of which six were conscripts, had to take less than ten minutes.

The Viggen's one-piece wrap-around windscreen was specially strengthened to survive bird strikes at high speeds and also gives the pilots an excellent forward view. Sweden's numerous dispersed underground hangars dictated that the Viggen's fin be capable of folding down for easier storage.

During the 1960s, the Swedish Air Force were expected to purchase more than 800 Viggens, but the final Viggen production total was 329 built in attack, trainer, two reconnaissance versions and the more powerful JA 37 fighter variant. The last of the Viggens, a fighter, was delivered to the Swedish Air Force in 1990. Since then the Viggen fighter has undergone several upgrades with better radar to track more targets simultaneously, new avionics and cockpit displays and extra weaponry in the form of the AIM-120 AAM.

The Viggen has been gradually replaced in Svenska Flygvapnet (Swedish Air Force) service by the Gripen.

ABOVE: **The last JA 37 interceptor version was delivered to the Swedish Air Force in 1990.** BELOW: **Able to operate from country roads and motorways, the Viggen protected Sweden for almost three decades.**

Saab JA 37 Viggen

First flight: February 8, 1967 (prototype)
Power: Volvo Flygmotor 12,750kg/28,110lb afterburning-thrust RM8B turbofan
Armament: One 30mm/1.18in cannon plus six external hardpoints for 6000kg/13,228lb of ordnance including two Sky Flash and four Sidewinder AAMs
Size: Wingspan – 10.6m/34ft 9.25in
Length – 16.4m/53ft 9.75in
Height – 5.9m/19ft 4.25in
Wing area – 52.2m^2/561.89sq ft, including canards
Weights: Empty – 15,000kg/33,060lb
Maximum take-off – 20,500kg/45,194lb
Performance: Maximum speed – 2195kph/1365mph
Ceiling – 18,290m/60,000ft
Range – 1000km/620 miles
Climb – 10,000m/32,810ft in 1minute, 24 seconds

Sud-Ouest Vautour

The Vautour (vulture) was initially developed as a medium bomber in the early to mid-1950s and from a modern perspective seemed an unusual choice for development as a fighter. The advanced high-performance twin-jet design was first tested in half-scale form in 1949 and the full-scale prototypes began testing in 1951. The trials were so promising that the type, very similar in layout to the Yak-28, was rapidly developed as the S.O. 4050 multi-role combat aircraft.

Three variants of the Vautour were developed: the single-seat cannon and bomb armed Vautour IIA attack aircraft, the two-seat Vautour IIB bomber equipped with a glazed nose for the navigator/bombardier, and the Vautour IIN – the N signifying nuit, or night. The latter was a two-seat all-weather/night attack fighter equipped with an interception radar in the nose, and it took off on its maiden flight on October 16, 1952. A total of 140 examples were ordered by the French but only 70 were produced between 1957 and 1959, armed with rockets, missiles and cannon, and these were mostly based at Tours with an all-weather fighter wing. They were gradually replaced from 1973 by the Mirage F1.

In the late 1950s, Israel wanted to develop a long-range fighter capability to tackle hostile aircraft deep in enemy territory. Following evaluation flights in early 1957 the Israeli Air Force selected the Vautour to replace the de Havilland Mosquito in the long-range attack role and to counter the Arabs' Ilyushin Il-28 light jet bombers. Eighteen Vautour bombers were first exported to Israel, followed by seven of the fighter version. Capable of supersonic speed in a dive, these

TOP: **The similarities between the Vautour and the Yak-28 are clear in this photograph.** ABOVE: **The Vautour IIB bomber version equipped the French equivalent of Strategic Air Command.**

aircraft saw considerable action with the Israeli Air Force (IAF) in the 1967 Six-Day War and were in constant use until 1970.

Two IAF squadrons were equipped with the Vautour – the "Bat" squadron at Tel-Nof operated the IIN variant. The 7 IINs were initially operated as night interceptors (alongside the IAF's Meteor NF.13s until 1960 when these were retired) but after the arrival of the Mirage IIIC in 1963 they were employed as attack aircraft. They did however continue to fly night interceptions as required, for example early in 1964 when they attempted to engage Egyptian MiG-19s.

The first encounter between the IAF Vautours and the MiG-19 had occurred some five years earlier on August 16, 1959 when two Vautours engaged four Egyptian MiGs on the Israeli-Egyptian border. Later in March 1962 a single Vautour chased an Ilyushin Il-28 all the way to Damascus before being ordered to turn back.

TOP: **This French Air Force Vautour IIN was modified to test a new radome installation.** ABOVE: **An unlikely fighter, the Vautour IIN was in front-line service with the Armée de l'Air for around 15 years.**

Sud-Ouest Vautour IIN

First flight: October 16, 1952
Power: Two SNECMA 3503kg/7716lb-thrust Atar 101E-3 turbojet engines
Armament: Four 30mm/1.18in cannon, internal bomb bay with provision for up to 240 unguided rockets, plus underwing pylons for air-to-air missiles or rockets
Size: Wingspan – 15.09m/49ft 6in
Length – 15.57m/51ft 2in
Height – 4.5m/14ft 9in
Wing area – 45m^2/484.4sq ft
Weights: Empty – 10,000kg/22,010lb
Maximum take-off – 20,000kg/44,093lb
Performance: Maximum speed – 1105kph/687mph
Ceiling – 15,000m/49,210ft
Range – 3200km/1990 miles
Climb – 3600m/11,800ft per minute

Sukhoi Su-9/11

The dominance of swept-wing fighters in the Korean War stimulated the ultimate development of the configuration – the delta. In the USSR, the TSAGI (National Aerodynamic Research Centre) endorsed the form and encouraged its development. Sukhoi's design bureau produced a prototype delta-winged aircraft, the T-3, and a whole range of nose configurations were tried, but it was the safe option that was chosen for the production aircraft – a circular intake with a small conical centrebody housing the radar.

Production began in 1958 and the first Su-9s joined air defence squadrons in 1959, equipped with four AA-1 "Alkali" air-to-air missiles. Two drop tanks were carried, as the internal fuel capacity of

2145 litres/472 gallons severely limited range. A special version, the T-431, set an altitude record of 28,852m/94,659ft in 1959. Su-9s were still in use in the early 1980s and many of the examples retired from service were converted to drones, or pilotless vehicles, and were used as aerial targets to test and train Soviet air defence personnel.

The 1961 Tushino Aviation Day display saw the first appearance of the T-43 prototype, an improved version of the Su-9. By 1965, production of the new version, by then called the Su-11, was underway with a more powerful engine, new radar and improved weaponry. The nose was lengthened and a much larger centrebody was needed to house the new Uragan 5B radar.

ABOVE: **This Su-9 was pictured at the 1967 Soviet Aviation Day display.** BELOW: **A total of 2000 Su-9/11s were built, but the Soviet Union chose to keep them all.**

The new weapons were the long-range Anab air-to-air missiles, carried in pairs, one equipped for infra-red homing (heat seeking) and the other radar-guided.

Combined Sukhoi Su-9/11 production is estimated at 2000 aircraft. None saw service with other Warsaw Pact countries and no examples of this potent fighter were exported.

Sukhoi Su-11

First flight: 1961 (T-43)

Power: Lyulka 10,000kg/22,046lb afterburning thrust AL-7F-1 turbojet

Armament: Two AA-3 Anab long-range air-to-air homing missiles

Size: Wingspan – 8.43m/27ft 8in
  Length – 17.4m/57ft 1in
  Height – 4.88m/16ft
  Wing area – 26.2m^2/282.02sq ft

Weights: Empty – 9100kg/20,062lb
  Maximum take-off – 14,000kg/30,865lb

Performance: Maximum speed – 1915kph/1190mph
  Ceiling – 17,000m/55,775ft
  Range – 1450km/900 miles with drop tanks
  Climb – 8230m/27,000ft per minute

Sukhoi Su-15

This very fast single-seat aircraft, codenamed "Flagon" by NATO, served from the 1960s into the 90s. Equipped with long-range air-to-air missiles, the Su-15 was an interceptor, whose sole role was the air defence of the USSR. Around 1500 served with Soviet PVO-Strany home defence units from 1967, deployed in areas where they were only likely to face attacking NATO bombers with little likelihood of ever having to dogfight.

Developed to replace the Su-11, the Su-15 Flagon-A was the first production version and was first seen at the 1967 Aviation Day display – it was clearly a twin-engine development of the Su-11 but with side intakes necessitated by the introduction of the large conical radome. The large rear-warning radar appeared on this model and was common to most of the Flagon family.

Flagon interceptor missions were almost always flown under ground control and this included the most infamous Su-15 mission of all, on September 1, 1983. At 03.20 local time, Su-15 pilot Major Vassily Kasmin launched two AA-3 Anab air-to-air missiles at a Korean Air Lines Boeing 747 airliner, which had strayed 400km/250 miles north of its planned route. The airliner was overflying

ABOVE: **The Sukhoi Su-15 was a very big fighter that protected the Soviet Union and Russia for around 30 years.** BELOW: **This picture of an example preserved in a Russian museum shows the size of the large nose radome.**

Soviet military installations and after reportedly firing warning shots with cannon, the Su-15, under instruction from ground control, attacked from a distance of 800m/2624ft and destroyed the airliner with the loss of all 269 passengers and crew.

The "Flagon-D" was the first version produced in large numbers and differed from the A by having bigger span wings with a kinked leading edge. The E model was also produced in quantity and was powered by more powerful engines (hence the larger air intakes), presumably to reduce the scramble time.

The "Flagon-F" was the ultimate version and entered service in 1975. It introduced bigger engines, gun pods and a more powerful radar, housed in an ogival-shaped radome designed to reduce drag and improve supersonic acceleration.

From the mid-1990s, the Su-15 was replaced by the Su-27 and MiG-31. Two-seat trainer versions and experimental versions with lift jets were also produced.

Sukhoi Su-15 Flagon-F

First flight: 1965

Power: Two Tumansky 7200kg/15,873lb afterburning thrust R-13F2-300 turbojets

Armament: Four AA-3 "Anab" medium-range air-to-air missiles carried on underwing pylons, two AA-8 "Aphid" short-range air-to-air missiles on inboard positions, plus two 23mm/0.9in gun pods

Size: Wingspan – 10.53m/34ft 6in
Length – 21.33m/70ft
Height – 5.1m/16ft 8.5in
Wing area – 36m^2/387.5sq ft

Weights: Empty – 11,000kg/24,250lb
Maximum take-off – 18,000kg/39,680lb

Performance: Maximum speed – 2230kph/1386mph
Ceiling – 20,000m/65,615ft
Range – 725km/450 miles
Climb – 10,670m/35,000ft per minute

Sukhoi Su-27 family

The arrival of the long-range Su-27 (codenamed "Flanker" by NATO) gave the USSR a formidable fighter that could escort its bomber force all the way to the UK. This high-performance aircraft, which also had the capability of intercepting aircraft over long distances, came as a shock to NATO planners when it was deployed in the mid-1980s. About 20 per cent larger than the F-15 Eagle, the Su-27 is one of the biggest and most imposing fighters of all time.

Development work began in 1969 under Pavel Sukhoi himself and the prototype first flew in 1977, but early models displayed serious instability problems and it was considerably redesigned. Nevertheless, the Su-27 in service today is considered by many to be the pinnacle of Russian fighter design and the masterpiece of the Sukhoi bureau.

The fast-climbing and superbly manoeuvrable fly-by-wire Flanker can carry up to 10 air-to-air missiles, including the 112km/70-mile-range AA-10C. That amount of missiles gives the Flanker "combat persistence" – it can keep on fighting long after other fighters would have had to turn for home. Huge internal fuel tanks give very long range (up to 4000km/ 2484 miles), with no need for drag-inducing external fuel tanks.

The Su-27's Zhuk radar can track targets while continuing to scan for others and perhaps most importantly gives the aircraft a look-down/shoot-down capability. Very advanced electronics enables the Flanker to detect and destroy an enemy fighter beyond visual range (BVR) at tree-top height, without the need to descend to that level and lose a height advantage. The Su-27 equips air arms in Russia, Belarus, Uzbekistan, Ethiopia, China, Vietnam and the Ukraine

TOP: **The large Su-27 first flew in April 1981 and came as a shock to potential adversaries of the Soviet Union.** ABOVE: **Preparing to land, this Su-27 has deployed its enormous dorsal airbrake which reduces the aircraft's speed most effectively.**

– China also negotiated manufacturing rights to produce its own Su-27s, which began to appear in December 1998.

The Su-27P is a single-seat air defence fighter, the Su-27S is a multi-role version capable of carrying a 4000kg/8820lb bomb load and the Su-27UB is a two-seat operational trainer. Specially modified versions have set more than 40 altitude and climb records.

The Su-30 is a two-seat air defence fighter capable of 10-hour missions and can also serve as an airborne command post for other Su-27s. India and China have ordered these aircraft, which like the derivative Su-37, have canards and thrust-vectoring nozzles for enhanced manoeuvrability.

The Su-27 spawned a whole family of fighter aircraft, including the Su-33, Su-35 and Su-37, but the Su-27 is likely

ABOVE: **This Ukrainian Air Force example shows the huge rear defensive radar boom which effectively gives the type's pilots eyes in the back of their head.**
LEFT: **The excellent Su-27 did much to remove the advantage enjoyed in the early 1980s by US fighter types like the F-15.**

to be the mainstay of the Russian aviation industry for some years to come.

The Russian Navy's carrier arm is equipped with the Su-33 Naval Flanker version (originally the Su-27K), with moveable foreplanes plus folding wings and tailplane. Deployed since 1995 and certainly the most modern fighters in the Russian inventory, Su-33s provide the Russian Admiral Kuznetsov carrier class with air defence. Landing gear is also strengthened and as a naval aircraft it does, of course, have an arrester hook. Because of the lower approach and take-off speeds a number of other changes were made – moveable foreplanes aid manoeuvrability and control in all aspects of flight.

BELOW: **The Su-34 fighter-bomber derivative first flew in 1990, and seats its two-man crew in a side-by-side cockpit.**

Sukhoi Su-27P

First flight: April 20, 1981
(T-10S-1 pre-production prototype)
Power: Two Saturn/Lyulka 12,516kg/27,557lb afterburning thrust AL-31F turbofans
Armament: One 30mm/1.18in cannon, plus ten hardpoints for up to ten air-to-air missiles from AA-8 "Aphids" to AA10Cs
Size: Wingspan – 14.7m/48ft 3in Length – 21.94m/72ft Height – 5.93m/19ft 6in Wing area – 62m²/667sq ft
Weights: Empty – 16,380kg/36,110lb
Maximum take-off – 33,000kg/72,750lb
Performance: Maximum speed – 2500kph/1553mph
Ceiling – 18,011m/59,055ft
Range – 3680km/2285 miles
Climb – 18,312m/60,040ft per minute

TOP: **The Su-37 version has canard foreplanes and agility-enhancing thrust vectoring nozzles.** ABOVE: **The performance and agility of the Su-37 Super Flanker makes it a potent dogfight adversary.**

Sukhoi Su-35/37

A version of the Su-27 fitted with canards first flew in May 1985 and was developed into what became the Su-35. The prototype of the first true Su-35, initially designated Su-27M, had its test flight in June 1988. The single-seat Su-35 differed from the Su-27 in a number of ways, apart from the all-moving canard foreplanes. Improved engines provided greater thrust while flight control was managed by a digital fly-by-wire system that boasted quadruple redundancy, that is the systems could find four alternative routes by which to send control commands throughout the aircraft. This kind of system is an insurance against combat damage – on-board systems will simply find another route by which to pass the information.

The extremely efficient Phazotron radar can search over 100km/62 miles, track 24 targets simultaneously and has a terrain-following mode to guide the aircraft automatically over undulating landscapes. Development of this and the fly-by-wire system considerably delayed the overall programme. The Su-35 tailcone also houses a radar, which scans and protects the aircraft's rear. The aircraft is equipped for inflight refuelling and auxiliary fuel tanks are fitted in the two tailfins. The cockpit Electronic Flight Information System (EFIS) consists of three TV screens and a Head-Up Display (HUD).

The Su-37 Super Flanker is a further improvement on the Su-35 and has two-dimensional thrust-vectoring nozzles controlled by the fly-by-wire system. The improved cockpit has a sidestick controller and four LCD multifunction displays. When the Su-37 appeared at the 1996 Farnborough air show piloted by Sukhoi test pilot Eugeny Frolov, it stole the show with the astounding manoeuvres made possible by thrust vectoring. The Su-37 was flipped on its back while flying at 350kph/217mph so that it faced the opposite direction, inverted and almost stationary. After pausing for two seconds (long enough to loose off a missile in combat) the thrust vectoring was used to complete the 360 degree rotation and the aircraft moved off in its original direction of flight at only 60kph/37mph.

Sukhoi's chief designer Mikhail Simonov is so confident about the advantage bestowed by the aircraft's thrust vectoring system, that he challenged any US aircraft to a mock dogfight "… any time, any place!" At the time of writing, the Su-37 was yet to be ordered into production.

Sukhoi Su-35

First flight: June 28, 1988
Power: Two Lyulka 12,500kg/27,557lb AL-31M turbofans
Armament: One 30mm/1.18in cannon and 14 hardpoints to carry a range of missiles and bombs up to 6000kg/13,228lb
Size: Wingspan – 14.7m/48ft 2.75in
Length – 22.2m/72ft 10in
Height – 6.36m/20ft 10in
Wing area – 46.5m²/500sq ft
Weights: Empty – 17,000kg/37,479lb
Maximum take-off – 34,000kg/74,956lb
Performance: Maximum speed – 2500kph/1550mph
Ceiling – 18,000m/59,055ft
Range – 4000km/2484 miles
Climb – not published

LEFT: **The tail-dragging straight-winged Attacker was the Fleet Air Arm's first front-line jet fighter.**

Supermarine Attacker F. Mk I

First flight: July 27, 1946
Power: Rolls-Royce 2271kg/5000lb-thrust Nene 3 turbojet
Armament: Four 20mm/0.78in cannon in wing
Size: Wingspan – 11.25m/36ft 11in
Length – 11.43m/37ft 6in
Height – 3.02m/9ft 11in
Wing area – 21m²/226sq ft
Weights: Empty – 3826kg/8434lb
Maximum take-off – 5539kg/12,211lb
Performance: Maximum speed – 950kph/590mph
Ceiling – 13,715m/45,000ft
Range – 950km/590 miles
Climb – 1936m/6350ft per minute

Supermarine Attacker

The Supermarine Attacker was designed to an RAF specification and combined a Nene jet engine with the laminar wing and landing gear of the piston-engined Spiteful. This approach was taken to bring another British single-seat jet fighter into service as soon as possible. Although the prototype first flew in July 1946, the type did not enter service until August 1951 and then with

the Royal Navy, who maintained interest in the Attacker long after the RAF abandoned it. The Attacker was an unremarkable aircraft and the tailwheel made deck landing difficult, but as the first Fleet Air Arm jet fighter in front-line use, the Attacker provided the Royal Navy with its first foothold in the jet age. The type was phased out of front-line use in 1954.

Attackers were also supplied to the Pakistani Air Force, who operated them as land-based aircraft.

LEFT: **The Scimitar was a large twin-engined fighter and although only produced in limited quantities, it served the Royal Navy well in a variety of roles for a decade.**

Supermarine Scimitar F.1

First flight: January 11, 1957
Power: Two Rolls-Royce 5105kg/11,250lb static thrust Avon 202 turbojets
Armament: Four 30mm/1.18in cannon, wing pylons for up to 96 air-to-air rockets or a range of other stores
Size: Wingspan – 11.33m/37ft 2in
Length – 16.87m/55ft 4in
Height – 5.28m/17ft 4in
Wing area – 45.06m²/485sq ft
Weights: Empty – 10,869kg/23,962lb
Maximum take-off – 15,513kg/34,200lb
Performance: Maximum speed – 1143kph/710mph
Ceiling – 14,020m/46,000ft
Range – 2288km/1422 miles
Climb – 3660m/12,000ft per minute

Supermarine Scimitar

This large and heavy fighter was the Royal Navy's first swept-wing single-seat fighter and was also the first Fleet Air Arm aircraft equipped to carry an atomic bomb. The Scimitar was equally at home carrying out low-level bombing attacks, high-altitude interception with air-to-air missiles and long-range fighter reconnaissance – it represented a quantum leap from the lacklustre Sea

Hawk which it replaced as the Navy's standard single-seat strike fighter.

The first operational squadron equipped with this very capable combat aircraft was No.803, formed at Lossiemouth in June 1958. Although only 76 were produced, the Scimitars gave the Royal Navy real punch and retained their nuclear role until 1969.

Supermarine Swift F. Mk 1

First flight: August 5, 1951
Power: Rolls-Royce 3406kg/7500lb-thrust Avon RA7 turbojet
Armament: Two 30mm/1.18in cannon
Size: Wingspan – 9.85m/32ft 4in
Length – 12.64m/41ft 5.5in
Height – 3.8m/12ft 0in
Wing area – 28.43m²/306sq ft
Weights: Empty – 5678kg/12,500lb
Maximum take-off – 7721kg/17,000lb
Performance: Maximum speed – 1110kph/690mph
Ceiling – 13,725m/45,500ft
Range – 1175km/730 miles
Climb – 3752m/12,300ft

Supermarine Swift

In 1946 Britain's Air Ministry asked manufacturers to propose a replacement for the Gloster Meteor. Supermarine's entry was a development of its Attacker, but featuring staged improvements including swept wings and tail, tricycle undercarriage and a Rolls-Royce Avon engine, which became the Swift F. Mk 1. This aircraft

was allocated, on a very restricted basis, to No.56 Squadron RAF in February 1954 but only to gain air experience with swept wings. High-speed and high-altitude manoeuvrability and control problems persisted with interim marks, but the FR. Mk 5 did enter RAF front-line service, equipping Nos.2 and 79 Squadrons in RAF

Germany from 1955 until 1961. This version of the Swift, an effective fighter reconnaissance aircraft, was the first reheat-engined swept-wing aircraft in RAF service.

Tupolev Tu-28P

First flight: 1957
Power: Two Lyulka 11,200kg/24,690lb afterburning thrust AL-21F turbojets
Armament: Four AA-5 "Ash" long-range air-to-air missiles
Size: Wingspan – 18.1m/59ft 4.5in
Length – 27.2m/89ft 3in
Height – 7m/23ft
Wing area – 80m²/861sq ft
Weights: Empty – 25,000kg/55,125lb
Maximum take-off – 40,000kg/88,185lb
Performance: Maximum speed – 1850kph/1150mph
Ceiling – 20,000m/65,615ft
Range – 5000km/3105 miles
Climb – 7500m/25,000ft per minute

Tupolev Tu-28

Codenamed "Fiddler" by NATO, this very large fighter provided the USSR with a long-range fighter capability from the 1960s until its gradual replacement by Su-27s and MiG-31s in the late 1980s. The Tu-28, designed to intercept Western missile-carrying aircraft before they had a chance to launch their deadly weapons, was the world's largest all-weather

interceptor. With a range of more than 3000km/1865 miles, the Tu-28 was deployed to protect the northern Soviet Union and was armed with four AA-5 "Ash" air-to-air missiles.

Production began in the early 1960s and the type entered service in the mid-1960s, although it was unknown to the West until Soviet Aviation Day in 1967. Two crew were carried in tandem.

The aircraft were phased out of service by 1992.

Vought F7U Cutlass

In 1945 the US Navy issued a requirement for a 965kph/600mph carrier-borne fighter. German wartime aerodynamic research data proved very useful to US aircraft designers in the immediate post-war years. Vought (or Chance Vought as it was then known) designers were particularly interested in the work carried out by the Arado company on tailless aircraft and this led directly to the rather unconventional F7U Cutlass, which had a 38-degree swept wing, twin tail fins but no conventional tail surfaces. The Cutlass helped the US Navy break new ground – it was the first supersonic production aircraft in the US Navy inventory.

The F7U-1 was the first version in service but only 14 were built and these were used for trials and training. The aircraft was very demanding in terms of maintenance and it also had a high accident rate but it was very popular with pilots and could pull 16G manoeuvres when making use of its excellent aerobatics.

The F7U-3 that ultimately equipped 13 US Navy and Marine Corps squadrons ashore and on carriers was not just modified and improved – it was effectively a new design. The F7U-1 version had not been considered robust enough for carrier use so the new model was considerably tougher, being re-stressed throughout. To reduce maintenance time over 100 extra doors and access panels were added. The nose was redesigned, twice, to improve pilot visibility and the tricycle undercarriage nosewheel was both lengthened and strengthened. This new version was introduced into US Navy service from 1954 and the

TOP: **Like the Douglas Skyray, the Cutlass was designed with the benefit of data derived from German wartime aerodynamic research. This Cutlass is preserved at the Museum of Naval Aviation at Pensacola in Florida.**
ABOVE: **An F7U-1 Cutlass.** BELOW LEFT: **The Cutlass is surely one of the oddest-looking fighters ever.**

F7U-3M variant was equipped to carry four laser-beam-riding Sparrow air-to-air missiles.

Most were withdrawn from service in 1956–7 as new, more capable aircraft became available. The F7U-3 was just as accident-prone as the F7U-1, with an incredible 25 per cent of all aircraft built being lost in accidents.

Vought F7U-3 Cutlass

First flight: September 29, 1948 (XF7U-1 prototype)
Power: Two Westinghouse 2767kg/6100lb afterburning thrust J46-WE-8A turbojet engines
Armament: Four 20mm/0.78in cannon, plus underwing attachments for rockets
Size: Wingspan – 12.09m/39ft 8in
    Length – 13.13m/43ft 1in
    Height – 4.46m/14ft 7.5in
    Wing area – 46.08m²/496sq ft
Weights: Empty – 8260kg/18,210lb
    Maximum take-off – 14,353kg/31,642lb
Performance: Maximum speed – 1094kph/680mph
    Ceiling – 12,190m/40,000ft
    Range – 1062km/660 miles
    Climb – 3960m/13,000ft per minute

Vought F-8 Crusader

The single-seat Crusader naval fighter began life as Vought's response to a 1952 US Navy requirement for a carrier-based supersonic fighter. The prototype first took to the air in March 1955 and exceeded Mach 1 during this initial flight, making it the first fighter designed for shipboard operation to fly faster than sound.

Carrier operations require that aircraft have very robust landing gear, an arrester hook, and folding wings but these features all add to the overall weight and thus can compromise

performance. Vought came up with a brilliant variable-incidence wing, which on take-off and landing could be pivoted up seven degrees. This gave the wing a high angle-of-attack and so reduced approach and take-off speeds. The raised centre section of the wing also acted as a speed brake to reduce landing speed further.

The armament consisted of four 20mm/0.78in cannon, two of the guns on either side of the fuselage. Behind the guns, on each side of the aircraft, was a launch rail for a single Sidewinder air-to-air missile. There were no wing stores pylons on the prototype, but these came on later production models.

The first production version of the F8U-1 Crusader, as it was then named, flew at the end of September 1955 and the US Navy accepted its first operational F8U-1 on December 28, 1956. The US Navy was eager to show off its new fighter and a series of speed and endurance records were bagged by Crusaders in 1956–7. On July 16, 1957 an F8U-1 and an F8U-1P reconnaissance model attempted to set a coast-to-coast speed record. The pilot of the F8U-1P that landed in New York after a flight of 3 hours and 23 minutes was Major John Glenn, later an astronaut and US senator.

The F8U-1E had an improved radar system that gave it limited all-weather capability while the more powerful F8U-2 incorporated a further improved radar and fire-control system, as well as an uprated J57-P-16 engine with 7670kg/16,900lb of afterburning thrust.

Next version was the F8U-2N, with new avionics, including a push-button autopilot, and the uprated J57-P-20 engine, with increased afterburning thrust of 8,170kg/18,000lb. Yet more versions followed. The first F8U-2NE flew at the end of June 1961 and carried an improved search and fire-control radar system for enhanced all-weather operation.

In September 1962, the US Navy introduced an aircraft designation system in line with US Air Force designations, so

ABOVE: **The last of the gunfighters – two US Navy Vought F-8 Crusaders, the top one flying in an inverted position.** BELOW: **The F-8's innovative variable-incidence wing reduced take-off and landing speeds.**

ABOVE: The French Aéronavale was the main overseas customer for the Crusader, and operated the type until 2000.

existing Crusader variant designations were changed. The F8U-1 became the F-8A and the later models changed thus: F8U-1E/F-8B, F8U-2/F-8C, F8U-2N/F-8D, F8U-2NE/F-8E, F8U-1P/RF-8A.

One final new-production model was built – the F-8E(FN), built for the French Aéronavale. However, French carriers were smaller than American carriers, and this dictated new engineering, including blown flaps to reduce the aircraft's landing speed.

The Aéronavale operated 42 Crusaders from the carriers *Clémenceau* and *Foch*. The French aircraft also had the capability to carry two Matra R.530 air-to-air missiles and eventually four Matra Magic R.550 heat-seeking missiles, in place of Sidewinders.

The Crusader was used by both US Marine and US Navy detachments during the war in Vietnam, its combat début coming on August 2, 1964. North Vietnamese patrol boats attacked the US Navy destroyer *Maddox* so four Crusaders from the carrier *Ticonderoga* attacked and sank one of the

patrol boats. The Marines used the aircraft largely in the attack role, but the US Navy used the Crusader as a dogfighter and in the period 1966–8 shot down at least 18 MiGs.

The Crusader proved so effective that in 1966 a re-engineering programme was established to refurbish and improve the type. Stronger wings and main landing gear plus blown flaps (devised for the French Crusaders) were added to a total of 446 rebuilt.

By 1972, fighter versions of the F-8 were being phased out of US Navy service but in 1978, 25 refurbished US Navy F-8Hs were sold on to the Philippine Air Force as F-8Ps, which finally retired in 1986. The Aéronavale Crusaders were the last of the type in service and were replaced by the Rafale from 2000, bringing more than four decades of Crusader service to an end.

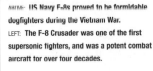

ABOVE: US Navy F-8s proved to be formidable dogfighters during the Vietnam War.

LEFT: The F-8 Crusader was one of the first supersonic fighters, and was a potent combat aircraft for over four decades.

Vought F-8E Crusader

First flight: March 25, 1955
Power: Pratt & Whitney 8165kg/18,000lb afterburning thrust J57-P-20A turbojet engine
Armament: Four 20mm/0.78in cannon, four AIM-9 Sidewinder air-to-air missiles, or two AGM-12B Bullpup missiles
Size: Wingspan – 10.72m/35ft 2in
Length – 16.61m/54ft 6in
Height – 4.8m/15ft 9in
Wing area – 32.52m^2/350sq ft
Weights: Empty – 9038kg/19,925lb
Maximum take off – 15,422kg/34,000lb
Performance: Maximum speed – 1800kph/1120mph
Ceiling – 17,983m/59,000ft
Range – 966km/600 miles
Climb – 17,374m/57,000ft in 6 minutes

LEFT: **The Yak-17 was the penultimate Yak jet fighter modified from an original piston-powered type.**

Yakovlev Yak-17

First flight: Early 1947
Power: Klimov 1000kg/2205lb thrust RD-10A turbojet
Armament: Two nose-mounted 23mm/0.9in cannon
Size: Wingspan – 9.2m/30ft 2.25in
Length – 8.78m/28ft 9.75in
Height – 2.1m/6ft 10in
Wing area – 14.85m²/159.85sq ft
Weights: Empty – 2430kg/5357lb
Maximum take-off – 3323kg/7326lb
Performance: Maximum speed – 750kph/466mph
Ceiling – 12,750m/41,830ft
Range – 717km/446 miles
Climb – 5000m/16,405ft in 5.8 minutes

Yakovlev Yak-17

The Yak-17 was developed from the earlier Yak-15 which itself had been a conversion of the taildragging Yak-3 piston fighter. The Yak-15 had been the first successful Soviet jet fighter in service having first flown in April 1946. About 200 Yak-15s were built before being succeeded by the much improved Yak-17 of which around 430 were built.

The Yak-17 differed from the Yak-15 by having a retractable tricycle under-carriage (thus eliminating the archaic tailwheel), and a more powerful engine. Structural strengthening also took place, and to improve the aircraft's range, drop-tanks were introduced too. A two-seat conversion trainer variant (YaK-17UTI) was also built.

The Yak-17 was also operated by Poland and Czechoslovakia and was phased out by all air forces by 1955.

LEFT: **The Yak-23 took the Yak-15 design as far as it could go.**

Yakovlev Yak-23

First flight: June 17, 1947
Power: Klimov 1590kg/3505lb thrust RD-500 turbojet
Armament: Two nose-mounted 23mm/0.9in cannon plus one 60kg/132lb bomb
Size: Wingspan – 8.73m/28ft 7.75in
Length – 8.12m/26ft 7.75in
Height – 3.31m/10ft 10.3in
Wing area – 13.5m²/145.32sq ft
Weights: Empty – 2000kg/4409lb
Maximum take-off – 3036kg/6693lb
Performance: Maximum speed – 975kph/606mph
Ceiling – 14,800m/48,555ft
Range – 1200km/745 miles
Climb – 2041m/6693ft per minute

Yakovlev Yak-23

The Yak-23 was the ultimate development of the Russian Yak-15/ -17 family. It differed from the Yak-17 by having the horizontal tail surfaces mounted higher up a much larger fin.

Designed as a lightweight day fighter, the Yak-23 first flew in June 1947 with power provided by an imported Rolls-Royce Derwent. It entered production,

powered by a Soviet copy of the Derwent (the RD-500), in early 1948. 310 were built and many were operated by other Eastern Bloc nations including Bulgaria, Romania, Czechoslovakia and Poland. The last of the barrel-bodied Yaks, this aircraft was always seen as a back up for the advanced swept wing fighters under development at the time

and this wonderfully agile fighter was indeed replaced throughout the Warsaw Pact by the MiG-15 in the mid-1950s.

LEFT: **The Yak-25, equipped with a heavyweight nose radar.**

Yakovlev Yak-25

First flight: June 19, 1952 (Yak-120)
Power: Two Tumansky 2633kg/5798lb-thrust RD-9 turbojet engines
Armament: Two 37mm/1.46in cannon
Size: Wingspan – 11m/36ft 1in
  Length – 15.67m/51ft 5in
  Height – 4.32m/14ft 2in
  Wing area – 28.94m²/311.51sq ft
Weights: Empty – 7300kg/16,095lb
  Maximum take-off – 10,900kg/24,030lb
Performance: Maximum speed – 1090kph/677mph
  Ceiling – 14,000m/45,900ft
  Range – 2730km/1696 miles
  Climb – 3000m/9800ft per minute

Yakovlev Yak-25

Codenamed "Flashlight" by NATO, the two-seat Yak-25 (not to be confused with the Yak-25 single-engine fighter prototype of 1947) was the Soviet Union's first all-weather radar-equipped jet fighter and took to the air in prototype form (Yak-120) in June 1952. The new aircraft was designed to loiter for up to 2½ hours and carry the new Sokol radar that weighed in at around 500kg/1100lb. Power was provided by two jets slung beneath a swept but untapered wing. Sole armament was a pair of 37mm/1.46in cannon housed under the fuselage.

Although production began in 1953, with the aircraft then designated Yak-25, the radar was not ready for service until late 1955. The type was deployed to protect the far north of the Soviet Union against NATO bombers, and the introduction of the Yak-25 was enough to persuade the USAF that overflights of the USSR were no longer an easy reconnaissance option.

Production ceased in 1958 after 480 had been built. It remained in front-line use until the mid-1960s.

LEFT: **The Yak-28 was a multi-role type, and appeared in a number of versions.**

Yakovlev Yak-28PM

First flight: March 5, 1958 (Yak 129)
Power: Two Tumansky 6128kg/13,492lb after-burning thrust R-11AF-2-300 turbojets
Armament: Two Anab missiles, one infra-red and one radar-homing, plus two short-range air-to-air missiles
Size: Wingspan – 11.64m/38ft 2.25in
  Length – 20.65m/67ft 9in
  Height – 3.95m/12ft 11.5in
  Wing area – 37.6m²/404.74sq ft
Weights: Maximum take-off – 15,700kg/34,612lb
Performance: Maximum speed – 1890kph/1174mph
  Ceiling – 16,000m/52,495ft
  Range – 2630km/1634 miles
  Climb – not known

Yakovlev Yak-28

At first glance the Yak-28 was similar to the Yak-25 in configuration but it was a wholly new design that first flew in prototype form during 1958 as the Yak-129. First versions developed were bomber/tactical attack aircraft but the Yak-28P was a dedicated all-weather interceptor with tandem cockpits for the two crew. It was designed to operate at low and medium altitude equipped with an Orel radar and armed with two air-to-air missiles, one radar-homing and one beam-riding.

Codenamed "Firebar" by NATO, the Yak-28 was capable of transonic flight and entered service in the winter of 1961–2. The aircraft was upgraded in numerous ways – its engines were uprated to have 6128kg/13,492lb after-burning thrust each and two short-range air-to-air missiles were added to the stores options, gaining the aircraft the designation Yak-28PM. Production ceased in 1967 after 437 fighters had been built and the type was phased out of service in the mid-1980s.

Glossary

AAM	air-to-air missile
Aerodynamics	study of how gases, including air, flow and how forces act upon objects moving through air
AEW	airborne early warning
Afterburner	facility for providing augmented thrust by burning additional fuel in the jet pipe
Ailerons	control surfaces at trailing edge of each wing used to make the aircraft roll
AMRAAM	advanced medium-range air-to-air missile
Angle of attack	angle of a wing to the oncoming airflow
ASRAAM	advanced short-range air-to-air missile
AWACS	Airborne Warning and Control System
Biplane	an aircraft with two sets of wings
BVR	beyond visual range
Canard wings	two small horizontal surfaces on either side of the front of an aircraft
CAP	combat air patrol
Ceiling	the maximum height at which an aircraft can operate
CRT	cathode ray tube
Delta wing	a swept-back triangular-shaped wing
Dihedral	the upward angle of the wing formed where the wings connect to the fuselage
Dorsal	pertaining to the upper side of an aircraft
Drag	the force that resists the motion of the aircraft through the air
ECM	electronic countermeasures
Elevators	control surfaces on the horizontal part of the tail, used to alter the aircraft's pitch
ELINT	electronic intelligence

FAA	Fleet Air Arm
FBW	fly-by-wire
Fin	the vertical portion of the tail
Flaps	moveable parts of a wing used to increase lift at slower air speeds
G	the force of gravity
HOTAS	hands on throttle and stick
HUD	Head-Up Display
IFF	identification friend or foe
IFR	inflight refuelling
Jet engine	an engine that works by creating a high velocity jet of air to propel it forward
Leading edge	the front edge of a wing or tailplane
Mach	speed of sound – Mach 1 = 1223kph/760mph at sea level
Monoplane	an aircraft with one set of wings
NATO	North Atlantic Treaty Organization
Pitch	rotational motion in which an aircraft turns around its lateral axis
Port	left side when looking forward
Radome	protective covering for radar made from material through which radar beams can pass
RAF	Royal Air Force
RATO	rocket-assisted take-off

RFC	Royal Flying Corps
RNAS	Royal Naval Air Service
Roll	rotational motion in which the aircraft turns around its longitudinal axis
Rudder	the parts of the tail surfaces that control an aircraft's yaw (its left and right turning)
SAC	Strategic Air Command (USAF)
SAM	surface-to-air missile
SLR	side-looking airborne radar
Starboard	right side when looking forward
STOL	short take-off and landing
Supersonic	indicating motion faster than the speed of sound
Swing wing	a wing capable of variable sweep
Tailplane	horizontal part of the tail, known as horizontal stabilizer in North America
Thrust	force produced by engine which pushes an aircraft forward
Triplane	an aircraft with three sets of wings
UHF	ultra high frequency
USAAC	United States Army Air Corps
USAAF	United States Army Air Forces
USAF	United States Air Force
V/STOL	vertical/short take-off and landing
Variable geometry	see Swing wing
Ventral	pertaining to the underside of an aircraft
VHF	very high frequency

Key to flags

For the specification boxes, the national flag that was current at the time of the aircraft's use is shown.

 Australia

 Britain

 Canada

 Czechoslovakia

 France

 Germany: World War I

 Germany: World War II

 Germany

 India

 Israel

 Italy

 Japan

 Netherlands

 Poland

 Romania

 South Africa

 Spain

 Sweden

 USA

 USSR

Acknowledgements

The author would like to give special thanks to Mike Bowyer, Peter March, Kazuko Matsuo and Hideo Kurihara for their help with picture research.

The publisher would like to thank the following individuals and picture libraries for the use of their pictures in the book (l=left, r=right, t=top, b=bottom, m=middle, um=upper middle, lm=lower middle). Every effort has been made to acknowledge the pictures properly, however we apologize if there are any unintentional omissions, which will be corrected in future editions.

Aerospace Publishing: 206t.

BAE Systems: 28b; 34t; 35t; 42t; 43bl; 43br; 156t; 157lm; 157b; 182t; 193um; 227m; 256.

B.J.M. & V. Aviation: 211t.

Michael J.F. Bowyer: 25tl; 47b; 53t; 58t; 60b; 63b; 65; 66t; 76b; 87bl; 89m; 95bl; 101m; 107mr; 155m; 158t; 158b; 159t; 160b; 161t; 161m; 162t; 163m; 163b; 165b; 168b; 169b; 169b; 170t; 171lm; 171b; 174b; 175m; 177um; 177b; 181m; 181b; 187b; 189m; 191lm; 192m; 200b; 201t; 202t; 202b; 206b; 209t; 221t; 221m; 222t; 223b; 225tl; 225tr; 227b; 228t; 228b; 233t; 235b; 246t.

Francis Crosby Collection: 60t; 74b; 81b; 86t; 114b; 147b; 179b; 198b.

Ken Duffey: 238b.

Chris Farmer: 164t; 166b; 172t; 173b; 191um; 195m; 195b; 214b.

Imperial War Museum Photograph Archive: 6t (CT 906); 6b (COL 195); 7t (TR 38450); 7m (CT 442); 10t (Q 67436); 10b (Q 67062); 11t (Q 67832); 12t (Q 69593); 12r (Q 42283); 13m (Q 114172); 13b (Q 64214); 14tr (Q 28180); 15tr (Q 68415); 15b (TR 516); 17tl (CH 3513); 17tr (EA 34177A); 18r (Q 63125); 19t (FRA 102960); 19m (TR 22); 19b (FRA 102079); 20t (HU 2742); 21l (GER 530); 22 (TR 139); 23tl (HU 1215); 23tr (HU 50153); 23b (CH 1299); 24b (CL 2332); 25tr (CH 16117); 25br (CH 16607); 27tl (TR 285); 27tr (NYF 18669); 27m (NYF 74296); 27b (A 9423); 30b (A 32268); 31br (A 31917); 32 (CT 62); 35m (CT 68); 36 (CT 72); 39t (CT 391); 41t (CT 57); 46tr (Q 61061); 50t (CH 886); 50b (CH 1101); 51t (COL 187); 51bl (CH 5105); 51br (TR 868); 52b (MH 165); 55t (Q79081); 55m (Q 68344); 55b (Q 11993); 56t (Q 66585); 58b (MH 5698); 59b (TR 978); 61tl (Q 11897); 62b (ATP 12184F); 63t (HU 1642); 64 (HU 2703); 67t (HU 2840); 69t (MA 6711); 69lm (HU 2395); 69b (MH 4190); 70b (Q 33847); 72b (Q 63153); 79tl (TR 284); 79tr (A 11644); 79b (A 24528); 81t (NYF 20500); 83m; 83b (CH 5093); 85m (C 1291); 85b (CH 17331); 88t (HU 4985); 89t (MH 4880); 90m (MH 4881); 96t (EA 15161); 97t (OEM 5182); 99b (Q 63808); 101tr (CH 15662); 101b (HU 2742); 102b (HU 5181); 103m (HU 2741); 103b (MH 4908); 104 (CT 842); 111tl (HU 63024); 111tr (HU 63022); 111bl (CF 899); 111br (HU 63021); 114t (C 1378); 115tr (Q 55974); 123m (CH 7059); 123b (NYP 21768A); 131m (HU 31375); 131br (EA 25060); 133um (Q 60550); 133b (Q 60608); 134t (Q 07104); 134m (Q 67249); 134b (Q 69650);

137tl (Q 67556); 137tr (Q 27508); 137bl (Q 57660); 137br (HU 68205); 139t (HU 39323); 140m (Q 67061); 142t (COL 188); 143tl (CH 24); 143m (TR 23); 143b (PMA 20625); 145t (EMOS 1214); 145br (CH 5005); 147um (A 25442); 147lm (A20026); 149m (RR 2219); 152b (CT 800); 153b (A 22930); 157um (GT 440); 160b (GLF 1092); 161b (GLF 1003); 178tr (ATP 15053C); 179t (Imperial War Museum Duxford); 179mr (A 34408), 180bl (COL 50); 180br (CAM 1473); 185 (CT 816); 192b (CT 915); 193t (CT 913); 193m (CT 916); 193lm (ATP 21301D); 194t (ATP 13595C); 209b (CT 70); 247m (A 33984); 250t (CT 72); 250b (TR 285); 251 (TR 22); 252 (COL 188); 253b (CT 800); 254 (TR 978); 255 (TR 38450).

Key Publishing Ltd: 48b; 49b; 98t.

Cliff Knox: 11um; 14b; 16; 24t; 29m; 33bl; 37b; 39b; 52t; 54b; 66b; 71b; 80bl; 84t; 84b; 85tl; 96b; 97m; 100t; 115b; 120t; 136t; 140b; 146t; 147t; 148b;

168t; 174t; 175b; 184t; 186t; 195t; 203ml; 208t; 211lm; 216b; 218t; 221b; 227t; 231t; 235t; 240t; 241b; 246b.

Kokujoho Magazine: 200tr; 118um; 118lm; 165t; 189b; 219b; 242b.

Hideo Kurihara: 110b; 117t.

Andrew March: 215b.

Daniel J. March: 26t; 37lm; 61tr; 176b; 192t; 242t.

Peter R. March: 2–3; 8–9; 11lm; 11b; 12l; 13t; 14tl; 18l; 20b; 21tr; 21b; 25bl; 26b; 28t; 29t; 30t; 31tr; 31bl; 34b; 37t; 37um; 38t; 38b; 39m; 40t; 41b; 43t; 44–5; 46tl; 48t; 49t; 53b; 54t; 56b; 57b; 59t; 62t; 67m; 69um; 70t; 71t; 72t; 73b; 74t; 75t; 75m; 75b; 76t; 77t; 78t; 78b; 80t; 81m; 82t; 82bl; 83t; 83b; 86t; 87br; 88t; 89b; 90b; 91t; 92t; 92b; 93t; 93m; 94m; 97b; 98b; 99t; 100b; 101tl; 102t; 103t; 105t; 106t; 106b; 107ml; 107b; 108b; 109; 110t; 113t; 113b; 115tl; 116b; 117b; 118t; 119b; 120m; 120b; 121t;

121b; 122t; 122b; 125t; 126t; 129t; 129m; 130t; 130b; 131t; 131bl; 132t; 132b; 133t; 135t; 135b; 136b; 138b; 139b; 140t; 141t; 141m; 141b; 142b; 143tr; 144b; 146b; 148t; 148m; 150–1; 152t; 154t; 154m; 154b; 155b; 156b; 157t; 162t; 163t; 164b; 166t; 167t; 167b; 169t; 170b; 171t; 171um; 172b; 173tr; 173m; 175t; 176t; 177t; 177lm; 178b; 180t; 181t; 182b; 183t; 183m; 183b; 184m; 186bl; 186br; 188m; 188b; 189t; 191b; 193b; 194b; 196b; 197t; 198t; 199t; 200tl; 201b; 203t; 203mr; 203b; 204; 205t; 205b; 207t; 207b; 208b; 209m; 210; 211um; 211b; 212t; 212b; 213t; 213m; 214t; 215t; 216t; 217t; 217b; 218b; 219t; 220t; 220b; 222b; 223t; 223m; 224t; 224m; 224b; 225b; 226t; 226b; 229t; 229b; 230b; 231b; 234t; 235um; 235lm; 236t; 237b; 239t; 239b; 240b; 241t; 241m; 243t; 243b; 244t; 244b; 245t; 247t; 247b; 248t; 248b; 249t; 249b.

Martin-Baker Aircraft Company: 42b.

Maru Magazine: 94t; 94b; 116t; 119tr.

Ministry of Defence: 153t.

Northrop Grumman: 15tl; 77b; 80br; 82br; 187t; 188t.

Bruce Robertson: 46b; 57t; 61b; 67b; 93b; 95t; 105b; 108t; 112t; 112b; 118b; 119tl; 126b; 128t; 128b; 129b; 138t; 144t; 149t; 149b; 155t; 178tl; 178m; 184b; 196t; 197b; 199b; 213b; 230t; 236b; 238t; 245m; 245b.

Rolls-Royce: 33br.

Saab: 7b; 29b; 35b; 232; 233b; 253t.

Geoff Sheward: 123t; 127t; 127b; 160t; 173tl; 190; 191t; 237t.

Brian Strickland Collection: 47t; 68; 73t; 87t; 90t; 91b; 95br; 107t; 124; 125b; 133lm; 145bl; 179ml.

USAF: 10b; 159m.

Index